Wine
FOR
DUMMIES®
4TH EDITION

by Ed McCarthy
Certified Wine Educator

and

Mary Ewing-Mulligan
Master of Wine

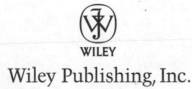

WILEY

Wiley Publishing, Inc.

Wine For Dummies®, 4th Edition

Published by
Wiley Publishing, Inc.
111 River St.
Hoboken, NJ 07030-5774
www.wiley.com

Copyright © 2006 by Wiley Publishing, Inc., Indianapolis, Indiana

Published by Wiley Publishing, Inc., Indianapolis, Indiana

Published simultaneously in Canada

For general information on our other products and services, please contact our Customer Care Department within the U.S. at 800-762-2974, outside the U.S. at 317-572-3993, or fax 317-572-4002.

For technical support, please visit www.wiley.com/techsupport.

Wiley also publishes its books in a variety of electronic formats. Some content that appears in print may not be available in electronic books.

Library of Congress Control Number: 2006927773

ISBN-13: 978-0-470-04579-4

ISBN-10: 0-470-04579-5

Manufactured in the United States of America

10 9 8 7 6 5 4 3 2

4O/QY/QZ/QW/IN

WILEY

About the Authors

Ed McCarthy and **Mary Ewing-Mulligan** are two wine lovers who met at an Italian wine tasting in New York City's Chinatown and subsequently merged their wine cellars and wine libraries when they married. They have since co-authored six wine books in the *Wine For Dummies* series (including two of their favorites, *French Wine For Dummies* and *Italian Wine For Dummies*) as well as their latest book, *Wine Style* (Wiley); taught hundreds of wine classes together; visited nearly every wine region in the world; run five marathons; and raised eleven cats. Along the way, they have amassed more than half a century of professional wine experience between them.

Mary is president of International Wine Center, a New York City wine school that offers credentialed wine education for wine professionals and serious wine lovers. As U.S. director of the Wine & Spirit Education Trust (WSET®), the world's leading wine educational organization, she works to make the courses she offers in New York available in more and more parts of the United States. She is also the long-standing wine columnist of the *NY Daily News*. Mary's most impressive credential is that she's the first female Master of Wine (MW) in the United States, and one of only 22 MW's in North America (with 251 worldwide).

Ed, a New Yorker, graduated from City University of NY with a master's degree in psychology. He taught high school English in another life, while working part-time in wine shops to satisfy his passion for wine and to subsidize his growing wine cellar. That cellar is especially heavy in his favorite wines — Bordeaux, Barolo, and Champagne. Besides co-authoring six wine books in the *For Dummies* series with Mary, Ed went solo as author of *Champagne For Dummies,* a topic on which he's especially expert.

Ed and Mary also share wine columns in *Nation's Restaurant News* and in *Beverage Media,* a trade publication. They are each columnists for the online wine magazine, *WineReviewOnline.com.* Ed and Mary are both accredited as Certified Wine Educators (CWE).

When they aren't writing, teaching, or visiting wine regions, Mary and Ed maintain a busy schedule of speaking, judging at professional wine competitions, and tasting as many new wines as possible. They admit to leading thoroughly unbalanced lives in which their only non-wine pursuits are hiking in the Berkshires and the Italian Alps. At home, they wind down to the tunes of U2, K.D. Lang, Bob Dylan, and Neil Young in the company of their feline roommates Dolcetto, Black & Whitey, Ponzi, and Pinot.

Authors' Acknowledgments

The wine world is dynamic — it's constantly changing. Because three years have passed since the third edition of *Wine For Dummies,* we decided to revise and update the book. We especially felt an obligation to write this fourth edition because of all the readers who have personally told us how valuable *Wine For Dummies* has been to them. We are grateful that we've been able to contribute to your knowledge about this wonderful beverage.

But this book would not have been possible without the team at Wiley. We sincerely thank Publisher Diane Steele, who engaged us to write the fourth edition of *Wine For Dummies,* along with Acquisitions Editor Stacy Kennedy. Really special thanks go to our Project Editor, Traci Cumbay, who made excellent suggestions to improve the text.

We thank our technical reviewer, colleague Igor Ryjenkov, MW, for his expertise. It's a better, more accurate book because of you.

Special thanks to Steve Ettlinger, our agent and friend, who brought us to the *For Dummies* series in the first place, and who is always there for us.

We thank all our friends in the wine business for your information and kind suggestions for our book; the book reviewers, whose criticism has been so generous; and our readers, who have encouraged us with your enthusiasm for our previous books in this series.

Mary offers special thanks to Linda Lawry and everyone else at International Wine Center, who enabled her to have the time and the peace of mind to work on this book. Thanks also to Elise McCarthy, E.J. McCarthy, Cindy McCarthy Tomarchio and her husband, David, for their encouragement and support.

Publisher's Acknowledgments

We're proud of this book; please send us your comments through our Dummies online registration form located at www.dummies.com/register/.

Some of the people who helped bring this book to market include the following:

Acquisitions, Editorial, and Media Development

Project Editor: Traci Cumbay

(Previous Edition: Joan Friedman)

Acquisitions Editor: Stacy Kennedy

Editorial Program Coordinator: Erin Calligan

Technical Editor: Igor Ryjenkov, MW

Editorial Manager: Michelle Hacker

Editorial Supervisor and Reprint Editor: Carmen Krikorian

Editorial Assistant: David Lutton

Cover Photos: © S.T. Yiap/Age Fotostock

Cartoons: Rich Tennant (www.the5thwave.com)

Composition

Project Coordinator: Tera Knapp

Layout and Graphics: Lauren Goddard, Denny Hager, Stephanie D. Jumper, Heather Ryan, Alicia South

Special Art: Akira Chiwaki

Proofreaders: Leeann Harney, Techbooks

Indexer: Techbooks

Publishing and Editorial for Consumer Dummies

 Diane Graves Steele, Vice President and Publisher, Consumer Dummies

 Joyce Pepple, Acquisitions Director, Consumer Dummies

 Kristin A. Cocks, Product Development Director, Consumer Dummies

 Michael Spring, Vice President and Publisher, Travel

 Kelly Regan, Editorial Director, Travel

Publishing for Technology Dummies

 Andy Cummings, Vice President and Publisher, Dummies Technology/General User

Composition Services

 Gerry Fahey, Vice President of Production Services

 Debbie Stailey, Director of Composition Services

Contents at a Glance

Table of Contents

Introduction

We love wine. We love the way it tastes, we love the fascinating variety of wines in the world, and we love the way wine brings people together at the dinner table. We believe that you and everyone else should be able to enjoy wine — regardless of your experience or your budget.

But we'll be the first to admit that wine people, such as many wine professionals and really serious connoisseurs, don't make it easy for regular people to enjoy wine. You have to know strange names of grape varieties and foreign wine regions. You have to figure out whether to buy a $20 wine or an $8 wine that seem to be pretty much the same thing. You even need a special tool to open the bottle once you get it home!

All this complication surrounding wine will never go away, because wine is a very rich and complex field. But you don't have to let the complication stand in your way. With the right attitude and a little understanding of what wine is, you can begin to buy and enjoy wine. And if, like us, you decide that wine is fascinating, you can find out more and turn it into a wonderful hobby.

Because we hate to think that wine, which has brought so much pleasure into our lives, could be the source of anxiety for anyone, we want to help you feel more comfortable around wine. Some knowledge of wine, gleaned from the pages of this book and from our shared experiences, will go a long way toward increasing your comfort level.

Ironically, what will *really* make you feel comfortable about wine is accepting the fact that you'll never know it all — and that you've got plenty of company.

You see, after you really get a handle on wine, you discover that *no one* knows everything there is to know about wine. There's just too much information, and it's always changing. And when you know that, you can just relax and enjoy the stuff.

About This Book

If you already have a previous edition of *Wine For Dummies,* you may be wondering whether you need this book. We believe that you do. We wrote

Wine For Dummies in 1995, and the world of wine has changed a lot since then. It has even changed since our third edition in 2003:

- ✔ Dozens of wineries have opened, a few have gone out of business, many have improved, and a few have slipped. Web sites on wine have come and gone. The wine auction scene bears almost no resemblance to what it was. Our recommendations reflect all these changes.

- ✔ Remember those prices that we listed for your favorite wines in our earlier editions? Well, big surprise: Just about all those prices have increased. But we point out some bargains, especially in Parts III, IV, and V.

- ✔ Several new vintages have occurred; we give you the lowdown on them throughout the book, and especially in our vintage chart in Appendix C.

- ✔ Great wine regions of yesterday, such as Spain, Hungary and Greece, have revitalized themselves, and we tell you about them. Also in this edition, we've updated the wine regions of Italy, California, Washington, Chile, and Argentina, among others.

We wrote this book to be an easy-to-use reference. You don't have to read it from cover to cover for it to make sense and be useful to you. Simply turn to the section that interests you and dig in.

Conventions Used in This Book

To help you navigate this book, we've established the following conventions:

- ✔ *Italic* is used for emphasis and to highlight new words or terms that are defined.

- ✔ `Monofont` is used for Web addresses.

- ✔ Sidebars, which are shaded boxes of text, consist of information that's interesting but not necessarily critical to your understanding of the topic.

Foolish Assumptions

We assume that you picked up this book for one of several reasons:

- ✔ You know very little about wine, but have a strong desire to learn more.

- ✔ You do know something about wine, more than most people, but you want to understand it better, from the ground up.

> ✔ You're already very knowledgeable but realize that you can always discover more or want to see whether we've made any mistakes so that you can brag to your friends that you caught us in a flagrant error. (Maybe you think that a particular vintage in Bordeaux wasn't nearly as good as we said, for example.)

We also assume that you don't have a lot of ego invested in wine — or maybe you do, and you're buying this book "for your sister-in-law." And we assume that you are someone who doesn't appreciate a lot of mumbo-jumbo and jargonistic language about wine, and that you're someone who wants straight talk instead.

How This Book Is Organized

This book is a wine textbook of sorts, a user's manual, and a reference book, all in one. We've included very basic information about wine for readers who know nothing (or next to nothing) about wine — but we have also included tips, suggestions, and more sophisticated information for seasoned wine drinkers who want to take their hobby to a more advanced level. Depending on where you fall on the wine-knowledge gradient, different chapters will be relevant to you.

Part I: Getting to Know Wine

The five chapters in Part I get you up and sipping even if you've never tasted wine in your life. We tell you the basic types of wine, how to taste it, which grapes make wine, why winemaking matters, and how wines are named.

Part II: Wine and You: Up Close and Personal

This part deals with practical wine matters — in the wine shop, in the restaurant, and in your home. Find out how to handle snooty wine clerks, restaurant wine lists, and those stubborn corks. In addition, we show you how to decipher cryptic wine labels.

Part III: The "Old World" of Wine

Visit this part for a tour of the major wine regions of Europe: France, Italy, Spain, Portugal, Germany, Switzerland, Austria, Hungary, and Greece.

Part IV: Discovering the New World of Wine

Here we adventure to Australia, New Zealand, Chile, Argentina, and South Africa, and then take a look at the major wine areas in the United States — California, Oregon, Washington, and New York — and end with a quick look at Canada's wines.

Part V: Wine's Exotic Face

Some of the most exciting and fascinating wines are in this part, including Champagne, Sherry, Port, Sauternes, and other exotic dessert wines.

Part VI: When You've Caught the Bug

You find a wealth of practical advice in this part, including recommendations on where and how you can buy wine beyond your local wine shops. We tell you how to describe and rate wines you taste, and how to pair food and wine. We also tell you how to store wine properly, and how to pursue your love and knowledge of wine beyond this book.

Part VII: The Part of Tens

What *For Dummies* book would be complete without this part? It's a synopsis of interesting tips and recommendations about wine to reinforce our suggestions earlier in the book. We're particularly happy to debunk ten prevalent myths about wine so that you can become a savvier consumer and a more satisfied wine drinker.

Part VIII: Appendixes

In Part VIII, we show you how to pronounce foreign wine words, and you can look up unfamiliar wine terms in our glossary. You can also consult our vintage chart to check out the quality and drinkability of your wine.

Icons Used in This Book

 This odd little guy is a bit like the two-year-old who constantly insists on knowing "Why, Mommy, why?" But he knows that you may not have the same level of curiosity that he has. Where you see him, feel free to skip over the technical information that follows. Wine will still taste just as delicious.

 Advice and information that will make you a wiser wine drinker or buyer is marked by this bull's-eye so that you won't miss it.

 There's very little you can do in the course of moderate wine consumption that can land you in jail — but you could spoil an expensive bottle and sink into a deep depression over your loss. This symbol warns you about common pitfalls.

 Some issues in wine are so fundamental that they bear repeating. Just so you don't think that we repeated ourselves without realizing it, we mark the repetitions with this symbol.

 Wine snobs practice all sorts of affectations designed to make other wine drinkers feel inferior. But you won't be intimidated by their snobbery if you see it for what it is. (And you can learn how to impersonate a wine snob!)

 A bargain's not a bargain unless you really like the outfit, as they say. To our tastes, the wines we mark with this icon are bargains because we like them, we believe them to be of good quality, and their price is low compared to other wines of similar type, style, or quality. You can also interpret this logo as a badge of genuineness, as in "This Chablis is the real deal."

 Unfortunately, some of the finest, most intriguing, most delicious wines are made in very small quantities. Usually, those wines cost more than wines made in large quantities — but that's not the only problem; the real frustration is that those wines have very limited distribution, and you can't always get your hands on a bottle even if you're willing to pay the price. We mark such wines with this icon, and hope that your search proves fruitful.

Part I

Getting to Know Wine

In this part . . .

To grasp the material in this part of the book, you need some preliminary knowledge: what a grape is, and where your tongue and nose are located.

If you have those bases covered, you're ready to begin understanding and enjoying wine — even if you've never tasted wine before in your life. We start slowly so that you can enjoy the scenery along the way.

Chapter 1

Wine 101

. . . .

In This Chapter

▶ What wine is

▶ Million-dollar words like *fermentation* and *sulfites*

▶ What red wine has that white wine doesn't

▶ Why color matters

▶ Differences between table wine, sparkling wine, and fortified wine

. . . .

*W*e know plenty of people who enjoy drinking wine but don't know much about it. (Been there, done that ourselves.) Knowing a lot of information about wine definitely isn't a prerequisite to enjoying it. But familiarity with certain aspects of wine can make choosing wines a lot easier, enhance your enjoyment of wine, and increase your comfort level. You can learn as much or as little as you like. The journey begins here.

How Wine Happens

Wine is, essentially, nothing but liquid, fermented fruit. The recipe for turning fruit into wine goes something like this:

1. **Pick a large quantity of ripe grapes from grapevines.**

   You could substitute raspberries or any other fruit, but 99.9 percent of all the wine in the world is made from grapes, because they make the best wines.

2. **Put the grapes into a clean container that doesn't leak.**

3. **Crush the grapes somehow to release their juice.**

   Once upon a time, feet performed this step.

4. **Wait.**

In its most basic form, winemaking is that simple. After the grapes are crushed, *yeasts* (tiny one-celled organisms that exist naturally in the vineyard and, therefore, on the grapes) come into contact with the sugar in the grapes' juice and gradually convert that sugar into alcohol. Yeasts also produce carbon dioxide, which evaporates into the air. When the yeasts are done working, your grape juice is wine. The sugar that was in the juice is no longer there — alcohol is present instead. (The riper and sweeter the grapes, the more alcohol the wine will have.) This process is called *fermentation*.

What could be more natural?

Fermentation is a totally natural process that doesn't require man's participation at all, except to put the grapes into a container and release the juice from the grapes. Fermentation occurs in fresh apple cider left too long in your refrigerator, without any help from you. In fact we read that milk, which contains a different sort of sugar than grapes do, develops a small amount of alcohol if left on the kitchen table all day long.

Speaking of milk, Louis Pasteur is the man credited with discovering fermentation in the nineteenth century. That's discovering, not inventing. Some of those apples in the Garden of Eden probably fermented long before Pasteur came along. (Well, we don't think it could have been much of an Eden without wine!)

Modern wrinkles in winemaking

Now if every winemaker actually made wine in as crude a manner as we just described, we'd be drinking some pretty rough stuff that would hardly inspire us to write a wine book.

But today's winemakers have a bag of tricks as big as a sumo wrestler's appetite. That's one reason why no two wines ever taste exactly the same.

The men and women who make wine can control the type of container they use for the fermentation process (stainless steel and oak are the two main materials), as well as the size of the container and the temperature of the juice during fermentation — and every one of these choices can make a big difference in the taste of the wine. After fermentation, they can choose how long to let the wine *mature* (a stage when the wine sort of gets its act together) and in what kind of container. Fermentation can last three days or three months, and the wine can then mature for a couple of weeks or a couple of years or anything in between. If you have trouble making decisions, don't ever become a winemaker.

The main ingredient

Obviously, one of the biggest factors in making one wine different from the next is the nature of the raw material, the grape juice. Besides the fact that riper, sweeter grapes make a more alcoholic wine, different *varieties* of grapes (Chardonnay, Cabernet Sauvignon, or Merlot, for example) make different wines. Grapes are the main ingredient in wine, and everything the winemaker does, he does to the particular grape juice he has. Chapter 3 covers specific grapes and the kinds of wine they make.

Local flavor

Grapes, the raw material of wine, don't grow in a void. Where they grow — the soil and climate of each wine region, as well as the traditions and goals of the people who grow the grapes and make the wine — affects the nature of the ripe grapes, and the taste of the wine made from those grapes. That's why so much of the information there is to learn about wine revolves around the countries and the regions where wine is made. In the five chapters that comprise Parts III and IV of this book, we cover all the world's major wine regions and their wines.

What Color Is Your Appetite?

Your inner child will be happy to know that when it comes to wine, it's okay to like some colors more than others. You can't get away with saying "I don't like green food!" much beyond your sixth birthday, but you can express a general preference for white, red, or pink wine for all your adult years.

(Not exactly) white wine

Whoever coined the term "white wine" must have been colorblind. All you have to do is look at it to see that it's not white, it's yellow. But we've all gotten used to the expression by now, and so *white wine* it is.

White wine is wine without any red color (or pink color, which is in the red family). This means that *White Zinfandel,* a popular pink wine, isn't white wine. But yellow wines, golden wines, and wines that are as pale as water are all white wines.

Wine becomes white wine in one of two ways. First, white wine can be made from white grapes — which, by the way, aren't white. (Did you see that one coming?) *White* grapes are greenish, greenish yellow, golden yellow, or some-times even pinkish yellow. Basically, white grapes include all the grape types that are not dark red or dark bluish. If you make a wine from white grapes, it's a white wine.

The second way a wine can become white is a little more complicated. The process involves using red grapes — but only the *juice* of red grapes, not the grape skins. The juice of most red grapes has no red pigmentation — only the skins do — and so a wine made with only the juice of red grapes can be a white wine. In practice, though, very few white wines come from red grapes. (Champagne is one exception; Chapter 14 addresses the use of red grapes to make Champagne.)

In case you're wondering, the skins are removed from the grapes by either *pressing* large quantities of grapes so that the juice flows out and the skins stay behind — sort of like squeezing the pulp out of grapes, the way kids do in the cafeteria — or by *crushing* the grapes in a machine that has rollers to break the skins so that the juice can drain away.

Is white always right?

You can drink white wine anytime you like — which for most people means as a drink without food or with lighter foods. Chapter 19 covers the dynamics of pairing wines with food.

The skinny on sulfites

Sulfur dioxide, a compound formed from sulfur and oxygen, occurs naturally during fermentation in very small quantities. Winemakers add it, too. Sulfur dioxide is to wine what aspirin and vitamin E are to humans — a wonder drug that cures all sorts of afflictions and prevents others. Sulfur dioxide is an antibacterial, preventing the wine from turning to vinegar. It inhibits yeasts, preventing sweet wines from refermenting in the bottle. It's an antioxidant, keeping the wine fresh and untainted by the demon oxygen. Despite these magical properties, winemakers try to use as little sulfur dioxide as possible because many of them share a belief that the less you add to wine, the better (just as many people prefer to ingest as little medication as possible).

Now here's a bit of irony for you:

Today — when winemaking is so advanced that winemakers need to rely on sulfur dioxide's help less than ever before — most wine labels in America state "Contains Sulfites" (meaning sulfur dioxide). That's because Congress passed a law in 1988 requiring that phrase on the label. So

now many wine drinkers understandably think that there's *more* sulfur in the wine than there used to be; but, in reality, sulfur dioxide use is probably at an all-time low.

Approximately 5 percent of asthmatics are extremely sensitive to sulfites. To protect them, Congress mandated that any wine containing more than 10 parts per million of sulfites carry the "Contains Sulfites" phrase on its label. Considering that about 10 to 20 parts per million occur naturally in wine, that covers just about every wine. (The exception is organic wines, which are intentionally made without the addition of sulfites; some of them are low enough in sulfites that they don't have to use the mandated phrase.)

Actual sulfite levels in wine range from about 30 to 150 parts per million (about the same as in dried apricots); the legal max in the United States is 350. White dessert wines have the most sulfur — followed by medium-sweet white wines and blush wines — because those types of wine need the most protection. Dry white wines generally have less, and dry reds have the least.

White wine styles: There's no such thing as plain white wine

White wines fall into four general taste categories, not counting sparkling wine or the really sweet white wine that you drink with dessert (see Chapter 15 for more on those). If the words we use to describe these taste categories sound weird, take heart — they're all explained in Chapter 2. We also explain the styles in plentiful detail in our book, *Wine Style* (Wiley). Here are the four broad categories:

- Some white wines are *fresh, unoaked whites* — crisp and light, with no sweetness and no oaky character. (Turn to Chapter 3 for the lowdown on oak.) Most Italian white wines, like Soave and Pinot Grigio, and some French whites, like Sancerre and some Chablis wines, fall into this category.

- Some white wines are *earthy whites* — dry, fuller-bodied, unoaked or lightly oaked, with a lot of earthy character. Some French wines, such as Mâcon or whites from the Côtes du Rhône region (covered in Chapter 9) have this taste profile.

- Some white wines are *aromatic whites*, characterized by intense aromas and flavors that come from their particular grape variety, whether they're *off-dry* (that is, not bone-dry) or dry. Examples include a lot of German wines, and wines from flavorful grape varieties such as Riesling or Viognier.

- Finally, some white wines are rich, oaky whites — dry or fairly dry, and full-bodied with pronounced oaky character. Most Chardonnays and many French wines — like many of those from the Burgundy region of France — fall into this group.

White wines are often considered *apéritif* wines, meaning wines consumed before dinner, in place of cocktails, or at parties. (If you ask the officials who busy themselves defining such things, an apéritif wine is a wine that has flavors added to it, as vermouth does. But unless you're in the business of writing wine labels for a living, don't worry about that. In common parlance, an apéritif wine is just what we said.)

A lot of people like to drink white wines when the weather is hot because they're more refreshing than red wines, and they're usually drunk chilled (the wines, not the people).

We serve white wines cool, but not ice-cold. Sometimes restaurants serve white wines too cold, and we actually have to wait a while for the wine to warm up before we drink it. If you like your wine cold, fine; but try drinking your favorite white wine a little less cold sometime, and we bet you'll discover it has more flavor that way. In Chapter 8, we recommend specific serving temperatures for various types of wine.

For suggestions of foods to eat with white wine, turn to Chapter 19; for really detailed information about white wine and food (and white wine itself, for that matter), refer to our book *White Wine For Dummies* (Wiley).

Red, red wine

In this case, the name is correct. Red wines really are red. They can be purple red, ruby red, or garnet, but they're red.

Red wines are made from grapes that are red or bluish in color. So guess what wine people call these grapes? Black grapes! We suppose that's because black is the opposite of white.

The most obvious difference between red wine and white wine is color. The red color occurs when the colorless juice of red grapes stays in contact with the dark grape skins during fermentation and absorbs the skins' color. Along with color, the grape skins give the wine *tannin*, a substance that's an important part of the way a red wine tastes. (See Chapter 2 for more about tannin.) The presence of tannin in red wines is actually the most important taste difference between red wines and white wines.

Red wines vary quite a lot in style. This is partly because winemakers have so many ways of adjusting their red-winemaking to achieve the kind of wine they want. For example, if winemakers leave the juice in contact with the skins for a long time, the wine becomes more *tannic* (firmer in the mouth, like strong tea; tannic wines can make you pucker). If winemakers drain the juice off the skins sooner, the wine is softer and less tannic.

Red wine styles: There's no such thing as just plain red wine, either

Here are four red wine styles:

- *Soft, fruity reds* are relatively light-bodied, with a lot of fruitiness and little tannin (like Beaujolais Nouveau wine from France, some Valpolicellas from Italy, and many under-$10 U.S. wines).

- *Mild-mannered reds* are medium-bodied with subtle, un-fruity flavors (like less expensive wines from Bordeaux, in France, and some inexpensive Italian reds).

- *Spicy reds* are flavorful, fruity wines with spicy accents and some tannin (such as some Malbecs from France or Argentina, and Dolcettos from Italy).

- *Powerful reds* are full-bodied and tannic (such as the most expensive California Cabernets; Barolo, from Italy; the most expensive Australian reds; and lots of other expensive reds).

Red wine sensitivities

Some people complain that they can't drink red wines without getting a headache or feeling ill. Usually, they blame the sulfites in the wine. We're not doctors or scientists, but we can tell you that red wines contain far less sulfur than white wines. That's because the tannin in red wines acts as a preservative, making sulfur dioxide less necessary. Red wines do contain histamine-like compounds and other substances derived from the grape skins that could be the culprits. Whatever the source of the discomfort, it's probably not sulfites.

Red wine tends to be consumed more often as part of a meal than as a drink on its own.

Thanks to the wide range of red wine styles, you can find red wines to go with just about every type of food and every occasion when you want to drink wine (except the times when you want to drink a wine with bubbles, because most bubbly wines are white or pink). In Chapter 19, we give you some tips on matching red wine with food. You can also consult our book about red wine, *Red Wine For Dummies* (Wiley).

One sure way to spoil the fun in drinking most red wines is to drink them too cold. Those tannins can taste really bitter when the wine is cold — just as in a cold glass of very strong tea. On the other hand, many restaurants serve red wines too warm. (Where do they store them? Next to the boiler?) If the bottle feels cool to your hand, that's a good temperature. For more about serving wine at the right temperature, see Chapter 8.

A rose is a rose, but a rosé is "white"

Rosé wines are pink wines. Rosé wines are made from red grapes, but they don't end up red because the grape juice stays in contact with the red skins for a very short time — only a few hours, compared to days or weeks for red wines. Because this *skin contact* (the period when the juice and the skins intermingle) is brief, rosé wines absorb very little tannin from the skins. Therefore, you can chill rosé wines and drink them as you would white wines.

Of course, not all rosé wines are called rosés. (That would be too simple.) Many rosé wines today are called *blush* wines — a term invented by wine marketers to avoid the word *rosé,* because back in the '80s, pink wines weren't very popular. Lest someone figures out that *blush* is a synonym for *rosé,* the labels call these wines *white.* But even a child can see that White Zinfandel is really pink.

The blush wines that call themselves *white* are fairly sweet. Wines labeled *rosé* can be sweetish, too, but some wonderful rosés from Europe (and a few from America, too) are *dry* (not sweet). Some hard-core wine lovers hardly ever drink rosé wine, but many wine drinkers are discovering what a pleasure a good rosé wine can be, especially in warm weather.

Which type when?

Your choice of a white wine, red wine, or rosé wine will vary with the season, the occasion, and the type of food that you're eating (not to mention your personal taste!). Choosing a color usually is the starting point for selecting a specific wine in a wine shop or in a restaurant. As we explain in Chapters 6 and 7, most stores and most restaurant wine lists arrange wines by color before making other distinctions, such as grape varieties, wine regions, or taste categories.

Although certain foods can straddle the line between white wine and red wine compatibility — grilled salmon, for example, can be delicious with a rich white wine or a fruity red — your preference for red, white, or pink wine will often be your first consideration in pairing wine with food, too.

Pairing food and wine is one of the most fun aspects of wine, because the possible combinations are almost limitless. (We get you started with the pairing principles and a few specific suggestions in Chapter 19.) Best of all, your personal taste rules!

Other Ways of Categorizing Wine

We sometimes play a game with our friends: "Which wine," we ask them, "would you want to have with you if you were stranded on a desert island?" In other words, which wine could you drink for the rest of your life without getting tired of it? Our own answer is always Champagne, with a capital *C* (more on the capitalization later in this section).

In a way, it's an odd choice because, as much as we love Champagne, we don't drink it *every day* under normal circumstances. We welcome guests with it, we celebrate with it after our team wins a Sunday football game, and we toast our cats with it on their birthdays. We don't need much of an excuse to drink Champagne, but it's not the type of wine we drink every night.

What we drink every night is regular wine — red, white, or pink — without bubbles. There are various names for these wines. In America, they're called *table* wines, and in Europe they're called *light* wines. Sometimes we refer to them as *still* wines, because they don't have bubbles moving around in them.

Ten occasions to drink rosé (and defy the snobs)

1. When she's having fish and he's having meat (or vice versa)

2. When a red wine just seems too heavy

3. With lunch — hamburgers, grilled cheese sandwiches, and so on

4. On picnics on warm, sunny days

5. To wean your son/daughter, mate, friend (yourself?) off cola

6. On warm evenings

7. To celebrate the arrival of spring or summer

8. With ham (hot or cold) or other pork dishes

9. When you feel like putting ice cubes in your wine

10. On Valentine's Day (or any other pink occasion)

In the following sections, we explain the differences between three categories of wines: table wines, dessert wines, and sparkling wines.

Table wine

Table wine, or light wine, is fermented grape juice whose alcohol content falls within a certain range. Furthermore, table wine is not bubbly. (Some table wines have a very slight carbonation, but not enough to disqualify them as table wines.) According to U.S. standards of identification, table wines may have an alcohol content no higher than 14 percent; in Europe, light wine must contain from 8.5 percent to 14 percent alcohol by volume (with a few exceptions). So unless a wine has more than 14 percent alcohol or has bubbles, it's a table wine or a light wine in the eyes of the law.

The regulations-makers didn't get the number 14 by drawing it from a hat. Historically, most wines contained less than 14 percent alcohol — either because there wasn't enough sugar in the juice to attain a higher alcohol level, or because the yeasts died off when the alcohol reached 14 percent, halting the fermentation. That number, therefore, became the legal borderline between wines that have no alcohol added to them (table wines) and wines that may have alcohol added to them (see "Dessert wine," in the next section).

Today, however, the issue isn't as clear-cut as it was when the laws were written. Many grapes are now grown in warm climates where they become so ripe, and have so much natural sugar, that their juice attains more than 14 percent alcohol when it's fermented. The use of gonzo yeast strains that continue working even when the alcohol exceeds 14 percent is another factor. Many red Zinfandels, Cabernets, and Chardonnays from California now have

14.5 or even 15.5 percent alcohol. Wine drinkers still consider them table wines, but legally they don't qualify. (Technically, they're dessert wines, and are taxed at a higher rate.) Which is just to say that laws and reality don't always keep pace.

Here's our own, real-world definition of table wines: They are the normal, non-bubbly wines that most people drink most of the time.

Dessert wine

Many wines have more than 14 percent alcohol because the winemaker added alcohol during or after the fermentation. That's an unusual way of making wine, but some parts of the world, like the Sherry region in Spain and the Port region in Portugal, have made quite a specialty of it. We discuss those wines in Chapter 15.

Dessert wine is the legal U.S. terminology for these wines, probably because they're usually sweet and often enjoyed after dinner. We find that term misleading, because dessert wines are not *always* sweet and not *always* consumed after dinner. (Dry Sherry is categorized as a dessert wine, for example, but it's dry, and we drink it before dinner.)

In Europe, this category of wines is called *liqueur wines,* which carries the same connotation of sweetness. We prefer the term *fortified,* which suggests that the wine has been strengthened with additional alcohol. But until we get elected to run things, the term will have to be *dessert wine* or *liqueur wine.*

How to (sort of) learn the alcohol content of a wine

Regulations require wineries to state a wine's alcohol percentage on the label (again, with some minor exceptions). It can be expressed in *degrees,* like 12.5 degrees, or as a percentage, like 12.5 percent. If a wine carries the words "Table Wine" on its label in the United States, but not the alcohol percentage, it should have less than 14 percent alcohol by law.

For wines sold within the United States — whether the wine is American or imported — there's a big catch, however. The labels are allowed to lie. U.S. regulations give wineries a 1.5 percent leeway in the accuracy of the alcohol level. If the label states 12.5 percent, the actual alcohol level can be as high as 14 percent or as low as 11 percent. The leeway does not entitle the wineries to exceed the 14 percent maximum, however.

If the alcohol percentage is stated as a number that's neither a full number nor a half-number — 12.8 or 13.2, for example, instead of 12.5 or 13 — odds are it's precise.

Sparkling wine (and a highly personal spelling lesson)

Sparkling wines are wines that contain carbon dioxide bubbles. Carbon dioxide gas is a natural byproduct of fermentation, and winemakers sometimes decide to trap it in the wine. Just about every country that makes wine also makes sparkling wine. In Chapter 14, we discuss how sparkling wine is made and describe the major sparkling wines of the world.

In the United States, Canada, and Europe, *sparkling wine* is the official name for the category of wines with bubbles. Isn't it nice when everyone agrees?

Champagne (with a capital *C*) is the most famous sparkling wine — and probably the most famous *wine,* for that matter. Champagne is a specific type of sparkling wine (made from certain grape varieties and produced in a certain way) that comes from a region in France called Champagne. It is the undisputed Grand Champion of Bubblies.

Unfortunately for the people of Champagne, France, their wine is so famous that the name *champagne* has been borrowed again and again by producers elsewhere, until the word has become synonymous with practically the whole category of sparkling wines. For example, until a recent agreement between the United States and the European Union, U.S. winemakers could legally call any sparkling wine *champagne* — even with a capital *C*, if they wanted — as long as the carbonation was not added artificially. Even now, those American wineries that were already using that name may continue to do so. (They do have to add a qualifying geographic term such as *American* or *Californian* before the word Champagne, however.)

Popular white wines

These types of white wine are available almost everywhere in the United States. We describe these wines in Parts III and IV of this book.

- **Chardonnay:** Can come from California, Australia, France, or almost any other place

- **Sauvignon Blanc:** Can come from California, France, New Zealand, South Africa, and other places

- **Riesling:** Can come from Germany, California, New York, Washington, France, Austria, Australia, and other places

- **Pinot Grigio** or **Pinot Gris:** Can come from Italy, France, Oregon, California, and other places

- **Soave:** Comes from Italy

Popular red wines

You find descriptions and explanations of these popular and widely available red wines all through this book.

- **Cabernet Sauvignon:** Can come from California, Australia, France, and other places

- **Merlot:** Can come from California, France, Washington, New York, Chile, and other places

- **Pinot Noir:** Can come from California, France, Oregon, New Zealand, and other places

- **Beaujolais:** Comes from France

- **Lambrusco:** Usually comes from Italy

- **Chianti:** Comes from Italy

- **Zinfandel:** Usually comes from California

- **Côtes du Rhône:** Comes from France

- **Bordeaux:** Comes from France

For the French, limiting the use of the name *champagne* to the wines of the Champagne region is a *cause célèbre*. European Union regulations not only prevent any other member country from calling its sparkling wines *champagne* but also prohibit the use of terms that even *suggest* the word *champagne*, such as fine print on the label saying that a wine was made by using the "champagne method." What's more, bottles of sparkling wine from countries outside the European Union that use the word champagne on the label are banned from sale in Europe. The French are that serious.

To us, this seems perfectly fair. You'll never catch us using the word *champagne* as a generic term for wine with bubbles. We have too much respect for the people and the traditions of Champagne, France, where the best sparkling wines in the world are made. That's why we stress the capital "C" when we say Champagne. *Those* are the wines we want on our desert island, not just any sparkling wine from anywhere that calls itself champagne.

When someone tries to impress you by serving a "Champagne" that's not French, don't rush to be impressed. Most respectable sparkling wine companies in America won't call their wines champagne out of respect for their French counterparts. (Of course, many of California's top sparkling wine companies are actually owned by the French — so it's no surprise that *they* won't call their wines champagne — but many other companies won't use the term, either.)

Chapter 2

These Taste Buds Are for You

We know they're out there — the cynics who are saying, right about now, "Hey, I already know how to taste. I do it every day, three to five times a day. All that wine-tasting humbug is just another way of making wine complicated."

And you know, in a way, those cynics are right. Anyone who can taste coffee or a hamburger can taste wine. All you need are a nose, taste buds, and a brain. Unless you're like our friend who lost his sense of smell from the chemicals he used every day as a cosmetology teacher, you, too, have all that it takes to taste wine properly.

You also have all that it takes to speak Mandarin. Having the ability to do something is different from knowing how to do it and applying that know-how in everyday life, however.

The Special Technique for Tasting Wine

You drink beverages every day, tasting them as they pass through your mouth. In the case of wine, however, drinking and tasting are not synonymous. Wine is much more complex than other beverages: There's more going on in a mouthful of wine. For example, most wines have a lot of different (and subtle) flavors, all at the same time, and they give you multiple sensations when they're in your mouth, such as softness and sharpness together.

If you just drink wine, gulping it down the way you do soda, you miss a lot of what you paid for. But if you *taste* wine, you can discover its nuances. In fact, the more slowly and attentively you taste wine, the more interesting it tastes.

And with that, we have the two fundamental rules of wine tasting:

1. **Slow down.**
2. **Pay attention.**

The process of tasting a wine — of systematically experiencing all the wine's attributes — has three steps. The first two steps don't actually involve your mouth at all. First you look at the wine, and then you smell it.

Savoring wine's good looks

We enjoy looking at the wine in our glass, noticing how brilliant it is and the way it reflects the light, trying to decide precisely which shade of red it is and whether it will stain the tablecloth permanently if we tilt the glass too far.

Tips for smelling wine

✔ Be bold. Stick your nose right into the airspace of the glass where the aromas are captured.

✔ Don't wear a strong scent; it will compete with the smell of the wine.

✔ Don't knock yourself out smelling a wine when there are strong food aromas around. The tomatoes you smell in the wine could really be the tomato in someone's pasta sauce.

✔ Become a smeller. Smell every ingredient when you cook, everything you eat, the fresh fruits and vegetables you buy at the supermarket, even the smells of your environment — like leather, wet earth, fresh road tar, grass, flowers, your wet dog, shoe polish, and your medicine cabinet. Stuff your mental database with smells so that you'll have aroma memories at your disposal when you need to draw on them.

✔ Try different techniques of sniffing. Some people like to take short, quick sniffs, while others like to inhale a deep whiff of the wine's smell. Keeping your mouth open a bit while you inhale can help you perceive aromas. (Some people even hold one nostril closed and smell with the other, but we think that's a bit kinky.)

To observe a wine's appearance, tilt a (half-full) glass away from you and look at the color of the wine against a white background, such as the tablecloth or a piece of paper (a colored background distorts the color of the wine). Notice how dark or how pale the wine is, what color it is, and whether the color fades from the center of the wine out toward the edge, where it touches the glass. Also notice whether the wine is cloudy, clear, or brilliant. (Most wines are clear. Some wines that are *unfiltered* — Chapter 5 explains filtering — can be less than brilliant but shouldn't be cloudy.) Eventually, you'll begin to notice patterns, such as deeper color in younger red wines.

If you have time to kill, at this point you can also swirl the wine around in your glass (see the following section, "The nose knows") and observe the way the wine runs back down the inside of the glass. Some wines form *legs* or *tears* that flow slowly down. Once upon a time, these legs were interpreted as the sure sign of a rich, high-quality wine. Today, we know that a wine's legs are a complicated phenomenon having to do with the surface tension of the wine and the evaporation rate of the wine's alcohol. If you're a physicist, this is a good time to show off your expertise and enlighten your fellow tasters — but otherwise, don't bother drawing conclusions from the legs.

The nose knows

Now we get to the really fun part of tasting wine: swirling and sniffing. This is when you can let your imagination run wild, and no one will ever dare to contradict you. If you say that a wine smells like wild strawberries to you, how can anyone prove that it doesn't?

Before we explain the smelling ritual, and the tasting technique that goes along with it (described in the next section), we want to assure you that: a) you don't have to apply this procedure to every single wine you drink; b) you won't look foolish doing it, at least in the eyes of other wine lovers (we can't speak for the other 90 percent of the human population); and c) it's a great trick at parties to avoid talking with someone you don't like.

To get the most out of your sniffing, swirl the wine in the glass first. But don't even *think* about swirling your wine if your glass is more than half full.

Keep your glass on the table and rotate it three or four times so that the wine swirls around inside the glass and mixes with air. Then quickly bring the glass to your nose. Stick your nose into the airspace of the glass, and smell the wine. Free-associate. Is the aroma fruity, woodsy, fresh, cooked, intense, light? Your nose tires quickly, but it recovers quickly, too. Wait just a moment and try again. Listen to your friends' comments and try to find the same things they find in the smell.

Wines have noses — and palates, too

With poetic license typical of wine tasters, someone once dubbed the smell of a wine its *nose* — and the expression took hold. If someone says that a wine has a huge nose, he means that the wine has a very strong smell. If he says that he detects lemon *in the nose* or *on the nose,* he means that the wine smells a bit like lemons.

In fact, most wine tasters rarely use the word *smell* to describe how a wine smells because the word *smell* (like the word *odor*) seems pejorative. Wine tasters talk about the wine's nose or aroma. Sometimes they use the word *bouquet,* although that word is falling out of fashion.

Just as a wine taster might use the term *nose* for the smell of a wine, he might use the word *palate* in referring to the taste of a wine. A wine's palate is the overall impression the wine gives in your mouth, or any isolated aspect of the wine's taste — as in "This wine has a harmonious palate," or "The palate of this wine is a bit acidic." When a wine taster says that he finds raspberries *on the palate,* he means that the wine has the flavor of raspberries.

As you swirl, the aromas in the wine vaporize, so that you can smell them. Wine has so many *aromatic compounds* that whatever you find in the smell of a wine is probably not merely a figment of your imagination.

The point behind this whole ritual of swirling and sniffing is that what you smell should be pleasurable to you, maybe even fascinating, and that you should have fun in the process. But what if you notice a smell that you don't like?

Hang around wine geeks for a while, and you'll start to hear words like *petrol, manure, sweaty saddle, burnt match,* and *asparagus* used to describe the aromas of some wines. "Yuck!" you say? Of course you do! Fortunately, the wines that exhibit such smells are not the wines you'll be drinking for the most part — at least not unless you really catch the wine bug. And when you do catch the wine bug, you may discover that those aromas, in the right wine, can really be a kick. Even if you don't learn to enjoy those smells (some of us do, honest!), you'll appreciate them as typical characteristics of certain regions or grapes.

Then there are the bad smells that nobody will try to defend. It doesn't happen often, but it does happen, because wine is a natural, agricultural product with a will of its own. Often when a wine is seriously flawed, it shows immediately in the nose of the wine. Wine judges have a term for such wines. They call them DNPIM — Do Not Put In Mouth. Not that you'll get ill, but why subject your taste buds to the same abuse that your nose just took? Sometimes it's a bad cork that's to blame, and sometimes it's some other sort of problem in the winemaking or even the storage of the wine. Just rack it up to experience and open a different bottle.

While you're choosing the next bottle, make up your own acronyms: SOTYWE (Serve Only To Your Worst Enemies) for example, or ETMYG (Enough To Make You Gag), or our own favorite, SLADDR (Smells Like A Dirty Dish Rag).

When it comes to smelling wine, many people are concerned that they aren't able to detect as many aromas as they think they should. Smelling wine is really just a matter of practice and attention. If you start to pay more attention to smells in your normal activities, you'll get better at smelling wine.

The mouth action

After you've looked at the wine and smelled it, you're finally allowed to taste it. This is when grown men and women sit around and make strange faces, gurgling the wine and sloshing it around in their mouths with looks of intense concentration in their eyes. You can make an enemy for life if you distract a wine taster just at the moment when he is focusing all his energy on the last few drops of a special wine.

 Here's how the procedure goes. Take a medium-sized sip of wine. Hold it in your mouth, purse your lips, and draw in some air across your tongue, over the wine. (Be utterly careful not to choke or dribble, or everyone will strongly suspect that you're not a wine expert.) Then swish the wine around in your mouth as if you are chewing it. Then swallow it. The whole process should take several seconds, depending on how much you are concentrating on the wine. (Wondering what to concentrate on? The next two sections tell you, along with the section "Parlez-Vous Winespeak?" later in this chapter.)

Ten aromas (or flavors) associated with wine

Fruits	Tobacco
Herbs	Butterscotch
Flowers	Toast
Earth	Vanilla
Grass	Coffee, mocha, or chocolate

Feeling the tastes

Taste buds on the tongue can register various sensations, which are known as the basic tastes. These include sweetness, sourness, saltiness, bitterness, and umami, a savory characteristic. Of these tastes, sweetness, sourness, and bitterness are those most commonly found in wine. By moving the wine around in your mouth, you give it a chance to hit all your taste buds so that you don't miss anything in the wine (even if sourness and bitterness sound like things you wouldn't mind missing).

As you swish the wine around in your mouth, you are also buying time. Your brain needs a few seconds to figure out what the tongue is tasting and make some sense of it. Any sweetness in the wine registers in your brain first because many of the taste buds on the front of your tongue — where the wine hits first — capture the sensation of sweetness; *acidity* (which, by the way, is what normal people call sourness) and bitterness register subsequently. While your brain is working out the relative impressions of sweetness, acidity, and bitterness, you can be thinking about how the wine feels in your mouth — whether it's heavy, light, smooth, rough, and so on.

Tasting the smells

Until you cut your nose in on the action, that's all you can taste in the wine — those three sensations of sweetness, acidity, and bitterness and a general impression of weight and texture. Where have all the wild strawberries gone?

They're still there in the wine, right next to the chocolate and plums. But to be perfectly correct about it, these flavors are actually *aromas* that you taste, not through tongue contact, but by inhaling them up an interior nasal passage in the back of your mouth called the *retronasal passage* (see Figure 2-1). When you draw in air across the wine in your mouth, you are vaporizing the aromas just as you did when you swirled the wine in your glass. There's a method to this madness.

Figure 2-1:
Wine flavors are actually aromas that vaporize in your mouth; you perceive them through the rear nasal passage.

Nasal cavities

The nasal passage

The retronasal passage

© Akira Chiwaki

Ten odors not associated with wine

Paint	Cannabis
New car	Magic Marker
Cigars	Elephant dung
Glue	Chanel No. 5
Gorgonzola	Fabric softener sheets

After you go through all this rigmarole, it's time to reach a conclusion: Do you like what you tasted? The possible answers are yes, no, an indifferent shrug of the shoulders, or "I'm not sure, let me take another taste," which means that you have serious wine-nerd potential.

Parlez-Vous Winespeak?

Now we have to confess that there is one step between knowing how to taste wine and always drinking wine that you like. And it's a doozy. That step is putting taste into words.

We wouldn't have to bother with this detail if only we could always choose our wines the way that customers choose cheese in a gourmet shop. ("Can I try that one? No, I don't like it; let me taste the one next to it. Good. I'll take half a pound.")

"Like/Don't Like" is a no-brainer once you have the wine in your mouth. But most of the time you have to buy the stuff without tasting it first. So unless you want to drink the same wine for the rest of your life, you're going to have to decide what it is that you like or don't like in a wine and communicate that to another person who can steer you toward a wine you'll like.

There are two hurdles here: Finding the words to describe what you like or don't like, and then getting the other person to understand what you mean. Naturally, it helps if we all speak the same language.

Unfortunately, Winespeak is a dialect with an undisciplined and sometimes poetic vocabulary whose definitions change all the time, depending on who's speaking. In case you really want to get into this wine thing, we treat you to some sophisticated wine language in Chapters 5 and 19. For now, a few basic words and concepts should do the trick.

The sequential palate

The tastes of a wine reveal themselves sequentially as the tongue detects them, and they register in your brain. We recommend that you follow this natural sequence when you try to put words to what you're tasting.

Sweetness

As soon as you put the wine into your mouth, you can usually notice sweetness or the lack of it. In Winespeak, *dry* is the opposite of sweet. Classify the wine you're tasting as either *dry, off-dry* (in other words, somewhat sweet), or *sweet.*

Acidity

All wine contains acid (mainly *tartaric acid,* which exists in grapes), but some wines are more acidic than others. Acidity is more of a taste factor in white wines than in reds. For white wines, acidity is the backbone of the wine's taste (it gives the wine firmness in your mouth). White wines with a high amount of acidity feel *crisp,* and those without enough acidity feel *flabby.*

You generally perceive acidity in the middle of your mouth — what wine-tasters call the *mid-palate.* You can also sense the consequences of acidity (or the lack of it) in the overall style of the wine — whether it's a tart little number or a soft and generous sort, for example. Classify the wine you're tasting as *crisp, soft,* or "couch potato."

Tannin

Tannin is a substance that exists naturally in the skins, seeds (or *pips*), and stems of grapes. Because red wines are fermented with their grape skins and pips, and because red grape varieties are generally higher in tannin than white varieties, tannin levels are far higher in red wines than in white wines. Oak barrels can also contribute tannin to wines, both reds and whites. Have you ever taken a sip of a red wine and rapidly experienced a drying-out feeling in your mouth, as if something had blotted up all your saliva? That's tannin.

Is it sweetness or fruitiness?

Beginning wine tasters sometimes describe dry wines as sweet because they confuse fruitiness with sweetness. A wine is *fruity* when it has distinct aromas and flavors of fruit. You smell the fruitiness with your nose; in your mouth, you "smell" it through your retronasal passage.

Sweetness, on the other hand, is a tactile impression on your tongue. When in doubt, try holding your nose when you taste the wine; if the wine really is sweet, you'll be able to taste the sweetness despite the fact that you can't smell the fruitiness.

Touchy-feely

Softness and firmness are actually *textural impressions* a wine gives you as you taste it. Just as your mouth feels temperature in a liquid, it feels texture. Some wines literally *feel* soft and smooth as they move through your mouth, while others feel hard, rough, or coarse. In white wines, acid is usually responsible for impressions of hardness or firmness (or crispness); in red wines, tannin is usually responsible. Low levels of either substance can make a wine feel pleasantly soft — or too soft, depending on the wine and your taste preferences. Unfermented sugar also contributes to an impression of softness, and alcohol can, too. But very high alcohol — which is fairly common in wines these days — can give a wine an edge of hardness.

To generalize a bit, tannin is to a red wine what acidity is to a white: a backbone. Tannins alone can taste bitter, but some tannins in wine are less bitter than others. Also, other elements of the wine, such as sweetness, can mask the perception of bitterness (see "Balance" later in this chapter). You sense tannin — as bitterness, or as firmness or richness of texture — mainly in the rear of your mouth and, if the amount of tannin in a wine is high, on the inside of your cheeks and on your gums. Depending on the amount and nature of its tannin, you can describe a red wine as *astringent, firm,* or *soft.*

Body

A wine's body is an impression you get from the whole of the wine — not a basic taste that registers on your tongue. It's the impression of the weight and size of the wine in your mouth, which is usually attributable principally to a wine's alcohol. We say "impression" because, obviously, one ounce of any wine will occupy exactly the same space in your mouth and weigh the same as one ounce of any other wine. But some wines *seem* fuller, bigger, or heavier in the mouth than others. Think about the wine's fullness and weight as you taste it. Imagine that your tongue is a tiny scale and judge how much the wine is weighing it down. Classify the wine as *light-bodied, medium-bodied,* or *full-bodied.*

The flavor dimension

Wines have flavors (er, we mean *mouth aromas*), but wines don't come in a specific flavor. While you may enjoy the suggestion of chocolate in a red wine that you're tasting, you wouldn't want to go to a wine store and ask for a chocolaty wine, unless you don't mind the idea of people holding their hands over their mouths and trying not to laugh aloud at you.

Is it acid or tannin?

Red wines have acid as well as tannin, and distinguishing between the two as you taste a wine can be a real challenge. When you're not sure whether it's mainly tannin or acid you're perceiving, pay attention to how your mouth feels *after* you've swallowed the wine. Acid makes you salivate (saliva is alkaline, and it flows to neutralize the acid). Tannin leaves your mouth dry.

Instead, you should refer to *families of flavors* in wine. You have your *fruity wines* (the ones that make you think of all sorts of fruit when you smell them or taste them), your *earthy wines* (these make you think of minerals and rocks, walks in the forest, turning the earth in your garden, dry leaves, and so on), your *spicy wines* (cinnamon, cloves, black pepper, or Indian spices, for example), your *herbal wines* (mint, grass, hay, rosemary, and so on), and so on, and so on. There are so many flavors in wine that we could go on and on (and we often do!), but you get the picture, don't you?

If you like a wine and want to try another wine that's similar but different (and it will always be different, we guarantee you), one method is to decide what families of flavors in the wine you like and mention that to the person selling you your next bottle. In Parts III, IV and V, you'll find wines that fit these specific flavors.

Another aspect of flavor that's important to consider is a wine's *flavor intensity* — how much flavor the wine has, regardless of what those flavors are. Some wines are as flavorful as a Big Mac, while others have flavors as subtle as fillet of sole. Flavor intensity is a major factor in pairing wine with food, as you can read in Chapter 19, and it also helps determine how much you like a wine.

The Quality Issue

Did you notice, by any chance, that nowhere among the terms we use to describe wines are the words *great, very good,* or *good?* Instead of worrying about crisp wines, earthy wines, and medium-bodied wines, wouldn't it just be easier to walk into a wine shop and say, "Give me a very good wine for dinner tonight"? Isn't *quality* the ultimate issue — or at least, quality within your price range, also known as *value?*

Wine producers constantly brag about the quality ratings that their wines receive from critics, because a high rating — implying high quality — translates into increased sales for a wine. But quality wines come in all colors, degrees of sweetness and dryness, and flavor profiles. Just because a wine is high quality doesn't mean that you will actually enjoy it, any more than two-thumbs-up means that you'll love a particular movie. We've purchased highly rated wines and ended up pouring them down the sink because we didn't care to drink them. Personal taste is simply more relevant than quality in choosing a wine.

Nevertheless, degrees of quality do exist among wines. But a wine's quality is not absolute: how great a wine is or isn't depends on who is doing the judging.

The instruments that measure the quality of a wine are a human being's nose mouth, and brain, and because we're all different, we all have different opinions on how good a wine is. The combined opinion of a group of trained, experienced palates (also known as wine experts) is usually considered a definitive judgment of a wine's quality. (Turn to Chapter 19 for more about expert opinion.)

What's a good wine?

A good wine is, above all, a wine that you like enough to drink — because the whole purpose of a wine is to give pleasure to those who drink it. After that, how good a wine is depends on how it measures up to a set of (more or less) agreed-upon standards of performance established by experienced, trained experts. These standards involve mysterious concepts like *balance, length, depth, complexity,* and *trueness to type* (*typicity* in Winespeak, *typicité* in Snobwinespeak). None of these concepts is objectively measurable, by the way.

Balance

Three words we talk about in the "Parlez-Vous Winespeak?" section in this chapter — sweetness, acidity, and tannin — represent three of the major *components* (parts) of wine. The fourth is alcohol. Besides being one of the reasons we usually want to drink a glass of wine in the first place, alcohol is an important element of wine quality.

Balance is the relationship of these four components to one another. A wine is balanced when nothing sticks out as you taste it, like harsh tannin or too much sweetness. Most wines are balanced to most people. But if you have any pet peeves about food — if you really hate anything tart, for example, or if you never eat sweets — you may perceive some wines to be unbalanced. If you perceive them to be unbalanced, then they are unbalanced for you. (Professional tasters know their own idiosyncrasies and adjust for them when they judge wine.)

Taste is personal

Literally! The perception of the basic tastes on the tongue varies from one person to the next. Research has proven that some people have more taste buds than others, and are therefore more sensitive to characteristics such as sourness or bitterness in food and beverages. The most sensitive tasters are called, somewhat misleadingly, "supertasters" — not because they are more expert, but because they perceive sensations such as bitterness more acutely. If you find diet sodas very bitter, or if you need to add a lot of sugar to your coffee to make it palatable, you may fall into this category — and you therefore may find many red wines unpleasant, even if other people consider them great.

Tannin and acidity are *hardening elements* in a wine (they make a wine taste firmer in the mouth), while alcohol and sugar (if any) are *softening elements.* The balance of a wine is the interrelationship of the hard and the soft aspects of a wine, and a key indicator of quality.

Length

When we call wines *long* or *short,* we're not referring to the size of the bottle or how quickly we empty it. *Length* is a word used to describe a wine that gives an impression of going all the way on the palate — you can taste it across the full length of your tongue — rather than stopping short halfway through your tasting of it. Many wines today are very up front on the palate — they make a big impression as soon as you taste them — but they don't go the distance in your mouth. They are *short.* Generally, high alcohol or excess tannin is to blame. Length is a sure sign of high quality.

Depth

This is another subjective, unmeasurable attribute of a high-quality wine. We say a wine has *depth* when it seems to have a dimension of verticality — that is, it does not taste flat and one-dimensional in your mouth. A "flat" wine can never be great.

Complexity

There's nothing wrong with a simple, straightforward wine, especially if you enjoy it. But a wine that keeps revealing different things about itself, always showing you a new flavor or impression — a wine that has *complexity* — is usually considered better quality. Some experts use the term *complexity* specifically to indicate that a wine has a multiplicity of aromas and flavors, while others use it in a more holistic (but less precise) sense, to refer to the total impression a wine gives you.

Balance in action

For firsthand experience of how the principle of taste balance works, try this. Make a very strong cup of tea, and chill it. When you sip it, the cold tea will taste bitter, because it's very tannic. Now add lemon juice; the tea will taste astringent (constricting the pores in your mouth), because the acid of the lemon and the tannin of the tea are accentuating each other. Now add a lot of sugar to the tea. The sweetness should counter-balance the acid–tannin impact, and the tea will taste softer than it did before.

Finish

The impression a wine leaves in the back of your mouth and in your throat after you have swallowed it is its *finish* or *aftertaste.* In a good wine, you can still perceive the wine's flavors — such as fruitiness or spiciness — at that point. Some wines may finish *hot,* because of high alcohol, or *bitter,* because of tannin — both shortcomings. Or a wine may have nothing much at all to say for itself after you swallow.

Typicity

In order to judge whether a wine is true to its type, you have to know how that type is supposed to taste. So you have to know the textbook characteristics of wines made from the major grape varieties and wines of the world's classic wine regions. (For example, the Cabernet Sauvignon grape typically has an aroma and flavor of blackcurrants, and the French white wine called Pouilly-Fumé typically has a slight gunflint aroma.) Turn to Chapter 3 and Chapters 9 through 15 for all those details.

What's a bad wine?

Strangely enough, the right to declare a wine "good" because you like it does not carry with it the right to call a wine "bad" just because you don't. In this game, you get to make your own rules, but you don't get to force other people to live by them.

The fact is there are very few bad wines in the world today compared to even 20 years ago. And many of the wines we could call bad are actually just bad *bottles* of wine — bottles that were handled badly, so that the good wine inside them got ruined.

Here are some characteristics that everyone agrees indicate a bad wine. We hope you never meet one.

- **Moldy fruit:** Have you ever eaten a raspberry from the bottom of the container that had a dusty, cardboardy taste to it? That same taste of rot can be in a wine if the wine was made from grapes that were not completely fresh and healthy when they were harvested. Bad wine.

- **Vinegar:** In the natural evolution of things, wine is just a passing stage between grape juice and vinegar. Most wines today remain forever in the wine stage because of technology or careful winemaking. If you find a wine that has crossed the line toward vinegar, it's bad wine.

- **Chemical or bacterial smells:** The most common are acetone (nail polish thinner) and sulfur flaws (rotten eggs, burnt rubber, bad garlic). Bad wines.

- **Oxidized wine:** This wine smells flat, weak, or maybe cooked, and it tastes the same. It may have been a good wine once, but air — oxygen — got in somehow and killed the wine. Bad bottle.

- **Cooked aromas and taste:** When a wine has been stored or shipped in heat, it can actually taste cooked or baked as a result. Often there's tell-tale leakage from the cork, or the cork has pushed up a bit. Bad bottle. (Unfortunately, every other bottle of that wine that experienced the same shipping or storage will also be bad.)

- **Corky wine:** The most common flaw, *corkiness* comes across as a smell of damp cardboard that gets worse with air, and a diminished flavor intensity. It's caused by a bad cork, and any wine in a bottle that's sealed with a cork is at risk for it. Bad bottle.

The Final Analysis: Do You Like It?

Let's not dwell too long on what can go wrong with a wine. If you find a bad wine or a bad bottle — or even a wine that is considered a good wine, but you don't like it — just move on to something you like better. Drinking a so-called great wine that you don't enjoy is as stupid as watching a television show that bores you. Change the channel. Explore.

Chapter 3

Pinot Envy and Other Secrets about Grape Varieties

In This Chapter
▶ Descriptions of major grape varieties and their wines
▶ Genus, species, variety, clone, and other grape terms
▶ Endangered species and mixed marriages
▶ Soils that grapes love

*W*e love to visit wine country. Gazing across manicured rows of grapevines in Napa Valley or pondering craggy terraces of rugged hillside vines in Portugal inspires us — and reinforces for us the fact that wine is an agricultural product, born of the earth, the grapevine, and the hard work of humans. Literally and emotionally, grapes are the link between the land and the wine.

Grapes also happen to give us one of the easiest ways of classifying wine and making sense of the hundreds of different types of wine that exist.

Why Grapes Matter

Grapes are the starting point of every wine, and therefore they are largely responsible for the style and personality of each wine. The grapes that make a particular wine dictate the genetic structure of that wine and how it will respond to everything that the winemaker does to it.

Think back to the last wine you drank. What color was it? If it was white, the odds are that's because it came from white grapes; if it was pink or red, that's because the wine came from red grapes.

Did it smell herbal or earthy or fruity? Whichever, those aromas came mainly from the grapes. Was it firm and tannic or soft and voluptuous? Thank the grapes — with a nod to Mother Nature and the winemaker.

The specific grape variety (or varieties) that makes any given wine is largely responsible for the sensory characteristics the wine offers — from its appearance to its aromas, its flavors, and its alcohol–tannin–acid profile. How the grapes grow — the amount of sunshine and moisture they get, for example, and how ripe they are when they're harvested — can emphasize certain of their characteristics rather than others. So can winemaking processes such as oak aging (see Chapter 5). Each grape variety reacts in its own way to the farming and winemaking techniques that it faces.

Of genus and species

By *grape variety,* we mean the fruit of a specific type of grapevine: the fruit of the Cabernet Sauvignon vine, for example, or of the Chardonnay vine.

The term *variety* actually has specific meaning in scientific circles. A variety is a subdivision of a species. Most of the world's wines are made from grape varieties that belong to the species *vinifera* — itself a subdivision of the genus *Vitis*. This species originated in Europe and western Asia; other distinct species of *Vitis* are native to North America.

Grapes of other species can also make wine; for example, the Concord grape, which makes Concord wine as well as grape juice and jelly, belongs to the native American species *Vitis labrusca*. But the grapes of this species have a very different flavor from vinifera grapes — *foxy* is the word used to describe that taste. The number of non-vinifera wines is small because their flavor is less popular in wine.

A variety of varieties

Snowflakes and fingerprints aren't the only examples of Nature's infinite variety. Within the genus *Vitis* and the species *vinifera,* there are as many as 10,000 varieties of wine grapes. If wine from every one of these varieties were commercially available and you drank the wine of a different variety every single day, it would take you more than 27 years to experience them all!

Not that you would want to. Within those 10,000 varieties are grapes that have the ability to make extraordinary wine, grapes that tend to make very ordinary wine, and grapes that only a parent could love. Most varieties are obscure grapes whose wines rarely enter into international commerce.

An extremely adventuresome grape nut who has plenty of free time to explore the back roads of Spain, Portugal, Italy, and Greece might be able to encounter 1,500 different grape varieties (only four years' worth of drinking) in his lifetime. The grape varieties you might encounter in the course of your normal wine enjoyment probably number fewer than 50.

> # The phylloxera threat
>
> If endangered species lists had existed at the end of the nineteenth century, *Vitis vinifera* certainly would've been on them. The entire species was nearly eradicated by a tiny louse called *phylloxera* that immigrated to Europe from America and proceeded to feast on the roots of vinifera grapevines, wiping out vineyards across the continent.
>
> To this day, no remedy has been found to protect vinifera roots from phylloxera. What saved the species was grafting vinifera vines onto rootstocks of native American species that are resistant to the bug. The practice of grafting the fruit-bearing part of *Vitis vinifera* onto the rooting part of other, phylloxera-resistant species continues today everywhere in the world where phylloxera is present and fine wine is made. (The fruit-bearing part is called a *scion,* and the rooting plant is called a *rootstock.*) Miraculously, each grape variety maintains its own character despite the fact that its roots are alien.

How grapes vary

All sorts of attributes distinguish each grape variety from the next. These attributes fall into two categories: personality traits and performance factors. *Personality traits* are the characteristics of the fruit itself — its flavors, for example. *Performance factors* refer to how the grapevine grows, how its fruit ripens, and how quickly it can get from 0 to 60 miles per hour.

Personality traits of grape varieties

Skin color is the most fundamental distinction among grape varieties. Every grape variety is considered either a white variety or a red (or "black") one, according to the color of its skins when the grapes are ripe. (A few red-skinned varieties are further distinguished by having red pulp rather than white pulp.)

Individual grape varieties also differ from one another in other ways:

- **Aromatic compounds:** Some grapes (like Muscat) contribute floral aromas and flavors to their wine, for example, while other grapes contribute herbaceous notes (as Sauvignon Blanc does) or fruity character. Some grapes have very neutral aromas and flavors and, therefore, make fairly neutral wines.

- **Acidity levels:** Some grapes are naturally disposed to higher acid levels than others, which influences the wine made from those grapes.

- **Thickness of skin and size of the individual grapes (called *berries*):** Black grapes with thick skins naturally have more tannin than grapes with thin skins; ditto for small-berried varieties compared to large-berried varieties, because their skin-to-juice ratio is higher. More tannin in the grapes translates into a firmer, more tannic red wine.

How grapes ripen

When grapes are not yet ripe, they contain high amounts of acid and very little sugar — which is true for any fruit — and their flavor is tart. As ripening progresses, they become sweeter and less acidic (although they always retain some acid), and their flavors become richer and more complex. Their skins get thinner, and even their seeds and stems "ripen," sometimes changing color from green to brown. In red grape varieties, the tannin in the skins, stems, and pips becomes richer and less astringent. The stage of ripeness that the grapes attain is a big factor in the style of the wine.

The composite personality traits of any grape variety are fairly evident in wines made from that grape. A Cabernet Sauvignon wine is almost always more tannic and slightly lower in alcohol than a comparable Merlot wine, for example, because that's the nature of those two grapes.

Performance factors of grape varieties

The performance factors that distinguish grape varieties are vitally important to the grape grower because those factors determine how easy or challenging it will be for him to cultivate a specific variety in his vineyard — if he can even grow it at all. The issues include

- How much time a variety typically needs to ripen its grapes. (In regions with short growing seasons, early-ripening varieties do best.)

- How dense and compact the bunches of grapes are. (In warm, damp climates, grape varieties with dense bunches can have mildew problems.)

- How much vegetation a particular variety tends to grow. (In fertile soils, a vine that's disposed to growing a lot of leaves and shoots can have so much vegetation that the grapes don't get enough sun to ripen.)

The reasons some grape varieties perform brilliantly in certain places (and make excellent wine as a result) are so complex that grape growers haven't figured them all out yet. The amount of heat and cold, the amount of wind and rain (or lack of it), and the slant of the sun's rays on a hillside of vines are among the factors affecting a vine's performance. In any case, no two vineyards in the world have precisely the same combination of these factors — precisely the same *terroir* (see Chapter 4). The issue simply defies simple generalizations.

Grape royalty and commoners

Bees have their queens, gorillas have their silverbacks, and humans have their royal families. In the grape kingdom, there are nobles, too — at least as interpreted by the human beings who drink the wine made from those grapes.

Noble grape varieties (as wine people call them) have the potential to make great — not just good — wine. Every noble grape variety can claim at least one wine region where it's the undisputed king. The wines made from noble grapes on their home turf can be so great that they inspire winemakers in far-flung regions to grow the same grape in their own vineyards. The noble grape might prove itself noble there, too — but frequently the grape does not. Adaptability isn't a prerequisite of nobility.

Classic examples of noble grape varieties at their best are

- The Chardonnay grape and the Pinot Noir grape in Burgundy, France
- The Cabernet Sauvignon grape in Bordeaux, France
- The Syrah grape in France's Northern Rhône Valley
- The Chenin Blanc grape in France's Loire Valley
- The Nebbiolo grape in Piedmont, Italy
- The Sangiovese grape in Tuscany, Italy
- The Riesling grape in the Mosel and Rheingau regions of Germany

TECHNICAL STUFF

Chardonnay, do you take this limestone soil?

One important factor in how a grape variety performs is the soil in the vineyard. Over the centuries, some classic compatibilities between grape varieties and types of soil have become evident: Chardonnay in limestone or chalk, Cabernet Sauvignon in gravelly soil, Pinot Noir in limestone, and Riesling in slatey soil. At any rate, these are the soils of the regions where these grape varieties perform at their legendary best.

Soil affects a grapevine in several ways (besides simply anchoring the vine): It provides nutrition for the grapevine; it can influence the temperature of the vineyard; and it's a water-management system for the plant.

A safe generalization is that the best soils are those that have good drainage and aren't particularly fertile. (An extreme example is the soil — if we can call it that — of the Châteauneuf-du-Pape district in France's Rhône Valley: It's just stones.) The wisdom of the ages dictates that the grapevine must struggle to produce the best grapes, and well-drained, less fertile soils challenge the vine to struggle, regardless of what variety the grapevine is.

Cloning the perfect grapevine

Hang around wine people long enough, and you're sure to hear them talk about *clones* or *clonal selection* of grape varieties. Has the Brave New World of grape growing arrived? Not really. In botanical terms, a *clone* is a subdivision of a variety. Within a single variety, such as Chardonnay, differences can exist from one plant to the next. Some vines might ripen their fruit slightly more quickly, for example, or produce grapes with slightly different aromas and flavors than the next vine.

Nurseries propagate grapevines asexually, by taking cuttings from a *mother plant* and allowing those cuttings to root (until the new plant is mature enough to be grafted onto a phylloxera-resistant rootstock). The new plants are genetically identical to the mother plant. Naturally, grape growers choose from the nursery the most ideal plants for their situation (in terms of ripening, fruit flavor, disease resistance, heartiness — or whatever it is they're looking for). Voilá! They've made a clonal selection. Increasingly, growers plant their vineyards with several different clones to foster complexity.

A Primer on White Grape Varieties

This section includes descriptions of the 12 most important white *vinifera* varieties today. In describing the grapes, naturally we describe the types of wine that are made from each grape. These wines can be varietal wines, or place-name wines that don't mention the grape variety anywhere on the label (a common practice for European wines; see Chapter 4). These grapes can also be blending partners for other grapes, in wines made from multiple grape varieties. (Turn to Chapter 2 for a quick review of some of the descriptors we use in this section.)

Chardonnay

Chardonnay is a regal grape for its role in producing the greatest dry white wines in the world — white Burgundies — and for being one of the main grapes of Champagne. Today it also ends up in a huge amount of everyday wine.

The Chardonnay grape grows in practically every wine-producing country of the world, for two reasons: It's relatively adaptable to a wide range of climates; and the name Chardonnay on a wine label is, these days, a surefire sales tool.

Because the flavors of Chardonnay are very compatible with those of oak — and because white Burgundy (the great prototype) is generally an oaked wine, and because many wine drinkers love the flavor of oak — most Chardonnay wine receives some oak treatment either during or after fermentation. (For the best Chardonnays, oak treatment means expensive barrels of French oak; but for lower-priced Chardonnays it could mean soaking oak chips in the wine or even adding liquid essence of oak. See Chapter 5 for more on oak.) Except for Northeastern Italy and France's Chablis and Mâconnais districts, where oak is usually not used for Chardonnay, oaky Chardonnay wine is the norm and unoaked Chardonnay is the exception.

Oaked Chardonnay is so common that some wine drinkers confuse the flavor of oak with the flavor of Chardonnay. If your glass of Chardonnay smells or tastes toasty, smoky, spicy, vanilla-like, or butterscotch-like, that's the oak you're perceiving, not the Chardonnay!

Chardonnay itself has fruity aromas and flavors that range from apple — in cooler wine regions — to tropical fruits, especially pineapple, in warmer regions. Chardonnay also can display subtle earthy aromas, such as mushroom or minerals. Chardonnay wine has medium to high acidity and is generally full-bodied. Classically, Chardonnay wines are dry. But most inexpensive Chardonnays these days are actually a bit sweet.

Chardonnay is a grape that can stand on its own in a wine, and the top Chardonnay-based wines (except for Champagne and similar bubblies) are 100 percent Chardonnay. But less expensive wines that are labeled *Chardonnay* — those selling for less than $10 a bottle in the United States, for example — are likely to have some other, far less distinguished grape blended in, to help reduce the cost of making the wine. Anyway, who can even tell, behind all that oak?

Riesling

The great Riesling wines of Germany have put the Riesling grape on the charts as an undisputedly noble variety. Riesling shows its real class only in a few places outside of Germany, however. The Alsace region of France, Austria, and the Clare Valley region of Australia are among the few.

Riesling wines are far less popular today than Chardonnay. Maybe that's because Riesling is the antithesis of Chardonnay. While Chardonnay is usually gussied up with oak, Riesling almost never is; while Chardonnay can be full-bodied and rich, Riesling is more often light-bodied, crisp, and refreshing. Riesling's fresh, vivid personality can make many Chardonnays taste clumsy in comparison.

Aliases and a.k.a.'s

The same grape variety will often go by different names in different countries or even in different districts within the same country. Often it's just a case of traditional local synonyms. But sometimes, grape growers call one variety by the name of another because they think that's what they're growing (until a specialized botanist called an *ampelographer* examines their vines and tells them otherwise). In California, for example, some of the so-called Pinot Blanc has turned out to be another grape entirely: Melon de Bourgogne. In Chile, much of what grape growers call Merlot is really the Carmenère grape — while in the Friuli region of Italy, some of what is called Cabernet Franc is actually Carmenère.

For more tales of viticultural intrigue, read Jancis Robinson's classic book on grape varieties, *Vines, Grapes and Wines* (Alfred A. Knopf), an indispensable and fascinating reference.

The common perception of Riesling wines is that they're sweet, and many of them are — but plenty of them aren't. Alsace Rieslings are normally dry, many German Rieslings are fairly dry, and a few American Rieslings are dry. (Riesling can be vinified either way, according to the style of wine a producer wants to make.) Look for the word *trocken* (meaning dry) on German Riesling labels and the word *dry* on American labels if you prefer the dry style of Riesling.

High acidity, low to medium alcohol levels, and aromas/flavors that range from ebulliently fruity to flowery to minerally are trademarks of Riesling.

Riesling wines are sometimes labeled as *White Riesling* or *Johannisberg Riesling* — both synonyms for the noble Riesling grape. With wines from Eastern European countries, though, read the fine print: Olazrizling, Laskirizling, and Welschriesling are from another grape altogether.

If you consider yourself a maverick who hates to follow trends, check out the Riesling section of your wine shop instead of the Chardonnay aisle.

Sauvignon Blanc

Sauvignon Blanc is a white variety with a very distinctive character. It's high in acidity with pronounced aromas and flavors. Besides herbaceous character (sometimes referred to as *grassy*), Sauvignon Blanc wines display mineral aromas and flavors, vegetal character, or — in certain climates — fruity character, such as ripe melon, figs, or passion fruit. The wines are light- to medium-bodied and usually dry. Most of them are unoaked, but some are oaky.

France has two classic wine regions for the Sauvignon Blanc grape: Bordeaux; and the Loire Valley, where the two best known Sauvignon wines are called Sancerre or Pouilly-Fumé (described in Chapter 9). In Bordeaux, Sauvignon Blanc is sometimes blended with Sémillon (described in Table 3-1); some of the wines that are blended about fifty-fifty from the two grapes and fermented in oak are among the great white wines of the world.

Sauvignon Blanc is also important in Northeastern Italy, South Africa, and parts of California, where the wines are sometimes labeled as "Fumé Blanc." New Zealand's Sauvignon Blanc wines in particular are renowned for their fresh, flavorful style.

Pinot Gris/Pinot Grigio

Pinot Gris (*gree*) is one of several grape varieties called *Pinot:* There's Pinot Blanc (white Pinot), Pinot Noir (black Pinot), Pinot Meunier (we don't know how that one translates), and Pinot Gris (gray Pinot), which is called *Pinot Grigio* in Italian. Pinot Gris is believed to have mutated from the black Pinot Noir grape. Although It's considered a white grape, its skin color is unusually dark for a white variety.

Wines made from Pinot Gris can be deeper in color than most white wines — although most of Italy's Pinot Grigio wines are quite pale. Pinot Gris wines are medium- to full-bodied, usually not oaky, and have rather low acidity and fairly neutral aromas. Sometimes the flavor and aroma can suggest the skins of fruit, such as peach skins or orange rind.

Pinot Gris is an important grape throughout Northeastern Italy and also grows in Germany, where it is called Ruländer. The only region in France where Pinot Gris is important is in Alsace, where it really struts its stuff. Oregon has had good success with Pinot Gris, and more and more winemakers in California are now taking a shot at it. Because Pinot Grigio is one of the best-selling inexpensive white wine in the United States, countries such as Chile and Australia now grow this grape for mass-market wines, and they often call the wine "Pinot Grigio."

Other white grapes

Table 3-1 describes some other grapes whose names you see on wine labels, or whose wine you could drink in place-name wines without realizing it.

Table 3-1	Other White Grapes and Their Characteristics
Grape Type	*Characteristics*
Albariño	An aromatic grape from the northwestern corner of Spain — the region called Rias Baixas — and Portugal's northerly Vinho Verde region, where it's called *Alvarinho*. It makes medium-bodied, crisp, appley-tasting, usually unoaked white wines whose high glycerin gives them silky texture.
Chenin Blanc	A noble grape in the Loire Valley of France, for Vouvray and other wines. The best wines have high acidity and a fascinating oily texture (they feel rather viscous in your mouth). Some good dry Chenin Blanc comes from California, but so does a ton of ordinary off-dry wine. In South Africa, Chenin Blanc is often called *Steen*.
Gewürztraminer *(geh-VAIRTZ-trah-mee-ner)*	A wonderfully exotic grape that makes fairly deep-colored, full-bodied, soft white wines with aromas and flavors of roses and lychee fruit. France's Alsace region is the classic domain of this variety; the wines have pronounced floral and fruity aromas and flavors, but are actually dry — as fascinating as they are delicious. A commercial style of U.S. Gewürztraminer is light, sweetish, and fairly insipid, but a few wineries in California, Oregon, and New York do make good, dry Gewürztraminer.
Grüner Veltliner	A native Austrian variety that boasts complex aromas and flavors (vegetal, spicy, mineral), rich texture, and usually substantial weight.
Muscat	An aromatic grape that makes Italy's sparkling Asti (which, incidentally, tastes *exactly* like ripe Muscat grapes). Extremely pretty floral aromas. In Alsace and Austria, makes a dry wine, and in lots of places (southern France, southern Italy, Australia) makes a delicious, sweet dessert wine through the addition of alcohol.
Pinot Blanc	Fairly neutral in aroma and flavors, yet can make characterful wines. High acidity and low sugar levels translate into dry, crisp, medium-bodied wines. Alsace, Austria, northern Italy, and Germany are the main production zones.
Sémillon *(seh-mee-yohn)*	Sauvignon Blanc's classic blending partner and a good grape in its own right. Sémillon wine is low in acid relative to Sauvignon Blanc and has attractive but subtle aromas — lanolin sometimes, although it can be slightly herbaceous when young. A major grape in Australia, and southwestern France, including Bordeaux (where it is the key player in the dessert wine, Sauternes).
Viognier *(vee-ohn-yay)*	A grape from France's Rhône Valley that's becoming popular in California, the south of France and elsewhere. Floral aroma, delicately apricot-like, medium- to full-bodied with low acidity.

A Primer on Red Grape Varieties

Here are descriptions of 12 important red vinifera grape varieties. You'll encounter these grapes in varietal wines and also in place-name wines. See Chapter 4 for a chart listing the grape varieties of major place-name wines.

Cabernet Sauvignon

Cabernet Sauvignon is a noble grape variety that grows well in just about any climate that isn't very cool. It became famous through the age-worthy red wines of the Médoc district of Bordeaux (which usually also contain Merlot and Cabernet Franc, in varying proportions; see Chapter 9). But today California is an equally important region for Cabernet Sauvignon — not to mention Washington, southern France, Italy, Australia, South Africa, Chile, Argentina, and so on.

The Cabernet Sauvignon grape makes wines that are high in tannin and are medium- to full-bodied. The textbook descriptor for Cabernet Sauvignon's aroma and flavor is *blackcurrants* or *cassis;* the grape can also contribute vegetal tones to a wine when or where the grapes are less than ideally ripe.

Cabernet Sauvignon wines come in all price and quality levels. The least-expensive versions are usually fairly soft and very fruity, with medium body. The best wines are rich and firm with great depth and classic Cabernet flavor. Serious Cabernet Sauvignons can age for 15 years or more.

Because Cabernet Sauvignon is fairly tannic (and because of the blending precedent in Bordeaux), winemakers often blend it with other grapes; usually Merlot — being less tannic — is considered an ideal partner. Australian winemakers have an unusual practice of blending Cabernet Sauvignon with Syrah. (More on that in Chapter 12.)

Cabernet Sauvignon often goes by just its first name, Cabernet (although it isn't the only Cabernet) or even by its nickname, *Cab*.

Merlot

Deep color, full body, high alcohol, and low tannin are the characteristics of wines made from the Merlot grape. The aromas and flavors can be plummy or sometimes chocolatey, or they can suggest tea leaves.

Some wine drinkers find Merlot easier to like than Cabernet Sauvignon because it's less tannic. (But some winemakers feel that Merlot isn't satisfactory in its own right, and thus often blend it with Cabernet Sauvignon, Cabernet Franc, or both.) Merlot makes both inexpensive, simple wines and, when grown in the right conditions, very serious wines.

Merlot is actually the most-planted grape variety in Bordeaux, where it excels in the Right Bank districts of Pomerol and St. Emilion. Merlot is also important in Washington, California, the Long Island district of New York, Northeastern Italy, and Chile.

Pinot Noir

The late Andre Tchelitscheff, the legendary winemaker of some of California's finest Cabernets, once told us that if he could do it all over again, he'd make Pinot Noir instead of Cab. He's probably not alone. Cabernet is the sensible wine to make — a good, steady, reliable wine that doesn't give the winemaker too much trouble and can achieve excellent quality — and Pinot Noir is finicky, troublesome, enigmatic, and challenging. But a great Pinot Noir can be one of the greatest wines ever.

The prototype for Pinot Noir wine is red Burgundy, from France, where tiny vineyard plots yield rare treasures of wine made entirely from Pinot Noir. Oregon, California, New Zealand, and parts of Australia and Chile also produce good Pinot Noir. But Pinot Noir's production is rather limited, because this variety is very particular about climate and soil.

Pinot Noir wine is lighter in color than Cabernet or Merlot. It has relatively high alcohol, medium-to-high acidity, and medium-to-low tannin (although oak barrels can contribute additional tannin to the wine). Its flavors and aromas can be very fruity — often like a mélange of red berries — or earthy and woodsy, depending on how it is grown and/or vinified. Pinot Noir is rarely blended with other grapes.

Syrah/Shiraz

The northern part of France's Rhône Valley is the classic home for great wines from the Syrah grape. Rhône wines such as Hermitage and Côte-Rôtie are the inspiration for Syrah's dissemination to Australia, California, Washington, Italy, and Spain.

Syrah produces deeply colored wines with full body, firm tannin, and aromas/flavors that can suggest berries, smoked meat, black pepper, tar, or even burnt rubber (believe it or not). In Australia, Syrah (called Shiraz) comes in several styles — some of them charming, medium-bodied, vibrantly fruity wines that are quite the opposite of the Northern Rhône's powerful Syrahs. Turn to Chapter 12 for more on Shiraz.

Syrah doesn't require any other grape to complement its flavors, although in Australia it is often blended with Cabernet, and in the Southern Rhône it is often part of a blended wine with Grenache and other varieties.

Zinfandel

White Zinfandel is such a popular wine — and so much better known than the red style of Zinfandel — that its fans might argue that Zinfandel is a white grape. But it's really red.

Zinfandel is one of the oldest grapes in California, and it therefore enjoys a certain stature there. Its aura is enhanced by its mysterious history: Although Zinfandel is clearly a vinifera grape, for decades authorities were uncertain of its origins. They have finally proven that Zinfandel's origin is an obscure Croatian grape.

Zin — as lovers of red Zinfandel call it — makes rich, dark wines that are high in alcohol and medium to high in tannin. They can have a blackberry or raspberry aroma and flavor, a spicy or tarry character, or even a jammy flavor. Some Zins are lighter than others and meant to be enjoyed young, and some are serious wines with a tannin structure that's built for aging. (You can tell which is which by the price.)

Nebbiolo

Outside of scattered sites in Northwestern Italy — mainly the Piedmont region — Nebbiolo just doesn't make remarkable wine. But the extraordinary quality of Barolo and Barbaresco, two Piedmont wines, prove what greatness it can achieve under the right conditions.

The Nebbiolo grape is high in both tannin and acid, which can make a wine tough. Fortunately, it also gives enough alcohol to soften the package. Its color can be deep when the wine is young but can develop orangey tinges within a few years. Its complex aroma is fruity (strawberry, cherry), earthy and woodsy (tar, truffles), herbal (mint, eucalyptus, anise), and floral (roses).

Lighter versions of Nebbiolo are meant to be drunk young — wines labeled Nebbiolo d'Alba, Roero, or Nebbiolo delle Langhe, for example — while Barolo and Barbaresco are wines that really deserve a *minimum* of eight years' age before drinking.

Sangiovese

This Italian grape has proven itself in the Tuscany region of Italy, especially in the Brunello di Montalcino and Chianti districts. Sangiovese makes wines that are medium to high in acidity and firm in tannin; the wines can be light-bodied to full-bodied, depending on exactly where the grapes grow and how the wine is made. The aromas and flavors of the wines are fruity — especially cherry, often tart cherry — with floral nuances of violets and sometimes a slightly nutty character.

Tempranillo

Tempranillo is Spain's candidate for greatness. It gives wines deep color, low acidity, and only moderate alcohol. Modern renditions of Tempranillo from the Ribera del Duero region and elsewhere in Spain prove what color and fruitiness this grape has. In more traditional wines, such as those of the Rioja region, much of the grape's color and flavor is lost due to long wood aging and to blending with varieties that lack color, such as Grenache.

Other red grapes

Table 3-2 describes additional red grape varieties and their wines, which you can encounter either as varietal wines or as wines named for their place of production.

Table 3-2	Other Red Grapes and Their Characteristics
Grape Type	**Characteristics**
Aglianico	From Southern Italy, where it makes Taurasi and other age-worthy, powerful red wines, high in tannin.
Barbera	Italian variety that, oddly for a red grape, has little tannin but very high acidity. When fully ripe, it can give big, fruity wines with refreshing crispness. Many producers age the wine in new oak to increase the tannin level of their wine.
Cabernet Franc	A parent of Cabernet Sauvignon, and often blended with it to make Bordeaux-style wines. Ripens earlier, and has more expressive, fruitier flavor (especially berries), as well as less tannin. A specialty of the Loire Valley in France, where it makes wines with place-names such as Chinon and Bourgeuil.
Gamay	Excels in the Beaujolais district of France. It makes grapey wines that can be low in tannin — although the grape itself is fairly tannic. Neither the grape called *Gamay Beaujolais* in California nor the grape called *Napa Gamay* is true Gamay.
Grenache	A Spanish grape by origin, called Garnacha there. (Most wine drinkers associate Grenache with France's southern Rhône Valley more than with Spain, however.) Sometimes Grenache makes pale, high-alcohol wines that are dilute in flavor. In the right circumstances, it can make deeply colored wines with velvety texture and fruity aromas and flavors suggestive of raspberries.

Chapter 4

Wine Names and Label Lingo

• •

In This Chapter

▶ A quick trick to decoding wine names

▶ The secret cult of *terroir*

▶ The truth behind impressive terms like *reserve* and *estate-bottled*

▶ AOC, DOC, DO, QbA, QWPSR, and other strange designations

• •

*W*e visit wine stores all the time, not just to shop for dinner but also to keep an eye on what kinds of wines are hitting the shelves. Never before have we seen such an astounding proliferation of wine labels! Since about 2003, it seems that new brands of wine have appeared out of the blue every week.

All this choice is terrific — or it's completely paralyzing, depending on how you approach the situation. One sure way to become more comfortable when confronted by shelf upon shelf of unfamiliar wine labels is to learn how to decode the information on those labels. This isn't difficult to do, because regulations specify what can and cannot appear on a label. Master that, and you'll be basking in the richness of choices that today's wine market offers.

The Wine Name Game

All sorts of names appear on wine labels. These names often include

- ✔ The name of the *grape* from which the wine was made.

- ✔ A *brand name,* which is traditionally the name of the company or person that made the wine (who is called the *producer*), but for less expensive wines is likely to be an invented name.

- ✔ Sometimes a special, fanciful name for that particular wine (called a *proprietary name*).

- ✔ The name of the *place,* or *places,* where the grapes grew (the wine region, and sometimes the name of the specific vineyard property).

Then there's the *vintage* year (the year the grapes for that wine grew), which is part of the wine's identity; and sometimes you see a descriptor like *reserve,* which either has specific legal meaning or means nothing at all, depending on where the wine came from.

Is it a grape? Is it a place?

Most of the wines that you find in your wine shop or on restaurant wine lists are named in one of two basic ways: either for their *grape variety* or for the *place where the grapes grew.* That information, plus the name of the producer, becomes the shorthand name we use in talking about the wine.

Robert Mondavi Cabernet Sauvignon, for example, is a wine made by Robert Mondavi Winery and named after the Cabernet Sauvignon grape. Fontodi Chianti Classico is a wine made by the Fontodi winery and named after the place called Chianti Classico.

You may recognize some names as grape names (see Chapter 3) and other names as place-names right off the bat; but if you don't, don't panic. That information is the kind of thing you can look up. (Chapters 9 through 15 will help.)

Hello, my name is Chardonnay

A *varietal* wine is a wine that is named after either the *principal* or the *sole* grape variety that makes up the wine.

Each country (and in the United States, some individual states) has laws that dictate the minimum percentage of the named grape that a wine must contain if that wine wants to call itself by a grape name. The issue is truth in advertising.

U.S. federal regulations fix the legal minimum percentage of the named grape at 75 percent (which means that your favorite California Chardonnay could have as much as 25 percent of some *other* grape in it). In Oregon, the minimum is 90 percent (except for Cabernet, which can be 75 percent). In Australia, it's 85 percent. And in the countries that form the European Union (EU), the minimum is 85 percent.

Some varietal wines are made *entirely* from the grape variety for which the wine is named. There's no law against that anywhere.

Most of the time, the labels of varietal wines don't tell you whether other grapes are present in the wine, what those grapes are, or the percentage of the wine that they account for. All you know is that the wine contains at least the minimum legal percentage of the named variety.

Interestingly, if a wine sold in the United States is named for two or more grape varieties — it's a Semillon-Chardonnay, for example — the label must state the percentages of each, and these percentages must total 100 percent. Now that's an honest varietal wine!

Why name a wine after a grape variety?

Grapes are the raw material of a wine. Except for whatever a wine absorbs from oak barrels (certain aromas and flavors, as well as tannin) and from certain winemaking processes described in Chapter 5, the juice of the grapes is what any wine *is*. So to name a wine after its grape variety is very logical.

Naming a wine for its grape variety is also very satisfying to exacting consumers. Knowing what grape a wine is made from is akin to knowing what type of oil is in the salad dressing, whether there are any trans-fats in your bread, and how much egg is in your egg roll.

Most California (and other American) wines carry varietal names. Likewise, most Australian, South American, and South African wines are named by using the *principal* principle. Even some countries that don't normally name their wines after grapes, such as France, are jumping on the varietal-name bandwagon for certain wines that they especially want to sell to Americans.

Varietal currency

A common perception among some wine drinkers is that a varietal wine is somehow *better* than a non-varietal wine. Actually, the fact that a wine is named after its principal grape variety is absolutely *no indication of quality.*

Hello, my name is Bordeaux

Unlike American wines, most European wines are named for the *region* where their grapes grow rather than for the grape variety itself. Many of these European wines come from precisely the same grape varieties as American wines (like Chardonnay, Cabernet Sauvignon, Sauvignon Blanc, and so on), but they don't say so on the label. Instead, the labels say Burgundy, Bordeaux, Sancerre, and so on: the *place* where those grapes grow.

The most common place-names

Beaujolais	Chianti	Rioja
Bordeaux	Côtes du Rhône	Sancerre
Burgundy (Bourgogne)	Mosel	Sauternes
Chablis	Port (Porto)	Sherry
Champagne	Pouilly-Fuissé	Soave
Châteauneuf-du-Pape	Rhine (Rheingau, Rheinhessen)	Valpolicella

Is this some nefarious plot to make wine incomprehensible to English-only wine lovers who have never visited Europe and flunked geography in school?

Au contraire! The European system of naming wines is actually intended to provide more information about each wine, and more understanding of what's in the bottle, than varietal naming does. The only catch is that to harvest this information, you have to learn something about the different regions from which the wines come. (Turn to Chapters 9 through 15 for some of that information.)

Why name a wine after a place?

Grapes, the raw material of wine, have to grow somewhere. Depending on the type of soil, the amount of sunshine, the amount of rain, the slope of the hill, and the many other characteristics that each *somewhere* has, the grapes will turn out differently. If the grapes are different, the wine is different. Each wine, therefore, reflects the place where its grapes grow.

In Europe, grape growers/winemakers have had centuries to figure out which grapes grow best where. They've identified most of these grape–location match-ups and codified them into regulations. Therefore, the name of a *place* where grapes are grown in Europe automatically connotes the grape (or grapes) used to make the wine of that place. The label on the bottle usually doesn't tell you the grape (or grapes), though. Which brings us back to our original question: Is this some kind of nefarious plot to make wine incomprehensible to non-Europeans?

The terroir game

Terroir (pronounced *ter wahr*) is a French word that has no direct translation in English, so wine people just use the French word, for expediency (not for snobbery).

There's no fixed definition of *terroir;* it's a concept, and, like most concepts, people tend to define it more broadly or more narrowly to suit their own needs. The word itself is based on the French word *terre,* which means soil; so some people define *terroir* as, simply, dirt (as in "Our American dirt is every bit as good as their French dirt").

Decoding common European place-names

Wine Name	Country	Grape Varieties
Beaujolais	France	Gamay
Bordeaux (red)	France	Cabernet Sauvignon, Merlot, Cabernet Franc, and others*
Bordeaux (white)	France	Sauvignon Blanc, Sémillon, Muscadelle*
Burgundy (red)	France	Pinot Noir
Burgundy (white)	France	Chardonnay
Chablis	France	Chardonnay
Champagne	France	Chardonnay, Pinot Noir, Pinot Meunier*
Châteauneuf-du-Pape*	France	Grenache, Mourvèdre, Syrah, and others*
Chianti	Italy	Sangiovese, Canaiolo, and others*
Côtes du Rhône*	France	Grenache, Mourvèdre, Carignan, and others*
Port (Porto)	Portugal	Touriga Nacional, Tinta Barroca, Touriga Franca, Tinta Roriz, Tinto Cão, and others*
Pouilly-Fuissé, Macon, Saint Véran	France	Chardonnay
Rioja (red)	Spain	Tempranillo, Grenache, and others*
Sancerre/Pouilly-Fumé	France	Sauvignon Blanc
Sauternes	France	Sémillon, Sauvignon Blanc*
Sherry	Spain	Palomino
Soave	Italy	Garganega and others*
Valpolicella	Italy	Corvina, Molinara, Rondinella*

*Indicates that a blend of grapes is used to make these wines.

But *terroir* is really much more complex (and complicated) than just dirt. *Terroir* is the combination of immutable natural factors — such as topsoil, subsoil, climate (sun, rain, wind, and so on), the slope of the hill, and altitude — that a particular vineyard site has. Chances are that no two vineyards in the entire world have precisely the same combination of these factors. So we consider *terroir* to be the *unique* combination of natural factors that a particular vineyard site has.

Terroir is the guiding principle behind the European concept that wines should be named after the place they come from (thought we'd gotten off the track, didn't you?). The thinking goes like this: The name of the place connotes which grapes were used to make the wine of that place (because the grapes are dictated by regulations), and the place influences the character of those grapes in its own unique way. Therefore, the most accurate name that a wine can have is the name of the place where its grapes grew.

It's not some nefarious plot; it's just a whole different way of looking at things.

Place-names on American wine labels

France may have invented the concept that wines should be named after their place of origin, but neither France nor even greater Europe has a monopoly on the idea. Wine labels from non-European countries also tell you where a wine comes from — usually by featuring the name of a place somewhere on the label. But a few differences exist between the European and non-European systems.

First of all, on an American wine label (or an Australian, Chilean or South African label, for that matter) you have to go to some effort to find the place-name on the label. The place of origin is not the fundamental name of the wine (as it is for most European wines); the grape usually is.

Second, place-names in the United States mean far less than they do in Europe. Okay, if the label says Napa Valley, and you've visited that area — and you loved eating at Mustards, and you'd like to spend the rest of your life in one of those houses atop a hill off the Silverado Trail — Napa Valley will mean something to you. But *legally,* the name Napa Valley means only that at least 85 percent of the grapes came from an area defined by law as the Napa Valley wine zone. The name Napa Valley does not define the type of wine, nor does it imply specific grape varieties, the way a European place-name does. (Good thing the grape name is there, as big as day, on the label.)

Place-names on labels of non-European wines, for the most part, merely pay lip service to the concept of *terroir.* In fact, some non-European wine origins are ridiculously broad. We have to laugh when we think how European winemakers must react to all those wine labels that announce a wine's place of origin simply as "California." *Great. This label says that this wine comes from a specific area that is 30 percent larger than the entire country of Italy! Some specific area!* (Italy has more than 300 specific wine zones.)

When the place on the label is merely *California,* in fact, that information tells you next to nothing about where the grapes grew. California's a big place, and those grapes could come from just about anywhere. Same thing for all those Australian wines labeled *South Eastern Australia* — an area only slightly smaller than France and Spain *combined.*

Wines named in other ways

Now and then, you may come across a wine that is named for neither its grape variety nor its region of origin. Such wines usually fall into three categories: *branded wines, wines with proprietary names,* or *generic wines.*

Branded wines

Most wines have brand names, including those wines that are named after their grape variety — like Cakebread (brand name) Sauvignon Blanc (grape) — and those that are named after their region of origin — like Masi (brand name) Valpolicella (place). These brand names are usually the name of the company that made the wine, called a *winery.* Because most wineries make several different wines, the brand name itself is not specific enough to be the actual name of the wine.

But sometimes a wine has *only* a brand name. For example, the label says *Salamandre* and *red French wine* but provides little other identification.

Wines that have *only* a brand name on them, with no indication of grape or of place — other than the country of production — are generally the most inexpensive, ordinary wines you can get. If they're from a European Union country, they won't even be *vintage dated* (that is, there won't be any indication of what year the grapes were harvested) because EU law does not entitle such wines to carry a vintage date.

Bigger than a breadbasket

When we travel to other countries, we realize that people in different places have different ways of perceiving space and distance. If someone tells us that we'll find a certain restaurant "just up ahead," for example, we figure it's the equivalent of about three blocks away — but they might mean three miles.

Discussing place-names for European wines can be just as problematic. Some of the *places* are as small as several acres, some are 100 square miles big, and others are the size of New Jersey. Certain words used to describe wine zones suggest the relative size of the place. In descending order of size and ascending order of specificity: country, region, district, subdistrict, commune, vineyard.

Grape names on European wines

Although most European wines are named after their place of origin, grape names do sometimes appear on labels of European wines. In Italy, for example, the official name of a wine could be a combination of place and grape — like the name Barbera d'Alba, which translates as Barbera (grape) of Alba (place).

In France, some producers have deliberately added the grape name to their labels even though the grape is already implicit in the wine name.

For example, a white Bourgogne (place-name) may also have the word Chardonnay (grape) on the label, for those wine drinkers who don't know that white Bourgogne is 100 percent Chardonnay. And German wines usually carry grape names along with their official place-names.

But even if a European wine does carry a grape name, the most important part of the wine's name, in the eyes of the people who make the wine, is the place.

Wines with proprietary names

You can find some pretty creative names on wine bottles these days: Tapestry, Conundrum, Insignia, Isosceles, Mythology, Trilogy. Is this stuff to drink, to drive, or to dab behind your ears?

Names like these are *proprietary names* (often trademarked) that producers create for special wines. In the case of American wines, the bottles with proprietary names usually contain wines made from a *blend* of grapes; therefore, no one grape name can be used as the name of the wine. (Remember the United States' 75 percent policy?) In the case of European wines, the grapes used to make the wine were probably not the approved grapes for that region; therefore, the regional name could not be used on the label.

Although a brand name can apply to several different wines, a proprietary name usually applies to one specific wine. You can find Zinfandel, Cabernet Sauvignon, Chardonnay, and numerous other wines under the Fetzer brand from California, for example, and you can find Beaujolais, Pouilly-Fuissé, Mâcon-Villages, and numerous other wines under the Louis Jadot brand from France. But the proprietary name Luce applies to a single wine.

Wines with proprietary names usually are made in small quantities, are quite expensive ($40 to $75 or more a bottle), and are high in quality.

Generic wines

A generic name is a wine name that has been used inappropriately for so long that it has lost its original meaning in the eyes of the government (exactly what Xerox, Kleenex, and Band-Aid are afraid of becoming).

Burgundy, Chianti, Chablis, Champagne, Rhine wine, Sherry, Port, and Sauterne are all names that rightfully should apply only to wines made in those specific places. After years of negotiation with the European Union, the U.S. government has finally agreed that these names can no longer be used for American wines. However, any wine that bore such a name prior to March 2006 may continue to carry that name. In time, generic names will become less common on wine labels.

Wine Labels, Forward and Backward

Many wine bottles have two labels. The front label names the wine and grabs your eye as you walk down the aisle, and the back label gives you a little more information, ranging from really helpful suggestions like "this wine tastes delicious with food" to oh-so-useful data such as "this wine has a total acidity of 6.02 and a pH of 3.34."

Now, if you're really on your toes, you may be thinking: How can you tell the difference between front and back on a round bottle?

The government authorities in the United States apparently haven't thought that one through yet. They (and other governments) require certain information to appear on the front label of all wine bottles — basic stuff, such as the alcohol content, the type of wine (usually *red table wine* or *white table wine*), and the country of origin — but they don't define *front label*. So sometimes producers put all that information on the smaller of two labels and call that one the front label. Then the producers place a larger, colorful, dramatically eye-catching label — with little more than the name of the wine on it — on the *back* of the bottle. Guess which way the back label ends up facing when the bottle is placed on the shelf?

We don't feel at all outraged about this situation. We'd rather look at colorful labels on the shelf than boring information-laden ones any day. And we're not so lazy that we can't just pick up the bottle and turn it around to find out what we need to know. Besides, we enjoy the idea that wine producers and importers — whose every word and image on the label is scrutinized by the authorities — have found one small way of getting even with the government.

The mandatory sentence

The federal government mandates that certain items of information appear on labels of wines sold in the United States. Such items are generally referred to as *the mandatory*. These include

- A brand name
- Indication of class or type (table wine, dessert wine, or sparkling wine)
- The percentage of alcohol by volume (unless it is implicit — for example, the statement "table wine" implies an alcohol content of less than 14 percent; see the section "Table wine" in Chapter 1)
- Name and location of the bottler
- Net contents (expressed in milliliters; the standard wine bottle is 750 ml, which is 25.6 ounces)
- The phrase *Contains Sulfites* (with very, very few exceptions)
- The government warning (that we won't dignify by repeating here; just pick up any bottle of wine and you'll see it on the back label)

Figure 4-1 shows you how all the details come together on a label.

American Viticultural Area (AVA)

GOBBLEDYGOOK

Sonoma Valley
Nonna's Vineyard

Select Reserve
Estate-Bottled

Chardonnay
White table wine
Net contents 750ml - 13.5% alcohol
Vinted and bottled by Gobbledygook Winery, Healdsburg, CA
CONTAINS SULFITES

Brand name
Quality designation
Estate-bottled designation
Wine name
Type
Alcohol by volume

Bottler information

Vineyard designation

Figure 4-1: The label of an American varietal wine.

© Akira Chiwaki

Will the real producer please stand up?

Although U.S. labeling laws require wine labels to carry the name and address of the bottler, this information doesn't necessarily tell you who made the wine.

Of the various phrases that may be used to identify the bottler on labels of wine sold in the United States, only the words *produced by* or *made by* indicate the name of the company that actually fermented 75 percent or more of the wine (that is, who really *made* the wine); words such as *cellared by* or *vinted by* mean only that the company subjected the wine to cellar treatment (holding it for a while, for example).

Wines made outside the United States but sold within it must also carry the phrase *imported by* on their labels, along with the name and business location of the importer.

Canadian regulations are similar. They require wine labels to indicate the *common name* of the product (that is, *wine*), the net contents, the percentage of alcohol by volume, the name and address of the producer, the wine's country of origin, and the container size. Many of these items must be indicated in both English and French.

The European mandate

Some of the mandatory information on American and Canadian wine labels is also required by the EU authorities for wines produced or sold in the European Union. But the EU regulations require additional label items for wines produced in its member countries.

The most important of these additional items is an indication of a wine's so-called quality level — which really means the wine's status in the European Union's hierarchy of place-names. In short, every wine made in an EU member country *must* carry one of the following items on the label:

- ✔ A registered place-name, along with an official phrase that confirms that the name is in fact a registered place-name (see the following section for a listing of those phrases)

- ✔ A phrase indicating that the wine is a *table wine,* a status lower than that of a wine with a registered place-name

For U.S. wines, the *table wine* category encompasses all non-sparkling wines that contain up to 14 percent alcohol. This is a distinctly different use of the term *table wine.*

Appellations of origin

A registered place-name is called an *appellation of origin.* In actuality, each EU place-name defines far more than just the name of the place that the grapes come from: The place-name connotes the wine's grape varieties, grape-growing methods, and winemaking methods. Each appellation is, therefore, a definition of the wine as well as the wine's name.

European wines with official place-names fall into a European category called QWPSR (Quality Wine Produced in a Specific Region). The following phrases on European labels confirm that a wine is a QWPSR wine and that its name is therefore a registered place-name:

✔ **France:** *Appellation Contrôlée* or *Appellation d'Origine Contrôlée* (AC or AOC, in short), translated as *regulated name* or *regulated place-name.* Also, on labels of wines from places of slightly lower status, the initials AO VDQS, standing for *Appellation d'Origine — Vins Délimités de Qualité Supérieure;* translated as *place-name, demarcated wine of superior quality.*

✔ **Italy:** *Denominazione di Origine Controllata* (DOC), translated as *regulated place-name;* or for certain wines of an even higher status, *Denominazione di Origine Controllata e Garantita* (DOCG), translated as *regulated and guaranteed place-name.*

✔ **Spain:** *Denominación de Origen* (DO), translated as *place-name;* and *Denomináción de Origen Calificada* (DOC), translated as *qualified-origin place-name* for regions with the highest status (of which there are only two, Rioja and Priorat).

✔ **Portugal:** *Denominação de Origem* (DO), translated as *place-name.*

✔ **Germany:** *Qualitätswein bestimmter Anbaugebiete* (QbA), translated as *quality wine from a specific region;* or *Qualitätswein mit Prädikat* (QmP), translated as *quality wine with special attributes,* for the best wines. (Read more about Germany's complex appellation system in Chapter 11.)

For European table wines — wines without an official appellation of origin — each European country has two phrases. One term applies to table wines with a geographic indication (actually Italy has two phrases in this category), and another denotes table wines with no geographic indication smaller than the country of production. These phrases are

- **France:** *Vin de pays* (country wine) followed by the name of an approved area; *vin de table*

- **Italy:** *Indicazione Geografica Tipica* (translated as *typical geographic indication* and abbreviated as IGT) and the name of an approved area, or *vino da tavola* (table wine) followed by a the name of a geographic area; *vino da tavola*

- **Spain:** *Vino de la tierra* (country wine) followed by the name of an approved area; *vino de mesa*

- **Portugal:** *Vinho Regional* (regional wine) and the name of an approved area; *vinho de mesa*

- **Germany:** *Landwein* (country wine) and the name of an approved area; *Deutscher tafelwein*

Table 4-1 lists the European wine designations for easy reference.

Table 4-1	European Wine Designations at a Glance		
Country	*QWPSR Designation(s)*	*Table Wine Designation with Geographic Indication*	*Table Wine Designation without Geographic Indication*
France	AOC	Vin de pays	Vin de table
	VDQS		
Italy	DOCG	IGT; Vino da tavola (and geographic name)	Vino da tavola
	DOC		
Spain	DOC	Vino de la tierra	Vino de mesa
	DO		
Portugal	DO	Vinho regional	Vinho de mesa
Germany	QmP	Landwein	Deutscher tafelwein
	QbA		

Figure 4-2 shows a European wine label as it would appear in the United States.

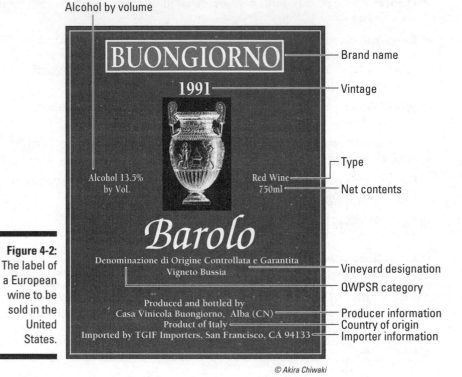

Alcohol by volume

BUONGIORNO — Brand name

1991 — Vintage

Type

Alcohol 13.5% by Vol.

Red Wine — 750ml — Net contents

Figure 4-2:
The label of
a European
wine to be
sold in the
United
States.

Barolo

Denominazione di Origine Controllata e Garantita
Vigneto Bussia — Vineyard designation
— QWPSR category

Produced and bottled by
Casa Vinicola Buongiorno, Alba (CN) — Producer information
Product of Italy — Country of origin
Imported by TGIF Importers, San Francisco, CA 94133 — Importer information

© Akira Chiwaki

TIP

The phrase for a registered place-name in the United States is *American Viticultural Area* (AVA). But the phrase does *not* appear on wine labels (refer to Figure 4-1). Nor does any such phrase appear on labels of Australian or South American wines.

Some optional label lingo

Besides the mandatory information required by government authorities, all sorts of other words can appear on wine labels. These words can be meaningless phrases intended to make you think that you're getting a special quality wine, or words that provide useful information about what's in the bottle. Sometimes the same word can fall into either category, depending on the label. This ambiguity occurs because some words that are strictly regulated in some producing countries are not at all regulated in others.

The EU hierarchy of wine

Although each country within the European Union makes its own laws regarding the naming of wine, these laws must fit within the framework of the European Union law. This framework provides two levels into which every single EU-produced wine must fit:

✔ **Quality wine:** Wines with official appellations of origin. (Each appellation regulation defines the geographic area, the grapes that may be used, grape-growing practices, winemaking and aging techniques, and so on.) This category is abbreviated as QWPSR in English (Quality Wine Produced in a Specific Region) or VQPRD in several other European languages. All AOC, DOC, DO, and QbA wines — to use the abbreviations mentioned previously in this chapter — fall into this category.

✔ **Table wine:** All other wines produced within the European Union. The table wine category has two subcategories: Table wines that carry a precise geographic indication on their labels, such as French *vin de pays* or Spanish *vino de la tierra* wines; and table wines with no geographic indication except the country of origin. These latter wines may not carry a vintage or a grape name.

All other wines sold in the European Union fall into a third category:

✔ **Wine:** Wines produced by countries outside the European Union, such as the United States, Canada, or Australia. If a wine has a geographic indication smaller than the country of origin, it enjoys higher status than otherwise.

Vintage

The word *vintage* followed by a year, or the year listed alone without the word *vintage,* is the most common optional item on a wine label (refer to Figure 4-2). Sometimes the vintage appears on the front label, and sometimes it has its own small label above the front label.

The *vintage year* is nothing more than the year in which the grapes for a particular wine grew; the wine must have 75 to 100 percent of the grapes of this year, depending on the country of origin. (*Nonvintage* wines are blends of wines whose grapes were harvested in different years.) But there is an aura surrounding vintage-dated wine that causes many people to believe that any wine with a vintage date is by definition better than a wine without a vintage date. *In fact, there is no correlation between the presence of a vintage date and the wine's quality.*

Generally speaking, *what* vintage a wine is — that is, whether the grapes grew in a year with perfect weather or whether the grapes were meteorologically challenged — is an issue you need to consider a) only when you buy top quality wines, and b) mainly when those wines come from parts of the world that experience significant variations in weather from year to year — such as many European wine regions.

Reserve

Reserve is our favorite meaningless word on American wine labels. The term is used to convince you that the wine inside the bottle is special. This trick usually works because the word *does* have specific meaning and *does* carry a certain amount of prestige on labels of wines from many other countries:

- In Italy and Spain, the word *reserve* (or its foreign language equivalent, which looks something like *reserve*) indicates a wine that has received extra aging at the winery before release. Implicit in the extra aging is the idea that the wine was better than normal and, therefore, worthy of the extra aging. Spain even has *degrees* of reserve, such as Gran Reserva.

- In France, the use of *reserve* is not regulated. However, its use is generally consistent with the notion that the wine is better in quality than a given producer's norm.

In the United States, the word *reserve* has historically been used in the same sense — as in Beaulieu Vineyards Georges de Latour Private Reserve, the best Cabernet that Beaulieu Vineyards makes. But these days, the word is bandied about so much that it no longer has meaning. For example, some California wines labeled *Proprietor's Reserve* sell for $6 a bottle. Those wines are not only the *least* expensive wines in a particular producer's lineup, but also some of the least expensive wines, period. Other wines are labeled Special Reserve, Vintage Reserve, Vintner's Reserve, or Reserve Selection — all utterly meaningless phrases.

Estate-bottled

Estate is a genteel word for a wine farm, a combined grape-growing and wine-making operation. The words *estate-bottled* on a wine label indicate that the company that bottled the wine also grew the grapes and made the wine. In other words, *estate-bottled* suggests accountability from the vineyard to the winemaking through to the bottling. In many countries, the winery does not necessarily have to own the vineyards, but it has to control the vineyards and perform the vineyard operations.

Estate-bottling is an important concept to those who believe that you can't make good wine unless the grapes are as good as they can possibly be. If *we* made wine, we'd sure want to control our own vineyards.

We wouldn't go so far as to say that great wines *must* be estate-bottled, though. Ravenswood Winery — to name just one example — makes some terrific wines from the grapes of small vineyards owned and operated by private landowners. And some large California landowners, such as the Sangiacomo family, are quite serious about their vineyards but do not make wine themselves; they sell their grapes to various wineries. None of those wines would be considered estate-bottled.

Sometimes French wine labels carry the words *domaine-bottled* or *château-bottled* (or the phrase *mis en bouteille au château/au domaine*). The concept is the same as estate-bottled, with *domaine* and *château* being equivalent to the American term *estate*.

Vineyard name

Some wines in the medium-to-expensive price category — costing about $25 or more — may carry on the label the name of the specific vineyard where the grapes for that wine grew. Sometimes one winery will make two or three different wines that are distinguishable only by the vineyard name on the label. Each wine is unique because the *terroir* of each vineyard is unique. These single vineyards may or may not be identified by the word *vineyard* next to the name of the vineyard.

Italian wines, which are really into the single-vineyard game, will have *vigneto* or *vigna* on their labels next to the name of the single vineyard. Or they won't. It's optional.

Other optional words on the label

You'll be pleased to know that we have just about exhausted our list of terms that you may find on a wine label.

One additional expression on some French labels is *Vieilles Vignes (vee yay veen),* which translates as *old vines,* and appears as such on some Californian and Australian labels. Because old vines produce a very small quantity of fruit compared to younger vines, the quality of their grapes and of the resulting wine is considered to be very good. The problem is, the phrase is unregulated. Anyone can claim that his vines are old.

The word *superior* can appear in French *(Supérieure)* or Italian *(Superiore)* as part of an AOC or DOC place-name (refer to the section "The mandatory sentence," earlier in this chapter, for a refresher on these acronyms). It means the wine attained a higher alcohol level than a nonsuperior version of the same wine would have. Frankly, it's a distinction not worth losing sleep over.

The word *Classico* appears on the labels of some Italian DOC and DOCG wines when the grapes come from the heartland of the named place.

Chapter 5

Behind the Scenes of Winemaking

The most frustrating thing about wine has to be the technical lingo. All you want is a crisp, fruity white wine to serve with tonight's fried chicken. But to find it, you have to fight your way through a jungle of jargon. You encounter it on the back labels of wine bottles, in the words the sales clerk uses to explain his recommendations, and on the signs all around the wine shop. Why on earth is everyone making wine so complicated?

Here's the story: Wine is two products. Some wine is just a beverage, and it should taste good — period. Other wine is an art form that fascinates and intrigues people. Many people who make and sell wine want you to think that their wines are in the second category, because such wines are more prestigious. Complicated technical language is supposed to make you think that a wine is special, more than just a beverage.

How much of this information (if any) is pivotal in helping you get the kind of wine you want, and how much is pretentious technobabble? Read on.

Grapegrowing, Winemaking, and the Jargon that Surrounds Them

Winemakers use numerous techniques to make wine. These techniques vary according to the grapes the winemakers have and the type of wine they're making. (If a winemaker is producing a huge quantity of a wine that will sell for $5.99, for example, he probably won't put the wine into new oak barrels because the cost of the barrels can add as much as $5 to the price of every bottle.)

No winemaking procedure is inherently good or inherently bad. Any technique can be right or wrong depending on the grapes and the type of wine being made — that is, the price level, the taste profile the winemaker is seeking, and the type of wine drinker the winery is targeting. Different wines appeal to different wine drinkers at different times:

- ✔ Some wines are intended to taste good right away, while others are intended to taste good down the road, after the wine has aged (see Chapter 16).

- ✔ Some are intended to taste good to casual wine drinkers, while others are intended for more experienced wine lovers.

How the wine tastes is the ultimate validation of any method used to produce a wine: The procedures themselves are meaningless if they don't create a wine that is appealing to the wine drinkers for whom that wine is intended.

The *taste* of the wine involves not just its flavors, but its aroma, body, texture, length, and so on (see Chapter 2). And the taste of a wine is a subjective experience.

Every winemaking technique does affect the taste of the wine in one way or another, however. Most of the technical words that are bandied about in wine circles represent procedures that *are* relevant to the taste of a wine. But — here's the key point — these technical words each represent isolated elements in the making of the wine, which are only *parts* of the total picture that begins with the grapes and ends when you put the wine in your mouth.

Viti-vini

Producing wine actually involves two separate steps: the growing of the grapes, called *viticulture,* and the making of the wine, called *vinification.* (In some wine courses, students nickname the dual process *viti-vini.*)

Sometimes one company performs both steps, as is the case with *estate-bottled* wines (see Chapter 4). And sometimes the two steps are completely separate. For example, some large wineries buy grapes from private grape growers. These growers don't make wine; they just grow grapes and sell them to whatever wine company offers them the highest price per ton.

In the case of the very least expensive wines, the winery named on the label may have purchased not even grapes but wine (from bulk wine producers), and then blended the wines and bottled the final product as his own. (As we mention in Chapter 4, only the terms *produced by* or *made by* on the label assure you that the company named on the label actually vinified most of that wine.)

Vine-growing variations

Growing grapes for wine is a fairly intricate process that viticulturalists are constantly refining to suit their particular soil, climate, and grape varieties. Many of the technical terms spill over into discussions about wine, or crop up on wine labels.

Here are the expressions that you're likely to encounter as you dig further into wine:

✔ **Microclimate:** Every wine region has climatic conditions (the amount and timing of sun, rain, wind, humidity, and so on) that are considered the norm for that area. But individual locations within a region — the south-facing side of a particular hill, for example — can have a climatic reality that is different from neighboring vineyards. The unique climatic reality of a specific location is usually called its *microclimate*. Technically, the correct term for what we have just described is *mesoclimate*, but microclimate is a more common term on back labels and in colloquial usage.

✔ **Canopy:** Left untended, grapevines would grow along the ground, up trees, wherever. (They're *vines,* after all!) Commercial viticulture involves attaching the shoots of vines to wires or trellises in a systematic pattern. The purpose of *training* the vine — as this activity is called — is to position the grape bunches so that they get enough sun to ripen well and so that the fruit is easy for the harvesters to reach.

An *open canopy* is a trellising method that maximizes the sunlight exposure of the grapes. *Canopy management,* the practice of maneuvering the leaves and fruit into the best position for a given vineyard, is a popular buzzword.

✔ **Ripeness:** Harvesting grapes when they're perfectly ripe is one of the crucial points in wine production. (See Chapter 3.) But ripeness is a subjective issue.

In cooler climates, a high degree of ripeness doesn't happen every year; wines from "riper" vintages should therefore be richer and fuller-bodied than the norm for that type of wine. In warmer climates, ripeness is almost automatic; the trick becomes not letting the grapes get too ripe too fast, which causes them to be high in sugar but still physiologically immature and undeveloped in their flavors (like a physically precocious but immature teenager). There's no fixed definition of perfect ripeness.

✔ **Low yields:** Generally speaking, the more grapes a grapevine grows (the higher its *yield* of grapes), the less concentrated the flavors of those grapes will be, and the lower in quality (and less expensive) their wine will be. Just about any wine producer anywhere can claim that his yields are low, because it's too complicated to prove otherwise. The proof is usually in the wine's concentration of flavor: If the wine tastes thin or watery, we'd be suspicious of the "low yield" claim.

✔ **Organic:** Grapegrowers increasingly farm their vineyards *organically,* that is without using chemical pesticides, herbicides and so forth. Their reasons have to do with the health of the land, and often their belief that organically grown grapes are superior to conventionally farmed grapes, and that they make better wine. For a wine label in the Unites States to state that the grapes for that wine were grown organically, the vineyard must be certified as organic by a government-approved organization.

A related term is *biodynamic;* this means that the vineyards are not only organic but also are farmed in keeping with the principles established in the early 20th century by Austrian philosopher Rudolph Steiner, which involve cosmic aspects such as respecting the movement of the moon and the planets in the timing of the work on the land. Biodynamic wines enjoy almost a cult following.

Winemaking wonders

The vinification end of wine production falls into two parts:

✔ **Fermentation,** the period when the grape juice turns into wine

✔ **Maturation** (or *finishing*), the period following fermentation when the wine settles down, loses its rough edges, goes to prep school, and gets ready to meet the world

Depending on the type of wine being made, the whole process can take three months or five years — or even longer if the bank isn't breathing down the winery's neck.

Winemakers don't have as many options in making wine as chefs do in preparing food — but almost! Of all the jargon you're likely to hear, information about oak is probably the most common.

When wood becomes magic

Oak barrels, 60 gallons in size, are often used as containers for wine during either fermentation or maturation. The barrels lend oaky flavor and aroma to the wine, which many people find very appealing; they can also affect the texture of the wine and its color. The barrels are expensive — about $800 per barrel if they're made from French oak. (Most people consider French oak to be the finest.) We suppose the expense is one good reason to boast about using the barrels.

But not all oak is the same. Oak barrels vary in the origin of their oak, the amount of *toast* (a charring of the inside of the barrels) each barrel has, how often the barrels have been used (their oaky character diminishes with use), and even the size of the barrels. Even if all oak *were* the same, a wine can turn out differently depending on whether unfermented juice or actual wine went into the barrels, and how long it stayed there.

In fact, the whole issue of oak is so complex that anyone who suggests that a wine is better simply because it has been oaked is guilty of gross oversimplification.

Barrel-fermented versus barrel-aged

You don't have to venture very far into wine before you find someone explaining to you that a particular wine was barrel-fermented or barrel-aged. What in the world does he mean, and should you care?

The term *barrel-fermented* means that unfermented juice went into barrels (almost always oak) and changed into wine there. The term *barrel-aged* usually means that wine (already fermented) went into barrels and stayed there for a maturation period — from a few months to a couple of years. Because most wines that ferment in barrels remain there for several months after fermentation ends, *barrel-fermented* and *barrel-aged* are often used together. Theterm *barrel-aged* alone suggests that the fermentation happened somewhere other than the barrel — usually in stainless steel tanks.

Classic barrel-fermentation — juice into the barrel, wine out — applies mainly to white wines, and the reason is very practical. As we mention in Chapter 2, the juice of red grapes ferments together with the grape skins in order to become red, and those solids are mighty messy to clean out of a small barrel! Red wines usually ferment in larger containers — stainless steel tanks or large wooden vats — and then *age* in small oak barrels after the wine has been drained off the grape skins. (Some light, fruity styles of red wine may not be oaked at all.) Some winemakers do partially ferment their reds in barrels; they start the fermentation in tanks, then drain the juice from the skins and let that juice finish its fermentation in barrels, without the skins. When a red wine is described as being barrel-fermented, that's usually the process.

Here's why you might care whether a white wine is barrel-fermented or just barrel-aged. Wines that ferment in barrels actually end up tasting *less* oaky than wines that simply age in barrels, even though they may have spent more time in oak. (A barrel-fermented and barrel-aged Chardonnay may have spent 11 months in oak, for example, and a barrel-aged Chardonnay may have spent only 5 months in oak.) That's because juice interacts differently with the oak than wine does.

A lot of people who are supposed to know more about wine than you confuse the effects of the two processes and tell you that the barrel-fermented wine tastes oakier. If you have a strong opinion about the flavor of oak in your wine, be sure that you know the real story.

Even More Winemaking Terms

Become a wine expert overnight and dazzle your friends with this amazing array of wine jargon. (Just don't fool yourself into believing that any one of the procedures described necessarily creates a high-quality wine. The merit of each procedure depends on the particular wine being made.)

- **Temperature control:** The modern age of winemaking began when winemakers were able to scientifically control the temperature of their fermentations by using stainless steel tanks rigged with cooling jackets or other computer-operated cooling devices. Because the temperature of the fermentation (about 54° to 77° F or 12° to 25° C for white wines and 77° to 93° F, or 25° to 34° C for reds) affects the final style of the wine, temperature control is critical. But, hey, this process was revolutionary and exciting almost half a century ago. Today it's just ho-hum par for the course.

- **Stainless steel:** Large tanks made of shiny, hygienic stainless steel are the vessels of choice for most fermentations, whether for red wine or white. When you hear a winemaker or wine expert say that a particular wine fermented in stainless steel, understand him to mean that one of three things is true:

  - The wine was not oaked at all (which is common for many aromatic-style white wines such as Rieslings, for example, to preserve the grapes' own flavors).

  - The wine was barrel-aged rather than barrel-fermented (see the previous section).

  - The winery sunk a lot of money into its equipment and wants you to know it.

- **Lees:** *Lees* is the name for various solids such as dead yeast cells that precipitate to the bottom of a wine after fermentation. These solids can interact with the wine and create more complex flavors in the wine. (Sometimes the winemaker stirs the lees around in the wine periodically to prevent off-flavors.) A white wine with extended lees contact is usually richer in texture and tastes less overtly fruity than it would otherwise.

- **ML or malolactic:** *Malolactic,* nicknamed *ML* or *malo,* is a secondary fermentation that weakens the acids in the wine, making the wine softer and less acidic. ML usually happens naturally, but a winemaker can also incite it or prevent it.

Red wines almost always undergo malolactic fermentation, but for white wines, ML is a stylistic judgment call on the winemaker's part. Sometimes, ML can contribute a buttery flavor to a white wine, but it diminishes the wine's fresh-fruitiness.

- **pH:** The chemical term *pH* means exactly the same thing for wine as it does in other scientific fields. ("Our facial cream is pH-balanced for sensitive skin.") If you want a technical explanation, look up your former chemistry teacher. If you'll settle for the general concept, pH is a measurement of acidity; wines with low pH (approximately 3.4 or less) have stronger acidity, and wines with high pH have weaker acidity.

- **Soft tannins:** Tannin in red wines varies not only in its quantity, but also in its nature. Some tannins give wines rich texture and an impression of substance without tasting bitter; other tannins are astringent and mouth-drying. *Soft tannins*, or *ripe tannins*, are buzzphrases for the good kind. Winemakers achieve soft tannins by harvesting fully ripe grapes, controlling fermentation time and temperature, and using other techniques.

- **Microxygenation:** This relatively new, high-tech winemaking technique involves feeding miniscule, controlled amounts of oxygen into a wine during or after fermentation. One effect is that it can mimic the gentle, steady exposure to oxygen that barrel-aged red wines receive as they mature in wood, and can thus help red wines develop softer tannins and more stable color without any actual use of oak. You hear this term, sometimes abbreviated as *microx,* thrown around in technical circles.

- **Fining** and **filtering:** Winemakers *fine* and *filter* most wines near the end of their maturation period. The purpose of these procedures is to *clarify* the wine — that is, to remove any cloudiness or solid matter in the wine — and to *stabilize* it — to remove any yeast, bacteria, or other microscopic critters that may change the wine for the worse after it is bottled.

There's a popular belief among anti-tech wine lovers that fining and filtration strip a wine of its character — and that unfined, unfiltered wines are inherently better, even if they're not brilliant in appearance. But it's a complex issue. (For one thing, there are *degrees* of fining and filtration, like *light* fining and *gentle* filtration.) These processes, when carried out carefully, are not detrimental to wine.

- **Blending:** This term usually applies to the process of making a wine from more than one grape variety. Winemakers generally ferment the different grapes separately and then blend their wines together.

The reasons for blending wines of different grapes are either to reduce costs — by diluting an expensive wine like Chardonnay with something else far less expensive, for example — or to improve the quality of the wine by using complementary grapes whose characteristics enhance each other. Many of Europe's traditional wines — such as red Rioja, red Bordeaux, Châteauneuf-du-Pape, and Champagne — are blended wines that owe their personalities to several grapes.

Wine terms that mean nothing

Sometimes winemakers or salespeople use words to describe their wines that, frankly, have no real meaning. When you hear these terms, understand them to mean that the person using them really wants you to believe that his wine is special. Then decide for yourself, by tasting, whether it is.

✔ handcrafted

✔ artisanal

✔ limited edition, limited selection, limited release

✔ vintner's select, vineyard select, "anything" select

Part II
Wine and You: Up Close and Personal

The 5th Wave   By Rich Tennant

WINE SALE

MYSTERY   HUMOR   ROMANCE
FICTION
NONFICTION

In this part . . .

With some of the basics under your belt — such as grape varieties, wine types, and wine names — you're ready to apply your knowledge at the practical level. Corkscrews, wine glasses, restaurant wine lists, and wine shops won't be any challenge at all, once you get the hang of them by browsing through the pages of the chapters that follow. We promise.

Chapter 6

Navigating a Wine Shop

*U*nless you enjoy a permanent, dependent relationship with an indulgent wine expert, the day will come when you have to purchase a bottle of wine yourself. If you're lucky, the shop owner will just happen to be some enlightened fellow or gal whose life's purpose is to make wine easy and accessible to others. The odds are, however, that most of the time you'll feel as if you're dancing in the dark.

Buying Wine Can Intimidate Anyone

Common sense suggests that buying a few bottles of wine should be less stressful than, say, applying for a bank loan or interviewing for a new job. What's the big deal? It's only grape juice.

But memories tell us otherwise. There was the time that one particular wine shop wouldn't take back one of the two bottles of inexpensive wine that we bought the week before, even when we explained how awful the first bottle had been. (Were *we* wrong about the wine or were *they* arrogant? We wasted days wondering.) And the time we pretended we knew what we were doing and bought a full case — 12 bottles — of a French wine based on the brand's general reputation, not realizing that the particular vintage we purchased was a miserable aberration from the brand's usual quality. (Why didn't we just ask someone in the store? We *might* have received good advice.) Then there were the many times we spent staring at shelves lined with bottles whose labels might as well have been written in Greek, for all that we could understand from them. Fortunately, our enthusiasm for wine caused us to persevere. We eventually discovered that wine shopping can be fun.

Our experience has taught us that the single most effective way to assure yourself of more good wine-buying experiences than bad ones is to come to terms with your knowledge — or lack thereof — of the subject.

Too much information about wine is constantly changing — new vintages each year, hundreds of new wineries, new brands, and so on — for *anyone* to presume that he knows it all, or for anyone to feel insecure about what he doesn't know.

If we'd all quit pretending that we know more than we do and give up our defensiveness about what we don't know, buying wine would become the simple exchange that it should be.

Wine Retailers, Large and Small

Buying wine in a store to drink later at home is great for a number of reasons, not the least of which is that stores usually have a much bigger selection of wines than restaurants do, and they charge you less for them. You can examine the bottles carefully and compare the labels. And you can drink the wine at home from the glass — and at the temperature — of your choosing.

On the other hand, you have to provide your own wine glasses, and you have to open the bottle yourself (see Chapter 8 for the lowdown on all that). And that big selection of wines in the store can be downright daunting.

Depending on where you live, you can buy wine at all sorts of stores: supermarkets, wine superstores, discount warehouses, or small specialty wine shops. Each type of store has its own advantages and disadvantages in terms of selection, price, or service.

Wine is a regulated beverage in many countries, and governments often get involved in deciding where and how wine may be sold. Some states within the United States and some provinces in Canada have raised government control of alcoholic beverage sales to a fine art, deciding not only *where* you can buy wine, but *which wines* are available for you to buy. If you love wine and live in one of those areas (you know who you are), take comfort in the fact that a) you have a vote; b) freedom of choice lies just across the border; and c) if the Iron Curtain can topple, there's hope for change in your local government, too.

We'll assume a healthy, open-minded, free-market economy for wine in our discussion of retail wine sales. We hope that scenario applies where you live, because your enjoyment of wine will blossom all the more easily if it does.

Supermarkets, superstores, and so on

In truly *open* wine markets, you can buy wine in supermarkets, like any other food product. Supermarkets and their large-scale brethren, discount warehouses, make wine accessible to everyone.

When wine is sold in supermarkets or discount stores, the mystique surrounding the product evaporates: Who can waste time feeling insecure about a wine purchase when there are much more critical issues at hand, such as how much time is left before the kids turn into monsters and which is the shortest line at the checkout? And the prices, especially in large stores, are usually quite reasonable.

The downside of buying wine in these stores is that your selection is often limited to wines produced by large wineries that generate enough volume to sell to supermarket chains. And you'll seldom get any advice on which wines to buy. Basically, you're on your own.

 We know for a fact that some people in the wine business disapprove of the straightforward attitude toward wine in supermarkets and discount stores; they think wine is sacrosanct and should always be treated like an elite beverage. At least you won't run into *them* as you browse the wine aisles in your supermarket.

 Discount stores are good places to find *private label* wines — wines that are created especially for the chain, and that carry a brand name that's owned by the store. These wines usually are decent (but not great), and if you like the wines, they can be excellent values. Some of the "club" chains may also offer — in smaller quantities — higher-end wines than supermarkets do.

 To guide you on your wine-buying journey, many stores offer plenty of *shelf-talkers* (small signs on the shelves that describe individual wines). These shelf-talkers should be taken with a very large grain of salt. They are often provided by the company selling the wine, which is more interested in convincing you to grab a bottle than in offering information to help you understand the wine. Most likely, you'll find flowery phrases, hyperbolic adjectives, impressive scores and safe, common-denominator stuff like "delicious with fish." (*Any* fish, cooked in *any* way?) The information will be biased and of limited value. We strongly recommend that you find a knowledgeable person from the store to help you, if at all possible, rather than rely on shelf-talkers.

Supermarket survival tips

If you're shopping in a supermarket where there's no one to turn to for advice, do one of the following:

✔ Consult a list of recommended wines from the last wine article that impressed you.

✔ Call a wine-knowledgeable friend on your cell phone (assuming that his or her palate and yours get along).

✔ Buy the wine with the prettiest label. What have you got to lose?

The bottom line is that supermarkets and discount warehouses can be great places to buy everyday wine for casual enjoyment. But if what you really want is to learn about wine as you buy it, or if you want an unusually interesting variety of wines to satisfy your rapacious curiosity, you will probably find yourself shopping elsewhere.

Wine specialty shops

Wine specialty shops are small- to medium-sized stores that sell wine and liquor and, sometimes, wine books, corkscrews (see Chapter 8 for more on those), wine glasses, and maybe a few specialty foods. The foods sold in wine shops tend to be gourmet items rather than just run-of-the-mill snack foods.

If you decide to pursue wine as a serious hobby, shops like these are the places where you'll probably end up buying your wine because they offer many advantages that larger operations cannot. For one thing, wine specialty shops almost always have wine-knowledgeable staffers on the premises. Also, you can usually find an interesting, varied selection of wines at all price levels.

Wine shops often organize their wines by country of origin and — in the case of classic wine countries, such as France, by region (Bordeaux, Burgundy, Rhône, and so on). Red wines and white wines are often in separate sections within these country areas. There may be a special section for Champagnes and other sparkling wines and another section for dessert wines. Some stores are now organizing their wine sections by style, such as "Aromatic Whites," "Powerful Reds," and so forth. A few organize the wines according to grape varieties.

Some wine shops have a special area (or even a super-special, temperature-controlled room) for the finer or more expensive wines. In some stores, it's a locked vault-like room. In others, it's the whole back area of the store.

Over in a corner somewhere, often right by the door to accommodate quick purchases, there's usually a *cold box,* a refrigerated cabinet with glass doors where bottles of best-selling white and sparkling wines sit. Unless you really *must* have an ice-cold bottle of wine immediately (the two of you have just decided to elope, the marriage minister is a mile down the road, and the wedding toast is only ten minutes away), avoid the cold box. The wines in there are usually too cold and, therefore, may not be in good condition. You never know how long the bottle you select has been sitting there under frigid conditions, numbed lifeless.

Near the front of the store you may also see boxes or bins of special *sale* wines. Sometimes, sale wines are those the merchant is trying to unload because he has had them for too long, or they're wines that he got a special deal on (because the distributor is trying to unload them). When in doubt, try one bottle first before committing to a larger quantity.

Sale displays are usually topped with *case cards* — large cardboard signs that stand above the open boxes of wine — or similar descriptive material. Our words of caution in the previous section on the credibility of shelf-talkers apply to case cards, too; but because case cards are a lot bigger, there's more of a chance that some useful information may appear on them.

Ten clues for identifying a store where you should *not* buy wine

1. The dust on the wine bottles is more than 1/8-inch thick.

2. Many of the white wines are dark gold or light-brown in color.

3. The most recent vintage in the store is 1997.

4. The colors on all the wine labels have faded from bright sunlight.

5. It's warmer than a sauna inside.

6. Most of the bottles are standing up.

7. All the bottles are standing up!

8. The selection consists mainly of jug wines or cheap "Bag-in-the-Box" wines.

9. The June Wine of the Month is a three-year-old Beaujolais Nouveau.

10. The owner resembles the stern teacher who always hated you.

Choosing the Right Wine Merchant

Sizing up a wine merchant is as simple as sizing up any other specialty retailer. The main criteria are fair prices, a wide selection, staff expertise, and service. Also, the shop must store its wines in the proper conditions.

No such species in your neighborhood? In Chapter 16, we talk about the advantages and disadvantages of buying wine by catalog, telephone, mail, or the Internet, which can be good alternatives if you don't have access to a decent wine shop where you live.

Putting price in perspective

When you're a novice wine buyer, your best strategy is to shop around *with an eye to service and reliable advice more than to price*. After you've found a merchant who has suggested several wines that you've liked, stick with him, even if he doesn't have the best prices in town. It makes better sense to pay a dollar or so more for wines recommended by a reliable merchant (wines that you'll probably like) than to buy wines in a cut-rate or discount store and save a buck, especially if that store has no special wine adviser or if the advice you receive is suspect.

When you have more knowledge of wine, you'll have enough confidence to shop at stores with the best prices. But even then, price must take a backseat to the storage conditions of the wine (see "Judging wine storage conditions," later in this chapter).

Evaluating selection and expertise

You won't necessarily know on your first visit whether a particular store's selection is adequate for you. If you notice many wines from many different countries at various prices, give the store's selection the benefit of the doubt. If you outgrow the selection as you learn more about wine, you can seek out a new merchant at that point.

Don't be too ready to give a merchant the benefit of the doubt when it comes to expertise, however. Some retailers are not only extremely knowledgeable about the specific wines they sell, but also extremely knowledgeable about wine in general. But some retailers know less than their customers. Just as you expect a butcher to know his cuts of meat, you should expect a wine merchant to know wine. Be free with your questions (such as, "Can you tell me something about this wine?" or "How are these two wines different?"), and judge how willing and able the merchant is to answer them.

Expect a wine merchant to have *personal* knowledge and experience of the wines he sells. These days, a lot of retailers use the ratings of a few critics as a crutch in selling wines. They plaster their shelves with the critics' scores (usually a number like 90 on a scale of 100) and advertise their wines by these numbers (see Chapter 18). We agree that selling by the numbers is one quick way of communicating an approximate sense of the wine's quality. (Remember, that doesn't mean you'll *like* the wine!) But the retailer's knowledge and experience of the wines simply must go beyond the critics' scores, or he's not doing his job properly.

Expecting service with a smile

Most knowledgeable wine merchants pride themselves in their ability to guide you through the maze of wine selections and help you find a wine that you will like. Trust a merchant's advice at least once or twice and see whether his choices are good ones for you. If he's not flexible enough — or knowledgeable enough — to suggest wine that suits your needs, obviously you need another merchant. All it will have cost you is the price of a bottle or two of wine. (Much less costly than choosing the wrong doctor or lawyer!)

Speaking of service, any reputable wine merchant will accept a bottle back from you if he has made a poor recommendation or if the wine seems damaged. After all, he wants to keep you as a customer. But with the privilege comes responsibility: Be reasonable. It's always a good idea to ask ahead of time about the store's defective and unopened wine policy. You should return an *open* bottle only if you think the wine is defective — in which case the bottle should be mostly full! Hold on to the store's receipt, and don't wait several months before returning an unopened bottle of wine. By that time, the store may have a hard time reselling the wine. After a week or two, consider the wine yours whether you like it or not.

Judging wine storage conditions

Here's a fact about wine that's worth learning early on: Wine is a perishable product. It doesn't go moldy like cheese, and it can't host e-coli bacteria, as meat can. It normally poses no health hazard beyond those associated with alcohol and certain individuals' sensitivities, even when it's past its prime. In fact, some wines — usually the more expensive ones — can get better and better as they get older. But if wine is not stored properly, its taste can suffer. (For advice on storing wine in your own home, see in Chapter 16.)

In sizing up a wine shop, especially if you plan to buy a lot of wine or expensive wine, check out the store's wine storage conditions. What you don't want to see is an area that's warm — for example, wines stored near the boiler so that they cook all winter, or wines stored on the top floor of the building where the sun can smile on them all summer.

The very best shops will have climate-controlled storerooms for wine — although, frankly, these shops are in the minority. If a shop does have a good storage facility, the proprietor will be happy to show it off to you because he'll be rightfully proud of all the expense and effort he put into it.

In better wine shops, you'll see most of the bottles (except for the inexpensive, large, jug-like bottles) lying *in a horizontal position,* so that their corks remain moist, ensuring a firm closure. A dry cork can crack or shrink and let air into the bottle, which will spoil the wine. A short time upright does not affect wine much, and so stores with a high turnover can get away with storing their fast-selling wines that way, but slower selling, expensive bottles, especially those intended for long maturation in your cellar will fare better in the long run lying down.

Unfortunately, the problem of wine spoilage doesn't begin at the retail outlet. Quite frequently, the *wholesaler* or *distributor* — the company from which the retailer purchases wine — doesn't have proper storage conditions, either. And there have certainly been instances when wine has been damaged by extremes of weather even before it got to the distributor — for example, while sitting on the docks in the dead of winter (or the dead of summer) or while traveling through the Panama Canal. A good retailer will check out the quality of the wine before he buys it, or he will send it back if he discovers the problem after he has already bought the wine.

Strategies for Wine Shopping

When you get beyond all the ego-compromising innuendo associated with buying wine, you can really have fun in wine shops. We remember when we first caught the wine bug. We spent countless hours on Saturdays visiting different wine stores near our home. (To a passionate wine lover, 50 miles can be near.) Trips to other cities offered new opportunities to explore. So many wines, so little time. . . .

We discovered good, reliable stores — and stores that we would Recommend Only To Our Worst Enemies (ROTOWE). Naturally, we made our share of mistakes along the way, but we learned a lot of good lessons.

How to avoid encounters with poorly stored wine

If you don't know how a wine has been stored — and let's face it, most of the time you don't — you can do two things to minimize the risk of getting a bad bottle.

First, patronize retailers who seem to care about their wine and who provide their customers with good service. Second, be attentive to seasonal weather patterns when buying wine or when having it shipped to you. We're very cautious about buying wine at the end of, or during, a very hot summer, unless the store has a good climate-control system. And we never have wine shipped to us (other than quick deliveries from our local shop) at the height of summer or winter.

Another way of knowing that the wine you are buying is sound is just to buy the best-selling, most popular wines — assuming you don't mind being a slave to taste trends. Wines that move through the distribution chain very quickly have less opportunity to be damaged along the way.

See a chance, take it

When we first started buying wine, our repertoire was about as broad as a two-year-old child's vocabulary. We'd buy the same brands again and again because we knew what to expect from them, and we liked them well enough — both good reasons to buy a particular wine. But in retrospect, we let ourselves get stuck in a rut because we were afraid to take a chance on anything new. If wine was really going to be fun, we realized, we had to be a little more adventuresome.

If you want to experience the wonderful array of wines in the world, experimenting is a must. New wines can be interesting and exciting. Now and then you might get a lemon, but at least you'll learn not to buy that wine again!

Explain what you want

The following scene — or something very much like it — occurs in every wine shop every day (and ten times every Saturday):

Customer: I remember that the wine had a yellow label. I had it in this little restaurant last week.

Wine Merchant: Do you know what country it's from?

Customer: I think it's Italian, but I'm not sure.

Wine Merchant: Do you recall the grape variety?

Customer: No, but I think it has a deer or a moose on the label. Maybe if I walk around, I can spot it.

Needless to say, most of the time that customer never finds the wine he or she is looking for.

When you come across a wine you like in a restaurant or at a friend's house, write down as much specific information about the wine from the label as you can. Don't trust your memory. If your wine merchant can see the name, he can give you that wine or — if he doesn't have that exact wine — he may be able to give you something very similar to it.

It's clearly to your advantage to be able to tell your wine retailer anything you can about the types of wine that you have liked previously or that you want to try. Describe what you like in clear, simple terms. For example, for white wine, you might use such words as "crisp, dry," or "fruity, ripe, oaky, buttery, full-bodied." For red wines, you might say "big, rich, tannic," or "medium-bodied, soft." Turn to Chapter 2 to learn other helpful descriptors. For detailed guidance in describing the taste of wines, read our book *Wine Style* (Wiley).

In-store samplings

In general, we're all for tasting wines before buying them, whenever possible. But the wine tastings that some retailers arrange in their stores do have their limitations. In addition to the fact that you usually get a miniscule serving in a little plastic cup more suited to dispensing pills in a hospital, you get to taste only the wines that the wine merchant (or one of his suppliers) happens to be pushing that day. Sometimes it's a wine that the store made an especially good buy on (translation: The store is making a good profit), or a wine that a local distributor is particularly interested in selling.

Whether you like the wine or not, you may feel some pressure to buy it after trying it. Our advice to you is not to succumb to any conscious or unconscious sales pressure. Buy the wine only if you really like it — and even then, buy only one bottle to start. The wine may taste completely different to you when you're having dinner that night. If it tastes even better than you thought, you can always buy more bottles later.

Five questions you should ask in a wine shop

- If a wine costs more than $10: What kind of storage has this wine experienced? Hemming and hawing on the part of the wine merchant should be taken to mean, "Poor."

- How long has this wine been in your store? This is especially important if the store does not have a climate-control system.

- What are some particularly good buys this month? (Provided you trust the wine merchant, and you don't think he's dumping some overstocked, closeout wine on you.)

- If applicable: Why is this wine selling at such a low price? The merchant might know that the wine is too old, or is otherwise defective; unless he comes up with a believable explanation, assume that's the case.

- Will this wine go well with the food I'm planning to serve? The more information about the recipe or main flavors you can provide, the better your chance of getting a good match.

Tell your wine merchant what kind of food you plan to have with the wine. This will narrow down your choices even more. The wine you drink with your flounder is probably not the one you want with spicy chili! A good wine merchant is invaluable in helping you match your wine with food. Chapter 19 tells you more about the subject.

Name your price

Because the price of a bottle of wine can range from about $4 to literally hundreds of dollars, it's a good idea to decide approximately how much you want to spend and to tell your wine merchant. Fix two price ranges in your mind: one for everyday purposes, and one for special occasions. These prices will probably change over time; the $6 to $10 range you start with for everyday wines often rises to $12 to $20 as you discover better wines. A good retailer with an adequate selection should be able to make several wine suggestions in your preferred price category.

A good wine merchant is more interested in the repeat business he'll get by making you happy than he is in trading you up to a bottle of wine that's beyond your limits. If what you want to spend is $10 a bottle, just say so, and stand firm, without embarrassment. There are plenty of decent, enjoyable wines at that price.

Chapter 7

Confronting a Restaurant Wine List

*W*hen you buy a bottle of wine in a restaurant, you get to taste it right then and there: instant gratification. If you've chosen well, you have a delicious wine that pairs beautifully with the food you've selected. You also can bask in the compliments of your family and friends during the whole meal and go home feeling good about yourself. If you haven't chosen well . . . well, we all know *that* feeling! Fortunately, practice *does* make perfect, at least most of the time.

The Restaurant Wine Experience

Here and there, you might come across a restaurant with a retail wine shop on the premises, a useful hybrid of a place where you can look over all the bottles, read the labels, browse through wine books and magazines, and then carry your chosen bottle to your table. Unfortunately, such establishments are rarer than four-leaf clovers. In most restaurants, you have to choose your wine from a menu that tells you only the names of the wines and the price per bottle — and manages to make even that little bit of information some-what incomprehensible. Welcome to the *restaurant wine list*.

Restaurant wine lists can be infuriating. Typically, they don't tell you enough about the wines. Sometimes, there's nothing worth drinking, at least in your price range; other times, you have so many choices that you're immobilized. All too frequently, the lists simply are not accurate; you spend ten good minutes of your life deciding which wine to order, only to discover that it's "not available tonight" (and probably hasn't been for months).

When you eat out, you may not feel like wading through the restaurant's wine list at all, knowing that it can be an ego-deflating experience. But don't give up without a fight. With a little guidance and a few tips, you can navigate the choppy waters of the wine list.

How Wine Is Sold in Restaurants

Believe it or not, restaurateurs really do want you to buy their wine. They usually make a sizable profit on every sale; their servers earn bigger tips and become happier employees; and you enjoy your meal more, going home a more satisfied customer.

But traditionally (and, we trust, unwittingly), many restaurants have done more to hinder wine sales than to encourage them. Fortunately, the old ways are changing. (*Un*fortunately, they're changing slowly.)

Wines available for sale in a restaurant these days generally fall into four categories:

- The *house wines,* usually one white and one red, and sometimes also a sparkling wine. These can be purchased *by the glass* or in a *carafe* (a wide-mouthed, handle-less pitcher). They are the wines you get when you simply ask for a glass of white or a glass of red.

- *Premium* wines, available by the glass. These offer a wider selection than the house wines and are generally better quality. (These wines are usually available also by the bottle.)

- Wines available by the bottle from the restaurant's *regular,* or standard, *wine list.*

- Older or rarer wines available by the bottle from a special wine list, sometimes called a *reserve wine list* (not every restaurant has this list).

The choice of the house

The wine list looks so imposing that you finally give up laboring over it. You hand it back to the server and say (either a bit sheepishly, because you're acknowledging that you can't handle the list, or with defiant bravado, signifying that you're not going to waste your time on this nonsense), "I'll just have a glass of white wine (or, 'Chardonnay')." Smart move or big mistake?

You'll probably know the answer to this question as soon as the house wine hits your lips. It might be just what you wanted — and you avoided the effort of plowing through that list. But in theory, we'd say, "Mistake."

Usually, a restaurant's *house wines* are inferior stuff that the restaurant owner is making an enormous profit on. (Cost-per-ounce is usually a restaurant owner's main criterion in choosing a house wine.) House wines can range in price from $4 up to $10 a glass (with an average of $6 to $8). Often, the entire bottle costs the proprietor the price of one glass or less! No wonder the "obliging" server fills your glass to the brim.

If you do choose a house wine, you usually save money if you buy it by the carafe, if it's offered that way. On the other hand, you may not want an entire carafe of the house wine!

We've found that only a small percentage of better restaurants — and wine-conscious restaurants, often located in enlightened places like Napa or Sonoma — offer a house wine worth drinking. And it's practically never a good value. Under most circumstances, avoid the house wine. For the same reasons, avoid asking for "a glass of Chardonnay" or "a glass of Merlot."

If circumstances are such that a glass of wine makes the most sense (if you're the only one in your group who's having wine with dinner, for example), chances are you'll need to order the house wine, unless you're at a restaurant that offers premium selections by the glass as well. If the house wine is your only option, ask the server what it is. Don't be satisfied with the response, "It's Chardonnay"; ask for specifics. Chardonnay from where? What brand? Ask to see the bottle. Either your worst fears will be confirmed (you've never heard of the wine, or it has a reputation for being inferior), or you'll be pleasantly surprised (you *have* heard of the wine, and it has a good reputation). At least you'll know what you're drinking, for future reference.

Premium pours

The word *premium* is used very loosely by the wine industry. You might think that it refers to a rather high-quality wine, but when annual industry sales statistics are compiled for the United States, *premium* indicates any wine that sells for more than $7 a bottle in stores!

As used in the phrase *premium wines by the glass,* however, *premium* usually does connote better quality. These are red and white wines that a restaurant sells at a higher price than its basic house wines. (Oh, we get it: You pay a premium for them!) Premium wines are usually in the range of $9 to $14 per glass.

The "wine-by-the-glass" challenge

We're delighted to see that many restaurants these days offer interesting selections of wine by the glass. Wine by the glass is a growing trend despite the challenges that it presents to restaurateurs. Their main problem is preserving the wine in all those open bottles. The more wines a restaurant offers by the glass, the greater the odds that there will be wine left over in each bottle at the end of the evening, and those wines won't be fresh enough to serve the next day. To solve this problem, restaurateurs must have some sort of wine preservation system — sometimes an attractive console behind the bar that injects inert gas into the open bottles to displace oxygen, or some simpler, behind-the-scenes gadget to protect the leftover wine from air. Otherwise, unless they're lucky enough to finish every bottle every night, they will waste an enormous amount of wine. Their wine profits will go right down the drain! (Or into the stew!)

A restaurant may offer just one premium white and one red, or it may offer several choices. These premium wines are not anonymous beverages, like the house red and white, but are identified for you somehow — on the wine list, on a separate card, verbally, or sometimes even by a display of bottles. (Why would you ever pay a premium for them if you didn't know what they were?) In some informal restaurants, wines by the glass are listed on a chalkboard.

Ordering premium wines by the glass is a fine idea, especially if you want to have only a glass or two or if you and your guests want to experiment by trying several wines. Sometimes we order a glass of a premium white wine or glass of Champagne as a starter and then go on to a bottle of red wine.

Of course, there's a catch. Not every restaurant offers premium wines by the glass. Also, you end up paying more for the wine if you order a bottle's worth of individual glasses than you would if you ordered a whole bottle to begin with.

If two or three of you are ordering the same wine by the glass — and especially if you might want refills — ask how many ounces are poured into each glass (usually five to eight ounces) and compare the price with that of a 25.4-ounce (750 ml) bottle of the same wine. (You usually do have the option of buying an entire bottle.) Sometimes, for the cost of only three glasses you can have the whole bottle.

Special, or reserve, wine lists

Some restaurants offer a special wine list of rare wines to supplement their regular wine list. These special lists appeal to two types of customers: very serious wine connoisseurs and "high rollers." If you're not in either category, don't even bother asking whether the restaurant has such a list. Then again, if you're not paying for the meal or if you seriously want to impress a client or a date, you may want to look at it! Try to get help with the list from some knowledgeable person on the restaurant staff, though: Any mistake you make can be a costly one.

The (anything but) standard wine list

Most of the time, you'll probably end up turning to the restaurant's standard wine list to choose your wine. Good luck!

We use the term *standard wine list* to distinguish a restaurant's basic wine list from its special, or reserve, wine list. Unfortunately, there's nothing standard about wine lists at all. They come in all sizes, shapes, degrees of detail, degrees of accuracy, and degrees of user-friendliness (the latter usually ranging from moderate to nil).

If you're still hung up on the emotional-vulnerability potential of buying wine, don't even pick up a wine list. (Instead, turn to Chapter 6 and re-read our pep talk about wine buying in the section, "Buying Wine Can Intimidate Anyone.") When you're ready, read the following section to get a wine you'll like — with minimum angst.

When the restaurant doesn't have an alcohol license, BYOB

In most places, establishments that sell alcohol beverages — both retail stores and restaurants — must be licensed by the government, to assure that appropriate taxes are paid and to aid in the enforcement of local laws. Some restaurants don't have liquor licenses due to circumstance or choice, and therefore cannot sell wine. In those restaurants, you can BYOB (bring your own bottle) to enjoy with your meal. (If you're not sure of the restaurant's policy on BYOB, call ahead.)

Many Chinese restaurants fall into this category, for example. (Asian cuisine can be difficult to match with wine, but Champagne and sparkling wine generally go well, as do Alsace Gewurztraminer or off-dry German Riesling.) Other examples include restaurants that have recently opened and have not yet received their liquor licenses, or restaurants that for some reason do not qualify for a license. (They may be located too close to a school or a church, for example.)

We love BYOB restaurants! Not only do we save money, but we can also bring the bottle of our choice, and not deal with the wine list. You may have to pay a small fee when you bring your own wine — after all, the service staff handles your bottle for you (see "Corkage fees" later in the chapter), but in most cases you still get a good deal.

How to Read a Wine List

Your first step in the dark encounter between you and the wine list is to size up the opposition. You can do this by noting how the wine list is organized.

Read the headings on the wine list the way you'd read the chapter titles in a book that you were considering buying. Figure out how the wines are categorized and how they're arranged within each category. Notice how much or how little information is given about each wine. Check out the style of the list: Does it seem pretentious or straightforward? Estimate the number of wines on it — there can be 12 or 200. (An indirect benefit of this procedure is that the purposeful look in your eyes as you peruse the list will convince your guests that you know what you're doing.)

Sometimes, the list is very small, with hardly any wines on it. It's tough to look purposeful for very long when you're studying a list like that.

As soon as your server comes to the table, ask to see the wine list. Besides communicating to the server that you feel comfortable with wine (whether it's true or not), your asking for the list quickly gives you more time to study it.

Sizing up the organization of the list

There's no way of predicting exactly what you'll find on the list, other than prices. Generally speaking, though, you may discover the wines arranged in the following categories:

- ✔ Champagne and sparkling wines
- ✔ (Dry) white wines
- ✔ (Dry) red wines
- ✔ Dessert wines

After-dinner drinks like Cognac, Armagnac, single-malt Scotches, grappas, or liqueurs usually do not appear on the list, or if they do, they have their own section near the back of the list.

Some restaurants further subdivide the wines on their list according to country, especially in the white and red wine categories: French red wines, Italian red wines, American reds, and so on. These country sections may then be subdivided by wine region. France, for example, may have listings of Bordeaux, Burgundy, and possibly Rhône all under *French red wines.* *USA reds* may be divided into California wines, Oregon wines, and Washington wines.

Or you may find that the categories under white wines and red wines are the names of grape varieties — for example, a Chardonnay section, a Sauvignon Blanc section, and a miscellaneous *other dry whites* section, all under the general heading of white wines. If the restaurant features a particular country's cuisine, the wines of that country, say Italian, may be listed first (and given certain prominence), followed by a cursory listing of wines from other areas.

We've noticed two recent trends in wine-conscious restaurants, and we applaud them both, because they make ordering easier and more fun:

- ✔ **The so-called progressive wine list, in which wines appear in a progressive sequence under each category heading.** For example, under "Chardonnays," the wines are arranged by weight and richness, progressing from the lightest wines to the most intense, regardless of price.

- ✔ **Lists that use wine styles as their basic form of organization.** In these lists, the category headings are neither varietal nor regional, but describe the taste of the wines in each category, such as "Fresh, crisp, unoaked whites," or "Full-bodied, serious reds."

Wine list power struggles

In many restaurants, the servers don't give you enough time to study the wine list. (Really good restaurants recognize that choosing a bottle of wine can take some time.) If your waiter asks, somewhat impatiently, "Have you selected your wine yet?" simply tell him (firmly) that you need more time. Don't be bullied into making a hasty choice.

Usually, your table will receive only one wine list. An outmoded convention dictates that only the host (the masculine is intentional) needs to see the list. (It's part of the same outmoded thinking that dictates that females should receive menus with no prices on them.) At our table of two, there are *two* thinking, curious, decision-making customers. We ask for a second list.

Invariably, the wine list is handed to the oldest or most important-looking male at the table. If you are a female entertaining business clients, this situation can be insulting and infuriating. Speak up and ask for a copy of the wine list for yourself. If it's important enough to you, slip away from the table and inform the server that you are the host of the table.

Getting a handle on the pricing

Often you'll find that within each category, the wines appear in ascending order of price with the least expensive wine first. Many a restaurateur is betting that you won't order that first wine out of fear of looking cheap. They figure you'll go for the second, third, or fourth wine down the price column or even deeper if you're feeling insecure and need the reassurance that your choice is a good one. (Meanwhile, that least expensive wine may be perfectly fine.)

What the wine list should tell you

The more serious a restaurant is about its wine selection, the more information it gives you about each wine.

Here's some information you're likely to find on the wine list:

- An *item number* for each wine. These are sometimes called *bin numbers,* referring to the specific location of each wine in the restaurant's cellar or wine storage room.

  Item numbers make it easier for the server to locate and pull the wine quickly for you. They're also a crutch to help the server bring you the right wine in case he doesn't have a clue about wine, not to mention a crutch for *you* in ordering the wine in case you don't have a clue how to pronounce what you've decided to drink. (And you can always pretend that you're using the number for the waiter's benefit.)

- The name of each wine. These names may be grape names or place-names (see Chapter 4), but they had better also include the name of each producer (Château this or that, or such-and-such Winery), or you'll have no way of knowing exactly which wine any listing is meant to represent.

- A vintage indication for each wine — the year that the grapes were harvested. If the wine is a blend of wines from different years, it may say *NV,* for *non-vintage.* (Chapter 4 tells you why non-vintage wines exist.) Sometimes, you'll see *VV,* which means that the wine is a vintage-dated wine, but you're not allowed to know *which* vintage it is unless you ask. The restaurateur just doesn't want to bother changing the year on the list when the wine's vintage changes. We're always annoyed when we see lists that don't name the wine's vintage.

- Sometimes, a brief description of the wines — but this is unlikely if dozens of wines are on the list.

- Sometimes, suggestions from the restaurateur for certain wines to pair with certain dinner entrées. In our experience, this information is helpful at times, but you may not always like — or agree with — their wine suggestion.

- Prices. There will *always* be a price for each wine.

The lowdown on high prices

Most restaurateurs count on wine and liquor sales to provide a disproportionate percentage of their business profit. The typical restaurant, therefore, charges two to two-and-a-half (sometimes three!) times the retail store price for a bottle of wine. That means that the restaurant is earning *three to four times* the price it paid for the bottle.

Admittedly, restaurateurs incur costs for wine storage, glasses, breakage, service, and so on. But those costs don't justify such extraordinary markups, in the eyes of most wine drinkers.

Some savvy restaurateurs have discovered that by marking up their wines less, they actually sell *more* wine and make *more money* in the end. We try to patronize *those* restaurants.

Assessing the list's style

Once upon a time, the best wine lists consisted of hand-lettered pages inside heavy leather covers embossed with the words *Carte des Vins* in gold. Today, the best wine lists are more likely to be laser-printed pages or cards that more than make up in functionality what they sacrifice in romance.

The more permanent and immutable a wine list seems, the less accurate its listings are likely to be — and the less specific. Such lists suggest that no one is really looking after wine on a day-to-day basis in that restaurant. Chances are that many of the wines listed will be out of stock.

Sometimes, the list of wines is actually included on the restaurant's menu, especially if the menu is a computer-printed page or two that changes from week to week or from month to month. Restaurants featuring immediate, up-to-date wine listings like this can be a good bet for wine.

Digital browsing

A few restaurants have dared to go where no wine list has gone before: into the digital realm. Their wine lists — at least a few copies of them — are on portable computer screens, or e-books, that enable you not only to see the list of available wines and their prices, but also to read background information by tapping a wine's name; you can even request a list of wines that are suitable for the food you're ordering. Of course, these lists have their downside: They're so much fun that you risk offending your friends by playing with the list for too long!

Many restaurants that are serious about wine publish their wine lists on the Internet. Before a special meal, you can go to the restaurant's Web site and make a short list of possible wines for your meal — guaranteed to boost your comfort level.

Ordering Your Wine

Plan to order the wine at the same time that you order the food — if not sooner; otherwise, you may be sipping water with your first course. If, after sizing up the wine list, you decide that you aren't familiar with most of the wines on it, ask for help with your selection.

If the restaurant is a fancy one, ask whether there's a *sommelier* (pronounced *som-mel-yay*) — technically, a specially trained, high-level wine specialist who is responsible for putting the wine list together and for making sure that the wines offered on the list complement the cuisine of the restaurant. (Unfortunately, not all restaurants employ one — usually only the most wine-conscious.) If the restaurant is not particularly fancy, ask to speak with the wine specialist. Often someone on the staff, frequently the proprietor, knows the wine list well.

If someone on the restaurant staff knows the wine list well, this person is your best bet to help you select a wine. He or she will usually know what wines go best with the food you are ordering. He will also be extremely appreciative of your interest in the list. For these reasons, even though we are familiar with wine, we often consult the sommelier, proprietor, or wine specialist for suggestions from the wine list.

Here are some face-saving methods of getting help choosing a wine:

- ✔ If you aren't sure how to pronounce the wine's name, point to it on the list, or use the wine's item or bin number (if there is one).

- ✔ Point out two or three wines on the list to the sommelier or server and say, "I'm considering these wines. Which one do you recommend?" This is also a subtle way of communicating your price range.

- ✔ Ask to *see* one or two bottles; your familiarity with the labels, seeing the name of an importer whose other wines you have enjoyed, or some other aspect of the label may help you make up your mind.

- ✔ Ask whether there are any half-bottles (375 ml) or 500 ml bottles available. Sometimes they're not listed, but smaller bottles give you wider possibilities in ordering: For example, you might drink one half-bottle of white wine and a half or full (750 ml) bottle of red wine.

- ✔ Mention the food you plan to order and ask for suggestions of wines that would complement the meal.

We realize that you can't remember *all* the wines that we recommend in this book when you're dining out, so we list, in Table 7-1, a few types of wine that are on most restaurant wine lists and that we believe are consistently reliable choices with food.

Table 7-1   Reliable wine choices when ordering in a restaurant

When you want:	*Order:*
A crisp, dry white wine that isn't very flavorful, to accompany delicately-flavored fish or seafood	Soave, Pinot Grigio, or Sancerre
Dry white wine with assertive flavor; perfect with mussels and other shellfish	Sauvignon Blanc from South Africa or New Zealand
Medium-bodied, characterful, dry white wine, for simple poultry, risotto, and dishes that are medium in weight	Mâcon-Villages, St.-Véran, or Pouilly-Fuissé
Full-bodied, rich white wine, for lobster or rich chicken entrées	California or Australian Chardonnay
Full-bodied white wine with a honeyed, nutty character; works with meaty fish, or veal, or pork entrées	Meursault
Medium-dry white wine, for Asian-inspired dishes	Chenin Blanc, Vouvray, or German Riesling
Easy-drinking, inexpensive red; perfect with roast chicken	Beaujolais (especially from a reputable producer, like Louis Jadot, Joseph Drouhin, or Georges Duboeuf)
Versatile, flavorful, relatively inexpensive red that can stand up to spicy food	California red Zinfandel
A lighter red that's delicious, young, and works with all sorts of light- and medium-intensity foods	Oregon or California Pinot Noir
The basic French version of Pinot Noir; try it with simple cuts of steak	Bourgogne Rouge
Dry, spicy, grapey, and relatively inexpensive red wine that's perfect with pizza	Barbera or Dolcetto
A very dry, medium-bodied red that's great with lots of foods	Chianti Classico

For more information on all these wines, refer to Chapters 9 through 13.

Handling the Wine Presentation Ritual

In many restaurants, the wine presentation occurs with such solemnity and ceremony that you'd think you were involved in high church or temple services. The hushed tones of the waiter, the ritualized performance — the seriousness of it all can make you want to laugh (but that seems wrong — like laughing in church). At the very least, you might be tempted to tell your waiter, "Lighten up! It's just a bottle of fermented fruit juice!"

Actually, though, there's some logic behind the Wine Presentation Ritual.

Step by step, the Ritual (and the logic) goes like this:

1. **The waiter or sommelier presents the bottle to you (assuming that you are the person who ordered the wine) for inspection.**

   The point of this procedure is to make sure that the bottle *is* the bottle you ordered. Check the label carefully. In our experience, 15 to 20 percent of the time it's the wrong bottle or not the vintage shown on the list. Feel the bottle with your hand, if you like, to determine whether its temperature seems to be correct. (This is also a good time for you to pretend to recognize something about the label, as if the wine is an old friend, even if you've never seen it before.) If you're satisfied with the bottle, nod your approval to the server.

2. **The server removes the cork and places it in front of you.**

   The purpose of this step is for you to determine, by smelling and visually inspecting the cork, whether the cork is in good condition, and whether the cork seems to be the legitimate cork for that bottle of wine.

   In rare instances, a wine may be so corky (see Chapter 2) that the cork itself will have an unpleasant odor. On even rarer occasions, the cork might be totally wet and shriveled or very dry and crumbly; either situation suggests that air has gotten into the wine and spoiled it.

   Once in your life, you may discover a vintage year or winery name on your cork. But most of the time, the presentation of the cork is inconsequential.

   If the cork does raise your suspicions, you should still wait to smell or taste the wine itself before deciding whether to reject the bottle.

   Once, when one of our wise-guy friends was presented the cork by the server, he proceeded to put it into his mouth and chew it, and then he pronounced to the waiter that it was just fine!

3. **If your wine needs decanting, the server decants it.**

   For more information on decanting, see Chapter 8.

4. **The server pours a small amount of wine into your glass and waits.**

At this point, you're *not* supposed to say, "Is that all you're giving me?!" You're expected to take a sniff of the wine, perhaps a little sip, and then either nod your approval to the waiter or murmur, "It's fine." Actually, this is an important step of the Ritual because if something is *wrong* with the wine, *now* is the time to return it — not after you've finished half of the bottle! For a review of wine-tasting technique, turn to Chapter 2 before you head out to the restaurant.

If you're not really sure whether the condition of the wine is acceptable, ask for someone else's opinion at your table and then make a group decision; otherwise, you risk feeling foolish by either returning the bottle later when it's been declared defective by one of your guests, or by drinking the stuff when it becomes clear to you later that there's something wrong with it. Either way, you suffer. Take as long as you need to on this step.

If you do decide that the bottle is out of condition, describe to the server what you find wrong with the wine, using the best language you can. (*Musty* or *dank* are descriptors that are easily understood.) Be sympathetic to the fact that you're causing more work for him, but don't be overly apologetic. (Why should you be? You didn't make the wine!) Let him smell or taste the wine himself if he would like. But don't let him make you feel guilty.

Depending on whether the sommelier or captain agrees that it's a bad bottle or whether he believes that you just don't understand the wine, he may bring you another bottle of the same, or he may bring you the wine list so that you can select a different wine. Either way, the Ritual begins again from the top.

5. **If you do accept the wine, the waiter pours the wine into your guests' glasses and then finally into yours.**

Now you're allowed to relax.

Twice the price

A few profit-minded restaurateurs train their servers to maximize wine sales in every way possible — even at the customers' expense. For example, some servers are trained to refill wine glasses liberally so that the bottle is emptied before the main course arrives. (This can happen all the more easily when the glasses are large.) Upon emptying the bottle, the server asks, "Shall I bring another bottle of the same wine?" Depending on how much wine is in everyone's glass and how much wine your guests tend to drink, you may not *need* another bottle, but your tendency will be to say *yes* to avoid looking stingy.

An even trickier practice is to refill the glasses starting with the host, so that the bottle runs dry before each of the guests has had a refill. How can you refuse a second bottle at the expense of your guests' enjoyment?! You'll have to order that second bottle — and you should let the manager know how you feel about it when you leave. (But remember, these nefarious restaurant practices are the exception rather than the rule.)

Ladies first?

Almost all restaurant waiters pour, and re-pour, wine for the women at the table first. What's wrong with that? Well, one of us, who otherwise is not a male chauvinist, doesn't like that idea because most of the time the females at the table are not drinking as much wine as he is. Quite frequently, the last part of the bottle will go into the glasses of the women, who often don't drink it, while the male(s) have empty glasses in front of them, forcing them to order another bottle or do without. Since we're all for equality between the sexes, how about pouring the wine into the emptiest glasses, regardless of sex?

Restaurant Wine Tips

Drinking wine in a restaurant requires so many decisions that you really do need a guidebook. Should you leave the wine in an ice bucket? What should you do if the wine is bad? And can you bring your own wine? Let the following tips guide you:

- ✔ **Can I kick the ice-bucket habit?** Most servers assume that an ice bucket is necessary to chill white wines and sparkling wines. But sometimes the bottle is already so cold when it comes to you that the wine would be better off warming up a bit on the table. If your white wine goes into an ice bucket and you think it's getting *too* cold, remove it from the bucket, or have the waiter remove it. Just because that ice bucket is sitting there on your table (or next to your table) doesn't mean that your bottle has to be in it!

  Sometimes, a red wine that's a bit too warm can benefit from five or ten minutes in an ice bucket. (But be careful! It can get too cold very quickly.) If the server acts as if you're nuts to chill a red wine, ignore him.

- ✔ **What's with these tiny glasses?** When various glasses are available, you can exercise your right to choose a different glass from the one you were given. If the restaurant's red wine glass is quite small, a stemmed water glass might be more appropriate for the red wine.

- ✔ **Should the wine "breathe"?** If a red wine you ordered needs aeration to soften its harsh tannins (see Chapter 8), merely pulling the cork will be practically useless in accomplishing that (because the air space at the neck of the bottle is too small). Decanting the bottle or pouring the wine into glasses is the best tactic.

- ✔ **Where's my bottle?** We prefer to have our bottle of wine on or near our table, not out of our reach. We can look at the label that way, and we don't have to wait for the server to remember to refill our glasses, either. (Okay, call us controlling.)

- ✔ **What if the bottle is bad?** Refuse any bottle that tastes or smells unpleasant (unless you brought it yourself!). A good restaurateur will always replace the wine, even if he thinks there's nothing wrong with it.

- ✔ **May I bring my own wine?** Some restaurants allow you to bring your own wine — especially if you express the desire to bring a special wine, or an older wine. Restaurants will usually charge a *corkage* fee (a fee for wine service, use of the glasses, and so on) that can vary from $10 to $25 a bottle, depending on the attitude of the restaurant. You should never bring a wine that is already on the restaurant's wine list; it's cheap and insulting. (Call and ask the restaurant when you're not sure whether the wine is on its list.) Anyway, you certainly should call ahead to determine whether it's possible to bring wine (in some places, the restaurant's license prohibits it) and to ask what the corkage fee is.

- ✔ **What if I'm traveling abroad?** If you journey to countries where wine is made, such as France, Italy, Germany, Switzerland, Austria, Greece, Spain, or Portugal, by all means try the local wines. They will be fresher than the imports, in good condition, and the best values on the wine list. It doesn't make sense to order French wines, such as Bordeaux or Burgundy, in Italy, for example. Or California Cabernets in Paris.

Wine bars

Wine bars are popping up everywhere, not just in London, Italy, and Paris. Wine bars are establishments that offer an extensive choice of wines by the glass — from 12 to 100 — as well as simple food to accompany the wines. The wine bottles are usually either hooked up to an inert-gas injection system after being opened, which keeps the wine fresh, or are topped up with inert gas from a free-standing dispenser at the end of each evening. The former system often makes a dramatic centerpiece behind the bar.

In wine bars, you are sometimes offered a choice of two different *sizes* of wines by the glass. You can have a *taste* of a wine (about two-and-a-half ounces) for one price, or a *glass* of a wine (often five ounces) for another price. And you can often order a *flight* of wines — several similar wines served side by side so that you can compare them.

Wine bars are the ideal way to try lots of different wines by the glass — an educational as well as a satisfying experience. We love them! Hopefully, their numbers will increase with the years.

Chapter 8

The Insider's Track to Serving and Using Wine

*H*ave you ever broken a cork while trying to extract it from the bottle, or taken an unusually long time to remove a stubborn cork, while your guests smiled at you uneasily? This has certainly happened to us from time to time and probably to just about everyone else who has ever pulled a cork out of a bottle of wine. It's enough to give anyone a case of corkophobia!

Removing the cork from a wine bottle is the first challenge that faces you in your quest to enjoy wine, and it's a big one. (Fortunately, once you get the hang of it, it's easy — most of the time.) Afterwards, there are the niggling details of wine service, such as which type of glass to use and what to do if you don't finish the whole bottle. But help is at hand for the wine-challenged!

Getting the Cork Out

Before you can even think about removing the cork from a wine bottle, you need to deal with whatever covers the cork. Most wine bottles have a colorful covering over the top of the bottle that's called a *capsule*. Wineries place capsules on top of the corks for two reasons: to keep the corks clean, and to create a fetching look for their bottles.

These days, many wineries use colored foil or plastic capsules rather than the traditional lead capsules. In keeping with the sheerness trend in fashion, some wineries use a transparent cellophane covering that lets the cork show through; sometimes, the sheer look graces special *flange-top* bottles, a fancy wine bottle with a protruding, flat lip at the top. (Some flange-top bottles sport colorful plastic plugs on top of the cork instead of cellophane.) The flange-top seems to be going out of style, and that's fortunate because many corkscrews just didn't fit over its wide top!

Whether the capsule is plastic, foil, or cellophane, we usually remove the entire capsule, so that no wine can possibly come into contact with the covering when we pour. (We use the small knife that's part of most *corkscrews* — the devices that exist solely for opening wine bottles.) When we encounter a plastic plug atop the cork instead of a capsule, we just flick it off with the tip of a knife.

After removing the capsule or plug, we wipe clean the top of the bottle with a damp cloth. Sometimes the visible end of the cork is dark with mold that developed under the capsule, and in that case, we wipe all the more diligently. (If you encounter mold atop the cork, don't be concerned. That mold is actually a good sign: It means that the wine has been stored in humid conditions. See Chapter 16 for information on humidity and other aspects of wine storage.)

Sometimes wine lovers just can't bring themselves to remove the whole capsule out of respect for the bottle of wine that they are about to drink. (In fact, traditional wine etiquette dictates that you not remove the entire capsule.) Many people use a gizmo called a foil cutter that sells for about $6 or $7 in wine shops, kitchen stores, or specialty catalogs. However, the foil cutter does not cut the capsule low enough, in our opinion, to prevent wine from dripping over the edge of the foil into your glass. If you want to leave the capsule on, use the corkscrew's knife to cut the foil under the second lip of the bottle, approximately three-fourths of an inch from the top.

The corkscrew not to use

The one corkscrew we absolutely avoid happens to be the most common type of corkscrew around. We don't like it for one very simple reason: It mangles the cork, almost guaranteeing that brown flakes will be floating in your glass of wine. (We also don't like it because it offends our sense of righteousness that an inferior product should be so popular.)

That corkscrew is the infamous Wing Type Corkscrew, a bright silver-colored, metal device that looks like a cross between a pair of pliers and a drill; when you insert this corkscrew into a cork, two "wings" open out from the side of the corkscrew. The major shortcoming of this device is its very short worm, or *auger* (the curly prong that bores into the cork), which is too short for many corks and overly aggressive on all of them.

Rather than finding out the hard way that this corkscrew just doesn't cut it (or, literally, cuts it too much!), as we did, invest a few dollars in a decent corkscrew right off the bat. The time and hassle you'll save will be more than worth the investment. Of the many types of wine-bottle openers available, we recommend the three described in the following sections.

The corkscrew to buy

The one indispensable corkscrew for every household is the Screwpull. It was invented in the early 1980s by a renowned Houston scientist, Dr. Herbert Allen, who was apparently tired of having a ten-cent piece of cork get the better of him.

The Screwpull is about six inches long. It consists of an arched piece of plastic (which looks like a clothespin on steroids) straddling an inordinately long, 5-inch worm that's coated with Teflon (see Figure 8-1).

To use this corkscrew, you simply place the plastic over the bottle top (having removed the capsule), until a lip on the plastic is resting on the top of the bottle. Insert the worm through the plastic, until it touches the cork. Hold on to the plastic firmly while turning the lever atop the worm clockwise. The worm descends into the cork. Then you simply keep turning the lever in the same clockwise direction, and the cork magically emerges from the bottle. To remove the cork from the Screwpull, simply turn the lever counterclockwise while holding on to the cork.

Figure 8-1:
The
Screwpull
corkscrew.

© Akira Chiwaki

The Screwpull comes in many colors and costs about $20 in wine shops, kitchen stores, and specialty catalogs. It's very simple to use, does not require a lot of muscle, and is our corkscrew of choice for most of the corks that we encounter.

It has one drawback; because it's made of plastic, it can break. But now a stainless steel version is available, for about $30. This Screwpull should last indefinitely.

Other corkscrews worth owning

Although we favor the Screwpull for removing corks, we have two other corkscrews for the remaining corks that the Screwpull can't remove. Flange-top bottles, for example, really challenge the Screwpull because of their unusual width at the top.

Our two alternative corkscrews are smaller devices that — besides working better now and then — can conveniently fit into your pants or apron pocket. Their size is one reason that servers in restaurants favor them.

The two-pronged type that they use in California

One is called, unofficially, the Ah-So because (according to wine legend, anyway) when people finally figure out how it works, they say, "Ah, so that's how it works!" (It's also known as the "Butler's Friend" — but where have all the butlers gone?)

It's a simple device made up of two thin, flat metal prongs, one slightly longer than the other (see Figure 8-2). To use it, you slide the prongs down into the tight space between the cork and the bottle (inserting the longer prong first), using a back-and-forth seesaw motion until the top of the Ah-So is resting on the top of the cork. Then you twist the cork while gently pulling it up.

Figure 8-2:
The Ah-So
corkscrew.

© Akira Chiwaki

One advantage of the Ah-So is that it delivers an intact cork — without a hole in it — that can be reused to close bottles of homemade vinegar, or to make cutesy bulletin boards.

Although more difficult to operate than the Screwpull, the Ah-So really comes into its own with very tight-fitting corks that no other corkscrews, including the Screwpull, seem to be able to budge. Also, the Ah-So can be effective with old, crumbly corks that don't give other corkscrews much to grip.

The Ah-So is useless with loose corks that move around in the bottle's neck when you try to remove them. It just pushes those corks down into the wine. At that point, you'll need another tool called a *cork retriever* (which we describe in the "Waiter, there's cork in my wine!" section, later in this chapter).

The Ah-So sells for around $6 to $9. It seems to be especially popular in California for no particular reason that we've ever been able to figure out.

The most professional corkscrew of them all

Our final recommended corkscrew, probably the most commonly used corkscrew in restaurants all over the world, is simply called the Waiter's Corkscrew. A straight or gently curved base holds three devices that fold into it, like a Swiss Army knife: a lever; a worm; and a small knife (see Figure 8-3). The latter is especially handy for removing the capsule from the bottle.

Figure 8-3:
The Waiter's
Corkscrew.

© Akira Chiwaki

Using the Waiter's Corkscrew requires some practice. First, wrap your fist around the bottle's neck. The trick then is to guide the worm down through the center of the cork, by turning the corkscrew; turn slowly at first, until you're sure that the worm is not off center and actually is descending down the middle of the cork. After the worm is fully descended into the cork, place the lever on the lip of the bottle and push against the lever while pulling the cork up. Give a firm tug at the very end or wiggle the bottom of the cork out with your hand.

Why is my cork blue?

Have you ever opened a bottle of wine and discovered that the "cork" is not cork at all, but plastic — and brightly colored, to boot?

While we appreciate the touch of whimsy that an orange or blue cork contributes, we are not fans of plastic corks. Winemakers are understandably disillusioned with cork itself because it can taint a wine with off-aromas. But if you're going to invent an alternative to cork, why plug the bottle neck with yet another closure that's a rude barrier between wine drinkers and their wine, demanding the same, complicated tool as a cork does — and can be even more difficult to remove?! Fortunately, some new versions of synthetic corks are relatively user-friendly compared to earlier types. But screwcaps are even more so.

If your cork ever breaks and part of it gets stuck in the neck of the bottle, the Waiter's Corkscrew is indispensable for removing the remaining piece. Use the method we just described, but insert the worm at a 45-degree angle. In most cases, you will successfully remove the broken cork.

The Waiter's Corkscrew sells for as little as $7, but designer versions can cost more than ten times that much.

The status corkscrews

You can buy some really fancy corkscrews, some that attach to a counter or a bar, which will cost you $100-plus. Yes, most of them work very well, after you get the hang of them, but frankly, we don't see the need to spend that much on a corkscrew. We'd rather spend it on the wine!

Waiter, there's cork in my wine!

Every now and then, even if you've used the right corkscrew and used it properly, you can still have pieces of cork floating in your wine. They can be tiny dry flakes that crumbled into the bottle, actual chunks of cork, or even the entire cork.

Before you start berating yourself for being a klutz, you should know that "floating cork" has happened to all of us at one time or another, no matter how experienced we are. Cork won't harm the wine. And besides, there's a wonderful instrument called a *cork retriever* (no, it's not a small dog from the south of Ireland!) available in specialty stores and in catalogs, although it's considerably more difficult to find than a corkscrew.

The cork retriever consists of three 10-inch pieces of stiff metal wire with hooks on the ends. This device is remarkably effective for removing floating pieces of cork from the bottle. We have even removed a whole cork from the neck with a cork retriever (fearing the whole time that the bottle neck would explode when we tried to force the cork *and* the retriever back up through the tiny diameter).

Alternatively, you can just pick out the offending piece(s) of cork with a spoon after you pour the wine into your glass. (That's one occasion when it's rude to serve your guest first, because the first glass has more cork pieces in it.) Or you can pour the wine through a paper coffee filter (preferably the natural brown-paper filter, or a filter rinsed with hot water to remove the chemicals) into a decanter or pitcher to catch the remaining pieces of cork.

A special case: Opening Champagne and sparkling wine

Opening a bottle of sparkling wine is usually an exciting occasion. Who doesn't enjoy the ceremony of a cold glass of bubbly? But you need to use a completely different technique than you'd use to open a regular wine bottle. The cork even looks different. Sparkling wine corks have a mushroom-shaped head that protrudes from the bottle and a wire cage that holds the cork in place against the pressure that's trapped inside the bottle.

Never, ever use a corkscrew on a bottle of sparkling wine. The pressure of the trapped carbonation, when suddenly released, can send the cork *and* corkscrew flying right into your eye.

Forget how they do it in locker rooms

If your bottle of bubbly has just traveled, let it rest for a while, preferably a day. Controlling the cork is difficult when the carbonation has been stirred up. (Hey, you wouldn't open a large bottle of soda that's warm and shaken up, either, would you? Sparkling wine has much more carbonated pressure than soda, and needs more time to settle down.)

If you're in the midst of a sparkling wine emergency and need to open the bottle anyway, one quick solution is to calm down the carbonation by submerging the bottle in an ice bucket for about 30 minutes. (Fill the bucket with one-half ice cubes and one-half ice-cold water.)

In any case, be careful when you remove the wire cage, and keep one hand on top of the cork as a precaution. (We had a hole in our kitchen ceiling from one adventure with a flying cork.) Be sure to point the bottle away from people and other fragile objects.

The comeback of the screwcap

Instead of imitation cork (see the sidebar "Why is my cork blue?"), we'd prefer to see real screwcaps on most wine bottles. Screwcaps are perfectly sound closures, technically speaking. And they prevent "cork taint," a chemical flaw affecting a small percentage of corks, and consequently the wine in those bottles. A "corky" wine — that is, one affected with cork taint — is damaged either slightly or flagrantly. In the worst-case scenarios, corky wines give off an offensive odor similar to moldy or damp cardboard.

Formerly, only cheap, lower-quality wines had screwcap closures. But in the past few years, more and more wine producers have switched from corks to screwcaps. For example, a number of New Zealand and Australian wineries are now using screwcaps, especially for their white wines. Some Swiss producers have been using screwcaps for their quality wines for years now, especially for half-bottles. And now some California producers, notably Bonny Doon, are dressing their bottles with screwcaps. Is this the start of a movement? Fine with us.

A sigh is better than a pop

If you like to hear the cork pop, just yank it out. When you do that, however, you'll lose some of the precious wine, which will froth out of the bottle. Also, the noise can interfere with your guests' conversation. Besides, it ain't too classy!

Removing the cork from sparkling wine with just a gentle sigh rather than a loud pop is fairly easy. Simply hold the bottle at a 45-degree angle with a towel wrapped around it if it's wet. (Try resting the base of the bottle on your hipbone.) Twist the bottle while holding on to the cork so that you can control the cork as it emerges. When you feel the cork starting to come out of the bottle, *push down against the cork* with some pressure, as if you don't want to let it out of the bottle. In this way, the cork will emerge slowly with a hiss or sigh sound rather than a pop.

Every once in a while, you'll come across a really tight sparkling wine cork that doesn't want to budge. Try running the top of the bottle under warm water for a few moments, or wrapping a towel around the cork to create friction. Either action will usually enable you to remove the cork.

Another option is to purchase a fancy gadget that you place around the part of the cork that's outside the bottle. (There are actually three gadgets: Champagne Pliers, a Champagne Star, and a Champagne Key.) Or you could probably try using regular pliers, although lugging in the toolbox will surely change the mood of the occasion.

Does Wine Really Breathe?

Most wine is alive in the sense that it changes chemically as it slowly grows older. Wine absorbs oxygen and, like our own cells, it oxidizes. When the grapes turn into wine in the first place, they give off carbon dioxide, just like us. So we suppose you could say that wine breathes, in a sense. But that's not what the server means when he asks, "Shall I pull the cork and let the wine breathe, sir (or madam)?"

The term *breathing* refers to the process of aerating the wine, exposing it to air. Sometimes the aroma and flavor of a very young wine will improve with aeration. But just pulling the cork out of the bottle and letting the bottle sit there is a truly ineffective way to aerate the wine. The little space at the neck of the bottle is way too small to allow your wine to breathe very much.

How to aerate your wine

If you really want to aerate your wine, do one or both of the following:

- ✔ Pour the wine into a *decanter* (a fancy word for a glass container that is big enough to hold the contents of an entire bottle of wine).
- ✔ Pour the wine into large glasses at least ten minutes before you plan to drink it.

Practically speaking, it doesn't matter what your decanter looks like or how much it costs. In fact, the very inexpensive, wide-mouthed carafes are fine.

Which wines need aerating?

Many red wines but only a few white wines — and some dessert wines — can benefit from aeration. You can drink most white wines upon pouring, unless they're too cold, but that's a discussion for later.

Young, tannic red wines

Young, tannic red wines (see Chapter 2 for more on tannin) — such as Cabernet Sauvignons, Bordeaux, many wines from the northern Rhône Valley, and many Italian wines — actually taste better with aeration because their tannins soften and the wine becomes less harsh.

The younger and more tannic the wine is, the longer it needs to breathe. As a general rule, most tannic, young red wines soften up with one hour of aeration. A glaring exception to the one-hour rule would be many young Barolos or Barbarescos (red wines from Piedmont, Italy, which you can read about in Chapter 10); these wines are frequently so tannic that they can really make your mouth pucker. They often can benefit from three or four hours of aeration.

Older red wines with sediment

Many red wines develop *sediment* (tannin and other matter in the wine that solidifies over time) usually after about eight years of age. You will want to remove the sediment because it can taste a bit bitter. Also, the dark particles floating in your wine, usually at the bottom of your glass, don't look very appetizing.

To remove sediment, keep the bottle of wine upright for a day or two before you plan to open it so that the sediment settles at the bottom of the bottle. Then decant the wine carefully: Pour the wine out of the bottle slowly into a decanter while watching the wine inside the bottle as it approaches the neck. You watch the wine so that you can stop pouring when you see cloudy wine from the bottom of the bottle making its way to the neck. If you stop pouring at the right moment, all the cloudy wine remains behind in the bottle.

To actually see the wine inside the bottle as you pour, you need to have a bright light shining through the bottle's neck. Candles are commonly used for this purpose, and they are romantic, but a flashlight standing on end works even better. (It's brighter, and it doesn't flicker.) Or simply hold the bottle up to a bright light, and pour slowly. Stop pouring the wine into the decanter when you reach the sediment, toward the bottom of the bottle.

The older the wine, the more delicate it can be. Don't give old, fragile-looking wines excessive aeration. (Look at the color of the wine through the bottle before you decant; if it looks pale, the wine could be pretty far along its maturity curve.) The flavors of really old wines will start fading rapidly after 10 or 15 minutes of being exposed to air.

If the wine needs aeration after decanting (that is, it still tastes a bit harsh), let it breathe in the open decanter. If the wine has a dark color, chances are that it is still quite youthful and needs to breathe more. Conversely, if the wine has a brick red or pale garnet color, it probably has matured and may not need much aeration.

A few white wines

Some very good, dry white wines — such as full-bodied white Burgundies and white Bordeaux wines, as well as the best Alsace whites — also get better with aeration. For example, if you open a young Corton-Charlemagne (a great white Burgundy), and it doesn't seem to be showing much aroma or flavor, chances are that it needs aeration. Decant it and taste it again in half an hour. In most cases, the wine dramatically improves.

Vintage Ports

One of the most famous fortified wines is Vintage Port (properly called "Porto"). We discuss this wine and others like it in Chapter 15.

For now, we'll just say that, yes, Vintage Port needs breathing lessons, and needs them very much, indeed! Young Vintage Ports are so brutally tannic that they demand many hours of aeration (eight would not be too many). Even older Ports improve with four hours or more of aeration. Older Vintage Ports require decanting for another reason: They're chock-full of sediment. (Often, large flakes of sediment fill the bottom 10 percent of the bottle.) Keep Vintage Ports standing for several days before you open them.

Exceptions to the "decant your red wines and Ports" rule

The exceptions prove the rule. The majority of red wines you drink don't require decanting, aeration, or any special preparation other than pulling out the cork and having a glass handy.

The following red wines *do not* need decanting:

- ✔ Light- and medium-bodied, less tannic red wines, such as Pinot Noirs, Burgundies, Beaujolais, and Côtes du Rhônes; lighter red Zinfandels; and less imposing Italian reds, such as Dolcettos, Barberas, and lighter Chiantis. These wines don't have much tannin and, therefore, don't need much aeration.

- ✔ Inexpensive (less than $12) red wines. Same reason as the preceding.

- ✔ Tawny ports — in fact, any other Ports except Vintage Ports. These wines should be free from sediment (which stayed behind in the barrels where the wine aged) and are ready to drink when you pour them.

Does the Glass Really Matter?

If you're just drinking wine as refreshment with your meal, and you aren't thinking about the wine much as it goes down, the glass you use probably doesn't matter too much. A jelly glass? Why not? Plastic glasses? We've used them dozens of times on picnics, not to mention in airplanes (where the wine's quality usually doesn't demand great glasses, anyway).

But if you have a good wine, a special occasion, friends who want to talk about the wine with you, or the boss for dinner, *stemware* (glasses with stems) is called for. And it's not just a question of etiquette and status: Good wine tastes better out of good glasses. Really.

Think of wine glasses as being like stereo speakers. Any old speaker brings the music to your ears, just like any old glass brings the wine to your lips. But (assuming that you care to notice it) can't you appreciate the sound so much more, aesthetically and emotionally, from good speakers? The same principle holds true with wine and wine glasses. You can appreciate wine's aroma and flavor complexities so much more out of a fine wine glass. The medium is the message.

The right color: none

Good wine glasses are always clear. (It's okay for jelly glasses to have pictures of the Flintstones on them, as long as the background is clear.) Those pretty pink or green glasses may look nice in your china cabinet, but they interfere with your ability to distinguish the true colors of the wine.

Thin but not tiny

Believe it or not (we didn't always), the taste of a wine changes when you drink the wine out of different types of glasses. A riot almost broke out at one wine event we organized because the same wine tasted so different in different glasses that the tasters thought we served them different wines — and that we had just pretended it was all the same wine, to fool them. We learned that three aspects of a glass are important: its size, its shape, and the thickness of the glass.

Size

For dry red and white wine, small glasses are all wrong — besides that, they're a pain in the neck. You just can't swirl the wine around in those little glasses without spilling it, which makes appreciating the aroma of the wine almost impossible. And furthermore, who wants to bother continually refilling them? Small glasses can work adequately only for sherry or dessert wines, which have strong aromas to begin with and are generally consumed in smaller quantities than table wines. In most cases, larger is usually better.

Matching glass size to wine works like this:

- ✔ Glasses for red wines should hold a minimum of 12 ounces; many of the best glasses have capacities ranging from 16 to 24 ounces, or more.

- ✔ For white wines, 10 to 12 ounces should be the minimum capacity.

- ✔ For sparkling wines, an 8 to 12 ounce capacity is fine.

Thickness and shape

Stemware made of very thin, fine crystal costs a lot more than normal glasses. That's one reason why many people don't use it, and why some people do. The better reason for using fine crystal is that the wine tastes better out of it. We're not sure whether the elegant crystal simply heightens the aesthetic experience of wine drinking or whether there's some more scientific reason.

The shape of the bowl also matters. Some wine glasses have very round bowls, while others have more elongated, somewhat narrower bowls. Often, when we're having dinner at home, we try our wine in glasses of different shapes, just to see which glass works best for that wine. We discuss the functions of various glass shapes in the next section.

Tulips, flutes, trumpets, and other picturesque wine-glass names

You thought that a tulip was a flower and a flute was a musical instrument? Well, they also happen to be types of glasses designed for use with sparkling wine. The tulip is the ideally shaped glass for Champagne and other sparkling wines (see Figure 8-4). It is tall, elongated, and narrower at the rim than in the middle of the bowl. This shape helps hold the bubbles in the wine longer, not allowing them to escape freely (the way the wide-mouthed, sherbet-cuplike, so-called Champagne glasses do).

Figure 8-4: Glasses for sparkling wine (from left): tulip, flute, trumpet.

© Akira Chiwaki

Half empty or half full?

"Fill 'er up" may be the rule for your gas tank, but not for your wine glass. We are annoyed when servers fill our glasses to the top. We guess they don't want to bother re-pouring the wine too often. Or maybe they want to give us our money's worth. But how can we stick our noses into full glasses without looking like idiots?

To leave some margin of safety for swirling and smelling the wine, fill the glass only partially. One-third capacity is the best fill-level for serious red wines. (This goes back to that idea of aerating the wine.) White wine glasses can be filled halfway, while sparkling wine glasses can be three-quarters full.

The flute is another good sparkling wine glass (see Figure 8-4); but it is less ideal than the tulip because it does not narrow at the mouth. The trumpet actually widens at the mouth, making it less suitable for sparkling wine but very elegant looking (see Figure 8-4). Another drawback of the trumpet glass is that, depending on the design, the wine can actually fill the whole stem, which means the wine warms up from the heat of your hand as you hold the stem. We avoid the trumpet glass.

An oval-shaped bowl that is narrow at its mouth (see Figure 8-5) is ideal for many red wines, such as Bordeaux, Cabernet Sauvignons, Merlots, Chiantis, and Zinfandels. On the other hand, some red wines, such as Burgundies, Pinot Noirs, and Barolos, are best appreciated in wider-bowled, apple-shaped glasses (see Figure 8-5). Which shape and size works best for which wine has to do with issues such as how the glass's shape controls the flow of wine onto your tongue. One glassmaker, Riedel Crystal, has designed a specific glass for every imaginable type of wine!

Figure 8-5: The Bordeaux glass (left) and the Burgundy glass.

© Akira Chiwaki

How many glasses do I need, anyway?

So what's a wine lover to do: Buy a different type of glass for each kind of wine? Fortunately, some all-purpose red and white wine glasses combine the best features, in terms of size, thickness, and shape, of most glasses. And you don't have to pay a fortune. Decent everyday wine glasses are available for as little as $3 a glass in wine shops and home furnishing stores.

If you want something finer, try Riedel or Spiegelau Crystal. Riedel is an Austrian glass manufacturer that specializes in making the right wine glass for each kind of wine. (Spiegelau, a German company now owned by Riedel, operates similarly, but its glasses are less expensive than Riedel's.) A new company, Ravenscroft Crystal, based in New York City, now also offers quality crystal wine glasses at moderate prices. You can buy these glasses in many department stores, specialty shops, or glass companies.

The more you care to pay attention to the flavor of the wine, the more you truly appreciate and enjoy wine from a good wine glass. If you just don't have an ear for music, that's okay, too.

Washing your wine glasses

Detergents often leave a filmy residue in glasses, which can affect the aroma and flavor of your wine. We strongly advise that you clean your good crystal glasses by hand, using washing soda or baking soda. (Washing soda is the better of the two; it doesn't cake up like baking soda.) Neither product leaves any soapy, filmy residue in your glass. You can find washing soda in the soap/detergent section of supermarkets.

Not Too Warm, Not Too Cold

Just as the right glass enhances your wine experience, serving wine at the ideal temperature is a vital factor in your enjoyment of wine. Frequently, we have tasted the same wine at different temperatures (and, believe it or not, at different barometric pressures) and have loved the wine on one occasion but disliked it the other time!

Most red wines are best at cool room temperature, 62° to 65°F (16° to 18°C). Once upon a time, in drafty old English and Scottish castles, that was simply room temperature. (Actually, it was probably warm, high noon room temperature!) Today when you hear room temperature, you think of a room that's about 70°F (21°C), don't you? Red wine served at this temperature can taste flat, flabby, lifeless, and often too hot — you get a burning sensation from the alcohol.

Ten or fifteen minutes in the fridge will do wonders to revive red wines that have been suffering from heat prostration. But don't let the wine get too cold. Red wines served too cold taste overly tannic and acidic, decidedly unpleasant. Light, fruity red wines, such as the most simple Beaujolais wines, are most delightful when served slightly chilled at about 58° to 60°F (14° to 15.5°C).

Are you wondering how to know when your bottle is 58° to 60°F? You can buy a nifty digital thermometer that wraps around the outside of the bottle and gives you a color-coded reading. Or you can buy something that looks like a real thermometer that you place into the opened bottle (in the bottle's mouth, you might say). We have both of those, and we never use them. Just feel the bottle with your hand and take a guess. Practice makes perfect.

Just as many red wines are served too warm, most white wines are definitely served too cold, judging by the service that we have received in many restaurants. The higher the quality of a white wine, the less cold it should be, so that you can properly appreciate its flavor. Table 8-1 indicates our recommended serving temperatures for various types of wines.

Table 8-1	Serving Temperatures for Wine	
Type of wine	*Temperature °F*	*Temperature °C*
Most Champagnes and sparkling wines	45°F	7°C
Older or expensive, complex Champagnes	52°–54°F	11°–12°C
Inexpensive sweet wines	50°–55°F	10°–12.8°C
Rosés and blush wines	50°–55°F	10°–12.8°C
Simpler, inexpensive, quaffing-type white wines	50°–55°F	10°–12.8°C
Dry Sherry, such as fino or manzanilla	55°–56°F	12°–13°C
Fine, dry white wines	58°–62°F	14°–16.5°C
Finer dessert wines, such as a good Sauternes	58°–62°F	14°–16.5°C
Light, fruity red wines	58°–60°F	14°–14.5°C
Most red wines	62°–65°F	16°–18°C
Sherry other than dry fino or manzanilla	62°–65°F	16°–18°C
Port	62°–65°F	16°–18°C

To avoid the problem of warm bubbly, keep an ice bucket handy. Or put the bottle back in the refrigerator between pourings.

Keeping Leftover Wine

A sparkling-wine stopper, a device that fits over an opened bottle, is really effective in keeping any remaining Champagne or sparkling wine fresh (often for several days) in the refrigerator. But what do you do when you have red or white wine left in the bottle?

You can put the cork back in the bottle if it still fits, and put the bottle into the refrigerator. (Even red wines will stay fresher there; just take the bottle out to warm up about an hour before serving it.) But four other methods are also reliable in keeping your remaining wine from oxidizing; these techniques are all the more effective if you put the bottle in the fridge after using them:

- If you have about half a bottle of wine left, simply pour the wine into a clean, empty half-sized wine bottle and recork the smaller bottle. We sometimes buy wines in half-bottles, just to make sure that we have the empty half-bottles around.

- Use a handy, inexpensive, miniature pump called a Vac-U-Vin in most wine stores. This pump removes oxygen from the bottle, and the rubber stoppers that come with it prevent additional oxygen from entering the bottle. It's supposed to keep your wine fresh for up to a week, but it doesn't always work that well, in our experience.

- Buy small cans of inert gas in some wine stores. Just squirt a few shots of the gas into the bottle through a skinny straw, which comes with the can, and put the cork back in the bottle. The gas displaces the oxygen in the bottle, thus protecting the wine from oxidizing. Simple and effective. Private Preserve is a good brand, and highly recommended.

- A new device, called WineSavor, is a flexible plastic disk that you roll up and insert down the bottle's neck. Once inside the bottle, the disk opens up and floats on top of the wine, blocking the wine from oxygen.

To avoid all this bother, just drink the wine! Or, if you're not too fussy, just place the leftover wine in the refrigerator and drink it in the next day or two — before it goes into a coma.

An aside about atmospheric pressure

File this under FYI ("For Your Information") — or maybe under "Believe It or Not."

Several years ago, we were enjoying one of our favorite red wines, an Italian Barbera, in the Alps. It was a perfect summer day in the mountains — crisp, clear, and cool. The wine was also perfect — absolutely delicious with our salami, bread, and cheese. A couple of days later, we had the very same wine at the seashore, on a cloudy, humid, heavy-pressure day. The wine was heavy, flat, and lifeless. What had happened to our wonderful mountain wine? We made inquiries among some of our wine-drinking friends and discovered that they had had similar experiences. For red wines, at least, atmospheric pressure apparently influences the taste of the wine: thin, light pressure, for the better; heavy pressure, heavy humidity, for the worse. So the next time one of your favorite red wines doesn't seem quite right, check the barometer! Believe it or not.

Entertaining with Wine

When you're hosting a dinner party, you probably serve more wines than you would in the course of a normal dinner. Instead of just one wine all through the meal, you may want to serve a different wine with every course. Many people serve two wines at the table: a white with the first course and a red with the entrée. (And if they love wine, they use a cheese course as an excuse to serve a second, knockout red.)

Because you want every wine to taste even better than the one before it — besides blending perfectly with the food you're serving — you should give some thought to the sequence in which the wines will be served. The classic guidelines are the following:

- ✔ White wine before red wine
- ✔ Light wine before heavy wine
- ✔ Dry wine before sweet wine
- ✔ Simple wine before complex, richly flavored wine

Each of these principles operates independently. You needn't go crazy trying to follow all of them together, or you'll be able to drink nothing but light, dry, simple whites and heavy, complex, sweet reds! A very light red wine served before a rich, full-bodied white can work just fine. If the food you're serving calls for white wine, there's really no reason that both wines couldn't be white: a simpler, lighter white first and a richer, fuller-bodied white second. Likewise, both wines could be red, or you could serve a dry rosé followed by a red.

First things first

Even if you don't plan to serve hors d'oeuvres, you probably want to offer your guests a drink when they arrive to set a relaxing tone for the evening.

We like to serve Champagne (notice the capital C) as the apéritif because opening the bottle of Champagne is a ceremony that brings together everyone in the group. Champagne honors your guests. And a glass of Champagne is compelling enough that to spend a thoughtful moment tasting it doesn't seem rude; even people who think it's absurd to talk about wine understand that Champagne is too special to be ignored. Also, Champagne is complex enough that it stands alone just fine, without food.

How much is enough

The necessary quantity of each wine depends on all sorts of issues, including the number of wines you serve (the more wines, the less you need of each), the pace of service (if you plan a long, leisurely meal, you need more of each wine), and the size of your wine glasses. If you're using oversized glasses, you need more of each wine, because it's easy to pour more than you realize into each glass.

Assuming a full-blown dinner that includes an apéritif wine, two wines with dinner, and another with cheese — and guests who all drink moderately — we recommend that you plan to have one bottle of each wine for every four people. That gives each person four ounces of each wine, with plenty left over in the 25-ounce bottle for refills. When serving two wines, plan one bottle of each wine per couple.

One simpler rule is to figure, in total, a full bottle of wine per guest (total consumption). That quantity may sound high, but if your dinner is spread over several hours and you're serving a lot of food, it really isn't immoderate. If you're concerned that your guests may overindulge, be sure that their water glasses are always full so that they have an alternative to automatically reaching for the wine.

If your dinner party is special enough to have several food courses and several wines, we recommend giving each guest a separate glass for each wine. The glasses can be different for each wine, or they can be alike. All those glasses really look festive on the table. And with a separate glass for each wine, no guest feels compelled to empty each glass before going on to the next wine. (You also can tell at a glance who is drinking the wine and who isn't really interested in it, and you can adjust your pouring accordingly.)

Part III
The "Old World" of Wine

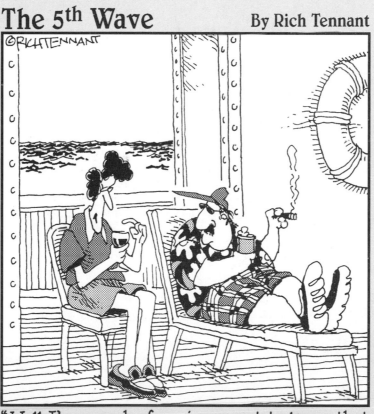

The 5th Wave
By Rich Tennant

"Well, I'm enough of a wine expert to know that if the boat were sinking, there'd be several cases of this Bordeaux that would go into a lifeboat before you would."

In this part . . .

We're flattered if you've gotten to this point by reading every word we've written so far. But we realize that you might have landed here by skipping a lot of stuff earlier in the book. That's okay with us — the meat and potatoes of the book start right here.

The three chapters in this part are chock-full of information about the world's original wine regions — those of France, Italy, Spain, and other European countries. We explain what the classic grape varieties are for each region and describe the wines, as well as name some top brands.

Chapter 9

Doing France

*F*rance. What comes to mind when you hear that word? Strolling along Paris's grand boulevard, the Champs Elysées? Romance? Sky blue water and golden sun on the French Riviera?

When we think of France, we think of wine. Bordeaux, Burgundy, Beaujolais, Chablis, Champagne, and Sauternes are not only famous wines, they're also places in France where people live, work, eat, and drink wine. France still has one of the highest per capita wine consumption rates of any major country in the world. The French have set the standard for the rest of us.

The French Model

Why did France become the most famous place in the world for wine? For one thing, the French have been doing it for a long time — making wine, that is. Even before the Romans conquered Gaul and planted vineyards, the Greeks arrived with their vines.

Equally important is French *terroir,* the magical combination of climate and soil that, when it clicks, can yield grapes that make breathtaking wines. And what grapes! France is the home of almost all the renowned varieties in the world — Cabernet Sauvignon, Chardonnay, Merlot, Pinot Noir, Syrah, and Sauvignon Blanc, just to name a few. (See Chapter 3 for more information on these grape varieties.)

France is the model, the standard setter, for the world's wines: Most wine-producing countries now make their own versions of Cabernet Sauvignon, Chardonnay, Merlot, Pinot Noir, and so on, thanks to the success of these grapes in France.

Understanding French wine law

France's system of defining and regulating wine regions — the *Appellation d'Origine Contrôlée,* or AOC (translated as *regulated place name* or *regulated origin name*) system, established in 1935 — has been the legislative model for most other European countries. The European Union's (EU's) framework of wine laws, within which the AOC system now operates, is also modeled on the French system.

To understand French wines and wine laws, you need to know four things:

- ✓ Most French wines are named after places. (These aren't arbitrary places; they're places registered and defined in French wine regulations.) When we talk about French wines and the regions they come from, most of the time the wine and the region have the same name (as in Burgundy, from Burgundy).

- ✓ The French wine system is hierarchical. Some wines (that is, the wines of some places) officially have higher rank than other wines.

- ✓ Generally, the smaller and more specific the place for which a wine is named, the higher its rank.

- ✓ Just because a wine carries a high rank doesn't necessarily mean that it's better than the next wine; it just means that it *should* be better. The laws rank the potential of the place where the wine comes from, and are not infallible indications of a wine's actual quality.

There are four possible ranks of French wine, according to French wine law. You can determine the rank of a French wine at a glance by seeing which of the following French phrases appears on the label. (Wines of higher rank generally cost more.) From highest to lowest, the rankings are

- ✓ **Appellation Contrôlée,** or AOC (or AC), the highest grade. On the label, the place-name of the wine usually appears between the two French words, as in Appellation Bordeaux Contrôlée.

- ✓ **Vin Délimité de Qualité Supérieure,** or VDQS wine (translated as *demarcated wine of superior quality*). These words appear on the label immediately below the name of the wine. This is a small category.

- ✓ **Vin de pays,** meaning *country wine*. On the label, the phrase is always followed by a place-name, such as *Vin de Pays de l'Hérault,* which indicates the area where the grapes grew; the places or regions are generally much larger than the places or regions referred to in the two higher rankings.

✔ **Vin de table,** ordinary French table wine that carries no geographic indication other than "France." By law, these wines may not indicate a grape variety or vintage. (See Chapter 4 for more about table wines.)

Here's how these four categories of French wines fit within the European Union's two-tier system described in Chapter 4:

✔ All AOC and VDQS wines fall into the EU's higher tier, QWPSR (Quality Wine Produced in a Specific Region, or simply *quality wine*).

✔ All *vins de pays* and *vins de table* fall into the EU's lower tier, table wines.

Fine distinctions in the ranks

France's system of place-naming its wines is actually a bit more complex than the four neat categories described in the preceding section may imply. Although all AOC wines/places hold exactly the same legal status — they're all generals in the French wine army, let's say — the market accords some AOCs higher regard (and higher prices) than others, based on the specificity of their terroir.

Some large AOC territories have smaller AOC zones nestled within them. When territories overlap, any wines produced from grapes grown within the larger area, such as Bordeaux, may carry that AOC place-name (assuming that the proper grape varieties are used and the wine conforms to the regulations for Bordeaux in all other respects). But wines whose grapes come from smaller territories within the larger area can be entitled to different, more specific AOC names, such as a district name, Haut-Médoc. That district can encompass even smaller AOC zones; wines made from grapes grown in these more limited zones may use yet another AOC name, such as Pauillac, a village. (They're all generals, but some of them have silver stars.)

The more specific the place described in the wine name, the finer the wine is generally considered to be in the eyes of the market, and the higher the price the winemaker can ask. Naturally, a winemaker will use the most specific name to which his wine is entitled.

In increasing order of specificity, an AOC name can be the name of

✔ A region (Bordeaux or Burgundy, for example)

✔ A district (Haut-Médoc or Côte de Beaune)

✔ A subdistrict (Côte de Beaune-Villages)

✔ A village or commune (Pauillac or Meursault)

✔ A specific vineyard (Le Montrachet)

Unfortunately, unless you're an expert at French geography and place-names, you won't know which type of place an AOC name refers to just by looking at the label.

France's Wine Regions

France has five wine regions that are extremely important for the quality and renown of the wines they produce, and it has several other regions that make interesting wines worth knowing about. The three major regions for red wine are Bordeaux, Burgundy, and the Rhône; for white wines, Burgundy is again a major region, along with the Loire and Alsace. Each region specializes in certain grape varieties for its wines, based on climate, soil, and local tradition. Table 9-1 provides a quick reference to the grapes and wines of these five regions. Later sections of this chapter describe the regions and their wines.

Table 9-1	Major Wine Regions of France and Their Wines	
Region/ Red Wines	**_White Wines_**	**_Grape Varieties_**
Bordeaux		
Bordeaux		Cabernet Sauvignon, Merlot, Cabernet Franc, Petite Verdot, Malbec*
	Bordeaux Blanc	Sauvignon Blanc, Sémillon, Muscadelle*
Burgundy		
Burgundy		Pinot Noir
	White Burgundy	Chardonnay
Beaujolais		Gamay
	Chablis	Chardonnay
Rhône		
Hermitage		Syrah
Côte-Rôtie		Syrah, Viognier*
Châteauneuf-du-Pape		Grenache, Mourvèdre, Syrah, (and many others)*
Côtes du Rhône		Grenache, Mourvèdre, Carignan, Syrah, (and many others)*
	Condrieu	Viognier

Region/ Red Wines	White Wines	Grape Varieties
Loire		
	Sancerre; Pouilly-Fumé	Sauvignon Blanc
	Vouvray	Chenin Blanc
	Muscadet	Melon de Bourgogne, a.k.a. Muscadet
Alsace		
	Riesling	Riesling
	Gewurztraminer	Gewurztraminer
	(Tokay)-Pinot Gris	Pinot Gris
	Pinot Blanc	Pinot Blanc

Wines are blended from several grape varieties.

Two other significant French wine regions are Provence and Languedoc-Roussillon, both in the South of France. And wine districts in Southwest France, such as Cahors, produce good-value wines and in some cases, seriously good wines.

We cover all these regions in this chapter, in more or less detail according to the importance of the region. For more specific information on French wines, see our book *French Wine For Dummies* (Wiley).

Bordeaux: The Incomparable

To really know wine, you must know French wine — French wines are that important in the wine world. Likewise, you must know Bordeaux to know French wine. Bordeaux is a wine region in western France named after the fourth-largest French city (see Figure 9-1). It produces 26 percent of all AOC wine. About 83 percent of Bordeaux wines are dry reds; 15 percent of the region's production is dry white, and 2 percent is sweet white wine, such as Sauternes.

Because the Bordeaux region is situated on the Atlantic coast, it has a maritime climate, with warm summers and fairly mild winters. The maritime weather brings rain, often during harvest time. The weather varies from year to year, and the character and quality of the vintages therefore also vary; when all goes well, such as in 1996, 2000, and 2005, the wines can be great.

© Akira Chiwaki

Bordeaux's reputation as one of the greatest wine regions in the world revolves around the legendary red wines of Bordeaux — *grands vins* (great wines) made by historic *chateaux* (wine estates) and capable of improving for many decades (see Chapter 16). Prices for these wines run to well over $500 a bottle for Château Pétrus — one of the most expensive red Bordeaux wines. (Old vintages of Pétrus cost even more!)

The taste of really great Bordeaux

When young, the finest red Bordeaux wines have a deep ruby hue and aromas of blackcurrants, plums, spice, cedar, and cassis. For the first ten years or so, these wines can be very dry in texture, almost austere, with tannin masking the fruity flavors. Eventually, the wines turn garnet, develop an extraordinarily complex bouquet and flavor, and soften in tannin. The very finest red Bordeaux wines will frequently take 20 years or more before reaching their maturity; some have lasted well over 100 years (see Chapter 16).

These legendary wines represent the pinnacle of a red Bordeaux pyramid; quantitatively, they're only a very small part of the region's red wine production, which also includes medium-priced and even inexpensive wines. Middle-level Bordeaux reds are ready to drink within 10 to 15 years of the harvest. Most fine Bordeaux wines, both red and white, start at about $25 a bottle when they're first available, two or three years after the vintage. The least expensive Bordeaux reds, which can cost as little as $8 a bottle, are enjoyable young, within two to five years of the vintage date.

The subregions of red Bordeaux

Two distinct red wine production zones exist within the Bordeaux region; these two areas have come to be called the Left Bank and the Right Bank — just as in Paris. While many of the least expensive Bordeaux reds are blended from grapes grown all through the Bordeaux region — and thus carry the region-wide AOC designation, Bordeaux — the better wines come from specific AOC *districts* or AOC *communes* that are located in either the Right Bank or the Left Bank.

The Left Bank vineyards lie west of the Garonne River (the more southerly of the two rivers depicted in the Bordeaux inset of Figure 9-1) and the Gironde Estuary into which the Garonne empties. The Right Bank vineyards lie east and north of the Dordogne River (the more northerly of the two rivers depicted in the inset), and east of the Gironde Estuary. (The middle ground in between the two rivers is more important for white wine than for red.)

Of the various wine districts on the Left Bank and the Right Bank, four (two on each bank) are the most important:

- Left Bank (the western area): Haut-Médoc, Pessac-Léognan
- Right Bank (the eastern area): St-Emilion, Pomerol

The Left Bank and the Right Bank differ mainly in soil composition: Gravel predominates on the Left Bank, and clay prevails on the Right Bank. As a result, Cabernet Sauvignon, which has an affinity for gravel, is the principal grape variety in the Haut-Médoc *(oh meh doc)* and Pessac-Léognan *(pay sac lay oh nyahn)*. Merlot, which does well in clay, dominates the St-Emilion *(sant em eel yon)* and Pomerol *(pohm eh roll)* wines. (Both areas grow Cabernet Sauvignon *and* Merlot, as well as Cabernet Franc and two less significant grapes. See Chapter 3 for more information on grape varieties.)

Left Bank and Right Bank Bordeaux wines are therefore markedly different from one another. But wines from the Haut-Médoc and Pessac-Léognan are quite similar; likewise, it can be difficult to tell the difference among wines from Pomerol and St-Emilion (on the Right Bank).

Each bank — in fact, each of the four districts — has its avid fans. The more established Left Bank generally produces austere, tannic wines with more pronounced blackcurrant flavor. Left Bank wines usually need many years to develop and will age for a long time, often for decades — typical of a Cabernet Sauvignon-based wine.

Bordeaux wines from the Right Bank are better introductory wines for the novice Bordeaux drinker. Because they're mainly Merlot, they're more approachable; you can enjoy them long before their Left Bank cousins, often as soon as five to eight years after the vintage. They're less tannic, richer in texture, and plummier in flavor, and they generally contain a bit more alcohol than Left Bank reds.

The Médoc mosaic

Historically, the Haut-Médoc has always been Bordeaux's most important district, and it deserves special attention. The Haut-Médoc is actually part of the Médoc peninsula. The name *Médoc* has two meanings. It refers to the entire area west of the wide Gironde Estuary (see Figure 9-1), and it's also the name for the northernmost district of the Left Bank. In other words (in the same word, actually), Médoc is frequently used as an umbrella term for the combined districts of Médoc and Haut-Médoc (the two districts that occupy the Médoc peninsula).

Of the two districts, the Haut-Médoc, in the south, is by far the more important for wine. The Haut-Médoc itself encompasses four famous wine communes: St. Estèphe *(sant eh steff)*, Pauillac *(poy yac)*, St-Julien *(san jhoo lee ehn)*, and Margaux *(mahr go)*. Table 9-2 gives a general description of each commune's wines.

Table 9-2	The Four Principal Communes in the Haut-Médoc
Commune	*Wine Characteristics*
St-Estèphe	Firm, tannic, earthy, chunky, and slow to mature; typical wine — Château Montrose
Pauillac	Rich, powerful, firm, and tannic, with blackcurrant and cedar aromas and flavors; very long-lived; home of three of Bordeaux's most famous wines — Lafite-Rothschild, Mouton-Rothschild, and Latour
St-Julien	Rich, flavorful, elegant and finesseful, with cedary bouquet; typical wine — Château Ducru-Beaucaillou
Margaux	Fragrant, supple, harmonious, with complex aromas and flavors; typical wine — Château Palmer

Two other communes in the Haut-Médoc — Listrac *(lee strahk)* and Moulis *(moo lees)* — make less well-known wines. Vineyards in the Haut-Médoc that aren't located in the vicinity of these six communes carry the district-wide appellation, *Haut-Médoc,* rather than that of a specific commune.

The names of these districts and communes are part of the official name of wines made there, and appear on the label.

Classified information

Have you ever wondered what a wine expert was talking about when he smugly pronounced a particular Bordeaux *second growth?* Wonder no more. He's talking about a chateau (as wine estates are called in Bordeaux) that made the grade about 150 years ago.

Back in 1855, when an Exposition (akin to a World's Fair) took place in Paris, the organizers asked the Bordeaux Chamber of Commerce to develop a classification of Bordeaux wines. The Chamber of Commerce delegated the task to the Bordeaux wine brokers, the people who buy and re-sell the wines of Bordeaux. These merchants named 61 top red wines — 60 from the Médoc and one from what was then called Graves (and today is known as Péssac-Leognan). According to the prices fetched by the wines at the time and the existing reputations of the wines, they divided these 61 wines into five categories, known as *crus* or *growths.* (In Bordeaux, a *cru* refers to a wine estate.) Their listing is known as the classification of 1855; to this day, these *classified growths* enjoy special prestige among wine lovers. (The Bordeaux wine brokers also classified Sauternes, the great Bordelais dessert wine; see Chapter 15 for info on Sauternes). The following list shows the five categories and names the first growths:

- **First Growths (5 chateaux)**

  Château Lafite-Rothschild
  Château Latour
  Château Margaux
  Château Haut-Brion
  Château Mouton-Rothschild (elevated from a Second Growth in 1973)
- **Second Growths (14 chateaux)**
- **Third Growths (14 chateaux)**
- **Fourth Growths (10 chateaux)**
- **Fifth Growths (18 chateaux)**

The 61 ranked wine estates are sometimes referred to as Great Growths or *Grands Crus Classés.* To appreciate the honor attached to being one of the Great Growths, bear in mind that there are about 8,000 chateaux (and over 13,000 wine producers) in Bordeaux!

The Mouton exception

The one dramatic exception to the "no changes in the 1855 classification" rule occurred in 1973. That year, the late Baron Philippe de Rothschild, finally (and rightfully) triumphed in his 50-year battle with the French government to have his beloved Château Mouton-Rothschild upgraded from a second growth to a first growth. The Minister of Agriculture (at that time, Jacques Chirac!) decreed that Château Mouton-Rothschild was indeed a first growth — which Bordeaux wine lovers considered it to be all along, in quality if not in official status. The Baron's motto, written in French on his family crest, had to change. Before 1973, it read

> First, I cannot be; second, I do not deign to be; Mouton, I am.

The Baron changed the motto on his 1973 Château Mouton-Rothschild to read

> First, I am; second, I was; Mouton does not change.

A postscript to this wonderful story: We adopted an adorable little kitten, a Blue Point Siamese, in 1973. Since Mouton-Rothschild is one of our favorite wines, and since our little kitten demonstrated the same firm, tenacious qualities as the wine, we named him Mouton. He was with us for 20 years, proving that he had the same longevity as the wine for which he was named. He is buried in our backyard, in an old wooden crate that once held 1973 Mouton-Rothschild.

The 1855 classification has held up remarkably well over time. Sure, a few of the 61 properties are not performing up to their classification today, while other unclassified chateaux now probably deserve to be included. But because of the politics involved, no changes in classification ranking have been made, with one dramatic exception (see "The Mouton exception" sidebar). Appendix B in our book *French Wine For Dummies* has a complete listing of the 61 wines in the 1855 classification.

Just to confuse things even more: Although the 1855 classification completely ignored the wines of St-Emilion, the AOC commission classified those wines a century later, in 1955. The wines fall into three quality categories, which are indicated on the labels:

- Currently, 13 chateaux have the highest ranking, *Premier Grand Cru Classé*. Two of the 13, Château Ausone and Château Cheval Blanc, are on their own pedestal as "Category A"; the other 11 are "Category B" *Premier Grand Cru Classé* wines.
- A middle category, *Grand Cru Classé*, consists of 55 chateaux.
- The third category, simply "*Grand Cru*," encompasses some 200 properties.

The wines of Pessac-Léognan were classified in 1953, and again in 1959. The wines of Pomerol have never been officially classified. (For more info on St-Emilion's and Pessac-Léognan's classified Bordeaux, see Chapter 4 of

French Wine For Dummies; also, in the same book, Appendix B lists the entire classification of *Premier Grand Cru Classé* and *Grand Cru Classé* St-Emilion wines and the 1959 classification of Pessac-Léognan wines.)

Bordeaux to try when you're feeling flush

If you're curious to try a prestigious red Bordeaux, let this list guide you. In addition to all five first growths listed in the previous section, we recommend the following classified growths from the Médoc, as well as some wines from the three other principal districts: Pessac-Léognan, St-Emilion, and Pomerol. Consult the "Practical advice on drinking red Bordeaux" section just ahead, before you drink the wine.

Médoc wines

Château Léoville-Las-Cases
Château Léoville-Barton
Château Rauzan-Ségla
Château Palmer
Château Cos D'Estournel
Château Léoville-Poyferré
Château Pontet-Canet
Château Haut-Batailley
Château Duhart-Milon-
    Rothschild

Château Clerc-Milon
Château Gruaud-Larose
Château Pichon-Lalande
Château Lagrange
Château Pichon-Baron
Château d'Armailhac
Château Prieuré-Lichine
Château Malescot-
    St-Exupéry
Château Calon-Ségur

Château Lynch-Bages
Château Montrose
Château Ducru-Beaucaillou
Château Grand-Puy-Lacoste
Château La Lagune
Château Branaire-Ducru
Château Batailley
Château Talbot

Pessac-Léognan wines

Château La Mission-Haut-Brion
Château Pape-Clément
Château La Tour-Haut-Brion

Château Haut-Bailly
Domaine de Chevalier
Château Smith-Haut-Lafitte

Château de Fieuzal
Château La Louvière

Pomerol wines

Château Pétrus*
Château Lafleur*
Château Latour à Pomerol
Château Certan de May
Château Lafleur-Pétrus

Château Trotanoy
Château Clinet
Vieux-Château-Certan
Château Gazin

Château L'Evangile
Château La Fleur de Gay
Château La Conseillante
Château l'Eglise Clinet

* Very expensive

St-Emilion wines

Château Cheval Blanc
Château Ausone
Château Figeac
Château Pavie- Macquin

Château La Dominique
Château Grand Mayne
Château Troplong Mondot
Château Magdelaine

Château Canon-La-Gaffelière
Château L'Arrosée
Château Clos Fourtet

The value end of the Bordeaux spectrum

As you may have suspected, the best buys in Bordeaux wines are not the illustrious classified growths. For really good values (and wines that you can drink within a few years of the vintage), look for Bordeaux wines that were not included in the 1855 classification.

Cru Bourgeois: The Middle Class of the Médoc

In 1932, a group of producers in the Médoc whose wines weren't recognized as *Grands Crus Classés* in the 1855 Bordeaux Classification obtained their own legally recognized classification, *Cru Bourgeois*. The wines in this category are considered just a bit less noble than the *Grands Crus Classé* wines, but sell at considerably lower prices, mainly in the $18 to $35 range; some of them are even as good as the lesser-quality classified growths.

In 2005, the Bordeaux Chamber of Commerce reclassified the *Cru Bourgeois* wines; 490 chateaux applied for classification, but only 247 made the grade. The jury divided the wineries into three categories: nine chateaux are now in the highest level, *Cru Bourgeois Exceptionnel*; 87 have *Cru Bourgeois Superieurs* status, and 151 chateaux are standard *Cru Bourgeois* wines. (Many of those whose chateaux were excluded brought the issue to court and their declassification was voided, but it is still unclear whether they may call their properties cru bourgeois or not.) The nine *Cru Bourgeois Exceptionnel* wines are the following:

Château Chasse-Spleen	Château Phélan-Ségur	Château Poujeaux
Château Les Ormes-de-Pez	Château Haut-Marbuzet	Château de Pez
Château Labegorce-Zédé	Château Potensac	Château Siran

Château Gloria, from St.-Julien, a wine often compared to *Grands Crus Classé* wines in quality, refused to apply for membership as a *Cru Bourgeois* wine, but critics generally agree that it would have been awarded *Cru Bourgeois Exceptionnel* status had it done so. In addition to the above wines, we recommend the following Cru Bourgeois wines:

Château Monbrison	Château Meyney	Château d'Angludet
Château Sociando Mallet	Château Coufran	Château Lanessan
Château Haut-Beauséjour	Château Loudenne	Château Fourcas-Hosten
Château Monbousquet	Château Bel Air	Château Greysac

January 2006 saw the revival of another category, *Cru Artisans du Médoc*, which was first formed in the 19th century. The Cru Artisan chateaux are a step below Cru Bourgeois wines; 44 chateaux in the Médoc have Cru Artisan status, and can place this designation on their labels beginning with the 2005 vintage. Prices for Cru Artisan Bordeaux are about $9 to $18.

Fronsac and Canon-Fronsac

When you leave the Médoc peninsula and the city of Bordeaux and cross over the Dordogne River into the Right Bank region, the first wine districts you encounter on your left are Fronsac and Canon-Fronsac. Of the lesser Bordeaux appellations, Canon-Fronsac and Fronsac have the highest reputations for quality, and they're priced accordingly, in the $20 to $30 range. Like St.-Emilion and Pomerol, Fronsac and Canon-Fronsac produce only red wines, and Merlot is the dominant grape variety. (For a list of the better wines from these districts, see Chapter 5 in *French Wine For Dummies*.)

Petits Chateaux

Petits chateaux is the general, catch-all term for the huge category of reasonably priced wines throughout the entire Bordeaux region that have never been classified. The term is somewhat of a misnomer because it suggests that the wines come from a specific chateau or vineyard estate; in fact, many *petits chateaux* do come from specific estates, but not all.

Some of these wines use grapes that have been sourced from all over the region, and others come from specific appellations. Ten *petit chateau* red appellations, all on the Right Bank, are noteworthy:

Côtes de Bourg   Puisseguin-St.-Emilion
Premières Côtes de Blaye   Lussac-St.-Emilion
Côtes de Castillon   Montagne-St.-Emilion
Côtes de Francs   St.-Georges-St.-Emilion
Lalande de Pomerol   Premières Côtes de Bordeaux

Lalande de Pomerol is a satellite district of Pomerol, and the four districts with "St.-Emilion" appended to their names surround St.-Emilion. The Côtes de Bourg and Premières Côtes de Blaye take their names from the port towns of Bourg and Blaye, on the Right Bank of the Gironde Estuary, opposite the Haut-Médoc. (A movement is afoot in Bordeaux to combine the five AOCs mentioned above that have the word "Côtes" in their name into a single, new appellation called Côtes de Bordeaux.)

We especially recommend wines from the Côtes de Bourg, Premières Côtes de Blaye, and Lalande de Pomerol as particularly good values. The wines from all ten appellations are mainly in the $12 to $22 range.

All these wines are primarily Merlot. They are generally fruitier, have softer tannins and are readier to drink sooner than the Cabernet Sauvignon-dominated wines of the Left Bank. In our recently published book, *Wine Style* (Wiley), we describe these wines as "Mild-mannered Reds." *Petits chateaux* are the Bordeaux wines of choice when you're looking for a young, inexpensive, approachable Bordeaux with dinner. (For a listing of recommended *petit chateaux* red Bordeaux wines, see Chapters 5 in *French Wine For Dummies*.)

Reverse chic: Drinking inexpensive Bordeaux

Some wine snobs wouldn't think of ordering anything but Classified Growth Bordeaux in restaurants. But if you're just getting acquainted with these wines, starting with an expensive, top-rated Bordeaux doesn't make any sense. Begin with inexpensive, easier-drinking Bordeaux wines first, so that you can develop a context for evaluating and appreciating the finer Bordeaux. The contrast of simpler Bordeaux really helps you understand the majesty of the great Bordeaux wines. Besides, every dinner doesn't call for a great Bordeaux. A modest Bordeaux is perfectly suitable for simpler fare, such as stew or a burger.

Generic Bordeaux

Red Bordeaux wines with no specific appellation carry the general "Bordeaux" or "Bordeaux Supérieur" appellations. Their grapes are predominantly Merlot and can grow anywhere throughout the Bordeaux region. These are fairly light-bodied wines ("Mild-mannered reds") that sell for $8 to $12. Sometimes the labels identify the wines as specifically Merlot or Cabernet Sauvignon. Two leading brands are Mouton-Cadet and Michel Lynch. Generic Bordeaux from good vintages, such as 2000 and 2005, can be really excellent buys.

Practical advice on drinking red Bordeaux

Because the finest red Bordeaux wines take many years to develop, they're often not good choices in restaurants, where the vintages available tend to be fairly recent. And when mature Bordeaux wines are available in restaurants, they're usually extremely expensive. Order a lesser Bordeaux when you're dining out, and save the best ones for drinking at home.

Red Bordeaux wines go well with lamb, venison, simple roasts, and hard cheeses, such as Comte, Gruyère, or Cheddar. If you plan to serve a fine red Bordeaux from a good but recent vintage (see Appendix C), you should decant it at least an hour before dinner and let it aerate (see Chapter 8); serve it at about 62° to 66°F (17° to 19°C). Better yet, if you have good storage conditions (see Chapter 16), save your young Bordeaux for a few years — it will only get better.

Fine recent Bordeaux vintages are 2005 (which shows promise of being truly great), 2000, 1996, 1995, 1990, 1989, 1986, and 1982. (Most 2005 Bordeaux will be available beginning in the fall of 2007 and in 2008.)

Bordeaux also comes in white

White Bordeaux wine comes in two styles, dry and sweet. The dry wines themselves are really in two different categories: inexpensive wines for enjoying young, and wines so distinguished and age-worthy that they rank among the great dry white wines of the world.

Two areas of the Bordeaux region are important for white wine production:

- The large district south of the city of Bordeaux is known as the Graves (*grahv*; see the Bordeaux inset in Figure 9-1). The Graves district and the Pessac-Léognan district, directly north (around the city of Bordeaux) are home to the finest white wines of Bordeaux, both dry and sweet. (We cover the great dessert wine from the southern Graves, Sauternes, in Chapter 15.)

- In the middle ground between the Garonne and Dordogne Rivers, east of Graves and Pessac-Léognan, a district called Entre-Deux-Mers (*ahn treh-douh-mare*) is also known for its dry, semi-dry, and sweet white Bordeaux wines.

A few white wines also come from the predominantly red-wine Haut-Médoc district, such as the superb Pavillon Blanc du Château Margaux. Although special and expensive, they qualify only for simple Bordeaux blanc appellation.

Sauvignon Blanc and Sémillon, in various combinations, are the two main grape varieties for the top white Bordeaux. It's a fortunate blend: The Sauvignon Blanc component offers immediate charm in the wine, while the slower-developing Sémillon gives the wine a viscous quality and depth, enabling it to age well. In general, a high percentage of Sémillon in the wine is a good indicator of the wine's ageworthiness. Many inexpensive white Bordeaux — and a few of the best wines — are entirely Sauvignon Blanc.

The top dry white Bordeaux wines are crisp and lively when they're young, but they develop richness, complexity, and a honeyed bouquet with age. In good vintages (see Appendix C), the best whites need at least ten years to develop and can live many years more. (See Chapter 16 for more information on older Bordeaux.)

Table 9-3 lists the top 12 white wines of Pessac-Léognan and Graves, in our rough order of preference, and shows their grape blends. We separated the wines into an A and B group because the four wines in the first group literally are in a class by themselves, quality-wise; they possess not only more depth and complexity but also more longevity than other white Bordeaux. Their prices reflect that fact — the A group wines range from $80 to $300 per bottle, whereas the B group wines cost between $30 and $70. (For more info about white Bordeaux, see Chapter 6 in *French Wine For Dummies*.)

Table 9-3	Top 12 Dry White Bordeaux
Wine	**Grape Varieties**
Group A	
Château Haut-Brion Blanc	Sémillon, 50 to 55%; Sauvignon Blanc, 45 to 50%
Château Laville-Haut-Brion	Sémillon, 60%; Sauvignon Blanc, 40%
Domaine de Chevalier	Sauvignon Blanc, 70%; Sémillon, 30%
Château Pape-Clément	Sémillon, 45%; Muscadelle, 10%; Sauvignon Blanc, 45%
Group B	
Château de Fieuzal	Sauvignon Blanc, 50 to 60%; Sémillon, 40 to 50 %
Château Smith-Haut-Lafitte	Sauvignon Blanc, 100%
Clos Floridene	Sémillon, 70%; Sauvignon Blanc, 30%
Château La Louvière	Sauvignon Blanc, 70%; Sémillon, 30%
Château La Tour-Martillac	Sémillon, 60%; Sauvignon Blanc, 30%; other, 10%
Château Couhins-Lurton	Sauvignon Blanc, 100%
Château Malartic-Lagravière	Sauvignon Blanc, 100%
Château Carbonnieux	Sauvignon Blanc, 65%; Sémillon, 35%

Burgundy: The Other Great French Wine

Burgundy, a wine region in eastern France, southeast of Paris (refer to Figure 9-1), stands shoulder-to-shoulder with Bordeaux as one of France's two greatest regions for dry, non-sparkling wines.

Unlike Bordeaux, Burgundy's fame is split nearly equally between its white and red wines. Also unlike Bordeaux, good Burgundy is often scarce. The reason is simple: Not counting Beaujolais (which is technically Burgundy, but really a separate type of wine), Burgundy produces only 25 percent as much wine as Bordeaux.

Burgundy's vineyards are more fragmented than Bordeaux's. The soils of the Burgundy region vary from hillside to hillside and even from the middle of each hill to the bottom. You can find two different vineyards growing the same grape but making distinctly different wines only two meters apart from each other across a dirt road!

Burgundy (or, as the French call it, *Bourgogne,* pronounced *bor guh nyeh*) is also a region of much smaller vineyard holdings than Bordeaux. The French Revolution in 1789 is partly to blame. French nobility and the Catholic Church were once the major vineyard owners, but after the Revolution, their lands were distributed to the populace. (Bordeaux, once owned by the English, and more distant from Paris, was considered somehow less French and wasn't really that affected by the Revolution.) France's Napoleonic Code, which requires all land to be equally divided among one's heirs, over time further fragmented each family's property in Burgundy.

The few large vineyards that do exist in Burgundy have multiple owners, with some families owning only two or three rows of vines in a particular vineyard. (One famous Burgundy vineyard, Clos de Vougeot, has about 82 owners!) The typical Burgundy winemaker's production varies from 50 cases to 1,000 cases of wine a year, per type — far from enough to satisfy wine lovers all over the world. Compare that to Bordeaux, where the average chateau owner makes 15,000 to 20,000 cases of his principal wine annually.

In Burgundy, the winemaker calls his property a *domaine,* certainly a more modest name than *chateau,* and a proper reflection of the size of his winery.

Chardonnay, Pinot Noir, Gamay

Burgundy has a *continental* climate (warm summers and cold winters) and is subject to localized summer hailstorms that can damage the grapes and cause rot. The soil is mainly limestone and clay. Burgundy's *terroir* is particularly suited to the two main grape varieties of the region, Pinot Noir (for red Burgundy) and Chardonnay (for white Burgundy). In fact, nowhere else in the entire world does the very fickle, difficult Pinot Noir grape perform better than in Burgundy.

In the southerly Beaujolais district of Burgundy, the soil becomes primarily granitic but also rich in clay and sand, very suitable for the Gamay grape of this area.

Districts, districts everywhere

Burgundy has five districts, all of which make quite distinct wines. The districts, from north to south, are the following (to see where in Burgundy each of these districts is situated, refer to the Burgundy inset in Figure 9-1):

- ✔ Chablis *(shah blee)*
- ✔ The Côte d'Or *(coat dor)*
- ✔ The Côte Chalonnaise *(coat shal oh naze)*
- ✔ The Mâconnais *(mack coh nay)*
- ✔ Beaujolais *(boh jhoe lay)*

The heart of Burgundy, the *Côte d'Or* (which literally means *golden slope*), itself has two parts: Côte de Nuits *(coat deh nwee)* in the north and the Côte de Beaune *(coat deh bone)* in the south.

The Chablis district makes only white wines, and the Mâconnais makes mainly white wines. Beaujolais makes almost exclusively red wines; even though Beaujolais is part of Burgundy, Beaujolais is an entirely different wine, because it is made with the Gamay grape rather than Pinot Noir. The same is true of Mâcon Rouge, from the Mâconnais district; even the small amount that's made from Pinot Noir rather than from Gamay does not resemble more northerly red Burgundies. (Actually, very little red Mâcon is exported; the world sees mainly white Mâcon.)

The term *red Burgundy* refers primarily to the red wines of the Côte d'Or and also to the less well-known — and less expensive — red wines of the Côte Chalonnaise. Likewise, when wine lovers talk about *white Burgundy,* they are usually referring just to the white wines of the Côte d'Or and the Côte Chalonnaise. They'll use the more precise names, Chablis and Mâcon, to refer to the white wines of those parts of Burgundy. On the other hand, when wine lovers talk about the region, Burgundy, they could very well be referring to the whole shebang, including Beaujolais, or all of Burgundy *except* Beaujolais. It's an imprecise language.

Don't ever mistake the inexpensive red California wine that calls itself *burgundy* — or the inexpensive California wine that calls itself *chablis* — for the real McCoys from France. These imposter wines are the products of various ordinary grapes grown in industrial-scale vineyards 6,000 miles away from the Côte d'Or. We'd be surprised if either one had even a drop of the true grapes of Burgundy — Pinot Noir or Chardonnay — in them.

From the regional to the sublime

Because soils vary so much in Burgundy, a wine's specific vineyard site becomes extremely relevant to the taste, quality, and price of that wine. A wine made from a tiny vineyard with its own particular characteristics is unique, more precious and rare than a wine blended from several vineyards or a wine from a less-favored site.

The AOC structure for Burgundy wines recognizes the importance of site. While there are region-wide AOCs, district-wide AOCs, and commune AOCs — just as in Bordeaux — *there are also AOC names that refer to individual vineyards.* In fact, some of these vineyards are recognized as better than others: Some of them are *premier cru (prem yay crew),* meaning first growth, while the very best are *grand cru,* meaning great growth.

Bordeaux producers use the terms *premier cru* and *grand cru*, too. In Bordeaux, however, except for St.Emilion, the terms represent status bestowed on a winery by a classification outside the AOC law (as when a First Growth calls itself a *Premier Grand Cru Classé* on its label, based on the 1855 Classification). In Burgundy, *premier cru* and *grand cru* are always official distinctions within the AOC law. Their meaning is extremely precise.

Table 9-4 gives examples of AOC names in Burgundy, listed in order of increasing specificity.

Table 9-4	The Structure of Burgundy AOC Names
Specificity of Site	*Examples*
Region-wide	Bourgogne Rouge
District-wide	Beaujolais; Mâcon
Village or commune	Pommard; Gevrey-Chambertin; Volnay
Premier cru*	Nuits-St. Georges Les Vaucrains; Beaune Grèves; Vosne-Romanée Les Suchots
Grand cru*	Musigny; La Tâche; Montrachet

* Refers to specific vineyard sites.

The availability and price of each category's wines vary in the following ways:

- ✔ The two broadest categories — regional and district place-names — account for 65 percent of all Burgundy wines. These wines retail for $11 to $25 a bottle. (You *can* buy affordable Burgundies at this level.)

- ✔ Commune-specific (also referred to as *village*) wines, such as Pommard or Gevrey-Chambertin, make up 23 percent of Burgundy and are in the $25 to $55 per bottle price range. Fifty-three communes in Burgundy have AOC status.

- ✔ Premier crus, such as Meursault Les Perrières or Nuits-St. Georges Les Vaucrains, account for 11 percent of Burgundy wines; 561 vineyards have premier cru status. Most of these wines cost from $35 to $90 per bottle — but a few cost over $100 per bottle.

- ✔ The 31 grand crus, such as Chambertin, represent only *1 percent* of Burgundy's wines. Prices for grand cru Burgundies — both red and white — start at around $75 and can go to well over $800 a bottle for Romanée-Conti, normally Burgundy's most expensive red wine.

The taste of fine red Burgundy

Red Burgundy is paler than Bordeaux, with a less dense ruby or garnet color, because Pinot Noir grapes do not have nearly as much pigmentation as Cabernet Sauvignon or Merlot grapes. It's rather full-bodied in terms of its alcohol and is relatively low in tannin. The characteristic aroma is of red or black berries and woodsy, damp-earth, or mushroomy scents. When a red Burgundy ages, it often develops a silky texture, richness, and a natural sweetness of fruit flavors; sometimes a bouquet of leather, coffee, and game emerges.

With some exceptions (for example, a powerful wine from a great vintage, such as 2002 or 1996), red Burgundy should be consumed within ten years of the vintage — and even sooner in a weaker vintage (see Appendix C for vintage ratings).

Thankfully, you can usually tell the difference between a premier cru and a grand cru Burgundy by looking at the label. Premier cru wines tend to carry the name of their commune plus the vineyard name — most often in the same-sized lettering — on the label and, often, the words *Premier Cru* (or *1er Cru).* If a vineyard name is in smaller lettering than the commune name, the wine is generally not a premier cru but a wine from a single-vineyard site in that commune. (Not all single vineyards have premier cru status.) Grand cru Burgundies carry only the name of the vineyard on the label. (For a complete listing of all grand cru Burgundies, see Appendix B in *French Wine For Dummies.*)

If a wine contains grapes from two or more premier crus in the same commune, it can be called a premier cru but it won't carry the name of a specific premier cru vineyard. The label will carry a commune name and the words *premier cru.*

The Côte d'Or: The heart of Burgundy

The Côte d'Or, a narrow 40-mile stretch of land with some of the most expensive real estate in the world, is the region where all the famous red and white Burgundies originate. The northern part of the Côte d'Or is named the Côte de Nuits, after its most important (commercial) city, Nuits-Saint-Georges. This area makes red Burgundies almost exclusively, although one superb white Burgundy, Musigny Blanc, and a couple other white Burgundies do exist on the Côte de Nuits. The following wine communes, from north to south, are in the Côte de Nuits; the names of these communes are also the names of their wines:

- **Marsannay** *(mahr sah nay):* Known for lighter-bodied reds and rosés
- **Fixin** *(fee san):* Sturdy, earthy, firm red wines
- **Gevrey-Chambertin** *(jehv ray sham ber tan):* Full-bodied, rich red wines; nine grand crus, such as Chambertin, Chambertin Clos de Bèze
- **Morey-Saint Denis** *(maw ree san d'nee):* Full, sturdy red wines; grand crus are Bonnes Mares (part), Clos de la Roche, Clos Saint-Denis, Clos de Tart, Clos des Lambrays
- **Chambolle-Musigny** *(shom bowl moo sih nyee):* Supple, elegant red wines; grand crus include Musigny and Bonnes Mares (part)
- **Vougeot** *(voo joe):* Medium-bodied red wines; grand cru is Clos de Vougeot
- **Vosne-Romanée** *(vone roh mah nay):* Elegant, rich, velvety red wines; the six grand crus are Romanée-Conti, La Tache, Richebourg, Romanée-Saint-Vivant, La Romanée, and La Grand Rue
- **Flagey-Échézeaux** *(flah jhay eh sheh zoe):* Hamlet of Vosne-Romanée; grand crus are Grands-Échézeaux and Échézeaux
- **Nuits-Saint-Georges** *(nwee san johrjes):* Sturdy, earthy, red wines; no grand crus; fine premier crus

Burgundy AOCs (Once again, with feeling)

Burgundies with regional, or region-wide, AOCs are easy to recognize — they always start with the word *Bourgogne (boor guh nyeh).* In the following list, read the AOC names down each column to see how the names change, becoming more specific from district to grand cru.

	Red Burgundy	*White Burgundy*
Region:	Bourgogne Rouge	Bourgogne Blanc
District:	Beaujolais	Côte de Beaune (also red)
Commune:	Chambolle-Musigny	Puligny-Montrachet
Premier cru:	Chambolle-Musigny Les Amoureuses	Puligny-Montrachet Les Pucelles
Grand cru:	Musigny	Montrachet

The taste of fine white Burgundy

White Burgundy combines a richness of flavor — peaches, hazelnuts, and honey in Meursault; floweriness and butterscotch in a Puligny or Chassagne-Montrachet — with lively acidity and a touch of oak. With age, even more flavor complexity develops. The wine leaves a lingering reminder of all its flavors. Chardonnay wines from other regions and countries can be good, but there's nothing else quite like a great white Burgundy.

The southern part of the Côte d'Or, the Côte de Beaune, is named after its most important city, Beaune (the commercial and tourist center of the Côte d'Or). The Côte de Beaune makes both white and red Burgundies, but the whites are more renowned. The following communes, from north to south, make up the Côte de Beaune:

- **Ladoix** *(lah dwah):* Seldom-seen, inexpensive red and white wines; part of the grand cru vineyards, Corton (red) and Corton-Charlemagne (white) are in this commune

- **Pernand-Vergelesses** *(per nahn ver jeh less):* Little-known red and white wines; good buys

- **Aloxe-Corton** *(ah luss cortohn):* Full, sturdy wines; several red grand crus that all include the name Corton and one magnificent white grand cru (Corton-Charlemagne) are here

- **Chorey-lès-Beaune** *(shor ay lay bone):* Mainly good-value red wine and a little white wine

- **Savigny-lès-Beaune** *(sah vee nyee lay bone):* Mostly red wines; fine values here, too

- **Beaune** *(bone):* Supple, medium-bodied reds; some whites; fine premier crus here

- **Pommard** *(pohm mahr):* Sturdy, full red wines; some good premier crus (Rugiens and Epénots)

- **Volnay** *(vohl nay):* Graceful, elegant red wines; good premier crus (Caillerets and Clos des Ducs)

- **Auxey-Duresses** *(awe see duh ress),* **Monthélie** *(mon tel lee),* **Saint-Romain** *(san roh man),* **Saint-Aubin** *(sant oh ban):* Four little-known villages producing mainly red wines; excellent values

- **Meursault** *(muhr so):* The northernmost important white Burgundy commune; full-bodied, nutty wines; some excellent premier crus (Les Perrières and Les Genevrières)

- **Puligny-Montrachet** *(poo lee nyee mon rah shay):* Home of elegant white Burgundies; grand crus include Montrachet (part), Chevalier-Montrachet,

Bâtard-Montrachet (part), and Bienvenues-Bâtard Montrachet, plus very fine premier crus

✔ **Chassagne-Montrachet** *(shah sahn nyah mon rah shay):* A bit sturdier than Puligny; the rest of the Montrachet and Bâtard-Montrachet grand crus are situated here, along with Criots-Bâtard Montrachet grand cru; also, some earthy, rustic reds

✔ **Santenay** *(sant nay):* Light-bodied, inexpensive red wines here

✔ **Maranges** *(ma rahnj):* Little-known, mainly red, inexpensive wines

All these red wines are entirely Pinot Noir, and the whites are entirely Chardonnay. The different characteristics from one wine to the next are due to the wines' individual terroirs.

Tables 9-5 and 9-6 list the best Burgundy producers and their greatest wines, in rough order of quality. For a more complete listing of Burgundy producers, see Chapter 7 in *French Wine For Dummies.*

Table 9-5	Best White Burgundy Producers and Their Greatest Wines
Producer	*Recommended Wines*
Domaine Ramonet*	Montrachet; Bâtard-Montrachet; Bienvenue-Bâtard-Montrachet; any of his Chassagne-Montrachet premier crus
Coche-Dury*	Corton-Charlemagne; Meursault premier cru (any)
Domaine des Comtes Lafon	Meursault premier crus (any); Le Montrachet
Domaine Leflaive	Chevalier-Montrachet; Bâtard-Montrachet; Puligny-Montrachet premier crus (any)
Domaine Étienne Sauzet	Bâtard-Montrachet; Bienvenue-Bâtard-Montrachet; Puligny-Montrachet Les Combettes
Louis Carillon	Bienvenue-Bâtard-Montrachet; Puligny-Montrachet premier crus (any)
Michel Niellon	Bâtard-Montrachet; Chevalier-Montrachet; Chassagne-Montrachet Les Vergers
Verget	Bâtard-Montrachet; Chevalier-Montrachet; Meursault premier crus (any)
Guy Amiot	Chassagne-Montrachet premier crus (any)
Louis Latour	Corton-Charlemagne; Puligny-Montrachet premier crus (any)

(continued)

Table 9-5 *(continued)*

Producer	Recommended Wines
Colin-Delégér	Chassagne-Montrachet premier crus (any); Puligny-Montrachet premier crus (any)
Jean-Noël Gagnard	Chassagne-Montrachet premier crus (any)
Louis Jadot	Corton-Charlemagne; Chassagne-Montrachet Les Caillerets; Beaune Grèves; Puligny-Montrachet premier crus (any)
Domaine François Jobard	Meursault premier crus (any)
Joseph Drouhin	All grand cru and premier crus
Domaine Bernard Morey	Chassagne-Montrachet Les Caillerets; Puligny-Montrachet La Truffierè
Domaine Marc Morey	Chassagne-Montrachet premier crus (any)

* These wines are very expensive and rare.

Table 9-6 Best Red Burgundy Producers and Their Greatest Wines

Producer	Recommended Wines
Domaine Leroy*	Musigny, Richebourg, Chambertin (*all* Leroy's grand crus and premier crus)
Domaine de la Romanée-Conti*	Romanée-Conti; La Tâche; Richebourg; Grands Echézeaux
Domaine Comte de Vogüé	Musigny (Vieilles Vignes); Bonnes Mares
Anne Gros	Richebourg; Clos de Vougeot
Georges et Christophe Roumier	Musigny; Bonnes Mares; Chambolle-Musigny Les Amoureuses
Ponsot	Clos de la Roche (Vieilles Vignes); Chambertin; Clos St-Denis (Vieilles Vignes); Griotte-Chambertin
Armand Rousseau	Chambertin (*all* his grand crus); Gevrey-Chambertin Clos St-Jacques
Méo-Camuzet	Vosne-Romanée premier crus (any of his three); Clos de Vougeot; Richebourg; Corton
Hubert Lignier	Clos de la Roche; Charmes-Chambertin

Producer	Recommended Wines
Domaine Dujac	Clos de la Roche; Bonnes Mares
Joseph Roty	Any of his grand cru Chambertins
Joseph Drouhin	All grand cru and premier crus
Jayer-Gilles	Échézeaux; Nuits-St.-Georges Les Damodes
Louis Jadot	Especially Romanée-St-Vivant; Chambertin Clos de Beze; Musigny
Domaine Jean et J.L. Trapet	Grand cru, premier cru Chambertins
Domaine Jean Grivot	Échézeaux; Nuits-St.-Georges premier crus
Michel Lafarge	Volnay premier crus; Beaune Les Grèves
Domaine Robert Chevillon	Nuits-St.-Georges Les St.-Georges; Nuits-Georges Les Vaucrains
Domaine/Maison J. Faiveley	Nuits-St.-Georges and Mercurey premier crus
Jacques-Fréderick Mugnier	Musigny; Bonnes Mares
Domaine Bruno Clair	Gevrey-Chambertin, Marsannay premier crus
Bouchard Pere & Fils	All grand cru and premier crus
Domaine Henri Gouges	Nuits-St.-Georges and Mercurey premier crus

* These wines are very expensive.

Practical advice on buying Burgundy

Nice of the Burgundians to make everything so stratified and clear, isn't it? Premier cru Burgundies are always better than commune wines, and grand crus are the best of all, right? Well, it ain't necessarily so! In order of importance, these are the criteria to follow when you're buying Burgundy:

✔ **The producer's reputation:** Based on wines he has made in recent years

✔ **The vintage year:** Quality fluctuates greatly from year to year

✔ **The appellation:** The name of the commune or vineyard and its specificity

The producer and the vintage are *considerably* more important than the appellation in Burgundy. Good vintages for red Burgundy are 2003, 2002, 1999, 1997, 1996, and 1995. For white Burgundy, 2002, 1999, 1997, 1996, 1995, and 1992 are quite good.

Côte Chalonnaise: Bargain Burgundies

The sad fact about Burgundy is that many of its best wines are costly. But one of Burgundy's best-kept secrets is the Côte Chalonnaise (the district that lies directly south of the Côte d'Or). Five villages here are home to some very decent Burgundies. True, Côte Chalonnaise Burgundies are not as fine as Côte d'Or Burgundies (they're a bit earthier and coarser in flavor and texture), but they can still be satisfying wines — and we're talking $20 to $35 retail per bottle here. Four villages or communes whose names appear as appellations on wine labels are the following:

- **Mercurey** *(mer cure ay):* Mostly red wine, and a small amount of white; the best wines of the Chalonnaise come from here, and also the most expensive ($24 to $35); three of the best producers of Mercurey are Aubert de Villaine , J.Faiveley, and Antonin Rodet.

- **Rully** *(rue yee):* Approximately equal amounts of red and white wine; the whites, although a bit earthy, are significantly better than the reds; look for the wines of the producer Antonin Rodet.

- **Givry** *(gee vree):* Mostly red wine, and a small amount of white; reds are better than the whites (but quite earthy); Domaine Joblot's Givry is especially worth seeking out.

- **Montagny** *(mon tah nyee):* All white wine; look for Antonin Rodet's and Louis Latour's Montagny.

Tips on drinking Burgundy

Red Burgundy is a particularly good wine to choose in restaurants. Unlike Bordeaux and other Cabernet Sauvignon-based wines, red Burgundy is usually approachable when young because of its softness and its enticing aromas and flavors of red fruits. Moreover, red Burgundy, like all Pinot Noirs, is a versatile companion to food. It's the one red wine that can complement fish or seafood; it is ideal with salmon, for example. Chicken, turkey, and ham are also good matches for Burgundy. With richer red Burgundies, beef and game (such as duck, pheasant, rabbit, or venison) all go well.

Red Burgundy is at its best when served at cool temperatures — about 60° to 62°F (17°C). It should *not* be decanted. Even older Burgundies seldom develop much sediment, and too much aeration would cause you to lose the wonderful Burgundy aroma, which is one of the greatest features of this wine.

On the other hand, white Burgundy often benefits from decanting, especially grand cru and premier cru white Burgundies from younger vintages (five years old or younger). Great young white Burgundies, such as Corton Charlemagne, just don't evolve completely in their first few years; the extra aeration will help bring out their aromas and flavors. And remember, don't serve them too cold! The ideal temperature range for serving the better white Burgundies is 58° to 62°F (15° to 17°C).

Another village specializes in the Aligoté grape (a second white grape permitted in Burgundy) that makes a particularly crisp and lively wine called Bouzeroon *(boo zer ohn)*. Aubert de Villaine is the quality producer here; try his Bourgogne Rouge, Bourgogne Blanc (made from Pinot Noir and Chardonnay respectively), or Bourgogne Aligoté de Bouzeron.

Chablis: Unique white wines

The village of Chablis, northwest of the Côte d'Or, is the closest Burgundian commune to Paris (about a two-hour drive). Although Chablis' wines are 100 percent Chardonnay just like the white Burgundies of the Côte d'Or, they're quite different in style. For one thing, almost all Côte d'Or white Burgundies ferment and age in oak barrels, but many Chablis producers use stainless steel tanks instead, at least for some of their wines. Also, Chablis' climate is cooler, producing wines that are intrinsically lighter-bodied, relatively austere in flavor, and crisper.

Chablis wine is classically very dry and sometimes has flinty flavors, without quite the richness and ripeness of Côte d'Or white Burgundies. (Recent Chablis vintages — such as 1997, 2000, and 2003 — have been so warm, however, that the wines have been tasting riper than usual.) For a classic, cool-climate Chablis, try a bottle from the 2004, 2002, or 1996 vintage. The 2005 Chablis vintage, by the way, is just being released as we write and is supposed to be fantastic!

Chablis is an ideal companion to seafood, especially oysters. Like all other white Burgundies, Chablis should be served cool (58° to 60°F, or 15°C), not cold.

The Chablis worth trying

Chablis is at its best at the premier cru and grand cru level. Simple village Chablis is less expensive — about $18 to $28 — but you can often find better white wines from Mâcon, the Chalonnaise, or the Côte d'Or (Bourgogne Blanc) at that price.

The seven grand cru Chablis vineyards are Les Clos, Valmur, Les Preuses, Vaudésir, Grenouilles, Bougros, and Blanchot. (Another vineyard that's actually — but not technically — grand cru is La Moutonne; this vineyard is a part of the Vaudésir and Les Preuses grand cru acreage but isn't recognized as a Grand Cru appellation.) Grand cru Chablis wines range in price from $60 to $95, depending on the producer. Grand cru Chablis from good vintages (see Appendix C) can age and improve for 15 years.

The Chablis district has 22 premier cru Chablis appellations, but the six most well-known are Fourchaume, Montée de Tonnerre, Vaillons, Mont de Milieu, Montmains, and Les Forêts (also known as Forest). Premier cru Chablis wines range in price from $32 to $55, depending on the producer, and can age up to ten years in good vintages.

Seven outstanding producers of Chablis

Seven producers really stand out in Chablis. For a true understanding of this underrated wine, try to buy their grand or premier cru Chablis. *Try* is the operative word here; these are small producers whose wines are available only in better stores:

- **Francois Raveneau** and **René et Vincent Dauvissat:** Both use oak for fermenting and aging; thus the wines are fairly rich and substantial.

- **Louis Michel:** Uses stainless steel only, making vibrant, crisp wines.

- **Jean Dauvissat:** Uses mainly stainless steel.

- **Jean Collet**, **Jean-Paul Droin**, and **Verget:** Other consistently fine producers of Chablis.

Mâcon: Affordable whites

If you're thinking that $20 or more sounds like too much to spend for a bottle of white Burgundy or Chablis for everyday drinking, we have an alternative wine for you: white Mâcon. Many of the best white wine buys — not only in France, but in the world — come from the Mâconnais district.

The Mâconnais lies directly south of the Chalonnaise and north of Beaujolais. It has a milder, sunnier climate than the Côte d'Or to the north. Wine production centers around the city of Mâcon, a gateway city to Provence and the Riviera. The hills in the Mâconnais contain the same chalky limestone beloved by Chardonnay that can be found in many Burgundy districts to the north. In Mâcon, you can even find a village called Chardonnay.

Mâcon's white wines, in fact, are 100 percent Chardonnay. Most of them are simply called *Mâcon* or *Mâcon-Villages* (a slightly better wine than Mâcon, because it comes from specific villages), and they retail for $11 to $17 a bottle. Often better are Mâcons that come from just one village; in those wines, the name of the village is appended to the district name, Mâcon (as in Mâcon-Lugny or Mâcon-Viré).

Celebration time: Beaujolais Nouveau

Each year on the third Thursday in November, the new vintage of Beaujolais — called Beaujolais Nouveau — is released all over the world with great fanfare. This youngster — only about six weeks old! — is a very grapey, easy-to-drink, delicious wine with practically no tannin but lots of fruitiness. In the United States, Beaujolais Nouveau graces many a Thanksgiving table because of the timing of its annual debut. It sells for $7 to $10 and is at its best within the first year of the vintage.

Mâcon whites are medium-bodied, crisp, fresh, and yet substantial wines, often with minerally flavor. They're usually unoaked. You should enjoy them while they're young, generally within three years of the vintage.

The best Mâcon whites come from the southernmost part of the district and carry their own appellations — Pouilly-Fuissé *(pwee fwee say)* and Saint-Véran *(san ver ahn)*.

- ✔ Pouilly-Fuissé is a richer, fuller-bodied wine than a simple Mâcon, is often oaked, and is a bit more expensive (around $20 to $25; up to $45 for the best examples). To try an outstanding example of Pouilly-Fuissé, buy Château Fuissé, which, in good vintages, compares favorably with more expensive Cote d'Or white Burgundies.

- ✔ Saint-Véran, at $14 to $19, is very possibly the best-value wine in all of Mâcon. Especially fine is the Saint-Véran of Verget, who is one of the best producers of Mâconnais wines.

Beaujolais: As delightful as it is affordable

The Beaujolais district is situated south of the Mâconnais, in the heart of one of the greatest gastronomic centers of the world; good restaurants abound in the area, as well as in the nearby city of Lyon. As a wine, Beaujolais is so famous that it stands apart from the other wines of Burgundy. It even has its own red grape, Gamay. The fact that Beaujolais is part of Burgundy is merely a technicality.

Beaujolais in action

To really get a feeling for being in France, visit a bistro in Paris or Lyon and order a carafe of young Beaujolais with your charcuterie, pâté, or chicken. No wine slides down the throat as easily! Young, uncomplicated Beaujolais wines should *definitely* be served chilled, at about 55°F (13°C), to capture their fruity exuberance. The fuller cru Beaujolais, on the other hand, are best at about the same temperature as red Burgundy (58° to 60°F; 14°C).

The easy-drinking Beaujolais

If you're a white wine, white Zinfandel, or rosé wine drinker (or even a non-wine drinker!), Beaujolais may be the *ideal* first red wine to drink — a bridge, so to speak, to more serious red wines. Beaujolais wines are the fruitiest red wines in France, although they're dry. Beaujolais is truly a fun wine that's delicious and doesn't require contemplation.

Beaujolais and *Beaujolais Supérieur* (one percent higher in alcohol) are the easiest Beaujolais wines. Their AOC territories extend across the whole Beaujolais district, but actually these wines come from the southern part of Beaujolais where the soil is mainly clay and sand. They're fresh, fruity, uncomplicated, fairly light-bodied wines that sell for $8 to $12 and are best a year or two after the vintage. They're fine wines for warm weather, when a heavier red wine would be inappropriate.

The serious versions

Beaujolais has its serious side, too. The best Beaujolais are made in the northern part of the Beaujolais district where the soil is granite-based. *Beaujolais-Villages* is a wine blended from grapes grown in (some of) 39 specific villages that produce fuller, more substantial wine than simple Beaujolais. It costs a dollar or two more, but can be well worth the difference.

Beaujolais that's even higher quality comes from ten specific areas in the north. The wines of these areas are known as *cru* Beaujolais, and only the name of the cru appears in large letters on the label. (The wines aren't actually named Beaujolais.) Cru Beaujolais have more depth and, in fact, need a little time to develop; some of the crus can age and improve for four or five years or more. They range in price from about $11 to $24. Table 9-7 lists the ten cru Beaujolais as they are geographically situated, from south to north, along with a brief description of each cru.

Table 9-7	The Ten Cru Beaujolais
Cru	*Description*
Brouilly *(broo yee)*	The largest cru in terms of production and the most variable in quality; light and fruity; drink within three years
Côte de Brouilly	Distinctly better than Brouilly, fuller and more concentrated; vineyards are higher in altitude; drink within three years
Regnié *(ray nyay)*	The newest village to be recognized as a cru; very similar to Brouilly; not quite as good as Côte de Brouilly
Morgon *(mor gohn)*	At its best, full and earthy; can age for five to seven years
Chiroubles *(sheh roob leh)*	One of our favorites; the quintessential, delicate, delicious, perfumed Beaujolais; tastes of young red fruits; very pretty; drink it within two years of the vintage
Fleurie *(flehr ee)*	Medium-bodied, rich, with a velvety fruitiness; the most popular cru (and, along with Moulin-á-Vent, the most expensive, at $16 to $22); quite reliable; can age for four years
Moulin-à-Vent *(moo lahn ah vahn)*	Clearly the most powerful, concentrated cru, and the one that can age the longest (ten years or more); this is one Beaujolais that really needs three or four years to develop
Chénas *(shay nahs)*	Bordering Moulin-à-Vent (in fact, much of it can be legally sold as the more famous Moulin-à-Vent); what is sold as Chénas is usually well priced; drink within four years
Juliénas *(jhool yay nahs)*	The insider's Beaujolais; often the most consistent and the best of the crus; full-bodied and rich, can last five years or more; seldom disappoints
Saint-Amour *(sant ah more)*	The most northerly cru in Beaujolais; perfectly named for loverson Valentine's Day (or any other day); supple, light to medium-bodied, delicious berry fruit; drink within two or three years

Most Beaujolais is sold by large *négociants* — firms that buy grapes and wine from growers and blend, bottle, and sell the wine under their own labels. Two of the largest and most reliable Beaujolais négociants are Georges Duboeuf and Louis Jadot; Jadot also owns a few very fine domaines, in Moulin-a-Vent and in Morgon. (For a list of other Beaujolais producers, see Chapter 8 in *French Wine For Dummies*.)

The Hearty Rhônes of the Valley

The Rhône *(rone)* Valley is in southeastern France, south of Beaujolais, between the city of Lyon in the north and Avignon directly south (just north of Provence). The growing season in the Rhône Valley is sunny and hot. The wines reflect the weather: The red wines are full, robust, and fairly high in alcohol. Even some of the white wines tend to be full and powerful. But the wines from the southern part of the Rhône are distinctly different from those in the northern Rhône Valley. (For a detailed explanation of how the Northern and Southern Rhône differ as wine districts, read Chapter 9 of *French Wine For Dummies*.)

For a good, reliable dry red wine that costs about $9 to $14, look no farther than the Rhône Valley's everyday red wine, Côtes du Rhône, which comes mainly from the southern part of the region. The Rhône Valley makes more serious wines — mostly red — but Côtes du Rhône is one of the best inexpensive red wines in the world.

Generous wines of the south

Most (in fact, about 95 percent of) Rhône wines come from the Southern Rhône, where the wines are generally inexpensive and uncomplicated. They're mainly blends of several grape varieties. The dominant grape variety in the southern Rhône is the prolific Grenache, which makes easygoing wines that are high in alcohol and low in tannin — but some blends contain significant amounts of Syrah or other varieties, which makes for somewhat gutsier wines. Almost all Côtes du Rhône wines are red (94 percent red, 3 percent white, 3 percent rosé).

Besides Côtes du Rhône, other southern Rhône wines to look for are

- **Côtes du Ventoux** *(vahn too),* which is similar to, but a bit lighter than, Côtes du Rhône
- **Côtes du Rhône-Villages,** from 95 villages, making fuller and a bit more expensive wines than Côtes du Rhône; 16 of these villages are entitled to use their names on the label, such as "Cairanne — Côtes du Rhône-Villages"
- The single-village wines **Gigondas** *(jhee gon dahs)* and **Vacqueyras** *(vah keh rahs)*

The last two wines are former Côtes du Rhône-Villages wines that graduated to individual appellations. Gigondas ($30 to $35) is particularly rich and robust and can live for ten years or more in good vintages. Vacqueyras is less powerful and robust than Gigondas but also less expensive (mainly $14 to $22); Vacqueyras is a particularly good buy.

Two interesting dry rosé wines of the southern Rhône are **Tavel** *(tah vel)* and **Lirac** *(lee rahk);* Lirac is less well known and therefore less expensive. (Tavel ranges from $17 to $30, Lirac a little less; Lirac can also be white or red.) Both are made from the Grenache and Cinsault grapes. They can be delightful on hot, summer days or at picnics. As with most rosé wines, they are best when they're very young.

But **Châteauneuf-du-Pape** *(shah toe nuf doo pahp)* is the king in the Southern Rhône. Its name recalls the fourteenth century, when nearby Avignon (not Rome) was the home of the Popes. Almost all Châteauneuf-du-Pape is red wine, and a blend of grapes: As many as 13 varieties can be used, but Grenache, Mourvèdre, and Syrah predominate. At its best, Châteauneuf-du-Pape is full-bodied, rich, round, and ripe. In good vintages, it will age well for 15 to 20 years. Most red Châteauneuf-du-Pape wines (a small amount of very earthy-style white Châteauneuf-du-Pape is also made) retail in the $28 to $45 price range, but the best ones can cost up $70 or more. Two of the finest Châteauneuf-du-Papes are *Château Rayas* (nearly 100 percent Grenache from very old vines) and *Château de Beaucastel* (which can age 20 years or more).

Noble wines of the north

The two best red wines of the entire Rhône — **Côte-Rôtie** *(coat roe tee)* and **Hermitage** *(er mee tahj)* — hail from the Northern Rhône Valley. Both are made from the noble Syrah grape (but some white Viognier grapes are sometimes used in Côte Rôtie).

Although both are rich, full-bodied wines, **Côte-Rôtie** is the more finesseful of the two. It has a wonderfully fragrant aroma — which always reminds us of green olives and raspberries — and soft, fruity flavors. In good vintages, Côte Rôtie can age for 20 years or more (see Appendix C). Most Côte-Rôties are in the $45 to $85 price range.

The most famous producer of Côte-Rôtie is Guigal; his single-vineyard Côte-Rôties — La Mouline, La Landonne, and La Turque — are legendary but rare and particularly expensive (over $200 a bottle!).

Red Hermitage is clearly the most full-bodied, longest-lived Rhône wine. It is a complex, rich, tannic wine that needs several years before it begins to develop, and it will age easily for 30 years or more in good vintages (2003, 1999, 1998, 1995, 1991, 1990, 1989, and 1988 were all excellent vintages in the Northern Rhone). The best red Hermitages sell today for $50 to $90, and a few are even over $100, although lesser Hermitages are as low as $40 to $45.

The three best producers of Hermitage are Jean-Louis Chave, Chapoutier, and Paul Jaboulet Aîné (for his top Hermitage, La Chapelle).

Jaboulet also makes a less expensive little brother to Hermitage, a **Crozes-Hermitage** (a separate appellation) called Domaine de Thalabert. It's as good as — if not better than — many Hermitages, can age and improve for 10 to 15 years in good vintages, and is reasonably priced at $28 to $30. It's a wine to buy.

Cornas, also made entirely from Syrah, is another fine Northern Rhône red wine. Cornas resembles Hermitage in that it is a huge, tannic wine that needs 10 to 20 years of aging. It ranges in price from $40 to $80. Two Cornas producers to look for are Domaine August Clape and Jean-Luc Colombo.

A small amount of white Hermitage is produced from the Marsanne and Roussanne grape varieties. White Hermitage is traditionally a full, heavy, earthy wine that needs eight to ten years to fully develop. Chapoutier's fine Hermitage Blanc, Chante-Alouette, however, is all Marsanne (about $80) and made in a more approachable style. The other great white Hermitage is Chave's; about $90, it's complex, rich, and almost as long-lived as his red Hermitage.

Condrieu *(cohn dree oo),* made entirely from Viognier, is the other white wine to try in the Northern Rhône. It's one of the most fragrant, floral dry wines in existence. Its flavors are delicate but rich, with delicious fresh apricot and peach notes; it makes a wonderful accompaniment to fresh fish. Condrieu (which sells for $45 to $60) is best young, however. And, because Condrieu is a small wine zone, the best Condrieu wines are hard to find. Look for them in finer wine shops and better French restaurants. (For more info on Rhône wines and producers, see Chapter 9 in *French Wine For Dummies.*)

The Loire Valley: White Wine Heaven

Have you been Chardonnay-ed out yet? If you're looking for white-wine alternatives to Chardonnay, discover the Loire *(l'wahr)* Valley wine region. A lot of white wines come from there, but virtually none of them are Chardonnay! For the record, you can find red wines and some dry rosés, too, in the Loire, but the region is really known for its white wines.

The Loire Valley stretches across northwest France, following the path of the Loire River from central France in the east to the Atlantic Ocean in the west. The rather cool climate, especially in the west, produces relatively light-bodied white wines. The Loire Valley has three sections: the Upper Loire, the Central Loire Valley, and the Pays Nantais *(pay ee nahn tay),* named after the city of Nantes, right where the Loire River empties into the Atlantic Ocean.

In the eastern end of the Valley (Upper Loire), just south of Paris, are the towns of Sancerre and Pouilly-sur-Loire, located on opposite banks of the Loire River. Here, the Sauvignon Blanc grape makes lively, dry wines that have spicy, green-grass and minerally flavors. The two principal wines in this area are **Sancerre** *(sahn sehr)* and **Pouilly-Fumé** *(pwee foo may).*

- Sancerre is the lighter, drier, and more vibrant of the two. It's perfect for summer drinking, especially with shellfish or light, freshwater fish, such as trout. Look for the Sancerres of Domaines Henri Bourgeois or Lucien Crochet.

- Pouilly-Fumé is slightly fuller than Sancerre and can have attractive gun-flint and mineral flavors. Pouilly-Fumé can be quite a fine wine when made by a good producer such as Didier Dagueneau or Ladoucette. Because of its fuller weight, Pouilly-Fumé goes well with rich fish, such as salmon, or with chicken or veal.

Most Sancerre and Pouilly-Fumé wines sell in the $20 to $35 range, but a few of the better Pouilly-Fumés can cost $50 or more. These wines are at their best when they're young; drink them within four years of the vintage.

The central Loire Valley is known for both its white and red wines. The Chenin Blanc grape makes better wine here than it does anywhere else in the world. The Anjou district produces arguably the world's greatest *dry* Chenin Blanc wine, Savennières (starts at about $20). A great dessert white wine made from Chenin Blanc, Coulée de Serrant, also comes from Anjou. Bonnezeaux and Quartz-de-Chaume are two other dessert white wine appellations from Anjou that are made from Chenin Blanc.

Near the city of Tours (where you can see beautiful chateaux of former French royalty), lies the town of Vouvray *(voo vray)*. **Vouvray** wines come in three styles: dry *(sec)*, medium-dry *(demi-sec)*, or sweet (called *moelleux,* pronounced *m'wah leuh*). Vouvray also can be a sparkling wine.

The best wines of Vouvray, the sweet *(moelleux),* can be made only in vintages of unusual ripeness, which occur infrequently. These wines need several years to develop and can last almost forever, thanks to their remarkable acidity; their prices begin at about $22. Three renowned Vouvray producers are Philippe Foreau of Clos Naudain, Gaston Huet-Pinguet, and Didier Champalou.

Less expensive Vouvrays, priced at about $14 to $15, are pleasant to drink young. Even the drier versions are not truly bone dry and are a good choice if you don't enjoy very dry wines. They go well with chicken or veal in cream sauce, spicy cuisines, or fruit and soft cheese after dinner.

The Loire Valley's best red wines also come from the Central Loire. Made mainly from Cabernet Franc, they carry the place-names of the villages the grapes come from: **Chinon** *(shee nohn),* **Bourgueil** *(boorguh'y),* **Saint-Nicolas-de-Bourgueil** *(san nee co lah deh boor guh'y),* and **Saumur-Champigny** *(saw muhr shahm pee n'yee).* They're all spicy, great-value ($12 to $35), medium-bodied reds that are famously food friendly.

Close to the Atlantic Ocean, the third wine district of the Loire Valley is the home of the Muscadet grape (also known as the Melon). The wine, also called **Muscadet** *(moos cah day),* is light and very dry, with apple and mineral flavors — perfect with clams, oysters, and river fish (and, naturally, ideal for summer drinking).

Here a Pouilly, there a Pouilly

You may get the two *Pouilly* wines — Pouilly-Fuissé and Pouilly-Fumé — confused, but they're very different wines. The Chardonnay-based Pouilly-Fuissé, from the Mâcon in Burgundy, is a full-bodied wine and usually oaky. Pouilly-Fumé, made from Sauvignon Blanc, is medium-bodied and crisper.

Most Muscadet comes from the Sèvre-et-Maine AOC zone, and those words appear on the label. Frequently you also see the term *sur lie*, which means that the wine aged on its *lees* (fermentation yeasts) and was bottled straight from the tank. This procedure gives the wine liveliness, freshness, and sometimes a slight prickle of carbon dioxide on the tongue.

The best news about Muscadet is the price. You can buy a really good Muscadet for $9 to $12. Buy the youngest one you can find because Muscadet is best within two years of the vintage; it isn't an ager. (See Chapter 12 in *French Wine For Dummies* for more on Loire Valley wines and producers.)

Alsace Wines: French, Not German

It's understandable that some wine drinkers confuse the wines of Alsace *(ahl zas)* with German wines. Alsace, in northeastern France, is just across the Rhine River from Germany. Originally a part of Germany, Alsace became French in the seventeenth century. Germany took the region back in 1871 only to lose it to France again in 1919 as a result of World War I. To complicate things further, both Alsace and Germany grow some of the same grapes (Riesling and Gewürztraminer, for example). But Alsace wines are distinctly different from German wines, generally dry, and fuller bodied.

Alsace wines are unique among French wines in that almost all of them carry a grape variety name as well as a place-name (that is, Alsace). All Alsace wines come in a long-necked bottle called a *flûte*. The wines of Alsace also happen to represent very good value.

Considering Alsace's northerly latitude, you'd expect the region's climate to be cool. But thanks to the protection of the Vosges Mountains to the west, Alsace's climate is quite sunny and temperate, and one of the driest in France — in short, perfect weather for grape growing.

Although some Pinot Noir exists, 91 percent of Alsace's wines are white. Four are particularly important: Riesling, Pinot Blanc, Pinot Gris, and Gewurztraminer. Each reflects the characteristics of its grape, but they all share a certain aroma and flavor, sometimes called a spiciness, that can only be described as the flavor of Alsace.

Riesling is the king of Alsace wines (remember that it's a *dry* wine here). Alsace Riesling has a fruity aroma but a firm, dry, almost steely taste. Although, like most Alsace wines, it can be consumed young, a Riesling from a good vintage can easily age and improve for ten years or more. Rieslings are in the $15 to $35 price range; a few of the best are over $35.

Alsace **Pinot Blanc** is the lightest of the four wines. Some producers make their Pinot Blanc medium-dry to appeal to wine drinkers who are unfamiliar with the region's wines, while others make classic, bone-dry Pinot Blanc. Either way, it's best young. Pinot Blanc is quite inexpensive, selling for $12 to $20.

Pinot Gris or **Tokay-Pinot Gris** (the "Tokay" part of the name is being dropped to avoid confusion with the famous Hungarian dessert wine, Tokaji) is made from Pinot Gris, the same variety that you find in Italy as Pinot Grigio. Here in Alsace, it makes a rich, spicy, full-bodied, characterful wine. Alsace's Pinot Gris retails for $15 to $30; it goes well with spicy meat dishes and can work with slightly sweet or sour flavors.

The **Gewürztraminer** grape has such intense, exotic, spicy aromas and flavors that it's a love-it-or-leave-it wine. (One of us loves it — the other leaves it!) But it certainly has its followers. And this grape is clearly at its best in Alsace. If you haven't tried an Alsace Gewurztraminer yet, you haven't tasted one of the most distinctive wines in the world. It's quite low in acidity and high in alcohol, a combination that gives an impression of fullness and softness. It goes best with *foie gras* and strong cheeses, and some people like it with spicy Asian cuisine. Gewurztraminer sells for about the same price as Riesling but doesn't age quite as well.

For more info on Alsace wines and producers, see Chapter 11 in *French Wine For Dummies*.

The South and Southwest

The most dynamic wine regions in France are all located in the southern part of the country. Ironically, this is the oldest wine-producing area in France: The Greeks made wine in Provence in the sixth century BC. The South is also the part of France that makes the most wine. Languedoc-Roussillon, a dual wine region, produces over 40 percent of France's wine!

Most southern French wines didn't get much international attention until the 1980s. Now the world has discovered that these wines are vastly improved in quality, as well as very affordable.

Southwest France, the huge area between Bordeaux and the Spanish border, also makes wine (well, it's French, isn't it?), and many wine regions here have also experienced a renaissance. Like the South, it's mainly red wine country, but you can find some interesting whites, rosés, sparkling wines, and dessert wines, as well. You might say that the South and Southwestern France are the country's "new" frontiers.

The Midi: France's bargain basement

The sunny, dry Languedoc-Roussillon *(lahn guh doc roo see yohn)* region, also known as the Midi *(mee dee),* has long been the country's largest wine-producing area. The region makes mainly red wines; in fact, more than half of France's red wines come from here. Traditionally, these robust red wines came from typical grape varieties of the South, such as Carignan, Cinsault, and Grenache. But in the last two decades, more serious varieties such as Syrah, Cabernet Sauvignon, and Merlot have become popular with growers. Winemakers use these grapes both for varietal wines and in blends.

In this region, look especially for the red wines from the AOC zones of **Corbières, Minervois, St-Chinian, Fitou**, and **Costières de Nîmes.** In addition, many varietal wines carrying the designation *Vin de Pays d'Oc* are often good values. They're made from grapes that can come from anywhere in the Languedoc-Roussillon region, rather than from a specific AOC zone.

The best news is that most of these wines are in the $8 to $15 price range, although a few of the better ones cost $20 or more. Two of the better-known brands of varietal wines (with the Vin de Pays d'Oc appellation) are Fortant de France and Réserve St. Martin. Even California's E. & J. Gallo winery now makes wines from Languedoc-Roussillon under the brand, Red Bicyclette.

Timeless Provence

Provence *(pro vahns)* — southeast of the Rhône Valley, east of Languedoc-Roussillon, and west of Northern Italy — may be France's most beautiful region. Home of the Riviera, Nice, and Cannes, it's certainly the country's most fashionable and touristy region. But it's also an ancient land, with a thriving old capital, Aix-en-Provence. The excellent light and climate have always attracted great artists — such as Vincent van Gogh — who painted many of their best works here.

Wine has always been part of Provence's culture and economy. Provence is best known for its rosés, which so many tourists enjoy on the Riviera, but Provence's red wines are now winning the most critical acclaim. Rosé wines still dominate in the region's largest AOC wine zone, **Côtes de Provence,** but in three other important AOC zones — **Coteaux d'Aix-en-Provence, Les Baux-de-Provence,** and **Bandol** — red wines rule. Bandol, and its foremost producer, Domaine Tempier, enjoy Provence's greatest reputation for reds. **Cassis** (no relation to the blackcurrant liqueur of the same name), a small AOC zone on the Mediterranean coast near Marseilles, makes distinctive, aromatic white wines.

Provence's reds and rosés derive from the same grape varieties used in Languedoc-Roussillon — Grenache, Cinsault, Mourvèdre, Carignan, Syrah, and Cabernet Sauvignon. The main varieties in white Cassis are Clairette and Marsanne.

For more info on the wines and producers of Languedoc-Roussillon and Provence, see Chapter 13 in *French Wine For Dummies.*

Southwest France

The large area that borders the Atlantic Ocean south of the Bordeaux region is known as Southwest France — but it's actually composed of many individual wine districts. Three of the most significant are situated near Bordeaux.

- **Bergerac** *(ber jhe rak)* makes Bordeaux-like red and white wines, without the Bordeaux prices. Merlot dominates Bergerac's red wines, while Sémillon and Sauvignon Blanc are the main varieties for its whites, some of which cost as little as $8 a bottle.

- **Monbazillac** *(mon bah zee yak)* specializes in sweet dessert wines similar to the Sauternes of the Bordeaux region (see Chapter 15 for more on Sauternes), but Monbazillac's wines are considerably less expensive — and less complex — than Sauternes.

- **Cahors** *(cah or)* is Southwest France's most prestigious red wine district. The main grape variety is Malbec, and that name increasingly appears on the labels. Nowhere else in the world, except Argentina, does this variety play such an important role. The best wines of the traditional Cahors producers, such as Château Lagrezette, are dark, tannic reds that need about ten years of aging before they mature. Prices for Château Lagrezette Cahors wines begin at about $23.

Two other districts in Southwest France, **Gaillac** *(gah yack)* and **Jurançon** *(joo rahn sohn),* specialize in white dessert wines — quite good in quality. Gaillac also makes fruity, lightly sparkling wines. The AOC red wine district of **Madiran** produces full-bodied, tannic reds, perfect for the local, hearty Gascony cuisine. Tannat is the main variety used in Madiran, along with Cabernet Sauvignon and Cabernet Franc. The last French AOC district before you cross the Pyrénées Mountains into Spain is **Irouléguy** *(ee roo leh gee);* spicy, tannic red wines are made here by natives who speak not French, but Basque. (Chapter 14 of *French Wine For Dummies* provides much more information on the wines and producers of Southwest France.)

Other French Wine Regions

Two of France's three least-known wine regions have something in common: They're located in the foothills and slopes of the Alps in eastern France, next to Switzerland. In fact, skiers are probably the most familiar with their wines. They are the **Jura** *(joo rah)* and **Savoie** *(sah v'wah)* — sometimes anglicized as *Savoy.*

Jura makes two interesting wines: "Yellow Wine" *(Vin Jaune)* — made nowhere else in France — and "Straw Wine" *(Vin de Paille),* a little of which is also made in the Northern Rhône. The Yellow Wine, from the Savagnin grape variety, is comparable to a light Spanish fino Sherry, but it's not fortified (see Chapter 15). Château-Chalon is the most famous example of Vins Jaunes *(van joh'n).* Vin de Paille *(van deh pah'ee)* is known as Straw Wine because of the traditional way in which it's made: The grapes (Savagnin, Chardonnay and others) are harvested late, arranged on straw mats or in baskets, and then placed in attics to dry — similar to Tuscany's specialty, Vin Santo (see Chapter 15). The resulting wine is rich, concentrated, nutty, and raisiny.

Savoie's wines, mainly white, are typically dry and light-bodied. Seyssel *(say sell),* Savoie's best-known appellation, is known for its slightly sparkling wines as well as its still whites.

Corsica, renowned historically as the birthplace of Napoleon, is a large, mountainous island 100 miles southeast of Provence. It's best known for its medium-bodied, well-priced red and rosé wines. (For more info on the wines and producers of France's minor wine regions, see Chapter 14 in *French Wine For Dummies.*)

Chapter 10

Italy, the Heartland of Vino

. . . .

. . . .

More than 2,000 years after Julius Caesar conquered Gaul, the Italians continue to take the world by storm. With passion, artistic flair, impeccable taste, and flawless workmanship as their weapons, the Italians have infiltrated the arenas of fashion, film, food, and of course, wine.

Thanks to the popularity of Italian restaurants, most of us have frequent opportunities to enjoy best-selling Italian wines such as Pinot Grigio, Soave, Valpolicella, and Chianti. But Italy makes other wines, too — many of them among the greatest wines on earth. And just about every one of Italy's thousand-something wines is terrific with food, because Italian wines are made specifically to be enjoyed during a meal. That's how the Italians drink them.

In this chapter, we focus on Italy's three most renowned wine areas — Piedmont, Tuscany, and Northeastern Italy. We also discuss some of the other Italian regions whose wines you are likely to find in your wine shop or *ristorante*. If you'd like detailed information on Italian wines, be sure to get our book *Italian Wine For Dummies* (Wiley).

The Vineyard of Europe

Tiny, overachieving Italy — 60 percent the size of France, three-quarters the size of California — makes more than 20 percent of the world's wines! Wine is the lifeblood of the Italian people. Vines grow all over, and no meal can possibly occur without a bottle of wine on the table.

The downside to wine's penetration into Italian culture is that Italians often take wine for granted. Italy took 28 years longer than France to develop a wine classification system, for example; and today, 40-plus years after creating that system, Italy has yet to incorporate official recognition of her best vineyard sites *(crus)* into her wine laws, as the French have done in Burgundy. Italy's casual attitude toward wine slowed the acceptance of even the top wines by many serious wine lovers around the world — although recognition of Italian wines has grown considerably over the past decade.

Another handicap of Italian wines, for wine drinkers in other countries who want to learn about them, is that most Italian wines are made from native grape varieties that don't exist elsewhere (and when transplanted, don't perform nearly as well as in Italy). Grapes such as Nebbiolo, Sangiovese, Aglianico, and Barbera, to name just a few, can make outstanding wine in Italy, but their names are unfamiliar. Table 10-1 lists the grape varieties behind some wines of Italy's most important wine regions.

Table 10-1	Grape Varieties of Some Major Italian Wine Regions	
Region/ Red Wine	*White Wine*	*Grape Varieties*
Piedmont		
Barolo		Nebbiolo
Barbaresco		Nebbiolo
Gattinara		Nebbiolo, Bonarda*
	Gavi	Cortese
Tuscany		
Chianti, Chianti Classico		Sangiovese, Canaiolo, and others*
Brunello di Montalcino		Sangiovese Grosso
Vino Nobile di Montepulciano		Sangiovese, Canaiolo, and others*
Carmignano		Sangiovese, Cabernet Sauvignon*
Super-Tuscans**		Cabernet Sauvignon, Sangiovese, and others*

Region/ Red Wine	White Wine	Grape Varieties
Veneto		
	Soave	Garganega, Trebbiano, and others*
Valpolicella		Corvina, Rondinella, Molinara*
Amarone		(Same grapes as Valpolicella; semi-dried)
Bardolino		Corvina, Rondinella, Molinara*
	Bianco di Custoza	Trebbiano, Garganega, Tocai*
	Lugana***	Trebbiano

  * *Blended wines, made from two or more grapes.*
  ** *Untraditional wines produced mainly in the Chianti district; see the discussion under Tuscany.*
  *** *Much of the Lugana wine zone is actually in Lombardy.*

On the upside, Italy is blessed with such a variety of soils and climates — from Alpine foothills in the north to Mediterranean coastlines — that the range of her wines is almost endless. (A curious wine lover could keep busy for a lifetime exploring the hundreds of wines in Italy!) Italy's hilly landscape provides plenty of high-altitude relief for grapevines even in the warm south.

The ordinary and the elite

Italy's wines, as we outside of Italy know them, fall into two distinct groups:

✔ Inexpensive red and white wines for everyday drinking with meals in the casual Italian fashion

✔ The better wines, which range from good to great in quality

One of the best-known Italian wines in the first category is Pinot Grigio, the ubiquitous dry white wine that has become the largest-selling type of imported wine in the United States. In the second category is Barolo, one of the world's finest red wines, along with many other fine Italian wines.

Categories of Italian wine, legally speaking

Because Italy is a member of the European Union, her official system of categorizing wines (her *appellation* system) must conform to the two-tier EU system. (See "The EU hierarchy of wine" in Chapter 4 for more information.) In the upper tier — Quality Wines Produced in a Specific Region (QWPSR) — Italy has two categories of wine:

- ✔ DOCG wines *(Denominazione di Origine Controllata e Garantita),* translated as *regulated and guaranteed place-name,* a small group of elite wines. The long Italian phrase corresponding to the initials DOCG appears on the labels of these wines.

- ✔ DOC wines *(Denominazione di Origine Controllata),* translated as *regulated place-name,* Italy's basic QWPSR wines. The phrase *Denominazione di Origine Controllata* appears on the labels of these wines.

The terms DOC and DOCG refer both to wine zones and the wines of those zones. The DOCG Soave, for example, is both a place (a specific production zone defined and regulated by Italian law, named after a town called Soave) and the wine of that place.

In the lower EU tier — table wine — Italy has another two categories of wine:

- ✔ IGT wines *(Indicazione di Geografica Tipica),* which are table wines with a geographic indication on the label. Most of these wines were previously labeled as *vino da tavola* followed by a geographic designation, and you still find this wording on some labels.

- ✔ Ordinary table wines that carry no geographical indication except "Italy."

Italy's wine regions

Italy is said to have 20 wine regions, which correspond exactly to her political regions (see Figure 10-1). In other words, wine is produced everywhere in Italy. What we would call a wine region in France, such as Burgundy or Alsace, we refer to as a wine *zone* in Italy to avoid confusion with the political region.

Figure 10-1:
The wine
regions of
Italy.

Many of the finest wines come from the north: the Piedmont region in the
northwest, Tuscany in north-central Italy, and the three regions (informally
called the Tre Venezie) of Northeastern Italy.

Reds Reign in Piedmont

Piedmont's claim to wine fame is the Nebbiolo *(neb bee OH lo)* grape, a noble red variety that produces great wine only in northwestern Italy. The proof of Nebbiolo's nobility is its wines: Barolo *(bah RO lo)* and Barbaresco *(bar bah RES co)* are two of the world's great red wines. Both are DOCG wines made entirely from the Nebbiolo grape in the Langhe hills around Alba, and each is named after a village within its production zone.

Both Barolo and Barbaresco are robust reds — very dry, full-bodied, and high in tannin, acidity, and alcohol. Their aromas suggest tar, violets, roses, ripe strawberries, and (sometimes) truffles — the kind that grow in the ground, not the chocolate! Barolo is more full-bodied than Barbaresco and usually requires a bit more aging; otherwise, the two wines are very similar. Like most Italian wines, they show at their best with food. Good Barolo and Barbaresco wines usually start at $40 and run to well over $100 per bottle.

Most Barolos and Barbarescos are not wines to drink young. Production rules stipulate that Barolo is not Barolo until it has aged for three years at the winery, or for five years if it is called *Riserva.* (Barbaresco's minimum aging is two years, or four for Riserva.) But both wines benefit from additional aging. When traditionally made, Barolo and Barbaresco often require 10 to 15 years' total aging, from the year of the vintage — and they usually benefit from a few hours of aeration before drinking to soften their somewhat tough tannins. (See Chapter 8 for instructions on aerating wine.)

Both Barbaresco and especially Barolo have something in common with Burgundy in France: *You must find a good producer to experience the wine at its best.* To guide you in that endeavor, we list the producers whom we consider the best of Barolo and Barbaresco, in our rough order of preference.

Tradition versus "new-style"

One Barolo can differ from another (and one Barbaresco from another) quite a lot according to the wineries' production methods. Traditionally made wines are more tannic and need more time to develop but typically have greater longevity than new-style wines do. The new-style wines are fruitier in flavor but often oaky-tasting, and are ready to drink sooner — as soon as three to five years after they are released. Some producers are in one winemaking camp or the other, while many producers make their wines in a middle-ground style.

Barolo
Giacomo Conterno
Giuseppe Mascarello
Giuseppe Rinaldi
Bartolo Mascarello
Vietti
Ceretto
Gaja
Bruno Giacosa
Roberto Voerzio
Aldo Conterno
Marcarini
Luciano Sandrone
Paolo Scavino
Podere Colla
Elvio Cogno
Clerico
Pio Cesare
Prunotto
Renato Ratti

Brovia
E. Pira & Figli
Elio Altare
Luigi Pira
Manzone
Marchesi di Barolo
Michele Chiarlo
Conterno-Fantino
Parusso
Giacomo Borgogno
Cordero di Montezemolo
Fontanafredda

Barbaresco
Bruno Giacosa
Gaja
Ceretto (a.k.a. Bricco Asili)
Marchesi di Gresy
Produttori del Barbaresco
DeForville

Some producers — including Giacomo Conterno, both Mascarellos, Giuseppe Rinaldi, and Bruno Giacosa — clearly make traditionally styled wines; others — such as Gaja, Altare, and Clerico — make modern-style wines; and some, such as Ceretto and Vietti, combine aspects of both winemaking styles. (We prefer the traditionally made wines, but all three styles have some excellent producers.)

Two other good Nebbiolo-based wines, the DOCGs Gattinara *(gah tee NAH rah)* and Ghemme *(GAE mae)*, come from northern Piedmont, where the Nebbiolo grape is called Spanna. Although Gattinara and Ghemme seldom get the praise that the two Big B's (Barolo and Barbaresco) enjoy, they offer the same enticing Nebbiolo aromas and flavors — especially Gattinara — in a less full-bodied style. Priced at $32 to $45 a bottle, Gattinara from a good producer may be one of the world's most underrated wines. Look for Antoniolo's, and Travaglini's Gattinaras; Antichi Vigneti di Cantalupo (about $40) is the leading Ghemme producer.

Weekday reds

The Piedmontese reserve serious wines like Barolo and Barbaresco for Sunday dinner or special occasions. What they drink on an everyday basis are the red wines Dolcetto *(dohl CHET to)*, Barbera *(bar BEAR ah)*, and Nebbiolo (grown outside of prestigious DOCG zones such as Barolo and Barbaresco). Of the three, Dolcetto is the lightest-bodied and is usually the first red wine served in a Piedmontese meal.

Dolcetto

If you know enough Italian to translate the phrase *la dolce vita,* you may think that the name Dolcetto indicates a sweet wine. Actually, the Dolcetto grape tastes sweet but the *wine* is distinctly dry and somewhat grapey with noticeable tannin. Dolcetto is often compared to Beaujolais (France's easy-drinking red wine; see Chapter 9), but it's drier and more tannic than most Beaujolais wines and goes better with food (at least in our opinion).

Dolcetto sells for $11 to $25. The best Dolcetto wines are from the zones of Dogliani, Diano d'Alba, and Alba; the labels of these wines carry the grape name, Dolcetto, along with the name of the area. Just about all our recommended Barolo producers make a Dolcetto, usually Dolcetto *d'Alba* (from Alba). A favorite producer of ours who happens to make only Dolcetto di Dogliani is Quinto Chionetti.

Barbera

While Dolcetto is unique to Piedmont, the Barbera grape is the second most widely planted red grape variety in all of Italy. (Sangiovese is *the* most planted red variety.) But it's in Piedmont — specifically the Asti and Alba wine zones — that Barbera excels. It's a rich, red wine with high acidity and generous black-cherry fruit character.

Barbera d'Alba is generally a bit fuller, riper, and richer than the leaner Barbera d'Asti — but Barbera d'Asti from certain old vineyards rivals Barbera d'Alba in richness and in power. (Link the *d'* with the word following it when pronouncing these names: *DAL ba, DAHS tee.*) Barbera happens to be our favorite everyday wine, especially with pasta or pizza — or anything tomatoe-y.

Barbera is more popular in the United States than it has ever been, and we couldn't be more delighted, as it's now easier to find. Two different styles of Barbera are available:

- ✔ The traditional style, aged in *casks* (large oak containers that impart little, if any, oak flavor to the wine), which sells for about $12 to $25

- ✔ The newer style, oak-influenced Barbera aged in *barriques* (small, new barrels of French oak), which sells in the $25 to $45 range (somebody has to pay for those expensive barriques!)

Although both types of Barbera are very good, with a few exceptions we prefer the simpler, less expensive, traditional style. Frankly, we're getting tired of the oak flavor in wines these days, although we do admit that some barrique-aged Barberas are quite good. Barbera is an unusual red grape variety in that it has practically no tannin, and so the tannins from the small oak barrels can complement Barbera wines.

Two particularly good producers of Barbera d'Alba are Vietti and Giacomo Conterno. Vietti also makes a terrific Barbera d'Asti called "La Crena."

Nebbiolo

A third weekday red from Piedmont is Nebbiolo (d'Alba or Langhe), made from Nebbiolo grapes grown in vineyards outside the prized Barolo or Barbaresco zones. The wine is lighter in body and easier to drink than either Barolo or Barbaresco, and it sells for about $15 to $20 a bottle. Another variation is Roero Rosso, made almost entirely from Nebbiolo. (For more specific information on Piedmontese wines, see Chapter 4 of *Italian Wine For Dummies.*)

Whites in a supporting role

Almost all Piedmont's wines are red, but the region does boast two interesting dry whites. Gavi, named for a town in southern Piedmont, is a very dry wine with pronounced acidity, made from the Cortese grape. Most Gavis sell for $13 to $24, while a premium Gavi, La Scolca's Black Label, costs around $45.

Arneis *(ahr NASE)* is a white wine produced in the Roero zone near Alba from a long-forgotten grape also called Arneis, which was rescued by Alfredo Currado, owner of Vietti winery, nearly 40 years ago. Arneis is a dry to medium-dry wine with rich texture. It's best when it is consumed within two years of the vintage; a bottle sells for $20 to $28. Besides Vietti's, look for Bruno Giacosa's and Ceretto's Arneis.

Tuscany the Beautiful

Florence, Siena, Michelangelo's David, the leaning tower of Pisa . . . the beautiful region of Tuscany has more than her share of attractions. Only one wine can possibly compare in fame — and that, too, comes from Tuscany: Chianti.

Chianti: Italy's great, underrated red

Chianti is a large wine zone extending through much of Tuscany. The zone — all of it DOCG status, deservedly or not — has eight districts. Chianti wines may use the name of the district where their grapes grow or the simpler appellation, Chianti, if their production does not qualify for a district name (if grapes from two districts are blended, for example).

The district known as *Chianti Classico* is the heartland of the zone, the best area, and — lucky for us — the one district whose wines are widely available. The only other Chianti district that comes close to rivaling Chianti Classico in quality is *Chianti Rufina (ROO fee nah;* not to be confused with the renowned Chianti producer Ruffino), whose wines are fairly available, especially from the well-known producer Frescobaldi.

Besides varying according to their district of production, Chianti wines vary in style according to their aging. *Riserva* wines must age for two years or more at the winery, and some of this aging is often in French oak; the best riservas have potential for long life. Chianti wines can also vary slightly according to their grape blend: Many top Chiantis are made almost entirely from the Sangiovese grape, while others use up to 25 percent of other varieties, including "international" varieties, such as Cabernet Sauvignon, Merlot, and Syrah.

Chianti is a very dry red wine that, like most Italian wines, tastes best with food. It ranges from light-bodied to almost full-bodied, according to the district, producer, vintage, and aging regime. It often has an aroma of cherries and sometimes violets, and has a flavor reminiscent of tart cherries. The best Chianti wines have very concentrated fruit character and usually taste best from five to eight years after the vintage — although in good vintages they have no problem aging for ten or more years.

Although Chianti is not a huge wine, today's Chianti wines, especially Chianti Classico, are richer and more concentrated than ever before — in some cases, too rich for us. Recent warm vintages in Europe, such as 1997, 2000, and 2003, have fed a trend toward ripeness, fleshiness of texture, and higher alcohol. The addition of international varieties and the use of barriques for aging — especially for riservas — has also affected the wines. More than ever, you must choose your Chianti producers with care.

The two exceptional vintages to look for in Chianti wines are 1999 and 2001 — two of the better Tuscan vintages of modern times.

We have compiled a list of our favorite producers, Group A (for us, the best) and Group B (our other favorites), in alphabetical order within each group (For more info on Chianti wines, see Chapter 8 in *Italian Wine For Dummies.*):

Another producer we admire is Montevertine, who chose to drop the Chianti name from its labels almost 30 years ago, but who produces excellent 100 percent Sangiovese wine in the Chianti Classico region.

Great Chianti Producers

Group A	**Group B**
Antinori	Carpineto
Badia a Coltibuono	Castello Banfi
Castellare	Castello d'Albola
Castell'in Villa	Castello di Ama
Castello dei Rampolla	Castello di Gabbiano
Castello di Brolio	Castello di Verrazzano
Castello di Fonterutoli	Castello di Volpaia
Fattoria La Massa	Cecchi-Villa Cerna
Felsina	Dievole
Fontodi	Fattoria di Viticcio
Frescobaldi	La Brancaia
Il Palazzino	Le Corti
Isole e Olena	Nittardi
Nozzole	Melini
Riecine	Monsanto-Il Poggio
Riseccoli	Querciabella
Ruffino	San Fabiano Calcinaia
San Giusto a Rentennano	San Felice
Selvapiana	Villa Cafaggio
Vecchie-Terre di Montefili	

From simple $10 to $15 Chianti to the more substantial Chianti Classico (generally between $15 and $25), Chianti remains one of the wine world's great values. Chianti Classico Riservas are a bit more costly, ranging from $28 to $45 per bottle.

Monumental Brunello di Montalcino

While Chianti has been famous for centuries, another great Tuscan wine, Brunello di Montalcino, exploded on the international scene only some 35 years ago, when the Biondi-Santi family, a leading producer, presented some of its oldest wines to writers. Their 1888 and 1891 vintages were still drinking well; in fact, they were in excellent shape! The rest is history, as they say.

Today, Brunello di Montalcino (brew NEL lo dee mon tahl CHEE no), a DOCG wine, is considered one of the greatest, long-lived red wines in existence. It has a price-tag to match: $45 to over $200 a bottle (for wines by the producer Soldera).

Brunello with American roots

The largest producer of Brunello di Montalcino is actually an American family — the Mariani family of Long Island, NY. In 1978, they established Castello Banfi in the southern part of the Montalcino zone, and today they are leaders in research into the grapes and terroirs of Montalcino.

The wine is named for the town of Montalcino, a walled fortress town south of the Chianti zone. Brunello di Montalcino comes from a particular clone, or strain, of Sangiovese, the grape of Chianti. It's an intensely concentrated, tannic wine that demands aging (up to 20 years) when traditionally made, and benefits from several hours of aeration before serving. Lately, some producers in Montalcino have been making a more approachable style of Brunello.

Rosso di Montalcino is a less expensive ($23 to $30), readier-to-drink wine made from the same grape and grown in the same production area as Brunello di Montalcino. Rosso di Montalcino from a good Brunello producer is a great value, offering you a glimpse of Brunello's majesty without breaking the bank.

To really appreciate Brunello di Montalcino, try a wine from one of the producers recommended in the following list (in our rough order of preference). Traditional winemakers, such as Biondi-Santi, Soldera, Costanti, Canalicchio di Sopra, and Pertimali, make wines that need at least 15 to 20 years of aging in good vintages (2001, 1999, 1997, 1995, 1990, 1988, 1985, and 1975 are recent great vintages for Brunello). Brunellos from avowed modern-style producers, such as Caparzo, Altesino, and Col d'Orcia, can be enjoyed in ten years. Younger than ten years — drink Rosso di Montalcino! (For a more complete listing of Brunello di Montalcino producers, see Chapter 8 in *Italian Wine For Dummies.*)

Great Brunello di Montalcino Producers

Soldera, Case Basse (very expensive)
Biondi-Santi (very expensive)
Altesino (especially Montosoli vineyard)
Costanti
Pertimali di Livio Sassetti
Castello Banfi
Canalicchio di Sopra

Il Greppone Mazzi
Il Poggione
Ciacci Piccolomini
Poggio Antico
Caparzo (especially "La Casa")
Castelgiocondo
La Torre

Vino Nobile, Carmignano, and Vernaccia

Three more Tuscan wines of note include two reds — Vino Nobile di Montepulciano *(NO be lay dee mon tay pul chee AH no)* and Carmignano *(car mee NYAH no)* — and Tuscany's most renowned white wine, Vernaccia di San Gimignano *(ver NAH cha dee san gee mee NYAH no)*. All three are DOCG wines.

The Montepulciano wine zone, named after the town of Montepulciano, is southeast of the Chianti zone. Vino Nobile's principal grape is the Prugnolo Gentile (a.k.a. Sangiovese). From a good producer, Vino Nobile di Montepulciano can rival the better Chianti Classicos. Nine producers we recommend are Boscarelli, Fattoria del Cerro, Avignonesi, Lodola Nuova, La Braccesca, Dei, Tenuta Trerose, Fassati, and Poliziano. Vino Nobile producers also make a lighter, readier-to-drink wine, Rosso di Montepulciano.

The Carmignano wine region is directly west of Florence. Although Sangiovese is the main grape of Carmignano — just as it is for Chianti — Cabernet Sauvignon is also one of this wine zone's traditional grapes. As a result, Carmignano's taste is rather akin to that of a Chianti with the finesseful touch of a Bordeaux. Two outstanding producers of Carmignano are Villa di Capezzana and Ambra.

Vernaccia di San Gimignano is named for the medieval walled town of San Gimignano, west of the Chianti Classico zone. Vernaccia is generally a fresh white wine with a slightly oily texture and an almond flavor, and it is meant to be drunk young. For an unusual interpretation, try Teruzzi & Puthod's oak-aged riserva, Terre di Tufo, a pricey but very good Vernaccia (about $18). Most Vernaccias are in the $11 to $13 range. Besides Teruzzi & Puthod, producers to seek are Montenidoli, Mormoraia, Cecchi, and Casale-Falchini.

Two more reds and a white

So many good Tuscan wines exist that we sometimes don't know when to stop talking about them (that's why we wrote *Italian Wine For Dummies!*). Three more deserve a mention here.

Pomino *(po MEE no)* is the name of a red and a white wine from a tiny area of the same name, which lies within the Chianti Rufina district. A hilly land with a particularly mild climate, Pomino has long been a stronghold of French varieties, right in the heart of Sangiovese-land. The Frescobaldi family, the major producer of Chianti Rufina, is also the main landowner in Pomino, and makes both a Pomino Rosso and a Pomino Bianco — but the red is the more noteworthy of the two. Pomino Rosso is a blend of Cabernet Sauvignon, Cabernet Franc, Merlot, Sangiovese, Canaiolo — and in Frescobaldi's case, also Pinot Nero (the Italian name for Pinot Noir). It sounds like a crazy blend, but it works! Pomino Bianco blends Chardonnay, Pinot Bianco, Trebbiano, and often Pinot Grigio. Besides Frescobaldi, another fine producer of Pomino is Fattoria Petrognano. Pomino costs about $24 to $30.

The new frontier for Tuscan wine is the Maremma (*mah REM mah*) in southwest Tuscany. Of the many wines coming from this area, two that impress us are the red, **Morellino di Scansano,** and the white, **Vermentino.** Morellino (*moh rehl LEE no*) is the name for Sangiovese in the hilly area around the town of Scansano (*scahn SAH no*). Most Morellino di Scansano wines offer an easy-drinking, inexpensive ($12 to $20) alternative to Chianti — although a few high-end examples exist. Look for Fattoria Le Pupille and Moris Farms.

Vermentino, an aromatic white varietal wine popular in Sardinia and Liguria, has suddenly become the hot new variety in Tuscany, especially along the coast. It's a crisp, medium-bodied, flavorful white that's usually unoaked, and sells for $15 to $20. Many leading Tuscan producers, such as Antinori and Cecchi, are making attractive Vermentino wines.

Super-Tuscans

When Chianti sales lost momentum in the 1970s, progressive producers caught the attention of the world by creating new red wines that are today collectively known as super-Tuscans. The pioneering examples include Sassicaia *(sas ee KYE ah),* from Marchese Incisa della Rocchetta, and Tignanello *(tee nyah NEL loh)* and Solaia *(so LYE ah)* from Marchesi Antinori. These and similar wines can't be called Chianti — either because they're produced outside the Chianti zone or because their grape blend (generally Cabernet Sauvignon, Cabernet Franc, Merlot, and/or Sangiovese) doesn't conform to DOC requirements for Chianti.

Today, dozens of super-Tuscan wines exist. Their grape blends vary; some producers use only native Tuscan grapes, while others use international varieties or a blend of Italian and international grapes. What these wines have in common is that they're expensive, ranging from $45 on up to $80, with a few well over $100 per bottle. The most famous super-Tuscan wines, Sassicaia, Ornellaia, Masseto, and Solaia, prized by wine collectors, can cost $200 in good vintages (see "Tuscany" in the vintage chart, Appendix C).

Super-Tuscan wines can range in taste from very good Chianti-like wines to Bordeaux-type or California Cabernet-type wines, depending on the varying amounts of Sangiovese, Cabernet Sauvignon, Merlot, and so on, and their specific vineyard areas.

Sangiovese at the table

Lighter Chianti wines go well with pasta, prosciutto, and roast chicken or squab. With Chianti Classicos and riservas, lamb, roast turkey, veal, steak, and roast beef are fine accompaniments. For the robust Brunello di Montalcino and super-Tuscan wines, try pheasant, steak, game, or chunks of fresh Parmesan cheese. Serve these wines at cool room temperature, 62° to 66° F (16° to19° C).

Now that Chianti has reestablished itself in the world market, these relatively new wines have become less prominent — but most major Chianti producers still make a super-Tuscan wine.

A dozen of our favorite super-Tuscan wines are the following (listed alphabetically, with their grape blend; the producer's name is in parentheses):

- ✔ Cepparello — all Sangiovese (Isole e Elena)
- ✔ Grattamacco — Sangiovese, Malvasia Nera, Cabernet Sauvignon (Grattamacco)
- ✔ Masseto — all Merlot (Tenuta dell'Ornellaia)
- ✔ Ornellaia — mainly Cabernet Sauvignon; some Merlot and/or Cabernet Franc (Tenuta dell'Ornellaia)
- ✔ Percarlo — 100 percent Sangiovese (San Giusto a Rentennano)
- ✔ Le Pergole Torte — entirely Sangiovese (Montevertine)
- ✔ Prunaio — mainly Sangiovese (Viticcio)
- ✔ Sammarco — 80 percent Cabernet Sauvignon, 20 percent Sangiovese (Castello dei Rampolla)
- ✔ Sassicaia — 75 percent Cabernet Sauvignon, 25 percent Cabernet Franc (Tenuta San Guido)
- ✔ I Sodi di San Niccolò — mostly Sangiovese (Castellare di Castellina)
- ✔ Solaia — 80 percent Cabernet Sauvignon, 20 percent Sangiovese (Antinori)
- ✔ Tignanello — 80 percent Sangiovese, 20 percent Cabernet Sauvignon (Antinori)

Decant young (less than ten years old) super-Tuscan wines two or three hours before serving. (For a more complete listing of super-Tuscan wines, see Chapter 8 in *Italian Wine For Dummies.*)

Tre Venezie

The three regions in the northeastern corner of Italy (refer to Figure 10-1) are often referred to as the *Tre Venezie* — the Three Venices — because they were once part of the Venetian Empire. Colorful historical associations aside, each of these regions produces red and white wines that are among the most popular Italian wines outside of Italy — as well as at home.

Three gentle wines from Verona

Chances are that if your first dry Italian wine wasn't Chianti or Pinot Grigio, it was one of Verona's big three: the white **Soave** *(so AH vay)* or the reds, **Valpolicella** *(val po lee CHEL lah)* or **Bardolino** *(bar do LEE noh)*. These enormously popular wines hail from Northeast Italy, around the picturesque city of Verona — Romeo and Juliet's hometown — and the beautiful Lake Garda.

Of Verona's two reds, Valpolicella has more body. (Bolla and Masi are two of the largest producers.) The lighter Bardolino is a pleasant summer wine when served slightly cool. Soave can be a fairly neutral-tasting unoaked white or a characterful wine with fruity and nutty flavor, depending on the producer.

Most Valpolicella, Bardolino, and Soave wines are priced from $9 to $14, as are two other white wines of the region, Bianco di Custoza and Lugana. Some of the better Veronese wines, from the following recommended producers, have slightly higher prices:

- **Soave:** Pieropan, Inama, Gini, Santa Sofia
- **Valpolicella:** Allegrini, Quintarelli, Dal Forno, Le Ragose, Bertani, Alighieri, Tommasi, Masi
- **Bardolino:** Guerrieri-Rizzardi, Cavalchina, Fratelli Zeni

Amarone della Valpolicella (also simply known as Amarone), one of Italy's most full-bodied red wines, is a variant of Valpolicella. It's made from the same grape varieties (refer to Table 10-1), but the ripe grapes dry on mats for several months before fermentation, thus concentrating their sugar and flavors. The resulting wine is a rich, potent (14 to 16 percent alcohol), long-lasting wine, perfect for a cold winter night and a plate of mature cheeses. Some of the best producers of Amarone are Quintarelli, Bertani, Masi, Tommasi, Le Ragose, Allegrini, and Dal Forno.

The Austrian-Italian alliance

If you have traveled much in Italy, you probably realize that in spirit Italy is not one unified country but 20 or more different countries linked together politically. Consider Trentino-Alto Adige. Not only is this mountainous region (the northernmost in Italy; refer to Figure 10-1) dramatically different from the rest of Italy, but also the mainly German-speaking Alto Adige (or South Tyrol) in the north is completely different from the Italian-speaking Trentino in the south. (Before World War I, the South Tyrol was part of the Austro-Hungarian Empire.) The wines of the two areas are different, too — yet the area is considered a single region!

Alto Adige produces red wine, but most of it goes to Germany, Austria, and Switzerland. The rest of the world sees Alto Adige's white wines — **Pinot Grigio, Chardonnay, Pinot Bianco, Sauvignon,** and **Gewürztraminer** — which are priced mainly in the $12 to $18 range.

One local red wine to seek out is Alto Adige's **Lagrein,** from a native grape variety of the same name. It's a robust, hearty wine, somewhat spicy and rustic in style, but it offers a completely unique taste experience. Hofstätter and Alois Lageder are two producers who make a particularly good Lagrein.

Pinot Grigio, marketing miracle

Pinot Grigio — the biggest-selling imported wine in the United States — is produced in all three of the Tre Venezie regions. The Cavit brand leads the way, but Folonari, MezzaCorona, and Santa Margherita all do very well in sales. Santa Margherita, in particular, was the first brand to establish itself solidly on the American market, and it still sells extremely well in restaurants. You could say that Pinot Grigio is the new Chardonnay.

Some people theorize that the musical name is part of the wine's success — that U.S. wine drinkers like to say, "Pinot Grigio," just as they once liked to say "Pouilly-Fuissé." But obviously people also like the taste of Pinot Grigio. It's fairly light-bodied, with crisp acidity and fairly neutral aromas and flavors — an easy-drinking wine that goes well with most foods. Pinot Grigio is so successful, in fact, that many California wineries are growing the Pinot Gris grape and using the Italian name, Pinot Grigio, on their wine labels. The Californian versions tend to be fruitier, fuller-bodied and sometimes ever so slightly sweet compared to the Italian wines.

Alto Adige produces Italy's best white wines, along with nearby Friuli. Four producers to look for are Alois Lageder, Hofstätter, Tiefenbrunner, and Peter Zemmer. Here are some highlights of each brand:

- ✔ Lageder's Pinot Bianco from the Haberlehof vineyard and his Sauvignon from the Lehenhof vineyard are exceptional examples of their grape varieties and are among the best wines from these two varieties that we've tasted.

- ✔ Hofstätter's Gewürztraminer, from the Kolbenhof vineyard, is as fine a wine as you can find from this tricky grape variety. Hofstätter also makes one of Italy's best Pinot Nero wines, Villa Barthenau.

- ✔ Tiefenbrunner's Müller Thurgau *(MOOL lair TOOR gow)* from his Feldmarschall Vineyard (the region's highest in altitude) could well be the wine world's best wine from this otherwise lackluster variety.

- ✔ Peter Zemmer produces reliable Chardonnay and Pinot Grigio wines in the $11 to $14 price range.

Trentino, the southern part of the Trentino-Alto Adige region, is not without its own notable wines. Some excellent **Chardonnay** wines come from Trentino, for example; two of the best are made by Pojer & Sandri and Roberto Zeni. (In fact, we recommend any of the wines from these two producers.) Elisabetta Foradori is a Trentino producer who specializes in red wines made from the local variety, **Teroldego** *(teh ROLL day go)* **Rotaliano.** Her best red wines, Granato and Sgarzon, are based on Teroldego and always get rave reviews from wine critics. Also, one of Italy's leading sparkling wine producers, Ferrari, is in Trentino. (See Chapter 14 for more information on sparkling wine producers.)

The far side: Friuli-Venezia Giulia

Italy has justifiably been known in the wine world for its red wines. But in the past 20 years, the region of Friuli-Venezia Giulia (refer to Figure 10-1), led by the pioneering winemaker, the late Mario Schiopetto, has made the world conscious of Italy's white wines as well.

Near the region's eastern border with Slovenia, the districts of Collio and Colli Orientali del Friuli produce Friuli's best wines. Red wines exist here, but the white wines have given these zones their renown. In addition to **Pinot Grigio, Pinot Bianco, Chardonnay,** and **Sauvignon,** two local favorites are **Tocai Friulano** and **Ribolla Gialla** (both fairly rich, full, and viscous).

A truly great white wine made here is Silvio Jermann's Vintage Tunina, a blend of five varieties, including Pinot Bianco, Sauvignon, and Chardonnay. Vintage Tunina is a rich, full-bodied, long-lived white of world-class status. It sells in the $35 to $45 range and, frankly, it's worth the money. Give the wine about ten years to age and then try it with rich poultry dishes or pasta.

We list our recommended producers in Friuli alphabetically:

Great Producers in Friuli

Abbazia di Rosazzo/Walter Filiputti	Ronco del Gelso
Borgo Conventi	Ronco del Gnemiz
Girolamo Dorigo	Ronco dei Rosetti, of Zamò
Livio Felluga	Ronco dei Tassi
Gravner	Russiz Superiore, of Marco Felluga
Jermann	Mario Schiopetto
Miani	Venica & Venica
Lis Neris-Pecorari	Vie di Romans
Plozner	Villa Russiz
Doro Princic	Volpe Pasini

For more info on the wines of Northeastern Italy, see Chapter 7 in *Italian Wine For Dummies.*

Snapshots from the Rest of Italy

Italy's wines are by no means confined to the five regions that we discuss individually. A quick tour of some of Italy's other regions proves the point. (For more complete info on the wines of Italy's other regions, see *Italian Wine For Dummies.*) Refer to Figure 10-1 for the location of each of the following regions:

- **Lombardy:** In the northern part of this northerly region, near the Swiss border, the Valtellina wine district produces four relatively light-bodied red wines from the Nebbiolo grape: Sassella, Inferno, Grumello, and Valgella. Most of these wines are inexpensive (about $10 to $20) and, unlike Barolo or Barbaresco, can be enjoyed young. Lombardy is also the home of Italy's best sparkling wine district, Franciacorta. (See Chapter 14 for more on Franciacorta and Italy's other sparkling wines.)

- **Emilia-Romagna:** This is the home of Lambrusco, one of Italy's most successful wines on export markets. For a different Lambrusco experience, try a dry one if you can find it. (You may have to go to Emilia-Romagna for that — but, hey, that's not so bad. Bologna and Parma, two gastronomic meccas, are in this region.)

- **Liguria:** This narrow region south of Piedmont, along the Italian Riviera, is also the home of Cinque Terre, one of Italy's most picturesque areas. The region's two fine white wines, Vermentino and Pigato, are just made for Liguria's pasta with pesto, its signature dish.

- **Marches** (also known as **Marche**): Verdicchio is a dry, inexpensive white wine that goes well with fish, is widely available, and improves in quality with every vintage. Try the Verdicchio dei Castelli di Jesi from Fazi-Battaglia, Colonnara, or Umani Ronchi, great values at $9 to $12. Marche's best red wine, Rosso Cònero, at $15 to $22, is one of Italy's fine red wine buys.

- ✔ **Umbria:** This region, home to the towns of Perugia and Assisi, makes some good reds and whites. Orvieto, a white, is widely available for around $11 from Tuscan producers such as Antinori and Ruffino. Two interesting red wines are Torgiano, a Chianti-like blend (try Lungarotti's Rubesco Riserva DOCG), and Sagrantino di Montefalco DOCG, a medium-bodied, characterful wine made from the local Sagrantino grape.

- ✔ **Latium:** This region around Rome makes the ubiquitous, inexpensive Frascati, a light, neutral wine from the Trebbiano grape; Fontana Candida is a popular brand.

- ✔ **Abruzzo:** Montepulciano d'Abruzzo, an inexpensive, easy-drinking, low tannin, low-acid red wine, comes from here; it's a terrific everyday red, especially from a quality producer such as Masciarelli. Abruzzo is also home to two other fine producers, Cataldi Madonna and the late, great Eduardo Valentini, whose sought-after Trebbiano d'Abruzzo is perhaps the world's greatest white wine from the otherwise ordinary Trebbiano grape.

- ✔ **Campania:** Some of the best wines in Southern Italy are produced here, around Naples. The full-bodied, tannic Taurasi, a DOCG wine from the Aglianico grape, is one of the great, long-lived red wines in Italy. Premium producers are Mastroberardino (look for his single-vineyard Taurasi, called Radici), Feudi di San Gregorio, and Terredora. The same producers also make two unique whites, Greco di Tufo and Fiano di Avellino. They're full-flavored, viscous wines with great aging capacity that sell in the $18 to $25 range. Falanghina ($12 to $16) is another exciting, light-bodied white Campania wine.

- ✔ **Basilicata:** The instep of the Italian boot, Basilicata has one important red wine, Aglianico del Vulture. It's similar to Taurasi, but not quite so intense and full-bodied. D'Angelo and Paternoster are leading producers.

- ✔ **Apulia:** This region makes more wine than any other in Italy. Generally, it is inexpensive, full-bodied red wine, such as Salice Salentino (from the native variety, Negroamaro) and Primitivo.

- ✔ **Sicily:** Once known only for its Marsala, a sweet, fortified wine, Sicily is now making quality reds and whites. Established wineries such as Corvo (a.k.a. Duca di Salaparuta) and Regaleali have been joined by exciting, new wineries such as Planeta, Morgante, Donnafugata, and Benanti to produce some of Italy's more intriguing wines — especially reds, many made from Sicily's superb variety, Nero d'Avola.

- ✔ **Sardinia:** This large island off the eastern coast of Italy makes delicate white wines and characterful reds from native grape varieties and from international varieties such as Cabernet Sauvignon. Sella & Mosca, Argiolas, and Santadi are three leading producers. Two of the more popular Sardinian wines are the white Vermentino and the red Cannonau (the local version of Grenache), both of which sell in the $11 to $16 range.

Chapter 11

Spain, Portugal, Germany, and Beyond

● ●

In This Chapter

▶ Spain comes of age

▶ Great finds from Portugal

▶ Germany's unique ways

▶ Austria, Hungary, and Greece

▶ Unusual wines from Alpine climes

● ●

*I*n the past, no one ever used the phrase *European wine* when talking generally about the wines of France, Italy, Spain, Portugal, and Germany. The wines had nothing in common.

But today, two factors have changed the way we look at the wines of these countries. First, Europe has unified, and the wines of the European Union member countries now share a common legislative umbrella. Second, non-European wines — from California, Australia, Chile, and South America — have inundated the U.S. market, popularizing a nomenclature (varietal names, such as Chardonnay) and flavors (fruity, fruitier, fruitiest) foreign to the European, or *Old World,* model.

When we compare Europe's wines to non-European, or *New World,* wines, we notice that the diverse wines of Europe have many things in common after all. Most European wines are usually named for their place of production instead of their grape (see Chapter 4); European winemaking is tethered to tradition and regulations; the wines for the most part have local flavor rather than con-forming to an international concept of how wine should taste (although, sadly, we're seeing an emerging "internationalization" of wine styles); and these wines are relatively low in fruitiness. European wines tend to embody the tra-ditions of the people who make them and the flavors of the place where their vines grow, unlike New World wines, which tend to embody grape variety and a general fruitiness of flavor.

Despite these similarities among European wines, the countries of Europe each make distinctly different wines. The importance of France and Italy has earned each of these countries a whole chapter, while the rest of Europe shares the spotlight here.

Intriguing Wines from Old Spain

Spain is a hot, dry, mountainous country with more vineyard land than any other nation on earth. It ranks third in the world in wine production, after France and Italy.

Spanish wine has awakened from a long period of dormancy and under-achievement. Spain is now one of the wine world's most vibrant arenas. For decades, only Spain's most famous red wine region, Rioja *(ree OH ha),* and the classic fortified wine region, Sherry, had any international presence for fine wines. (For more on Sherry, see Chapter 15.) Now, many other wine regions in Spain are making seriously good wines. Besides Rioja, the following regions are an important part of the wine quality picture in Spain today, and their wines are generally available (see Figure 11-1):

- ✔ **Ribera del Duero** *(ree BEAR ah dell DWAIR oh),* now famous for its high quality red wines, has helped to ignite world interest in Spanish wines.

- ✔ **Priorato** *(pree or AH toe),* mountainous and inaccessible, and one of the world's hot new regions for red wine, is north of the city of Tarragona, in northeast Spain.

- ✔ **Penedés** *(pen eh DAIS)* is a large producer of both red and white wines, as well as being famous for its sparkling wines (known as *Cava;* see Chapter 14).

- ✔ The **Rías Baixas** *(REE ahse BYCHE ahse)* region of Galicia *(gah LEETH ee ah)* is gaining acclaim for its exciting white wine, Albariño.

- ✔ **Navarra** *(nah VAR rah),* an area long known for its dry rosé wines, is an increasingly strong red wine region.

- ✔ **Toro** is quickly emerging as one of Spain's best red wine regions.

- ✔ **Rueda** *(ru AE dah)* is known for well-made, inexpensive white wines.

Spain's wine laws, like Italy's, provide for a bi-level QWPSR category: *Denominaciónes de Origen* (DO) and a higher classification, *Denominaciónes de Origen Calificada* (DOC), the latter created in 1991. So far, Rioja and Priorato are the only two regions that have been awarded the DOC (also known as DOCa). Wines that do not qualify as DO fall into the table wine category *Vino de la Tierra* (equivalent to the French *Vins de Pays*). See Chapter 4 for more about appellation systems.

Figure 11-1:
The wine regions of Spain.

© Akira Chiwaki

Rioja rules the roost

Rioja, in north-central Spain (see Figure 11-1), has historically been the country's major red wine region (even if today Ribera del Duero and Priorato are catching up — fast!). Three-quarters of Rioja's wine is red, 15 percent *rosado* (rosé), and 10 percent white.

The principal grape in Rioja is Tempranillo *(tem prah NEE yoh),* Spain's greatest red variety. But regulations permit another three varieties for reds — Garnacha (Grenache), Graciano (Carignan), and Mazuelo — and red Rioja wine is typically a blend of two or more varieties. Regulations aside, some producers now also use Cabernet Sauvignon in their red Rioja.

The Rioja region has three districts: the cooler, Atlantic-influenced Rioja Alavesa and Rioja Alta areas and the warmer Rioja Baja zone. Most of the best Riojas are made from grapes in the two cooler districts, but some Riojas are blended from grapes of all three districts.

Traditional production for red Rioja wine involved many years of aging in small barrels of American oak before release, which created pale, gentle, sometimes tired (but lovely) wines that lacked fruitiness. The trend has been to replace some of the oak aging with bottle aging, resulting in wines that taste much fresher. Another trend, among more progressive winemakers, is to use barrels made of French oak along with barrels of American oak — which has traditionally given Rioja its characteristic vanilla aroma. (See Chapter 5 for a discussion of oak barrels.)

Regardless of style, red Rioja wines have several faces according to how long they age before being released from the winery. Some wines receive no oak aging at all and are released young. Some wines age (in oak and in bottle) for two years at the winery and are labeled *crianza;* these wines are still fresh and fruity in style. Other wines age for three years and carry the designation *reserva.* The finest wines age for five years or longer, earning the status of *gran reserva.* These terms appear on the labels — if not on the front label, then on a rear label which is the seal of authenticity for Rioja wines.

Prices start at around $12 for crianza reds and go up to about $45 for some gran reservas. The best recent vintages for Rioja are 2004, 2001, 1995, 1994, 1989, 1982, and 1981.

The following Rioja producers are particularly consistent in quality for their red wines:

- ✔ CVNE (Compañía Vinícola del Norte de España), commonly referred to as CUNE *(COO nay)*

- ✔ Bodegas Muga

- ✔ R. Lopez de Heredia

- ✔ La Rioja Alta

- ✔ Marqués de Murrieta Ygay

- ✔ Marqués de Riscal

Most white Riojas these days are merely fresh, neutral, inoffensive wines, but Marqués de Murrieta and R. Lopez de Heredia still make a traditional white Rioja, golden-colored and oak-aged, from a blend of local white grape varieties, predominantly Viura. We find both of these traditional whites fascinating: flavorful, voluptuous, with attractive traces of oxidation, and capable of aging. They're not everybody's cup of tea, true, but the wines sure have character! They have so much presence that they can accompany foods normally associated with red wine, as well as traditional Spanish food, such as paella or seafood. The Murrieta white sells for about $16, and the Lopez de Heredia is about $20.

Ribera del Duero challenges

Ribera del Duero, two hours north of Madrid by auto, is one of Spain's most dynamic wine regions. Perhaps nowhere else in the world does the Tempranillo grape variety reach such heights, making wines with body, deep color, and finesse. For many years, one producer, the legendary Vega Sicilia, dominated the Ribera del Duero area. In fact, Spain's single most famous great wine is Vega Sicilia's Unico (Tempranillo, with 20 percent Cabernet Sauvignon) — an intense, concentrated, tannic red wine with enormous longevity; it ages for ten years in casks and then sometimes ages further in the bottle before it's released. Unico is available mainly in top Spanish restaurants; if you're lucky enough to find it in a retail shop, it can cost about $300 — a bottle, that is. Even Unico's younger, less intense, and more available sibling, the Vega Sicilia Valbuena, retails for about $100.

Vega Sicilia is no longer the only renowned red wine in Ribera del Duero. Alejandro Fernández's Pesquera, entirely Tempranillo, has earned high praise over the past 15 years. Pesquera is a big, rich, oaky, tannic wine with intense fruit character. The reserva sells for about $28, while the younger Pesquera is $20. The reserva of Fernández's other winery in the area, Condado de Haza, sells for about $35. Three other fine producers of Ribera del Duero are Bodegas Mauro, Viña Pedrosa, and Bodegas Téofilo Reyes, who all make red wines that rival Pesquera.

Priorato: Emerging from the past

Back in the twelfth century, monks founded a monastery (or "priory") in the harsh, inaccessible Sierra de Montsant Mountains, about 100 miles southwest of Barcelona in the Catalonia region, and planted vines on the steep hillsides. As time passed, the monastery closed, and the vineyards were abandoned because life was simply too difficult in this area (which in time became known as Priorat, or Priorato).

Cut to the twentieth century — in fact about 25 short years ago. Enterprising winemakers, among them Alvaro Palacios, rediscovered the area and decided that conditions are ideal for making powerful red wines, especially from old vines planted by locals early in the twentieth century.

No Spanish wine region has been in the spotlight lately more than Priorato. And yet Priorato hasn't become a tourist destination, because it's so inaccessible. The region's volcanic soil, composed mainly of slate and schist, is so infertile that not much other than grapes can grow there. The climate is harshly continental: very hot, dry summers and very cold winters. The steep slopes must be terraced; many vineyards can be worked only by hand. And grape yields are very low.

Amazingly rich, powerful red wines — made primarily from Garnacha and Carignan, two of Spain's native varieties — have emerged from this harsh landscape. Many are as rugged as the land, with high tannin and alcohol; some wines are so high in alcohol that they have an almost Port-like sweetness. Because winemaking in Priorato isn't cost-effective, to say the least, and the quantities of each wine are so small, the wines are necessarily quite expensive; prices begin at about $40.

Priorat reds to look for include Clos Mogador, Clos Erasmus, Alvaro Palacios, Clos Martinet, l'Hermita, Morlanda, Mas d'En Gil, and Pasanau.

Five other Spanish regions to watch

The action in Spanish wines — especially when value is your concern — definitely doesn't end with Rioja, Ribera del Duero, and Priorato.

Penedés

The Penedés wine region is in Catalonia, south of Barcelona (refer to Figure 11-1). It's the home of most Spanish sparkling wines, known as *Cava*, which we discuss in Chapter 14.

Any discussion of Penedés' still wines must begin with Torres, one of the world's great family-owned wineries. Around 1970, Miguel Torres pioneered the making of wines in Spain from French varieties, such as Cabernet Sauvignon and Chardonnay, along with local grapes, such as Tempranillo and Garnacha.

All the Torres wines are clean, well made, reasonably priced, and widely available. They start in the $10 range for the red Sangre de Toro (Garnacha–Carignan) and Coronas (Tempranillo–Cabernet Sauvignon) and the white Viña Sol. The top-of-the-line Mas La Plana Black Label, a powerful yet elegant Cabernet Sauvignon, costs about $45.

Freixenet, the leading Cava producer, is now also in the still wine business. Its wines include the inexpensive René Barbier brand varietals and two fascinating wines from Segura Viudas (a Cava brand owned by Freixenet), both $15 to $16. Creu de Lavit is a subtle but complex white that's all Xarel-lo (pronounced *sha REL lo*), a native grape used mainly for Cava production. The red Mas d'Aranyo is mainly Tempranillo. We particularly recommend Creu de Lavit.

Rías Baixas: The white wine from Galicia

Galicia, in northwest Spain next to the Atlantic Ocean and Portugal (refer to Figure 11-1), was not a province known for its wine. But from a small area called Rías Baixas *(REE ahse BYCHE ahse)*, tucked away in the southern part of Galicia, an exciting, new white wine has emerged — Albariño, made from the Albariño grape variety. Rías Baixas is, in fact, one of the world's hottest white wine regions. We use "hot" to mean "in demand," not to describe the climate, because Rías Baixas is cool and damp a good part of the year, and verdant year-round.

This region now boasts about 200 wineries, compared to only 60 just a decade ago. Modern winemaking, the cool climate, and low-yielding vines have combined to make Albariño wines a huge success, especially in the United States, its leading market. We love this lively, (mainly) unoaked white, with its vivid, floral aromas and flavors reminiscent of apricots, white peaches, pears, and green apples. It's a perfect match with seafood and fish. The Albariño grape — known as Alvarinho in northern Portugal (south of Rías Baixas) — makes wines that are fairly high in acidity, which makes them fine *apéritif* wines.

Albariños to look for include Bodega Morgadío, Lusco, Bodegas Martin Codax, Fillaboa, Pazo de Señorans, Pazo San Mauro, Pazo de Barrantes, and Vionta; all are in the $16 to $23 range.

Decoding Spanish wine labels

You see some of the following terms on a Spanish wine label:

Blanco: White

Bodega: Winery

Cosecha *(coh SAY cha)* or **Vendimia** *(ven DEE me yah):* The vintage year

Crianza *(cree AHN zah):* For red wines, this means that the wine has aged for two years with at least six months in oak; for white and rosé wines, crianza means that the wines aged for a year with at least six months in oak. (Some regions have stricter standards.)

Gran reserva: Wines produced only in exceptional vintages; red wines must age at least five years, including a minimum of two years in oak; white gran reservas must age at least four years before release, including six months in oak.

Reserva: Wines produced in the better vintages; red reservas must age a minimum of three years, including one year in oak; white reservas must age for two years, including six months in oak.

Tinto *(TEEN toe):* Red

Navarra

Once upon a time, the word *Navarra* conjured up images of inexpensive, easy-drinking dry rosé wines (or, to the more adventurous, memories of running the bulls in Pamplona, Navarra's capital city). Today, Navarra, just northeast of Rioja, is known for its red wines, which are similar to, but somewhat less expensive than, the more famous wines of Rioja.

Many Navarra reds rely on Tempranillo, along with Garnacha, but you can also find Cabernet Sauvignon, Merlot, and various blends of all four varieties in the innovative Navarra region. Look for the wines of the following three Navarra producers: Bodegas Julian Chivite *(HOO lee ahn cha VEE tay)*, Bodegas Guelbenzu *(gwel ben ZOO)*, and Bodegas Magana.

El Toro

The Toro region in northwest Spain, west of Ribera del Duero, made wines in the Middle Ages that were quite famous in Spain. But it's a hot, arid area with poor soil, so winemaking was practically abandoned there for centuries. In Spain's current wine boom, Toro has been rediscovered. Winemakers have determined that the climate and soil are actually ideal for making powerful, tannic red wines — mainly from the Tempranillo variety — which rival the wines of Toro's neighbors in Ribera del Duero. Toro producers to buy include Bodegas Fariña, Vega Sauco, Estancia Piedra, Bodegas y Viñas Dos Victorias, Gil Luna, and Dehesa La Granja (owned by Pesquera's Alejandro Fernandez).

The Verdejo from Rueda

The Rueda region, west of Ribera del Duero, produces one of Spain's best white wines from the Verdejo grape. The wine is clean and fresh, has good fruit character, and sells for an affordable $9 to $10. The Rioja producer Marquis de Riscal makes one of the leading and most available examples.

Portugal: More Than Just Port

Portugal is justifiably famous for its great dessert wine, Port (which we discuss in Chapter 15). But gradually, wine lovers are discovering the other dimensions of Portuguese wine — its dry wines, especially its reds. Most of these wines come from native Portuguese grape varieties, of which the country has hundreds. We expect Portugal's well-priced wines to play a larger role in world wine markets in the twenty-first century.

Portugal's highest rank for wines is _Denominação de Origen_ (DO), which has been awarded to the wines of 32 regions. The table wine category includes eight _Vinho Regional_ (VR) regions, equivalent to France's _Vin de Pays,_ and the simple _Vinho de Mesa_ (table wines).

Portugal's "green" white

On hot summer evenings, the most appropriate wine can be a bottle of bracing, slightly effervescent, white Vinho Verde _(VEEN yo VAIRD)_. The high acidity of Vinho Verde refreshes your mouth and particularly complements grilled fish or seafood.

The Minho region, Vinho Verde's home, is in the northwest corner of Portugal, directly across the border from the Rías Baixas wine region of Spain. (The region is particularly verdant because of the rain from the Atlantic Ocean — one theory behind the wine's name.)

Two styles of white Vinho Verde exist on the market. The most commonly found brands (Aveleda and Casal Garcia), which sell for $7 or $8, are medium-dry wines of average quality that are best served cold.

The more expensive Vinho Verdes ($15 to $20) are varietal wines made from either the Alvarinho grape (Rías Baixas's Albariño), Loureiro, or Trajadura. They're more complex, dryer, and more concentrated than basic Vinho Verde, and are Portugal's best whites. Unfortunately, these finer wines are more difficult to find than the inexpensive ones; look for them in better wine shops or in Portuguese neighborhoods — or on your next trip to Portugal!

The majority of wines from Vinho Verde are red. However, these wines are _highly_ acidic; you definitely need to acquire a taste for them. (We haven't acquired it yet!)

Noteworthy Portuguese red wines

Possibly the best dry red wine in Portugal, Barca Velha, comes from the Douro region, where the grapes for Port (officially known as _Porto_) grow. Made by the Ferreira Port house, Barca Velha is a full-bodied, intense, concentrated wine that needs years to age — Portugal's version of Vega Sicilia's Unico, but at a considerably lower price ($65 to $70). Like Unico, not much is made, and it's produced only in the best vintages.

Recognizing Portuguese wine terms

The following terms may appear on Portuguese wine labels:

Colheita *(col YAY tah):* Vintage year

Garrafeira *(gar rah FAY rah):* A reserva that has aged at least two years in a cask and one in a bottle if it's red; six months in a cask, six months in a bottle if it's white

Quinta *(KEEN ta):* Estate or vineyard

Reserva: A wine of superior quality from one vintage

Tinto *(TEEN toe):* Red

Fortunately, the Port house of Ramos Pinto (now owned by Roederer Champagne) makes inexpensive, top-quality, dry red Douro wines that are readily available. Duas Quintas (about $12) has ripe, plummy flavors and a velvety texture; it's surprisingly rich but supple, and it's a great value.

The Douro region boasts other terrific dry red wines, most of them fairly new and based on grapes traditionally used for Port. Brands to look for include Quinta do Vale D. Maria, Quinta do Vallado, Quinta do Crasto, Quinta do Cotto, Quinta de la Rosa, Quinta do Vale Meão, Quinta de Roriz, Quinta da Leda Vale do Bomfim and Chryseia.

Other good red Portuguese wines to try include

- ✔ **Quinta do Carmo:** The majority owner of this estate in the dynamic Alentejo region in southern Portugal is Château Lafite-Rothschild. A rich, full-bodied wine, it sells for $25. Don Martinho, a second-label wine from the estate, is less than half the price of Quinta do Carmo.

- ✔ **Quinta de Pancas:** One of the few Cabernet Sauvignons in Portugal, Quinta de Pancas comes from the Alenquer region, north of Lisbon; it sells for about $15.

- ✔ **Quinta de Parrotes:** Made from the local Castelão Frances grape variety, Quinta de Parrotes, from the same estate in Alenquer as the Quinta de Pancas, is a steal at $10.

- ✔ **Quinta da Bacalhôa:** An estate-bottled Cabernet Sauvignon-Merlot from the esteemed Portuguese winemaker Joào Pires in Azeitao (south of Lisbon), Bacalhôa has the elegance of a Bordeaux; it sells for $27.

✔ **The red wines of J.M. da Fonseca Successores** (no relation to the Fonseca Port house): This firm is producing some of the best red wines in Portugal. Look for Quinta da Camarate, Morgado do Reguengo, Tinto Velho Rosado Fernandes, and all da Fonseca's Garrafeiras.

✔ **The wines of Joao Portugal Ramos:** A tireless winemaker who consults for various wineries and also owns three properties, Ramos has a golden touch and yet maintains the typicity of his wines. Some wines sell under his own name; others are Marquês de Borba and Vila Santa.

Germany: Europe's Individualist

German wines march to the beat of a different drummer. They come in mainly one color: white. They're fruity in style, low in alcohol, rarely oaked, and often off-dry or sweet. Their labels carry grape names, which is an anomaly in Europe.

Germany is the northernmost major wine-producing country in Europe — which means that its climate is cool. Except in warmer pockets of Germany, red grapes don't ripen adequately, which is the reason most German wines are white. The climate is also erratic from year to year, meaning that vintages do matter for fine German wines. Germany's finest vineyards are situated along rivers such as the Rhine and the Mosel, and on steep, sunny slopes, to temper the extremes of the weather and help the grapes ripen.

Riesling and its cohorts

In Germany's cool climate, the noble Riesling (*REESE ling*) grape finds true happiness. Riesling represents little more than 20 percent of Germany's vineyard plantings.

Another major, but less distinguished, German variety is Müller-Thurgau (pronounced *MOOL lair TOOR gow*), a crossing between the Riesling and Silvaner (or possibly Chasselas) grapes. Its wines are softer than Riesling's with less character and little potential for greatness.

After Müller-Thurgau and Riesling, the most-planted grapes in Germany are Silvaner, Kerner, Scheurebe (*SHOY reb beh*), and Ruländer (Pinot Gris). Among Germany's red grapes, Spätburgunder (Pinot Noir) is the most widely planted, mainly in the warmer parts of the country.

Germany's wine laws and wine styles

Germany's classification system is not based on the French AOC system, as those of most other European countries are. Like most European wines, German wines are in fact named after the places they come from — in the best wines, usually a combination of a village name and a vineyard name, such as Piesporter (town) Goldtröpfchen (vineyard).

Unlike most European wines, however, the grape name is also usually part of the wine name (as in Piesporter Goldtröpfchen *Riesling*). And the finest German wines have yet another element in their name — a *Prädikat (PRAY di cat),* which is an indication of the ripeness of the grapes at harvest (as in Piesporter Goldtröpfchen Riesling *Spätlese*). Wines with a Prädikat hold the highest rank in the German wine system.

Germany's system of assigning the highest rank to the ripest grapes is completely different from the concept behind most other European systems, which is to bestow the highest status on the best vineyards or districts. Germany's system underscores the country's grape-growing priority: Ripeness — never guaranteed in a cool climate — is the highest goal.

German wine law divides wines with a Prädikat into six levels. From the least ripe to the ripest (that is, from the lowest to the highest), they are

- Kabinett *(KAB ee net)*
- Spätlese *(SHPATE lay seh)*
- Auslese *(OUSE lay seh)*
- Beerenauslese *(BEER en OUSE lay seh),* abbreviated as *BA*
- Eiswein *(ICE vine)*
- Trockenbeerenauslese *(TROH ken BEER enOUSE lay seh),* abbreviated as *TBA*

At the three highest Prädikat levels, the amount of sugar in the grapes is so high that the wines are inevitably sweet. Many people, therefore, mistakenly believe that the Prädikat level of a German wine is an indication of the wine's sweetness. In fact, the Prädikat is an indication of the amount of sugar in the *grapes at harvest,* not the amount of sugar in the wine. At lower Prädikat levels, the sugar in the grapes can ferment fully, to dryness, and for those wines there is no direct correlation between Prädikat level and sweetness of the wine.

Wines whose (grape) ripeness earns them a Prädikat are categorized as QmP wines *(Qualitätswein mit Prädikat),* translated as *quality wines with special attributes* (their ripeness). They are QWPSR wines in the eyes of the EU (see Chapter 4). When the ripeness of the grapes in a particular vineyard is not sufficient to earn the wine a Prädikat name, the wine can still qualify as a "quality wine" in Germany's second QWPSR tier, called QbA *(Qualitätswein bestimmter Anbaugebiet),* translated as *quality wine from a special region.* (Refer to the section, "Germany's wine regions," for the names of the main regions.) Often just the term *Qualitätswein* appears on labels of QbA wines, without the words *bestimmter Anbaugebiet* — and the name of the region will always appear.

Less than 10 percent of Germany's wine production falls into the lower, table wine categories *Landwein* (table wines with geographic indication) or *Deutscher Tafelwein.* Most of the inexpensive German wines that you see in wine shops are QbA wines.

Dry, half-dry, or gentle

The common perception of German wines is that they are all sweet. Yet many German wines taste dry, or fairly dry. In fact, you can find German wines at just about any sweetness or dryness level you like.

Most inexpensive German wines, such as Liebfraumilch, are light-bodied, fruity wines with pleasant sweetness — wines that are easy to enjoy without food. The German term for this style of wine is *lieblich,* which translates as "gentle" — a poetic but apt descriptor. The very driest German wines are called *trocken* (dry). Wines that are sweeter than trocken but dryer than lieblich are called *halbtrocken* (half-dry). The words *trocken* and *halbtrocken* sometimes appear on the label, but not always.

You can make a good stab at determining how sweet a German wine is by reading the alcohol level on the label. If the alcohol is low — about nine percent, or less — the wine probably contains grape sugar that didn't ferment into alcohol and is therefore sweet. Higher alcohol levels suggest that the grapes fermented completely, to dryness.

Although we generally prefer dry white wines, we find that a bit of sweetness in German wines can be appealing — and in fact can improve the quality of the wine. That's because sweetness undercuts the wines' natural high acidity and gives the wines better balance. In truth, most off-dry German wines don't really taste as sweet as they are, thanks to their acidity.

One way that German winemakers keep some sweetness in their wines is called the *süssreserve* (sweet reserve) method. In this method, a winemaker holds back as much as 25 percent of his grape juice and doesn't allow it to ferment. He then ferments the rest of his juice fully, until it's dry wine. Later, he blends the unfermented grape juice into his dry wine. The grape juice (the süssreserve) contributes a natural, juicy sweetness to the wine.

What's noble about rot?

Wine connoisseurs all over the world recognize Germany's sweet, dessert-style wines as among the greatest wines on the face of the earth. Most of these legendary wines owe their sweetness to an ugly but magical fungus known as *botrytis cinerea,* pronounced *bo TRY tis sin eh RAY ah,* commonly called *noble rot.*

Noble rot infects ripe grapes in late autumn if a certain combination of humidity and sun is present. This fungus dehydrates the berries and concentrates their sugar and their flavors. The wine from these infected berries is sweet, amazingly rich, and complex beyond description. It can also be expensive: $100 a bottle or more.

Wines at the BA and TBA Prädikat levels are usually made entirely from grapes infected with noble rot (called *botrytised* grapes) and are generally richly textured and sweet. *Auslese* level wines often come from some partially botrytised grapes, and when they do, they are likely to be sweet, although never to the extent of a BA or TBA.

Another way that Nature can contribute exotic sweetness to German wines is by freezing the grapes on the vine in early winter. When the frozen grapes are harvested and pressed, most of the water in the berries separates out as ice. The sweet, concentrated juice that's left to ferment makes a luscious sweet Prädikat-level wine called *Eiswein* (literally, ice wine). Eisweins differ from BAs and TBAs because they lack a certain flavor that derives from botrytis, sometimes described as a honeyed character.

Both botrytised wines and Eisweins are referred to as *late-harvest wines,* not only in Germany but all over the world, because the special character of these wines comes from conditions that normally occur only when the grapes are left on the vine beyond the usual point of harvest.

Germany's wine regions

Germany has 13 wine regions — 11 in the west and two in the eastern part of the country (see Figure 11-2).

The most famous of these 13 are the Mosel-Saar-Ruwer region, named for the Mosel River and two of its tributaries, along which the region's vineyards lie; and the Rheingau region, along the Rhine River. The Rhine River lends its name to three other German wine regions, Rheinhessen, the Pfalz (formerly called the Rheinpfalz), and the tiny Mittelrhein region.

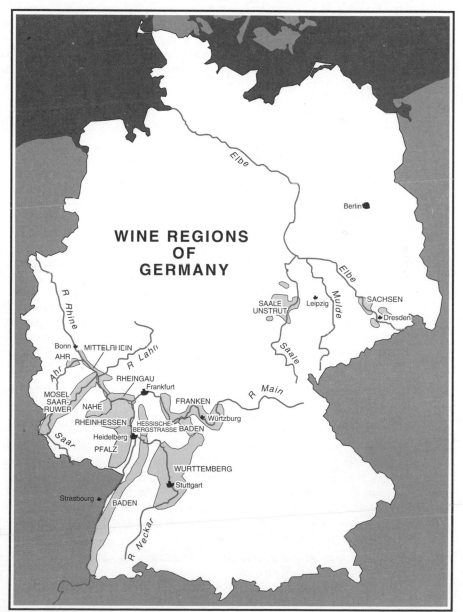

Figure 11-2:
The wine regions of Germany.

© Akira Chiwaki

Mosel-Saar-Ruwer

The Mosel-Saar-Ruwer *(MO zel zar ROO ver)* is a dramatically beautiful region, its vineyards rising steeply on the slopes of the twisting and turning Mosel River. The wines of the region are among the lightest in Germany (usually containing less than 10 percent alcohol); they're generally delicate, fresh, and charming. Riesling dominates the Mosel-Saar-Ruwer with 57 percent of the plantings. Wines from this region are instantly recognizable because they come in green bottles rather than the brown bottles that other German regions use.

The Mosel boasts dozens of excellent winemakers who produce really exciting Riesling wines. Some of our favorites include, in alphabetical order:

Egon Müller	Meulenhof
Dr. Fischer	J.J. Prüm
Friedrich Wilhelm Gymnasium	Reichsgraf Von Kesselstatt
Karlsmühle	Willi Schaefer
Dr. Loosen	Selbach-Oster
Maximin Grünhauser	Zilliken
Merkelbach	

Rheingau

The Rheingau *(RYNE gow)* is among Germany's smaller wine regions. It, too, has some dramatically steep vineyards bordering a river, but here the river is Germany's greatest wine river, the Rhine. The Riesling grape occupies more than 80 percent of the Rheingau's vineyards, many of which are south-facing slopes that give the Riesling grapes an extra edge of ripeness. Rheingau wine styles tend toward two extremes: trocken wines on the one hand and sweet late-harvest wines on the other. Recommended Rheingau producers include Georg Breuer, Knyphausen, Franz Küntsler, Schloss Schönborn, Leitz, and Robert Weil.

A secret code of German place-names

If you don't speak German and you don't know German geography intimately, deciphering German wine names is tricky, to say the least. But here's a bit of information that can help. In the German language, the possessive is formed by adding the suffix *-er* to a noun. When you see names like Zeller or Hochheimer — names that end in *-er* — on a wine label, the next word is usually a vineyard area that "belongs" to the commune or district with the *-er* on its name (Zell's Swartze Katz, Hochheim's Kirchenstück). The name of the region itself always appears on labels of QbA and Prädikat wines.

Rheinhessen

Rheinhessen *(RYNE hess ehn)* is Germany's largest wine region, producing huge quantities of simple wines for everyday enjoyment. Liebfraumilch originated here, and it's still one of the most important wines of the region, commercially speaking. The Rheinhessen's highest quality wines come from the Rheinterrasse, a vineyard area along the river. Producers from that area who are particularly good include Gunderloch, Heyl Zu Herrnsheim, and Strub.

Pfalz

Almost as big as the Rheinhessen, the Pfalz *(fallz)* has earned somewhat more respect from wine lovers for its fairly rich and full-bodied white wines and its very good reds — all of which owe their style to the region's relatively warm climate. Müller-Thurgau, Riesling, Silvaner, and Kerner are among the most planted grape varieties of the Pfalz, but qualitatively Scheurebe and Blauburgunder (Pinot Noir) are important. To experience the best of the Pfalz, look for wines from Dr. Bürklin-Wolf, Rainer Lingenfelder, Müller-Catoir, and Basserman-Jordan.

Nahe

One other German region of importance for the quality of its wines is Nahe *(NAH heh),* named for the Nahe River and situated west of Rheinhessen. The Riesling wines here are relatively full and intense. Favorite producers include Diel, Kruger-Rumpf, Prinz zu Salm-Dahlberg, and Dönnhoff.

Switzerland's Stay-at-Home Wines

Nestled between Germany, France, and Italy, Switzerland is in a perfectly logical location for growing grapes and making fine wine. Vineyards grace the country's three faces — French-speaking, German-speaking, and Italian-speaking. But few wine lovers outside of Switzerland have much opportunity to taste Swiss wines because the production is tiny and because the wines are so popular within Switzerland itself.

About half of Switzerland's wines are white; most are made from Chasselas — a grape cultivated with much less distinction in Germany, eastern France, and the Loire Valley. In Switzerland, Chasselas wines tend to be dry, fairly full-bodied, and unoaked, with mineral and earthy flavors. Other white grapes include Pinot Gris, Sylvaner, Marsanne, Petit Arvine, and Amigne — the latter two indigenous to Switzerland. Merlot is an important red grape (especially in the Italian-speaking Ticino region), along with Pinot Noir and Gamay.

Because of Switzerland's varied terrain (hills of varying altitudes, large lakes, sheltered valleys), numerous microclimates exist. Wine styles therefore vary, from relatively full-bodied reds and whites to delicate, crisp white wines.

Switzerland's major wine regions include the Vaud, along Lake Geneva; Valais, to the east, along the Rhône River; Neuchâtel, in western Switzerland, north of the Vaud; Ticino, in the south, bordering Italy; and Thurgau in the north, bordering Germany.

When you do find a bottle of Swiss wine, you may be surprised to discover how costly it is — $20 to $40 in the United States, reflecting high production costs. (But quality is generally also high.)

Austria's Exciting Whites (and Reds)

Austria is one of the wine countries that most excites us. Apart from the gorgeous vineyard regions, the warmth of the people, and the classic beauty of Vienna, we love many of the wines. What makes Austrian wines all the more interesting is how they are evolving, as winemakers gradually discover how to best express their land and their grapes through wine.

Austria makes less than one percent of all the wine in the world — about 28 million cases a year. All of it comes from the eastern part of the country, where the Alps recede into hills, and most of it comes from small wineries. Although some inexpensive Austrian wines do make their way to export markets, the Austrians have embraced a high-quality image, and most of their wines therefore command premium prices.

While the excellence of Austria's sweet whites has long been recognized, her dry whites and reds have gained recognition only in the past two decades. Reds are in the minority, claiming about 25 percent of the country's production, because many of Austria's wine regions are too cool for growing red grapes. Red wines hail mainly from the area of Burgenland, bordering Hungary, one of the warmest parts of the country. They're medium- to full-bodied, often engagingly spicy, with vivid fruity flavor — and often the international touch of oaky character. Many of them are based on unusual, native grape varieties such as the spicy Blaufrankish (Lemberger), the gentler St. Laurent, or Blauer Zweigelt (a crossing of the other two).

Austria's white wines — apart from the luscious, late-harvest dessert wines made from either botrytised, extremely ripe, or dried grapes — are dry wines ranging from light- to full-bodied that are generally unoaked.

The country's single most important grape variety is the native white Grüner Veltliner. Its wines are full-bodied yet crisp, with rich texture and herbal or sometimes spicy-vegetal flavors (especially green pepper). They're extremely food-friendly, and usually high quality. Some people in the wine trade have nicknamed Grüner Veltliner "GruVe"; we agree with that characterization!

Riesling, grown mainly in the region of Lower Austria, in the northeast, is another key grape for quality whites. In fact, some experts believe that Austria's finest wines are its Rieslings (while others prefer Grüner Veltliner). Other grape names that you may see on bottles of Austrian wine include Müller-Thurgau, which makes characterful dry whites; Welschriesling, a grape popular in Eastern Europe for inexpensive wines that achieves high quality only in Austria; Pinot Blanc, which can excel here; and Muscat. Sauvignon Blanc is a specialty of the region of Styria, in the south, bordering Slovenia.

In some parts of Austria, for example in the Wachau district, along the Danube River, wines are named in the German system — a town name ending in *-er* followed by a vineyard name and a grape variety. In other parts of Austria, the wine names are generally a grape name (or, increasingly, a proprietary name) followed by the name of the region.

Austria's wine laws draw from the German model, with QWPSR wine divided into *Qualitätswein* and *Prädikatswein* categories. (One difference is that *Kabinett* falls into the *Qualitätswein* category.) But some people believe that an appellation system based on terroir rather than ripeness levels would better express the diversity of Austria's vineyard regions. Authorities introduced a new system called *Districtus Austria Controllatus* (DAC) on a limited basis in early 2003.

The Re-emergence of Hungary

Of all the wine-producing countries in Eastern Europe that broke free from Communism in the late 1980s and early 1990s and have resumed wine production under private winery ownership, Hungary seems to have the greatest potential. In addition to a winemaking tradition that dates back to pre-Roman times, Hungary has a wealth of native and international grape varieties and plenty of land suited to vineyards, with a wide range of climates, soils, and altitudes.

The Hungarians are a proud and creative people — or so we concluded on a trip there when our guide mentioned (more than once) that Hungarians invented the hologram, the carburetor, contact lenses, and the ballpoint pen, among other essentials of modern life. Their wine consumption has increased significantly since the country gained independence, fueling an improvement in wine quality. International investment in vineyards and wineries has also made a huge contribution.

Hungary produces the equivalent of about 68 million cases of wine a year, most of which is white. Although the country is northerly — its capital, Budapest, sits at the same latitude as Quebec City — its climate is relatively warm because the country is landlocked and nearly surrounded by mountains. Three large bodies of water do affect the microclimate of certain wine regions: Lake Neusiedel, between Hungary and Austria in the northwest; Lake Balaton, Europe's largest lake, in the center of Hungary's western half (which is called Transdanubia); and the Danube River, which runs north to south right through the middle of the country. Hungary has 22 official wine regions, but their names are not yet particularly important outside Hungary.

The one Hungarian wine region that does have international fame is Tokaj-Hegyalja *(toe KYE heh JAH yah),* which takes its name from the town of Tokaj and owes its reputation to its world-class dessert wine, Tokaji Azsu *(toe KYE as ZOO).* The word *Aszu* refers to botrytised grapes (described earlier in this chapter in the section "What's noble about rot?"). The wine comes from Furmint and Harslevelu grapes, both native white varieties, and sometimes Muscat grapes, that have been infected by botrytis. This region also makes dry table wines, such as the varietal Tokaji Furmint.

Tokaji Azsu wines are labeled as three, four, five, or six Puttonyos, according to their sweetness, with six Puttonyos wines being the sweetest. *(Puttonyos* are baskets used to harvest the botrytised grapes, as well as a measure of sweetness.) All Tokaji Azsu wines sell in 500 ml bottles, and they range in price from about $35 to $150 per bottle, depending on their sweetness level.

Tokaji Azsu wines vary not only according to their sweetness, but also according to their style. Some wines have fresher, more vibrant fruity character, for example; some have aromas and flavors that suggest dried fruits; some have the smoky character and tannin of new oak barrels; and some have complex non-fruity notes such as tea leaves or chocolate. This range of styles is due mainly to different winemaking techniques among producers.

Tokaji Azsu has a complicated production method that involves using a certain amount of botrytised grapes (which are compressed into a paste of sorts) as well as healthy, non-moldy grapes; the more moldy grapes that are used, the sweeter the wine. The production method leaves plenty of room for individual interpretation. Some of the issues that winemakers differ on — besides the normal issues of grape blend — include

✔ What the botrytised grapes soak in to create the liquid that then ferments into the final wine: partially-fermented wine or simply juice (in either case, from non-moldy grapes)

✔ Whether the wine should mature in new or old oak barrels

✔ Whether the wine should be exposed to oxygen during aging (by leaving airspace in the barrels)

Beyond the famous Tokaj-Hegyalja region, Hungary has numerous other wine regions that produce a range of dry and semi-dry wines, both white and red, Most of these wines are named for their grape variety and are quite inexpensive. Kadarka is Hungary's best-known native red grape variety.

Hungary is now a member of the European Union, and its categories of wine therefore resemble those of EU countries (see Chapter 4). Wines at the highest level are classified as *Minosegi Bor (mih no SHAY ghee BOR)*, followed by *Tájbor* (country wine) and *Asztali Bor* (table wine).

The Glory That Is Greece

We find it hard to comprehend that a country which practically invented wine, way back in the seventh century BC, could be an emerging wine region today. But that's the way it is. Greece never stopped making wine for all those centuries, but her wine industry took the slow track, inhibited by Turkish rule, political turmoil, and other real-life issues. The modern era of Greek winemaking began only in the 1960s, and it has made particularly strong strides in the past decade. Today, Greek wines are worth knowing.

Although Greece is a southern country and famous for its sunshine, its grape-growing climate is actually quite varied, because many vineyards are situated at high altitudes where the weather is cooler. (Most of Greece is mountainous, in fact.) Its wines are mainly (60 percent) white; some of those whites are sweet dessert wines, but most are dry.

One of Greece's greatest wine assets — and handicaps, at the same time — is its abundance of native grape varieties, over 300 of them. Only Italy has more indigenous grape varieties. These native grapes make Greek wines particularly exciting for curious wine lovers to explore, but their unfamiliar names make the wines difficult to sell. Fortunately for the marketers, Greece also produces wines from internationally-famous grape varieties such as Chardonnay, Merlot, Syrah, and Cabernet Sauvignon, and those wines can be very good. These days, however, producers seem more committed than ever to their native varieties rather than to international grapes.

Of Greece's many indigenous grape varieties, four in particular stand out as the most important — two white and two red varieties:

- **Assyrtiko** (*ah SEER tee koe*): A white variety that makes delicate, bone dry, crisp, very long-lived wines with citrusy and minerally aromas and flavors. Although Assyrtiko grows in various parts of Greece, the best Assyrtiko wines come from the volcanic island of Santorini. Any wine called Santorini is made at least 90 percent from Assyrtiko.

- **Moschofilero** (*mos cho FEEL eh roe*): A very aromatic, pink-skinned variety that makes both dry white and pale-colored dry rosé wines grows mainly around Mantinia, in the central, mountainous Peloponnese region. If a wine is named Mantinia, it must be at least 85 percent Moschofilero. Wines made from Moschofilero have high acidity and are fairly low in alcohol, with aromas and flavors of apricots and/or peaches. Because they're so easy to drink, Moschofilero wines are a great introduction to Greek wines.

- **Agiorghitiko** (*eye your YEE tee koe*): The name of this grape translates in English to "St. George," and a few winemakers call it that on the labels of wines destined for English-speaking countries. Greece's most-planted and probably most important native red variety, it grows throughout the mainland. Its home turf, where it really excels, is in the Nemea district of the Peloponnese region; any wine named Nemea is entirely from Agiorghitiko. Wines from this variety are medium to deep in color, have complex aromas and flavors of plums and/or black currants, and often have a resemblance to Cabernet Franc or spicy Merlot wines. Agiorghitiko also blends well with other indigenous or international varieties.

- **Xinomavro** (*ksee NO mav roe*): The most important red variety in the Macedonia region of Northern Greece. Xinomavro produces highly tannic wines with considerable acidity that have been compared to Nebbiolo wines of Piedmont, Italy. Wines made from Xinomavro have complex, spicy aromas, often suggesting dried tomatoes, olives, and/or berries. Xinomavro wines are dark in color but lighten with age, and have great longevity. Their home base is the Naoussa district of Macedonia; any wine named Naoussa is entirely from Xinomavro.

Other important white indigenous varieties in Greece include Roditis (actually a pink-skinned grape), which makes Patras white; and Savatiano, the most widely planted white grape. Retsina, a traditional Greek wine made by adding pine resin to fermenting grape juice (resulting in a flavor not unlike some oaky Chardonnays), is made mainly from Savatiano. Mavrodaphne is an indigenous Greek red variety that is becoming increasingly important, both for dry and sweet red wines.

Some of the wine regions of Greece whose names you are likely to see on wine labels include

- **Macedonia:** The northernmost part of Greece, with mountainous terrain and cool climates. Naoussa wine comes from here.

- **The Peloponnese:** A large, mainly mountainous, peninsula in southwestern Greece with varied climate and soil. Noteworthy wines include the soft, red Nemea; the dry whites Patras and Mantinia; and the sweet wines Mavrodaphne de Patras (red) and Muscat de Patras (white).

- **Crete:** The largest Greek island, which makes both white and red wines, many of which are varietally-named along with the place-name of Crete.

- **Other Greek Islands:** Besides Crete, the four most important islands that make wine are Santorini, Rhodes, Samos, and Cephalonia.

Many Greek wines today are top-quality, especially the wines of small, independent wineries. The following are some of our favorite Greek wine producers (listed alphabetically within regions):

- From Macedonia: Alpha Estate, Domaine Gerovassilou, Kir Yianni Estate, and Tsantali-Mount Athos Vineyards

- From the Peloponnese: Antonopoulos Vineyards, Gaia Estate (pronounced *YEA ah,* has wineries also in Santorini), Katogi & Strofilia (with operations also in Macedonia), Mercouri Estate, Papantonis Winery, Domaine Skouras, Domaine Spiropoulos, and Domaine Tselepos

- From the islands: Boutari Estates (six estates throughout Greece, including Crete and Santorini), Gentilini (in Cephalonia), and Domaine Sigalas (Santorini)

Greece is a member of the European Union, and its appellation system for wine therefore conforms to the EU's two-tiered structure. At the top (QWPSR) level Greece has two categories:

- AOQS, *Appellation d'Origine de Qualité Supérieure* (yes, that's French!) for dry and off-dry wines

- AOC, *Appellation d'Origine Contrôlée,* for dessert and fortified wines

Table wines with a geographic name are called *vins de pays* (regional wines). Many of Greece's better wines in fact carry a *vins de pays* appellation. Other terms that have formal definitions under Greek wine regulations include *reserve* (QWPSR wines with a minimum two or three years aging, for whites and reds respectively), *grande reserve* (one additional year of aging), and *cava* (a table wine — in the EU sense of being at the lower appellation tier — with the same aging requirements as reserve).

Part IV
Discovering the New World of Wine

The 5th Wave   By Rich Tennant

"Mr. Rotgut! Mr. Rotgut! A car's coming! A car's coming, and he sure doesn't look lost to me!"

In this part . . .

Like Columbus in 1492, we set sail for the land of opportunity, where winemakers grow whichever grapes they like and make fresh, modern, flavorful wines that electrify wine drinkers.

This part contains only two chapters, but the countries represented in them are white-hot in the wine marketplace — the United States, Australia, New Zealand, Chile, Argentina, and South Africa, for example. We guide you to the most exciting wines and explain what makes them special.

Chapter 12

The Southern Hemisphere Arises

What do the wines of North and South America, South Africa, Australia, and New Zealand have in common? For one thing, none of them are produced in Europe. In fact, you could say that they are the wines of "Not Europe."

The name most often used in wine circles for Not Europe is the *New World*. Undoubtedly this phrase, with its ring of colonialism, was coined by a European. Europe, home of all the classic wine regions of the world, producer of more than 60 percent of the world's wine, is the Old World. Everything else is nouveau riche.

When we first heard the expression *New World* applied to wines, we thought it was absurd. How can you lump together wine regions as remote as Napa Valley, the Finger Lakes, Coonawarra, and Chile's Maipo Valley? But then we started thinking about it. In Europe, they've been making wines for so long that grape-growing and winemaking practices are now codified into detailed regulations. Which hillsides to plant, which grapes should grow where, how dry or sweet a particular wine should be — these decisions were all made long ago, by the grandparents and great-great-grandparents of today's winemakers. But in Not Europe, the grape-growing and winemaking game is wide open; every winery owner gets to decide for himself where to grow his grapes, what variety to plant, and what style of wine to make. The wines of the New World do have that in common.

The more we thought about it, the more similarities we found among New World wine regions as they compared to Europe. We concluded that the New World is a winemaking entity whose legislative reality, spirit, and winemaking style are unique from those of the Old World — as generalizations go.

We could easily fill 400 pages on the wines of the United States, Canada, Chile, Argentina, Australia, New Zealand, and South Africa alone, if only we had the space. Fortunately, New World wines are easy for you to explore without a detailed road map: In the New World, there's little encoded tradition to decipher and relatively little historical backdrop against which the wines need to be appreciated.

In this chapter, we explore the wines of Australia, New Zealand, Chile, Argentina, and South Africa. We devote the next chapter to the wines of the United States, with a short look at Canada, too.

The old and the new

In wine terms, the New World is not just geography but also an attitude toward wine. Some winemakers in Europe approach wine the liberated New World way, and some winemakers in California are dedicated Old World traditionalists.

Keep that in mind as you look over the following comparison between the Old and the New. And remember, we're talking generalizations here — and generalizations are never always true.

New World	Old World
Innovation	Tradition
Wines named after grape varieties	Wines named after region of production
Expression of the fruit is the primary winemaking goal	Expression of *terroir* (the particular place where the grapes grow, with its unique growing conditions) is the winemaking goal
Technology is revered	Traditional methods are favored
Wines are flavorful and fruity	Wines have subtle, less fruity flavors
Grape-growing regions are broad and flexible	Grape-growing regions are relatively small and fixed
Winemaking resembles science	Winemaking resembles art
Winemaking processes are controlled	Intervention in winemaking is avoided as much as possible
The winemaker gets credit for the wine	The vineyard gets the credit

Australian Wine Power

Make no mistake about it: Australia is one of the world powers of wine. The wine industry of Australia is perhaps the most technologically advanced, forward-thinking on earth, and the success of Australian wines around the world is the envy of wine producers in many other countries.

Australia has no native vines. Vinifera grapevines first came to the country in 1788, from South Africa. At first, most Australian wines were rich and sweet, many of them fortified, but today Australia is famous for its fresh, fruity red and white table wines that manage to be extremely consistent in quality. Australia now ranks sixth in the world in wine production — making slightly more than half as much wine as the United States — and fourth in exports.

Approximately the same size as the continental United States, Australia has about 2,000 wineries. Many of these wineries are small, family-owned companies, but four mega-companies — Foster's Wine Group, Constellation Wines, Pernod Ricard, and McGuigan Simeon Wines — together with one family-owned winery, Casella Wines, are responsible for about two-thirds of Australia's wine production.

Winemaking, grapes, and terroir

Australia's wine regions are mainly in the southern, cooler part of the country, with many of them clustered in the state of Victoria, the southern part of South Australia, the southern part of Western Australia, and the cooler parts of New South Wales.

The success of Australia's wines stems from a generally warm, dry climate, which provides winemakers with excellent raw material for their work. The country's research programs in grape-growing and winemaking also contribute greatly by enabling winemakers to stay on the cutting edge of their craft.

Australia's number-one grape for fine wine is Syrah, locally called *Shiraz,* followed by Cabernet Sauvignon, Chardonnay, Merlot, Semillon (pronounced *SEM eh lon* in Australia, as opposed to the French *sem ee yon* elsewhere in the world), Pinot Noir, Riesling, and Sauvignon Blanc. The wines are generally labeled with the name of their grape variety, which must constitute at least 85 percent of the wine.

Shiraz wines are particularly interesting because they come in numerous styles, from inexpensive, juicy wines brimming with ripe plum and blackberry fruit to serious wines that express specific regional characteristics, such as spice and pepper from cool-climate areas (such as Yarra Valley and the Adelaide Hills) or sweet-fruit ripeness from warmer areas (such as McLaren Vale, Barossa, and Clare).

The wines of Australia have two distinct faces:

✔ Most Australian wines in export markets are inexpensive varietal wines that sell for $10 a bottle or less. These wines are generally labeled simply as coming from *South Eastern Australia,* meaning that the grapes could have come from any of three states, a huge territory. Often sporting whimsical labels, they are user-friendly wines that preserve the intense flavors of their grapes and are soft and pleasant to drink young.

✔ Higher-priced wines carry more focused regional designations, such as single states (South Australia or Victoria, for example) or even tighter region-specific designations (such as Coonawarra or Yarra Valley). Although these wines are also enjoyable when released, they are more serious wines that can also age. Australia now has 60 wine regions and more than 100 Geographic Indications (GIs).

We mention some of the more famous regions of Australia, state by state, in the following section. If you're interested in learning about these regions — and the many others that we don't mention — in more detail, read Oz Clarke's *Australian Wine Companion* (Websters International, 2004) or James Halliday's excellent *Wines of Australia* (Mitchell Beazley, 2003).

Australia's wine regions

Australia's most important state for wine production is South Australia, whose capital is Adelaide (see Figure 12-1). South Australia makes about 50 percent of Australia's wine. While many vineyards in South Australia produce inexpensive wines for the thirsty home market, vineyards closer to Adelaide make wines that are considered among the country's finest. Among these fine wine regions are

✔ **Barossa Valley:** North of Adelaide, this is one of Australia's oldest areas for fine wine; it's a relatively warm area famous especially for its robust Shiraz, Cabernet Sauvignon, and Grenache, as well as rich Semillon and Riesling (grown in the cooler hills). Most of Australia's largest wineries, including Penfolds, are based here.

✔ **Clare Valley:** North of the Barossa Valley, this climatically diverse area makes the country's best Rieslings in a dry, weighty yet crisp style, as well as fine Shiraz and Cabernet Sauvignon.

✔ **McLaren Vale:** South of Adelaide, with a mild climate influenced by the sea, this region is particularly admired for its Shiraz, Cabernet, Sauvignon Blanc, and Chardonnay.

✔ **Adelaide Hills:** Situated partially within the Adelaide city limits, this fairly cool region sits between the Barossa and McLaren Vale areas and is the home to rather good Sauvignon Blanc, Chardonnay, Pinot Noir, and Shiraz.

✔ **Limestone Coast:** This unique zone along the southern coast of South Australia is an important area for fine wine, both red and white, thanks to the prevalence of limestone in the soil. Two of the six regions within the Limestone Coast zone are famous in their own right — the cool **Coonawarra** for some of Australia's best Cabernet Sauvignon wines, and **Padthaway** for its white wines, particularly Chardonnay, Sauvignon Blanc, and Riesling.

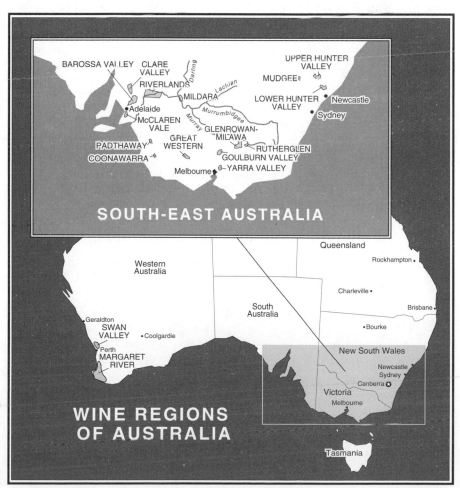

Figure 12-1: The wine regions of Australia.

© Akira Chiwaki

Odd couples

Although winemakers all over the world make blended wines — wines from more than one grape variety — generally the grape combinations follow the classic French models: Cabernet Sauvignon with Merlot and Cabernet Franc, for example, or Sémillon with Sauvignon Blanc. Australia has invented two completely original formulas:

✔ Shiraz with Cabernet Sauvignon

✔ Semillon with Chardonnay

The grape in the majority is listed first on the wine label for wines sold in the United States, and the percentages of each grape are indicated.

Adjoining South Australia to the east is Victoria, a smaller state that makes 15 percent of Australia's wines. While South Australia is home to most of Australia's largest wineries, Victoria has more wineries (over 500), most of them small. Victoria's fine wine production ranges from rich, fortified dessert wines to delicate Pinot Noirs. Principal regions include, from north to south

✔ **Murray River:** This area stretching into New South Wales includes the Mildura region, where Lindemans, one of Australia's largest wineries is situated. This region is particularly important for growing grapes for Australia's good-value wines.

✔ **Rutherglen:** In the northeast, this long-established, warm climate zone is an outpost of traditional winemaking and home of an exotic Australian specialty, fortified dessert Muscats and Tokays.

✔ **Goulburn Valley:** In the center of the state, Goulburn Valley is known especially for its full-bodied reds, especially Shiraz.

✔ **Heathcote**: East of Goulburn and due north of Melbourne (the capital), this area boasts unusual soils that make distinctive, rich-yet-elegant Shirazes and also Cabernet.

✔ **Yarra Valley:** In southern Victoria, and close to Melbourne, Yarra Valley boasts a wide diversity of climates due to altitude differences of its vineyards. The Yarra is noted for its Cabernet, Pinot Noir, Shiraz, Chardonnay, and Sauvignon Blanc.

✔ **Mornington Peninsula and Geelong**: South of Melbourne and separated from each other by Port Phillip Bay, these two cool, maritime regions specialize in fine Pinot Noir and Chardonnay.

New South Wales, with its capital, Sydney, is Australia's most populous state, and the first to grow vines; today it makes 31 percent of Australia's wine. High-volume production of everyday wines comes from an interior area called the Riverina. (We get a kick trying to pronounce its alternate name, Murrumbidgee.) Fine wine, for now, comes from three other areas:

✔ **Hunter Valley:** An historic grape-growing area that begins 80 miles north of Sydney. The Lower Hunter, with a warm, damp climate and heavy soils, produces long-lived Semillon as its best wine. The Upper Hunter is a drier area farther from the coast.

✔ **Mudgee:** An interior area near the mountains. Mudgee specializes in reds such as Merlot and Cabernet Sauvignon but also makes Chardonnay.

✔ **Orange:** A cool, high-altitude area making distinctive white wines and also very good reds.

Western Australia, the country's largest state, with its most isolated wine area — in the southwest corner — makes little wine compared to the preceding three states, but quality is high. The warm, dry Swan Valley is the state's historic center of wine production, but two cooler climate regions have become more important:

✔ **Margaret River:** This is a relatively temperate region near the Indian Ocean. Among the wines that various wineries here excel in are Sauvignon Blanc-Semillon blends (especially Cape Mentelle), Chardonnay (especially Leeuwin Estate), and Cabernet Sauvignon (from Mosswood, Voyager, Cape Mentelle, and Howard Park).

✔ **Great Southern:** Cooler than Margaret River, Great Southern's specialty is crisp, age-worthy Riesling. This huge, diverse region produces intense, aromatic Cabernet Sauvignon as well as fine Shiraz and Chardonnay; on the southern coast, Pinot Noir is successful.

Tasmania, an island south of Victoria, has some cool microclimates where producers such as Pipers Brook are proving what potential exists for delicate Pinot Noirs, Chardonnays, and sparkling wines.

The Rise of New Zealand

The history of fine winemaking in New Zealand is relatively short, having been hampered by conservative attitudes towards alcohol. In the 1980s, New Zealand finally began capitalizing on its maritime climate, ideal for producing high-quality wines, and started planting grapes in earnest. Today, it makes less than one-tenth of the wine of its nearest neighbor, Australia, but its production is increasing every year. And, unlike Australia, New Zealand has managed to maintain an elite image for its wines, as opposed to a good-value-for-everyday image.

Situated farther south than Australia, New Zealand is, in general, cooler. Of New Zealand's two large islands, the North Island is the warmer. Red grapes grow around the capital city, Auckland, in the north and around Hawkes Bay (especially known for its Cabernet Sauvignon) farther south on the North Island; Müller-Thurgau, Chardonnay, and Sauvignon Blanc are that island's main white varieties. Martinborough, a cooler district at the southern end of North Island, makes very good Pinot Noir.

On the South Island, Marlborough — the country's largest and commercially most important wine region — is New Zealand's top production zone for Chardonnay and, especially, Sauvignon Blanc.

The first New Zealand Sauvignon Blancs to be exported were generally unoaked wines with pronounced flavor, rich texture, and high acidity. They were so distinctive — pungent, herbaceous, with intense flavors suggestive of asparagus, lime, or cut grass — that New Zealand became recognized almost overnight in the late 1980s for a new prototype of Sauvignon Blanc. This style of New Zealand Sauvignon Blanc is still very popular worldwide. These are the least expensive "Kiwi" (as the locals call themselves, being among the world's major kiwi growers) Sauvignon Blancs, retailing for $12 to $18, with many priced around $15.

Another style of New Zealand Sauvignon Blanc has evolved in the last decade. Riper, less assertive, and softer in texture, this style is often achieved through the use of oak barrels and/or blending with Semillon, and it has fruitier flavors, usually passion fruit or ripe grapefruit. New Zealand wine producers correctly foresaw that wine drinkers may need an alternative to the herbaceous style. The riper, fruitier, less herbaceous New Zealand Sauvignon Blancs are frequently labeled as "Reserve" wines or as single-vineyard wines. They generally retail for $18 to $30.

Pinot Noir is increasingly significant in New Zealand. In addition to its stronghold in Martinborough, on the North Island, Pinot Noir is now being made in Marlborough and throughout the South Island, and this grape has now surpassed Cabernet Sauvignon as New Zealand's most planted red variety. New Zealand Pinot Noirs vary in taste from region to region; the wines of Martinborough, for example, are a bit more savory and minerally than those of Marlborough, which tend to be soft and fruity. In time, as the producers of each region refine their styles, the regional differences should become more evident.

In the central part of the South Island, Central Otago, home of the world's most southerly grapevines, has emerged as one of New Zealand's top regions for Pinot Noir. Vines are planted on hillsides for more sunshine and less risk of frost. The low-yielding vines here produce highly-concentrated Pinot Noir wines. Mt. Difficulty and Felton Road, both from Central Otago, are currently two of New Zealand's best Pinot Noir producers.

Four large producers dominate New Zealand's wine production: Montana (sold in the United States under the Brancott label, to avoid confusion with the state of Montana), Corbans, Villa Maria, and Nobilo. But in the past 20 years, numerous small, boutique wineries have sprung up, especially on the South Island, and are making excellent wine.

Current trends in kiwi land

New Zealand Sauvignon Blancs are still hot, and Pinot Noir seems to be the next Big Thing. But New Zealand is more than just a two-grape country. In the white wine category, we're impressed with the improved Chardonnays, Rieslings, and Pinot Gris wines. The biggest surprise could be New Zealand's really fine Cabernet Sauvignons, Merlots, and Bordeaux-blends, not only from established warmer-climate North Island regions such as Hawke's Bay and its Gimblett Road zone, but also from Waiheke Island, a few miles east of the city of Auckland, where the climate is mild enough to grow Cabernet Franc and Petit Verdot.

New Zealand's final surprise is that it's making excellent sparkling wines by using the classic method (see Chapter 14 for an explanation of this winemaking method). Most of the better New Zealand sparkling wines also use the two main grape varieties of Champagne, Pinot Noir and Chardonnay. Highfield Estate is one of New Zealand's many fine sparkling wine producers.

Chile Discovers Itself

Chile's wine industry wears the mantle *New World* somewhat uncomfortably. The Spanish first established vineyards in Chile in the mid-sixteenth century, and the country has maintained a thriving wine industry for its home market for several centuries. Nothing new about that. What *is* new about Chile, however, is the growth of her wine industry since the mid-1980s, her rapid development of a strong export market, and her shift toward French grape varieties such as Cabernet Sauvignon, Merlot, and Chardonnay — with an almost-forgotten red Bordeaux variety called Carmenère definitely in the running, on the outside post position.

With the Pacific Ocean to the west and the Andes Mountains to the east, Chile is an isolated country. This isolation has its advantages in terms of grape growing: Phylloxera hasn't yet taken hold in Chile — as it's done in just about every other winemaking country — and vinifera vines can therefore grow on their own roots. (For an explanation of phylloxera, see Chapter 3.) Chile's other viticultural blessings include a range of mountains along the coast, which blocks the ocean dampness from most vineyards, and the ocean's general tempering influence on a relatively hot climate.

Chile's wine regions

As in every other country, grape growers and wine producers in Chile originally planted vineyards in the most obvious locations, where grapes would grow prolifically. Trial and error have gradually enabled them to discover the less obvious locations — many of them cooler and less accessible areas — that offer the opportunity to make truly distinctive wines.

Initially considered the ideal place to plant grapes, Maipo Valley is part of Chile's vast Central Valley, which lies between the coastal range and the Andes. Convenience played a large role: The Maipo Valley surrounds Santiago, Chile's capital and its largest and most important city. Most of Chile's vineyards are still in the Central Valley, but today, vineyards also exist in regions that no one had heard of just ten years ago.

From north to south, here's a summary of Chile's wine regions today, both old and new:

- **Limari Valley:** A small region northwest of Santiago, near the Pacific Ocean. Although the climate is hot and dry — it's nearer to the equator than any of Chile's other important regions and close to the Atacama Desert — its unique microclimate, caused by its proximity to the Pacific, features cooling morning fog and ocean breezes that blow through the Valley during the day. Chile's three largest wineries, Concha y Toro, San Pedro, and Santa Rita, all have bought land in Limari. Promising wines so far are Sauvignon Blanc, Chardonnay, and Syrah. This is one of the country's hot emerging regions.

- **Aconcagua Valley:** North of Santiago, Aconcagua Valley is named for the country's highest mountain, the magnificent Mount Aconcagua and is one of the warmest areas for fine grapes. But Aconcagua also includes many cooler high-altitude sections. Cabernet Sauvignon grows especially well here, and more recently, Syrah. Viña Errázuriz is Aconcagua Valley's most important winery.

- **Casablanca Valley:** Once considered part of the Aconcagua Valley, the cooler Casablanca valley, near the Pacific Ocean, now has its own identity. The first-established of the newer Chilean wine regions, it's still one of the best. Some of Chile's finest Chardonnays and Sauvignon Blancs grow in one part of Casablanca, while good Merlots and Pinot Noirs come from a more mountainous part. Veramonte is Casablanca's best-known winery, but many other wineries own vineyards in this region.

- ✔ **San Antonio Valley:** Along with nearby Leyda Valley, tiny San Antonio Valley, south of Casablanca Valley and next to the ocean, is arguably Chile's most exciting new region. Pinot Noir and Syrah are growing especially well on its cool, steep slopes. Now making one of the world's best Pinot Noirs outside of Burgundy and a fine Syrah, Viña Matetic is the winery to watch in San Antonio Valley.

- ✔ **Maipo Valley:** Chile's most-established wine region, just south of Santiago, Maipo Valley is home to most of the country's wineries. Concha y Toro, Santa Rita, and Almaviva are a few of Maipo's premium producers. Cabernet Sauvignon is king in this region, and Merlot also does very well.

- ✔ **Cachapoal Valley:** The large Rapel Valley, south of Maipo Valley, has two main wine regions, Cachapoal Valley and Colchagua Valley. Cachapoal Valley, nearer the Andes, is a red wine region, and is strong in Merlot and Cabernet Sauvignon. Morandé and Altair are two rising star wineries here.

- ✔ **Colchagua Valley:** Ocean breezes have transformed the formerly quiet Colchagua Valley into one of Chile's most important new red wine regions. Carmenère, Cabernet Sauvignon, Merlot, and Syrah grow especially well here. Colchagua's two leading wineries are Casa Lapostolle and Montes.

- ✔ **Curicó Valley:** One of Chile's oldest and largest wine regions, the Curicó Valley is directly south of Rapel Valley. Because of its diverse microclimates, both red and white varieties grow well here. The huge San Pedro Winery and Viña Miguel Torres are located in Curicó.

- ✔ **Maule:** Maule Valley is Chile's largest wine region in area, and also the southernmost of its important wine regions. Because it's so huge, it has many diverse microclimates, and both red and white varieties grow well, especially Sauvignon Blanc, Cabernet Sauvignon, and Merlot. Viña Calina is Maule Valley's best-known winery.

The face and taste of the wines

Stylistically, Chile's wines generally lack the exuberant fruitiness of Californian and Australian wines. And yet they're not quite as subtle and understated as European wines. Although red wines have always been Chile's strength, today the white wines, especially those from cooler regions, are very good. Chile's Sauvignon Blancs are generally unoaked, while most of the Chardonnays are oaked.

Like most New World wines, Chile's wines are generally named for their grape varieties; they carry a regional (or sometimes a district) indication, too. The reasonable prices of the basic wines — mainly from $6 to $10 in the United States — make these wines excellent values. The most important wineries for the export market include, in alphabetical order, Calina, Caliterra, Carmen, Casa Lapostolle, Concha y Toro, Cousiño Macul, Errazuriz, Haras de Pirque, Los Vascos, Montes, Mont Gras, Santa Carolina, Santa Rita, and Undurraga. Viña Matetic, a rising star from the San Antonio Valley, is just beginning to appear on the export markets.

Chile's new challenge is to produce good-quality high-end wines along with its inexpensive varietals. Many of the top producers now make a super-premium red wine in the $45 to $90 price range. These elite Chilean reds are often blends rather than varietal wines, and many are styled along international lines — made from very ripe grapes that give rich, fruity flavors and high (14 percent or higher) alcohol levels, and aged in small French oak barrels. What many (but not all) of them lack, however, is a sense of place: They don't taste particularly Chilean. With time, Chile will undoubtedly reach its goal and begin producing fine wines that merit their high prices.

Keep an eye out for some of Chile's top super-premium red wines:

- ✔ Concha y Toro's Don Melchor Cabernet Sauvignon (about $45)

- ✔ Errázuriz's Don Maximiano Founder's Reserve (mainly Cabernet Sauvignon, about $50)

- ✔ Albis, a wine from a joint venture between the Chilean Haras de Pirque winery and the Italian Antinori company (Cabernet Sauvignon and Carmenère, about $52)

- ✔ Montes Alpha M (a "Bordeaux blend," about $75)

- ✔ Almaviva (a sleek and subtle red, mainly Cabernet Sauvignon with Carménère and Cabernet Franc, about $90)

- ✔ Casa Lapostolle's Clos Apalta (a blend of Carménère, Merlot, and Cabernet Sauvignon, about $80)

- ✔ Seña, from an estate in Aconcagua that was originally a partnership between the Robert Mondavi and Eduardo Chadwick (of Viña Errázuriz) families and is now owned by the Chadwicks (Cabernet Sauvignon, Merlot, and Carmenère, about $65)

Argentina, a Major League Player

Argentina produces about four times as much wine as Chile does — almost as much as the entire United States. It boasts the largest wine production in South America and the fifth-largest wine production in the world. In recent years, winemaking has shifted away from large-volume wines suited to the domestic market and toward higher-quality wines that suit wine drinkers outside Argentina. Not only is Argentina now a major player in the world wine market, but it's one of the world's most exciting countries for wine production.

Wine grapes have grown in Argentina since the mid-sixteenth century, as they have in Chile. But Argentina's source of vines was more diverse; for example, many vines were brought over by the vast numbers of Italian and Basque immigrants. As a result, Argentina boasts grape varieties such as Bonarda and Malbec that are insignificant in Chile.

Regions and grapes

Argentina's wine regions are situated mainly in the western part of the country, where the Andes Mountains divide Argentina from Chile. High altitude tempers the climate, but the vineyards are still very warm by day, cool by night, and desert dry. Rivers flow through the area from the Andes and provide water for irrigation.

The vast majority of Argentina's vineyards are in the state of Mendoza, Argentina's largest wine region, which lies at roughly the same latitude as Santiago, Chile. Within the Mendoza region are various wine districts (the names of which sometimes appear on wine labels) such as Maipú, San Martín, Tupungato, and Luján de Cuyo. Most of Argentina's oldest wineries and their vineyards are clustered close to Mendoza city, but the Uco Valley, south of the city, has attracted many newcomers who are building impressive wineries.

San Juan, just north of Mendoza and considerably hotter, is Argentina's second-largest wine region. La Rioja, Argentina's oldest wine-producing region, is east of San Juan.

San Juan is particularly famous for Torrontés, a variety that's probably indigenous to Galicia, Spain. It produces an inexpensive ($6 to $10), light-bodied, high-acid, aromatic white wine that's one of Argentina's signature white wines. It's especially fine with appetizers, seafood, and fish.

Argentina's red wines are generally higher in quality than its whites. The little-known Malbec grape variety — now seldom used in Bordeaux, where it originated — has emerged as Argentina's flagship variety. Malbec has adapted extremely well to the Mendoza region, and winemakers are learning how it varies in Mendoza's subzones. Arguments continue as to which variety makes Argentina's greatest red wines, Cabernet Sauvignon or Malbec. But the fact remains that good Cabernet wines come from almost every wine-producing country; only Argentina and Cahors, a small region in Southwest France, have had success with Malbec. The same logic suggests that Bonarda and Barbera, two northern Italian varieties that are widely planted in Argentina (especially Bonarda), have a good future there.

Names to know

Thanks in part to its high altitudes and sunny days, Argentina's natural resources for grape growing are among the strongest in the world. Increasingly, foreign investment continues to bring the capital and the winemaking know-how to make the most of these natural resources. Bodega Norton, for example, a winery that was purchased by an Austrian crystal producer in 1989, now makes some of the country's best wines. Moët & Chandon, another immigrant, is already Argentina's largest sparkling wine producer; it also makes the Terrazas varietal table wines. A Dutchman owns the state-of-the-art Bodegas Salentein winery and its sister winery, Finca El Portillo. Kendall Jackson has a presence, with its Viña Calina, as do several Bordeaux producers, such as Bordeaux's Lurton family, which owns Bodega J. & F. Lurton.

French enologist Michel Rolland has worked wonders at Trapiche; try Trapiche's great-value Oak Cask Cabernet Sauvignon or Oak Cask Malbec, both about $10. In fact Rolland, who knows the world's vineyards as well as anyone, has personally invested in an Argentine winery, Clos de los Siete; *that* says something about Argentina's potential!

The homegrown Catena Zapata has emerged as one of Argentina's top wine producers. At $10 a bottle, its Alamos Malbec is one of the greatest wine values around. Catena Cabernet Sauvignon or Malbec (both about $21), and the super-premium Malbec Alta or Cabernet Sauvignon Alta, both about $50, are higher-end wines, among the finest being made in South America today.

Other Argentine producers we recommend include Bodega Norton, Bodega J. & F. Lurton, Bodegas Salentein, Bodega Weinert, Trapiche, Etchart, Finca Sophenia, Achaval Ferrer, Pascual Toso, Michel Torino, Las Terrazas, Navarro Correas, Santa Julia, El Portillo, Dona Paula, and Valentín Bianchi. Some of Argentina's basic wines are priced the same as Chile's, in the $6 to $10 range, but a few wineries make pricier wines starting in the $18 to $20 range.

South African Wine Safari

Vines came to South Africa in the 1650s with the Dutch, the first European settlers; in the same period, French Huguenots (Protestants) escaping religious persecution brought winemaking expertise. At the end of the eighteenth century, South Africa was producing a luscious fortified wine called Constantia, which became sought after in European royal courts. The country began focusing seriously on table wine production only in the 1980s. Today, South Africa ranks ninth in the world in wine production.

Most of South Africa's table wines come from an area known as the Coastal Region, around the Cape of Good Hope. Traditionally, large firms dominated South Africa's wine industry, and they continue to do so. KWV, formerly a wine growers' cooperative, is one of the country's largest wineries. South Africa's largest winery, the gigantic Distell firm, owns two groups of wineries that had been among the country's largest wine companies — Stellenbosch Farmers' Winery Group and the Bergkelder Group.

South Africa's principal wine regions

South Africa has some vineyard areas with cool microclimates, especially around the southern coast (near the Cape of Good Hope) and in higher altitudes, but the climate in most of its wine regions is warm and dry.

South Africa's Wine of Origin legislation in 1973 created various wine regions, districts and wards. Almost all the country's vineyards are near its southwestern coast, in Cape Province, within 90 miles of Cape Town, the country's most fascinating and picturesque city.

South African style

Although we technically place South Africa in the New World, we must admit that its wines are rather reminiscent of European wines. The taste of a South African Cabernet Sauvignon, for example, may remind you of a French wine — but not quite. On the other hand, it doesn't really resemble a New World red from California or Australia, either. South African wines manage to combine the subtlety and finesse of French wines along with a touch of the voluptuous ripeness of California wines. In short, they are somewhat between both worlds.

The five major districts — mainly in the Coastal Region area — are

- **Constantia:** The oldest wine-producing area in the country (located south of Cape Town)
- **Stellenbosch:** East of Cape Town; the most important wine district in quantity and quality
- **Paarl:** North of Stellenbosch; home of the KWV and the famous, beautiful Nederburg Estate; the second-most important wine district
- **Franschhoek Valley:** A subdistrict of Paarl; many innovative winemakers here
- **Robertson:** East of Franschhoek, the only major district not in the Coastal Region; a hot, dry area, known mainly for its Chardonnays

The small, cool Hermanus/Walker Bay area, bordering the Indian Ocean, is also showing promise with Pinot Noir and Chardonnay, led by the innovative Hamilton Russell Winery. A newly added (11th) wine district, Elgin, is on the coast between Stellenbosch and Walker Bay. A cool area, Elgin shows promise for its intensely flavored Sauvignon Blancs and for Pinot Noirs. The latest area to show promise is Darling Hills, north of Cape Town, led by an up-and-coming winery, Groote Post.

Varietal wines in South Africa must contain at least 75 percent of the named grape variety; exported wines (complying with the stricter European Union regulations) must contain 85 percent of the named variety. About 35 percent of South Africa's wines qualify as Wine of Origin (WO). Wine of Origin regulations are based on the French *Appellation Contrôlée* laws (see Chapter 9), and they strictly designate vineyards, allowable grape varieties, vintage-dating, and so on.

Steen, Pinotage, and company

The most-planted grape variety in South Africa is Chenin Blanc, often locally called *Steen*. This versatile grape primarily makes medium-dry to semi-sweet wines, but also dry wines, sparkling wines, late harvest botrytis wines, and rosés.

Cabernet Sauvignon, Merlot, Shiraz, and Pinot Noir have become increasingly important red varieties, while Sauvignon Blanc and Chardonnay are popular white varieties. Cabernet Sauvignon and Sauvignon Blanc do particularly well in South Africa's climate. (Producers here make a very assertive version of Sauvignon Blanc.)

South Africa: The future

Chenin Blanc and Pinotage represent South Africa's recent past — although both are undergoing a revival today. Cabernet Sauvignon, Merlot, and Chardonnay are definitely making fine wines here now, but Sauvignon Blanc and Shiraz seem to hold the most promise in this country. Sauvignon Blanc is a no-brainer; some of the world's best Sauvignon Blanc varietal wines are already being made here. The flavorful character of Sauvignon Blanc asserts itself in South Africa, especially in Constantia and in a new cool-climate district, Elim, in Cape Agulhas.

Although South African Sauvignon Blancs resemble those from New Zealand, they are easier to drink and not quite as assertive. Shiraz has become the hot, new variety of the Southern Hemisphere, and indeed throughout the world. What South African winemakers love about Shiraz is its versatility. It can grow well in cool and in warm climates. Right now, Shiraz is the fastest-growing variety being planted in South Africa. In ten years or less, it may be the country's biggest-selling varietal wine.

And then you have Pinotage. Uniquely South African, Pinotage is a grape born as a crossing between Pinot Noir and Cinsaut (the same as Cinsault, the Rhône variety) back in 1925. However, Pinotage didn't appear as a wine until 1959. Pinotage wine combines the cherry fruit of Pinot Noir with the earthiness of a Rhône wine. It can be a truly delicious, light- to medium-bodied red wine that makes for easy drinking, or a more powerful red. Although many good Pinotage wines sell for $12 to $16, the best Pinotages cost more. Kanonkop Estate, a specialist in this variety, makes a $30 Pinotage. Simonsig Estate makes a fine Pinotage for $13 to $14.

While Pinotage is a pleasant wine, certainly worth trying, we believe South Africa's future is with Cabernet Sauvignon, Merlot, and Shiraz (and blends of these grapes) for its red wines and Sauvignon Blanc and Chardonnay for its whites.

Chapter 13

America, America

*W*hen the *conquistadors* came to the New World of America in search of gold, Spanish missionaries accompanied them and planted the first wine grapevines in what is now southern California. These "Mission" grapes, as they were called, still exist, but the noble grape varieties — Cabernet Sauvignon, Chardonnay, and the rest of the gang — have supplanted them to produce today's fine wines. One thing that hasn't changed is that California is still the focus of the American wine scene, although most of the wine business has moved north; southern California is now mainly filled with cars and people!

In this chapter, we cover American wines, paying particular attention to California's special wine regions, Napa Valley and Sonoma, but also discussing California's other wine regions, along with Oregon, Washington, and New York. We end with a quick look at Canada's up-and-coming wines.

The New World of American Wine

Even though the United States produced wine commercially in the nineteenth century, the U.S. wine industry made it big only beginning in the 1970s. Prohibition from 1920 to 1933, the Great Depression, and WWII were serious blows to the wine business — and recovery was slow.

Before 1970, only a few dozen operating wineries existed in California; today, the state has well over 800 bonded wineries (about a dozen or so "giants," but mainly small, family-owned operations).

California's growth has stimulated interest in wine all across the country. Today, wineries exist in all the 50 United States. But wine production is an important industry in only four states: California (the largest wine producing state, by far), Washington, Oregon, and New York. The United States currently is fourth in world wine production — although well behind the two leaders, Italy and France. (Spain is a distant third.)

Homegrown ways

The wines of the United States — especially California — are the essence of New World wine-think. Winemakers operate freely, planting whatever grape variety they wish, wherever they wish to plant it. They blend wines from different regions together as they wish. (Blending among states is trickier, because of federal rules.)

U.S. wines have elevated grape varieties to star status. Until California began naming wines after grapes, Chardonnay, Merlot, Pinot Noir, and Cabernet Sauvignon were just behind-the-scenes ingredients of wine — but now they *are* the wine. Lest anyone think that all wines from a particular grape are the same, however, winemakers have emerged as celebrities who put their personal spin on the best wines. In the California scenario especially, the land — the terroir — has been secondary, at least until recently.

American winemakers have embraced technology in their efforts to create wines that taste like fruit. California's two important universities for winemaking — California State University at Fresno and, especially, the University of California at Davis — have become world leaders in the scientific study of wine. Even European winemakers now make pilgrimages to California to study at U.C. Davis.

Playing by their own rules

An appellation system for wines does exist in the United States, and like the classic French model, the country defines various vineyard regions. But the U.S. system of American Viticultural Areas (AVAs) establishes only the geographical boundaries of wine zones; it doesn't stipulate which grape varieties can be planted, the maximum yield of grapes per acre (see Chapter 5), or anything else that would link the geography to a particular style of wine. AVA names, the names of the regions of production, therefore logically have secondary importance on wine labels after the name of the grape.

A smorgasbord of AVAs

In naming their wines, winemakers often choose to use a broader AVA designation rather than a smaller, more specific one, in order to widen their options in buying grapes and wine. A winery in Alexander Valley, within Sonoma County, for example, may use the broader *Sonoma County* AVA instead of Alexander Valley if it buys grapes from (or owns vineyards in) other areas of the county and wishes to use those grapes in its wine. It can use the larger *North Coast* AVA if it blends in grapes or wine from neighboring counties, like Napa. And if low price is a goal, the winery will use the even broader *California* AVA in order to buy cheaper grapes from the industrially-farmed vineyards of the Central Valley (the San Joaquin Valley) or other parts of the state where grapes and wine are less expensive than in Sonoma County.

Sometimes wineries use the *California* appellation even for their better wines, to give themselves complete freedom in sourcing their grapes. (This practice doesn't occur in smaller viticultural areas, such as southern Pennsylvania, where there are few alternative sources of grapes.) While specificity of place is admired, on the one hand, making a good wine at a good price through geographical blending is also admired. The relative merits depend on who's doing the admiring.

Traditional or not, America's way of making and naming wine sits just right with its local wine drinkers: American wines now account for about 70 percent of all wine sales in the United States.

Wines labeled with the name of a grape variety in the United States must contain at least 75 percent of that grape variety, according to federal law. Wines with an AVA indication must be made least 85 percent from grapes from that viticultural area. Wines with vintage years must derive at least 85 percent from the named vintage.

California, USA

When most wine drinkers think about American wine, they think of California. That's not surprising — the wines of California make up about 88 percent of U.S. wine production.

California's Gallo winery is the largest winery in the state — in fact, until recently, it was the largest wine company in the world — producing one out of every four bottles of wine sold in the United States. (Recently, a large New York-based corporation, Constellation Brands, became the world's largest wine company through a series of acquisitions.)

Signifying nothing

The words *reserve, special selection, private reserve, barrel select, vintners reserve, classic,* and so on have no legal definition in the United States. Although many premium wineries use these terms to indicate their special or better wines, most of the larger wineries use the same terms on their inexpensive bottlings as marketing tools (see Chapter 4).

It was the Robert Mondavi Winery, however, that stimulated fine wine production in the United States. Robert Mondavi left his family's winery (Charles Krug Winery) to start his own operation in 1966, a winery dedicated to making premium wines. These finer wines — his own, and those of the many producers who would follow in his steps — would be varietally named Cabernet Sauvignon, Chardonnay, and so on. Identifying the wines by their grape varieties was a reaction against the low-priced jug wines that were then popular, wines labeled with names borrowed from Europe's wine regions, such as Burgundy and Chablis. Today, even Gallo is very much in the varietal wine business. And Robert Mondavi Winery is part of the huge Constellation Wines Corporation.

Where California wines grow

In sunny California, there's no lack of warm climate for growing grapes. For fine wine production, the challenge is to find areas cool enough, with poor enough soil, so that grapes don't ripen too quickly, too easily, without full flavor development (see "Vine-growing vernacular" in Chapter 5). Nearness to the Pacific Coast and higher altitudes both assure cooler climates more so than latitude does. Fine wines therefore come from vineyards up and down almost the whole length of the state.

The most important fine wine areas and districts include the following (see Figure 13-1):

✔ **North Coast:**

> Napa Valley
> Sonoma County
> Mendocino and Lake Counties

✔ **North-Central Coast:**
   Livermore and Santa Clara Valleys (San Francisco Bay area)
   Santa Cruz Mountains
   Monterey County

✔ **Sierra Foothills**

✔ **South-Central Coast:**
   San Luis Obispo County
   Santa Barbara County

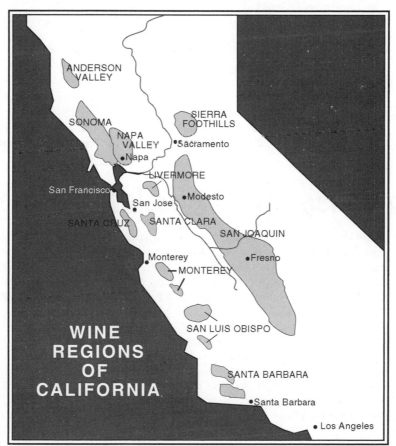

Figure 13-1:
The wine
regions of
California.

© Akira Chiwaki

Red wines finally catching up with Chardonnay

Chardonnay has been the perennial sales leader among varietal wines in the United States for the past 20 years or so. But Americans are drinking more red wine these days, and red wines are finally catching up to the big C. In addition to the usual suspects — Cabernet Sauvignon (still the leading seller), Cabernet blends, and Merlot — Pinot Noir, red Zinfandel and Shiraz (or Syrah, depending on the winery's inclination for naming) are growing in popularity.

When the wines are good

Weather variations from year to year are far less dramatic in California than they are in most European wine regions. One major reason is that rain doesn't fall during the growing season in much of California. (Rain at the wrong time is the usual cause of Europe's poorer vintages.) Using irrigation, winemakers, in effect, control the water to the vines. Ironically, one factor that can cause vintage variation in California is lack of water for irrigation due to drought.

Napa Valley: As Tiny as It Is Famous

Napa Valley is about a 90-minute drive northeast of the beautiful bay city of San Francisco. Many of California's most prestigious wineries — and certainly its most expensive vineyard land — are in the small Napa Valley, where about 240 wineries have managed to find space. (In 1960, Napa Valley had only 25 wineries.) The region's size is actually much tinier than its reputation: Napa produces less than five percent of California's wine grapes.

The southern part of the Valley, especially the Carneros district, is the coolest area, thanks to ocean breezes and mists from the San Pablo Bay. Carneros — which extends westward into Sonoma County — has become the vineyard area of choice for grape varieties that enjoy the cool climate: Chardonnay, Pinot Noir, Merlot, and grapes for sparkling wines. North towards Calistoga — away from the bay influence — the climate gets quite hot (but always with cool nights).

Wineries and vineyards occupy almost every part of Napa Valley. Many vineyards are on the valley floor, some are in the hills and mountains to the west (the Mayacamas Mountains), and some are in the mountains to the east (especially Howell Mountain). Napa winemakers and grape growers have established 14 AVAs besides the broad Napa Valley AVA itself and the even broader (six-county) North Coast AVA:

- Spring Mountain, Diamond Mountain and Mt. Veeder (all in the western mountains)

- Howell Mountain, Stags Leap District, Atlas Peak (all hilly or mountainous areas in eastern Napa Valley)

- Chiles Valley (in the easternmost part of Napa Valley)

- Oak Knoll District, Yountville, Oakville, Rutherford, and St. Helena (from south to north on the valley floor; Calistoga, a fifteenth AVA, is pending)

- Wild Horse Valley (in southeastern Napa Valley)

- Los Carneros (part in Napa Valley, part in Sonoma)

The grapes of Napa

Almost everyone in Napa who makes table wine makes a Cabernet Sauvignon and a Chardonnay, and many Napa producers now also make Merlot.

The six most important wines in Napa are the two whites, Chardonnay and Sauvignon Blanc (often labeled Fumé Blanc), and the four red wines, Cabernet Sauvignon, Merlot, Pinot Noir (mainly from cool Carneros), and Zinfandel. But blended wines have become increasingly important in the last 15 years. If red, these blends are usually made from red Bordeaux varieties (Cabernet Sauvignon, Cabernet Franc, Merlot, and sometimes even Malbec and Petit Verdot). If white, they're usually made from the white Bordeaux grapes (Sauvignon Blanc and Sémillon). Some of these blends are referred to as Meritage wines — not just in Napa but across the United States — although few carry the word *Meritage* on their labels.

Who's who in Napa (and for what)

If just about every winery in Napa makes a Chardonnay and a Cabernet Sauvignon, how can you distinguish the wineries from one another? Good question — with no easy answer. The following alphabetical list indicates some of the better wine producers in Napa Valley, as well as their best wines, and can help steer you in the right direction. We know the list looks overwhelming, but . . . that's Napa!

Our list includes Napa classics as well as some personal favorites. We cover sparkling wine producers in Chapter 14.

From $6 to $100-plus

You can find Chardonnays, Cabernets, Pinot Noirs, and Merlots from California at prices as low as $6 a bottle. Better wines can be quite expensive, however. Most mid-range varietal wines are in the $25 to $60 range. Reserves, single-vineyard wines, and special selection wines generally cost $50 to $100 and up.

Sauvignon Blancs — somewhat less in demand than Chardonnay, Cabernet, Pinot Noir, and Merlot — are the best values among California's premium wines. You can find many good ones for around $18, although a few are priced as high as $40. Red Zinfandels are also still a bargain, but their prices are climbing as they become more popular. You can still find many red Zins from $12 to $20, although a few premium Zinfandels are well over $20. If you like White Zinfandels, which are distinctly sweeter than the reds, you can save yourself a bundle; they're in the $5 to $8 range.

Although all the wineries in the following list are situated in Napa Valley, their wines are not necessarily always made with Napa-grown grapes; the geographic name on the label tells you where the grapes came from.

- **Acacia Winery:** Pinot Noir, Chardonnay
- **Anderson's Conn Valley:** Cabernet Sauvignon, Chardonnay
- **Araujo Estate:** Cabernet Sauvignon (Eisele Vineyard), Syrah
- **Beaulieu Vineyard:** Cabernet Sauvignon Private Reserve (Georges de Latour), Cabernet Sauvignon (Rutherford)
- **Beringer Vineyards:** Cabernet Sauvignon (single-vineyard wines), Chardonnay Private Reserve, Merlot (Bancroft Ranch)
- **Bryant Family Vineyard:** Cabernet Sauvignon (small winery; scarce)
- **Burgess Cellars:** Zinfandel, Cabernet Sauvignon
- **Cain Cellars:** Cain Five (five Bordeaux varieties), Cain Cuvée
- **Cakebread Cellars:** Cabernet Sauvignon, Sauvignon Blanc, Chardonnay
- **Caymus Vineyard:** Cabernet Sauvignon (especially *Special Selection*)
- **Chappellet:** Chenin Blanc, Cabernet Sauvignon
- **Charles Krug:** Cabernet Sauvignon, Chardonnay (Family Reserves)
- **Chateau Montelena:** Cabernet Sauvignon, Calistoga Cuvée Red, Chardonnay

- **Clos du Val:** Cabernet Sauvignon, Sémillon, Chardonnay

- **Corison:** Cabernet Sauvignon

- **Cuvaison:** Chardonnay, Cabernet Sauvignon

- **Dalla Valle:** Cabernet Sauvignon, Maya (blend of Cabernet Franc/ Cabernet Sauvignon)

- **Diamond Creek:** Cabernet Sauvignon

- **Dominus Estate:** Dominus (mainly Cabernet Sauvignon), Napanook

- **Duckhorn:** Merlot, Cabernet Sauvignon, Sauvignon Blanc

- **Dunn Vineyards:** Cabernet Sauvignon (especially Howell Mountain)

- **Far Niente:** Cabernet Sauvignon, Chardonnay

- **Fife Vineyards:** Zinfandel, Cabernet Sauvignon, Petite Sirah

- **Flora Springs:** Trilogy (blend of Cabernet Sauvignon, Merlot, Cabernet Franc), Cabernet Sauvignon Reserve, Soliloquy (Sauvignon Blanc)

- **Forman Vineyard:** Chardonnay, Cabernet Sauvignon

- **Franciscan Estate:** Chardonnay, Magnificat Red, Cabernet Sauvignon

- **Franus Winery:** Zinfandel, Cabernet Sauvignon

- **Freemark Abbey:** Cabernet Sauvignon (Bosché and Sycamore Vineyards)

- **Frog's Leap Winery:** Cabernet Sauvignon, Zinfandel, Sauvignon Blanc

- **Grace Family Vineyards:** Cabernet Sauvignon (small production; mailing list only)

- **Grgich Hills Cellar:** Chardonnay, Cabernet Sauvignon, Zinfandel, Fumé Blanc

- **Groth Vineyards:** Cabernet Sauvignon (especially Reserve)

- **Harlan Estate:** Cabernet Sauvignon (small winery; very scarce)

- **Heitz Wine Cellars:** Cabernet Sauvignon (Martha's Vineyard)

- **Hendry Ranch:** Zinfandel (all single-vineyard wines)

- **Hess Collection Winery:** Cabernet Sauvignon, Chardonnay

- **Lang & Reed:** Cabernet Franc

- **Long Vineyards:** Chardonnay, Riesling, Pinot Grigio

- **Markham Vineyards:** Chardonnay, Merlot, Cabernet Sauvignon

- ✔ **Mayacamas Vineyards:** Cabernet Sauvignon, Sauvignon Blanc

- ✔ **Mount Veeder Winery:** Cabernet Sauvignon, Reserve Red

- ✔ **Newton Vineyard:** Chardonnay, Merlot, Cabernet Sauvignon

- ✔ **Nickel & Nickel:** Cabernet Sauvignon (all single-vineyard wines)

- ✔ **Opus One:** Opus One (mainly Cabernet Sauvignon)

- ✔ **Pahlmeyer Winery:** Red (Cabernet blend), Merlot, Chardonnay

- ✔ **Patz & Hall:** Chardonnay

- ✔ **Joseph Phelps Vineyards:** Insignia (Cabernet blend), Cabernet Sauvignon

- ✔ **Pine Ridge Winery:** Cabernet Sauvignon, Chardonnay

- ✔ **Quintessa Estate:** Quintessa (Bordeaux blend)

- ✔ **Robert Mondavi:** Cabernet Sauvignon Reserve, Pinot Noir Reserve

- ✔ **Rubicon Estate** (formerly Niebaum-Coppola)**:** Rubicon (mainly Cabernet Sauvignon), Edizone Pennino Zinfandel

- ✔ **Rudd Estate:** Chardonnay, Sauvignon Blanc, Cabernet Sauvignon

- ✔ **Saddleback Cellars:** Cabernet Sauvignon

- ✔ **Saintsbury:** Pinot Noir (all), Chardonnay

- ✔ **Selene:** Merlot, Sauvignon Blanc

- ✔ **Shafer Vineyards:** Cabernet Sauvignon, Merlot

- ✔ **Silver Oak Cellars:** Cabernet Sauvignon

- ✔ **Silverado Vineyards:** Cabernet Sauvignon, Chardonnay (Carneros)

- ✔ **Smith-Madrone:** Riesling, Chardonnay, Cabernet Sauvignon

- ✔ **Spottswoode Winery:** Cabernet Sauvignon, Sauvignon Blanc

- ✔ **Staglin Family Vineyard:** Cabernet Sauvignon

- ✔ **Stag's Leap Wine Cellars:** Cask 23 (Cabernet blend), Cabernet Sauvignon (Fay Vineyard and SLV), Chardonnay

- ✔ **Stony Hill Vineyard:** Chardonnay, Riesling

- ✔ **Storybook Mountain:** Zinfandel

- ✔ **Swanson Vineyards:** Cabernet Sauvignon, Merlot, Syrah

- ✔ **Trefethen Vineyards:** Cabernet Sauvignon, Chardonnay, Riesling (dry)

- ✔ **Turley Wine Cellars:** Zinfandel (all single-vineyard Zinfandels)

- ✔ **Turnbull Cellars:** Cabernet Sauvignon, Turnbull Red "Black Label"

- ✔ **Viader Vineyards:** Viader Red (Cabernet Sauvignon/Cabernet Franc)

- ✔ **ZD Wines:** Cabernet Sauvignon, Chardonnay

Down-to-Earth in Sonoma

If you leave San Francisco over the beautiful Golden Gate Bridge, you'll be in Sonoma in an hour. The differences between Napa and Sonoma are remarkable. Many of Napa's wineries are showy (even downright luxurious), but most of Sonoma's are rustic, country-like, and laid-back. The millionaires bought into Napa; Sonoma is just folks (with some exceptions, of course).

On the other hand, the famously successful Gallo is also in Sonoma, and so are Sebastiani, Glen Ellen, Korbel, Kendall-Jackson, Simi, and Jordan wineries — not exactly small time operations! We have the sneaking impression that if we visit Sonoma in ten years, it will bear a striking resemblance to Napa. But we hope not; we like it just the way it is.

Sonoma's AVAs

Sonoma is more than twice as large as Napa, it's more spread out, and it has almost as many wineries — more than 200. Its climate is similar to Napa's, except that some areas near the coast are definitely cooler. Although there's plenty of Chardonnay, Cabernet Sauvignon, and Merlot in Sonoma, the region's varied microclimates and terrain have allowed three other varieties — Pinot Noir, Zinfandel, and Sauvignon Blanc — to excel.

The following are the viticultural areas (AVAs) of Sonoma County listed roughly from south to north with their principal grape varieties and wines:

- **Los Carneros** (part in Napa Valley): Pinot Noir, Chardonnay, sparkling wine, and Merlot
- **Sonoma Valley:** Chardonnay (to a lesser extent, Pinot Noir, Cabernet Sauvignon, Zinfandel)
- **Sonoma Mountain:** Cabernet Sauvignon
- **Bennett Valley:** Chardonnay, Sauvignon Blanc, Merlot
- **Russian River Valley:** Pinot Noir, Chardonnay, sparkling wine, Zinfandel
- **Sonoma-Green Valley** (within Russian River Valley): Sparkling wine, Chardonnay, Pinot Noir
- **Chalk Hill** (within Russian River Valley): Chardonnay, Sauvignon Blanc
- **Dry Creek Valley:** Zinfandel, Cabernet Sauvignon
- **Alexander Valley:** Cabernet Sauvignon, Chardonnay, Sauvignon Blanc
- **Knight's Valley:** Cabernet Sauvignon, Sauvignon Blanc
- **Rockpile** (a new AVA, in the northwestern part of the county): Zinfandel, Cabernet Sauvignon, Syrah, Petite Sirah

Sonoma County has two more AVAs: Northern Sonoma, a patchwork area encompassing Russian River Valley, Alexander Valley, Dry Creek Valley, and Knight's Valley; and Sonoma Coast, a hodgepodge of land in western Sonoma, along the coast. Also, the North Coast AVA takes in Sonoma County.

Pinot Noir lovers should look for wines from Russian River Valley producers, such as Williams & Selyem, Rochioli, Gary Farrell, Lynmar, and Dehlinger. We agree with those who say that the Russian River Valley is the source of some of the best Pinot Noir in the entire New World.

Sonoma producers and wines

The following list of recommended producers includes some of Sonoma's better wineries, listed alphabetically, along with their best wines. It's *slightly* less staggering than the Napa list.

Although these wineries are all in Sonoma County, some of their wines are made from grapes grown elsewhere. Cline Cellars, for example, uses grapes from Contra Costa County, east of San Francisco. Check the labels to find out.

- **Arrowood Vineyards:** Chardonnay, Cabernet Sauvignon, Syrah
- **B.R. Cohn:** Cabernet Sauvignon (Olive Hill Vineyard)
- **Benziger Family Winery:** Cabernet Sauvignon, Sauvignon Blanc
- **Chalk Hill Estate:** Sauvignon Blanc, Chardonnay, Cabernet Sauvignon
- **Chateau Souverain:** Cabernet Sauvignon, Sauvignon Blanc
- **Chateau St. Jean:** Chardonnay (Robert Young, Belle Terre Vineyards), Cabernet Sauvignon (Cinq Cépages)
- **Cline Cellars:** Mourvèdre, Zinfandel
- **Clos du Bois:** Marlstone (Cabernet blend), Chardonnay
- **Dehlinger Winery:** Pinot Noir, Chardonnay, Syrah
- **Dry Creek Vineyard:** Fumé Blanc, Chenin Blanc, Zinfandel
- **Ferrari-Carano:** Chardonnay, Fumé Blanc, Cabernet Sauvignon
- **Fisher Vineyards:** Chardonnay, Cabernet Sauvignon
- **Flowers Vineyard & Winery:** Pinot Noir, Chardonnay
- **Foppiano Vineyards:** Petite Sirah, Cabernet Sauvignon, Merlot
- **Gallo Family Vineyards:** Chardonnay (Laguna Ranch), Zinfandel (Frei Ranch)
- **Gary Farrell Wines:** Pinot Noir, Chardonnay, Zinfandel
- **Geyser Peak Winery:** Chardonnay, Cabernet Sauvignon

- **Hanna Winery:** Sauvignon Blanc, Zinfandel, Cabernet Sauvignon
- **Hanzell Vineyards:** Chardonnay
- **Hartford Court:** Pinot Noir (all), Zinfandel
- **Jordan Vineyard:** Cabernet Sauvignon, Chardonnay
- **Kendall-Jackson:** Cabernet Sauvignon, Chardonnay, Zinfandel
- **Kenwood Vineyards:** Cabernet Sauvignon (Artist Series), Zinfandel
- **Kistler Vineyards:** Chardonnay, Pinot Noir
- **Joseph Swan Vineyards:** Pinot Noir, Zinfandel
- **La Crema Winery:** Chardonnay, Pinot Noir
- **Laurel Glen Vineyard:** Cabernet Sauvignon, Reds, Terra Rosa
- **Lynmar Winery:** Pinot Noir, Chardonnay
- **Marcassin:** Chardonnay (all vineyards; very scarce, by mailing list)
- **Marietta Cellars:** Petite Sirah, Zinfandel, Old Vine Red (Zin blend)
- **Marimar Torres Estate:** Chardonnay, Pinot Noir
- **Martin Ray Winery:** Cabernet Sauvignon, Merlot, Chardonnay
- **Martinelli Vineyard:** Zinfandel, Chardonnay (Russian River Valley)
- **Matanzas Creek Winery:** Chardonnay, Sauvignon Blanc, Merlot
- **Paul Hobbs:** Cabernet Sauvignon, Chardonnay, Pinot Noir
- **Peter Michael Winery:** Chardonnay, Les Pavots (Cabernet blend)
- **Preston of Dry Creek:** Zinfandel, Syrah, Barbera
- **Quivira Vineyards:** Zinfandel, Syrah, Petite Sirah
- **A. Rafanelli Winery:** Zinfandel, Cabernet Sauvignon (mailing list)
- **Ravenswood:** Zinfandel (single-vineyards), Merlot (Sangiacomo Vineyard), Pickberry (Cabernet Sauvignon/Merlot blend)
- **J. Rochioli Vineyard:** Pinot Noir (all), Sauvignon Blanc, Zinfandel
- **Saint Francis Winery:** Zinfandel, Merlot, Cabernet Sauvignon
- **Sausal Winery:** Zinfandel (all), Sangiovese
- **Sebastiani Vineyards:** Cabernet Sauvignon, Merlot, Chardonnay
- **Seghesio Family Estates:** Zinfandel (all), Sangiovese, Barbera
- **Sonoma-Cutrer Vineyards:** Chardonnay (all selections)
- **Stonestreet:** Cabernet Sauvignon (all), Chardonnay, Sauvignon Blanc
- **Trentadue Winery:** Petite Sirah, Old Patch Red
- **Williams Selyem Winery:** Pinot Noir (all), Zinfandel, Chardonnay (all wines very scarce; sold by mailing list)

Mendocino and Lake Counties

Lake County, dominated by Clear Lake, is Napa's neighbor to the north, and Mendocino County is directly north of Sonoma.

If you have the chance, it's worth your while to drive up the beautiful California coastline from San Francisco on Route 1 to the quaint, old town of Mendocino — perhaps with a side trip to view the magnificent, giant redwoods of the Pacific Coast. Tourists are scarcer up here than in Napa or Sonoma, and that makes it all the nicer: You'll be genuinely welcomed at the wineries.

The cool Anderson Valley in Mendocino County is ideal for growing Chardonnay, Pinot Noir, Gewürztraminer, and Riesling, and for the production of sparkling wine. The wily Louis Roederer Champagne house bypassed Napa and Sonoma to start its sparkling wine operation here and has done extremely well in a short time — as have Scharffenberger and Handley, two other successful sparkling wine producers in Anderson Valley (see Chapter 14 for more sparkling wine producers).

The following list includes recommended producers and their best wines. We list the producers alphabetically, by county.

Mendocino County

- **Edmeades:** Zinfandel (especially single-vineyards)
- **Fetzer Vineyards:** Pinot Noir Reserve, Cabernet Sauvignon Reserve
- **Greenwood Ridge Vineyards:** Riesling, Pinot Noir, Zinfandel
- **Handley Cellars:** Chardonnay, Gewürztraminer, Sauvignon Blanc
- **Lazy Creek Vineyards:** Gewürztraminer, Riesling
- **Lolonis Winery:** Cabernet Sauvignon (all), Zinfandel
- **McDowell Valley Vineyards:** Syrah, Viognier
- **Navarro Vineyards:** Gewürztraminer, Chardonnay (Reserve)

Lake County

- **Guenoc Winery:** Cabernet Sauvignon, Chardonnay, Langtry Meritage Red (Cabernet blend), Petite Sirah Reserve
- **Steele Wines:** Chardonnay, Zinfandel, Pinot Noir, Pinot Blanc
- **Wildhurst Vineyards:** Cabernet Sauvignon, Chardonnay, Merlot

San Francisco Bay Area

The San Francisco Bay area includes wine regions north, east, and south of the city: Marin County to the north; Alameda County and Livermore Valley to the east; and Santa Clara Valley and San Mateo County to the south.

The urban spread east and south of San Francisco, from the cities of Palo Alto to San Jose (Silicon Valley) and eastward, has taken its toll on vineyards in the Livermore and Santa Clara Valleys. These two growing regions, both cooled by breezes from the San Francisco Bay, are now relatively small.

In Livermore, directly east of San Francisco, Sauvignon Blanc and Sémillon have always done well. In Santa Clara Valley, south of San Francisco with the Santa Cruz Mountains on its western side, Chardonnay, Cabernet Sauvignon, and Merlot are the three big grape varieties (and wines).

We list our recommended wineries alphabetically, by locality.

Marin County

- ✔ **Kalin Cellars:** Sauvignon Blanc, Sémillon, Chardonnay, Pinot Noir; grapes from diverse areas, including Livermore
- ✔ **Sean H. Thackrey:** Orion Old Vines Red (Syrah blend), Sirius (Petite Sirah); grapes come from several different areas, including Napa

Alameda County

- ✔ **Edmunds St. John:** Syrah, Rocks and Gravel (Rhône blend); grapes are sourced from throughout the state
- ✔ **Rosenblum Cellars:** Zinfandel (especially single-vineyards); uses mainly Sonoma Valley and Napa Valley fruit

Livermore Valley

- ✔ **Concannon Vineyard:** Chardonnay, Petite Sirah
- ✔ **Murrietta's Well:** Zinfandel, Red Meritage (Cabernet blend)
- ✔ **Wente Family Estates:** Chardonnay, Sauvignon Blanc

Santa Clara Valley (other than Santa Cruz Mountains)

- ✔ **J. Lohr Winery:** Chardonnay, Cabernet Sauvignon (Paso Robles)

San Mateo County

- ✔ **Cronin Vineyards:** Chardonnay (all selections)
- ✔ **Thomas Fogarty Winery:** Gewürztraminer, Chardonnay, Pinot Noir

Santa Cruz Mountains

Standing atop one of the isolated Santa Cruz Mountains, you can quickly forget that you're only an hour's drive south of San Francisco. The rugged, wild beauty of this area has attracted quite a few winemakers, including some of the best in the state. (Paul Draper of Ridge Vineyards and Randall Grahm of Bonny Doon are but two.) The climate is cool on the ocean side, where Pinot Noir thrives. On the San Francisco Bay side, Cabernet Sauvignon is the important red variety. Chardonnay is a leading variety on both sides.

We list our recommended Santa Cruz Mountains wine producers alphabetically, along with their best wines:

- **Bargetto:** Chardonnay, Cabernet Sauvignon, Merlot
- **Bonny Doon Vineyard:** Le Cigare Volant Red (Rhône blend), Old Telegram (Mourvèdre)
- **David Bruce Winery:** Pinot Noir (Santa Cruz), Zinfandel (Paso Robles)
- **Cinnabar Vineyards:** Chardonnay, Cabernet Sauvignon
- **Kathryn Kennedy Winery:** Cabernet Sauvignon, Syrah
- **Mount Eden Vineyards:** Chardonnay Estate, Cabernet Sauvignon Estate, Pinot Noir Estate
- **Ridge Vineyards:** Cabernet Sauvignon Monte Bello, Geyserville (Zin blend), Zinfandel (all)
- **Santa Cruz Mountain Vineyard:** Pinot Noir, Cabernet Sauvignon

What's New in Old Monterey

Monterey County has a little bit of everything — a beautiful coastline, the chic town of Carmel, some very cool (as in temperature, not chicness) vineyard districts and some very warm areas, mountain wineries and Salinas Valley wineries, a few gigantic wine firms and lots of small ones. Like most California wine regions, Monterey has been changing rapidly during the past two decades, and now seven official viticultural areas (AVAs) exist here, covering about 75 wineries:

- Arroyo Seco
- Carmel Valley
- Chalone
- Hames Valley
- Monterey

✔ San Luca

✔ Santa Lucia Highlands

Santa Lucia Highlands, in particular, has been garnering attention as the "hot" new region for California Pinot Noir.

Chardonnay is the leading varietal wine in Monterey County — as it is in most of the state. But the cooler parts of Monterey are also principal sources of Riesling and Gewürztraminer. Cabernet Sauvignon, and Pinot Noir are the leading red varieties in the mountain areas.

The following are our recommended producers in Monterey County, listed alphabetically, along with one producer from neighboring San Benito County:

✔ **Bernardus Winery:** Chardonnay, Sauvignon Blanc, Marinus (mainly Cabernet Sauvignon), Pinot Noir

✔ **Calera** (San Benito County): Pinot Noir (especially single-vineyard selections), Viognier, Chardonnay

✔ **Chalone Vineyard:** Chardonnay, Pinot Blanc, Pinot Noir

✔ **Chateau Julien:** Chardonnay, Merlot, Cabernet Sauvignon

✔ **Estancia Estates:** Chardonnay, Cabernet Sauvignon, Merlot, Pinot Noir

✔ **Morgan Winery:** Chardonnay, Pinot Noir, Pinot Gris, Syrah

✔ **Paraiso Vineyards:** Pinot Noir, Chardonnay, Riesling, Syrah

✔ **Robert Talbott Vineyards:** Chardonnay

Santa Lucia Highlands

The quest for the next great Pinot Noir region in the world is somewhat akin to the quest for the Holy Grail. The latest "hot" region, although it's definitely cool, is the Santa Lucia Highlands, a remote area perched high in the southwest part of Monterey County and sheltered from the Pacific Ocean by the majestic Santa Lucia Mountains. Most of the Santa Lucia Highlands area, which has vineyards up to 1,400 feet in altitude, lies above the morning fog line, and enjoys plenty of sunshine, with afternoon breezes coming from Monterey Bay. The relatively cool temperatures, low rainfall, well-drained granitic soils, and a long growing season combine to provide ideal conditions for Chardonnay and Pinot

Noir. But it's the Pinot Noir that excites wine lovers and critics — after all, good Chardonnay is not such a rarity. The Pinots generally have plenty of acidity and intensely flavored fruit character, including mineral notes. Most of the wineries in the region are smallish, so you have to search a while to find them, but if you're a Pinot Noir lover, you may not mind; half of the fun is in the quest. Some Santa Lucia Highlands wineries we recommend for Pinot Noir include Morgan Winery, Paraiso Vineyards, Pisoni Vineyard, Sea Smoke Winery, Siduri Wines, and Testarossa Vineyards. Some of the very best of these Pinot Noirs are sourced from Pisoni's vineyards, and are identified as such on the labels.

Thar's Wine in Them There Foothills

No wine region in America has a more romantic past than the Sierra Foothills. The Gold Rush of 1849 carved a place in history for the foothills of the Sierra Nevada Mountains. It also brought vineyards to the area to provide wine for the thirsty miners. One of the vines planted at that time was certainly Zinfandel — still the region's most famous wine. Many of the oldest grapevines in the United States, some over 100 years old — mainly Zinfandel — are here in the Sierra Foothills.

In fact, very little has changed in the Sierra Foothills over the years. This is clearly most rustic wine region on the West Coast — and perhaps in the country. Therein lies its charm. A visit to the Foothills is like a trip into the past, when life was simple.

The Sierra Foothills is a sprawling wine region east of Sacramento, centered in Amador and El Dorado Counties, but spreading north and south of both. Two of its best-known viticultural areas are Shenandoah Valley and Fiddletown. Summers can be hot, but many vineyards are situated as high as 1,500 feet — such as around Placerville in El Dorado — and evenings are very cool. Soil throughout the region is mainly volcanic in origin.

The following are our recommended producers in the Sierra Foothills (listed alphabetically), along with their best wines:

- **Amador Foothill Winery:** Zinfandel

- **Boeger Winery:** Zinfandel, Barbera, Sauvignon Blanc

- **Karly:** Zinfandel, Syrah, Sauvignon Blanc, Marsanne

- **Lava Cap Winery:** Barbera, Cabernet Sauvignon, Petite Sirah

- **Monteviña:** Zinfandel, Syrah

- **Renaissance Vineyard:** Cabernet Sauvignon, Riesling (Late Harvest) Sauvignon Blanc

- **Renwood Winery:** Barbera, Zinfandel (especially Grandpère Vineyard)

- **Shenandoah Vineyards:** Zinfandel, Sauvignon Blanc

- **Sierra Vista Winery:** Zinfandel, Syrah

- **Sobon Estate:** Zinfandel, Viognier

- **Stevenot Winery:** Syrah, Tempranillo, Zinfandel

Contrasts in San Luis Obispo

San Luis Obispo County is an area of vastly diverse viticultural areas. These include, for example, the warm, hilly Paso Robles region (north of the town of San Luis Obispo) where Zinfandel and Cabernet Sauvignon reign, and the cool, coastal Edna Valley and Arroyo Grande (south of the town), home of some very good Pinot Noirs and Chardonnays.

Paso Robles, with over 90 wineries, is in the heart of California's Central Coast, about equidistant from San Francisco and Los Angeles. Its wines are so different from those of the two coastal areas that we name the producers separately. We recommend the following producers in San Luis Obispo (listed alphabetically, along with their best wines):

Paso Robles

- **Adelaida Cellars:** Pinot Noir, Zinfandel, Cabernet Sauvignon
- **Eberle Winery:** Zinfandel, Cabernet Sauvignon, Viognier
- **EOS Estate Winery:** Zinfandel, Cabernet Sauvignon, Petite Sirah
- **Justin Vineyards:** Isosceles (Cabernet blend), Cabernet Sauvignon, Cabernet Franc, Chardonnay
- **Meridian Vineyards** (also has vineyards in Edna Valley and Santa Barbara)**:** Chardonnay (especially Reserve), Syrah
- **Peachy Canyon Winery:** Zinfandel
- **Rabbit Ridge Vineyards:** Zinfandel, Primitivo, Syrah, Pinot Grigio
- **Tablas Creek Vineyard:** Mourvèdre, Grenache, Syrah, Roussanne
- **Treana Winery:** Red (mainly Cabernet Sauvignon, Merlot, Syrah), White (mainly Marsanne and Viognier)
- **Wild Horse Winery:** Pinot Noir, Merlot, Cabernet Sauvignon

Edna Valley and Arroyo Grande

- **Alban Vineyards:** Viognier (Estate), Roussanne, Syrah, Grenache
- **Claiborne & Churchill:** Riesling, Pinot Gris, Pinot Noir
- **Edna Valley Vineyard:** Chardonnay, Pinot Noir, Cabernet Sauvignon
- **Laetitia Vineyard:** Chardonnay, Pinot Noir
- **Saucelito Canyon Vineyard:** Zinfandel
- **Talley Vineyards:** Chardonnay, Pinot Noir

Santa Barbara, Californian Paradise

The most exciting viticultural areas in California — if not in the entire country — are in Santa Barbara County. Even though Spanish missionaries planted vineyards there 200 years ago, it wasn't until 1975 that the first major winery (Firestone Vineyards) opened. In light of what we now know — that is, how well-suited Santa Barbara is to grape growing — 1975 was a late start.

The cool Santa Maria, Santa Ynez, and Los Alamos Valleys — which lie north of the city of Santa Barbara — run east to west, opening toward the Pacific Ocean and channeling in the ocean air. The cool climate is ideal for Pinot Noir and Chardonnay. In the Santa Maria Valley, one of the main sources of these varieties, the average temperature during the growing season is a mere 74°F. Farther south, in the Santa Ynez Valley, Riesling also does well.

Long before the film *Sideways* brought new attention and tourists to Santa Barbara wineries and restaurants, Pinot Noir had earned Santa Barbara much of its acclaim as a wine region. Santa Barbara is generally recognized as one of the six great American wine regions for this variety — the other five being Carneros, the Russian River Valley, Santa Lucia Highlands, Mendocino County's Anderson Valley and Oregon's Willamette Valley. In Santa Barbara, Pinot Noir wines seem to burst with luscious strawberry fruit, laced with herbal tones. These wines tend to be precocious; they're delicious in their first four or five years — not the "keepers" that the sturdier, wilder-tasting Russian River Pinot Noirs seem to be. But why keep them when they taste so good?

The following are some recommended producers in Santa Barbara (listed alphabetically), and their best wines:

- **Alma Rosa:** Chardonnay, Pinot Gris and Pinot Noir

- **Au Bon Climat:** Pinot Noir, Chardonnay (especially single-vineyard bottlings of both), Pinot Gris/Pinot Blanc

- **Babcock Vineyards:** Sauvignon Blanc, Chardonnay, Pinot Noir

- **The Brander Vineyard:** Sauvignon Blanc

- **Byron Vineyard:** Chardonnay (especially Nielson Vineyard), Pinot Noir

- **Cambria Winery:** Chardonnay, Pinot Noir (Julia's Vineyard), Syrah

- **Cottonwood Canyon:** Pinot Noir

- **Daniel Gehrs:** Chenin Blanc, Dry Riesling, Gewürztraminer, Syrah

- **Fess Parker Winery:** Chardonnay, Syrah, Pinot Noir

- **Fiddlehead Cellars:** Pinot Noir, Sauvignon Blanc

- ✔ **Firestone Vineyard:** Chardonnay, Sauvignon Blanc
- ✔ **Foley Estate:** Chardonnay, Pinot Noir
- ✔ **Foxen Vineyard:** Pinot Noir, Syrah, Viognier, Chenin Blanc
- ✔ **Gainey Vineyard:** Chardonnay, Pinot Noir, Sauvignon Blanc
- ✔ **Hitching Post**: Pinot Noir, Syrah
- ✔ **IO Wines:** IO (Rhône blend, Syrah/Grenache/Mourvèdre), Syrah
- ✔ **Lane Tanner:** Pinot Noir, Syrah
- ✔ **Lincourt Vineyards:** Pinot Noir, Syrah, Chardonnay
- ✔ **Longoria Wines:** Chardonnay, Pinot Noir, Cabernet Franc, Syrah
- ✔ **The Ojai Vineyard:** Pinot Noir, Syrah, Chardonnay
- ✔ **Qupé Cellars:** Syrah, Chardonnay, Roussanne, Marsanne, Viognier
- ✔ **Sanford Winery:** Pinot Noir (especially Sanford & Benedict Vineyard), Chardonnay, Sauvignon Blanc
- ✔ **Santa Barbara Winery:** Pinot Noir, Chardonnay, Syrah
- ✔ **Zaca Mesa Winery:** Syrah, Roussanne, Chardonnay

Elsewhere in California

One interesting winery in California's Central Valley, one in the Dunnigan Hills (north of the Central Valley), and one in southern California complete our portrait of recommended California wineries. Although these locations are normally too warm to grow grapes for fine wine, variables such as altitude — or, in the case of southern California, cool ocean breezes — create microclimates conducive to the production of fine wine.

Central Valley

- ✔ **Bogle Vineyards:** Petite Sirah, Sauvignon Blanc, Zinfandel, Merlot

Dunnigan Hills (Yolo County)

- ✔ **R. H. Phillips Vineyard:** Syrah, Sauvignon Blanc, Viognier, and Tempranillo (all under the "EXP" brand); Chardonnay Estate (Toasted Head)

Southern California (Bel Air, Los Angeles)

- ✔ **Moraga Vineyards:** Red (Cabernet Sauvignon, Merlot), White (Sauvignon Blanc)

Oregon, A Tale of Two Pinots

Because Oregon is north of California, most people assume that Oregon's wine regions are cool. And they're right. But the main reason for Oregon's cool climate is that no high mountains separate the vineyards from the Pacific Ocean. The ocean influence brings cool temperatures and rain. Grapegrowing and winemaking are really completely different in Oregon and California.

Winemaking is a fairly new industry in Oregon, but it's growing rapidly. From a handful of wineries in the early 1970s, the state had 314 wineries in 2005 — an increase of 140 wineries in the past four years! Most of Oregon's wineries are small, family-owned operations. The exception in terms of size is King Estate, Oregon's largest winery, but even King Estate is relatively small compared to some of the wine behemoths of California.

Oregon first gained respect in wine circles for its Pinot Noir, a grape that needs cool climates to perform at its best (see "A Primer on Red Grape Varieties" in Chapter 3). The Eyrie Vineyards released Oregon's first Pinot Noir in 1970, but national recognition for the state's Pinots came only after the excellent 1983 and 1985 vintages. Pinot Noir is still Oregon's flagship wine, and a vast majority of the state's wineries make this wine. Oregon's Pinot Noirs, with their characteristic black-fruit aromas and flavors, depth and complexity, have won accolades as among the very best Pinots in the United States.

Red wine encompasses 60 percent of Oregon's wine production today; the 40 percent of production that is white wine features mainly Pinot Gris, Chardonnay, and Riesling.

Oregon's other Pinot

Because Chardonnay is the companion grape to Pinot Noir in France's Burgundy region (see Chapter 9), and because Chardonnay wine is hugely popular in America, it's an important variety in Oregon. However, a second white grape variety has emerged to challenge Chardonnay's domination: Pinot Gris. A natural mutation of its ancestor, Pinot Noir, the Pinot Gris variety has grapes that are normally pale pink–yellowish in color when ripe.

David Lett, founder and winemaker of The Eyrie Vineyards and Oregon's Pinot Noir pioneer, is also the man who made Oregon's first Pinot Gris around 1970, followed by Ponzi Vineyards and Adelsheim Vineyards. Today, over 75 wineries in Oregon make Pinot Gris.

Two styles of Oregon Pinot Gris exist:

- A lighter, fruity style (for which the grapes are picked early) is always unoaked and can be consumed as soon as six to eight months after the autumn harvest.

- A medium-bodied, golden-colored wine from grapes left longer on the vine sometimes has a little oak aging and can age for five or six years or longer.

In general Oregon Pinot Gris is light- to medium-bodied, with aromas reminiscent of pears, apples, and sometimes of melon, and surprising depth for an inexpensive wine. It's an excellent food wine, even when it's slightly sweet; it works well especially with seafood and salmon, just the kind of food that it's paired with in Oregon. And the best news is the price. Most of Oregon's Pinot Gris wines are in the $12 to $18 range in retail stores.

Now, more and more California wineries are also making Pinot Gris — but in California, wineries are producing a lighter style, which they often call by the Italian name, Pinot Grigio, hoping to capitalize on the popularity of the Italian wine. Oregon's richer Pinot Gris wines resemble Alsace's flavorful Pinot Gris style. In the year 2000, Pinot Gris overtook Chardonnay as Oregon's number-one white variety planted, and it now also outsells Oregon Chardonnay.

Who's who in Willamette Valley

The main home of Pinot Noir and Pinot Gris in Oregon is the Willamette (*will AM ett*) Valley, directly south of the city of Portland in northwest Oregon. The cool Willamette Valley has established itself in the last 30 years as the most important wine region in Oregon; in fact, over 200 wineries, about two-thirds of the state's wineries, are situated there.

Willamette Valley is a convenient wine destination to visit because the vibrant city of Portland, with all its fine restaurants, hotels, and shops, is 30 minutes north of this wine region.

Willamette Valley is huge and encompasses several counties. Yamhill County, directly southwest of Portland, has the greatest concentration of wineries, all of which produce Pinot Noir. But quite a few wineries are located in Washington County, west of Portland, and in Polk County, south of Yamhill. Six AVAs now exist in the Willamette Valley: Chehalem Mountain, Dundee Hills, Yamhill-Carlton District, Ribbon Ridge, McMinnville Foothills, and Eola Hills.

Here are some of the better producers in the Willamette Valley, primarily for Pinot Noir and Pinot Gris (but sometimes also Chardonnay or Riesling), listed alphabetically:

Adelsheim Vineyard

Amity Vineyards

Anne Amie

Archery Summit

Argyle Winery

Beaux Frères

Benton Lane Winery

Bethel Heights Vineyard

Brick House Vineyards

Broadley Vineyards

Cameron Winery

Chehalem

Cooper Mountain Vineyards

Cristom Vineyards

Domaine Drouhin Oregon

Domaine Serene

Duck Pond Cellars

Edgefield Winery

Elk Cove Vineyards

Eola Hills Wine Cellars

Erath Vineyards

Evesham Wood Winery

The Eyrie Vineyards

Firesteed Winery

Hamacher Wines

Hinman Vineyards/Silvan Ridge

Ken Wright Cellars

King Estate Winery

Kramer Vineyards

Lange Winery

Montinore Vineyards

Oak Knoll Winery

Panther Creek Cellars

Patricia Green Cellars

Penner-Ash Wine Cellars

Ponzi Vineyards

Redhawk Vineyard

Rex Hill Vineyards

St. Innocent Winery

Shafer Vineyard

Sokol Blosser Winery

Stangeland Vineyards

Torii Mor Winery

Tualatin Vineyards

Van Duzer Vineyards

Willakenzie Estates

Willamette Valley Vineyards

Witness Tree Vineyard

Yamhill Valley Vineyards

Two other Oregon wine regions

Two other wine regions of note in Oregon are both in the southwest part of the state: the Umpqua Valley (around the town of Roseburg) and farther south, next to California's northern border, the Rogue River Valley.

Considerably warmer than Willamette, the Umpqua Valley is the site of Oregon's first winery, Hillcrest Vineyard, founded in 1962. The main grape varieties in Umpqua are Pinot Noir, Chardonnay, Riesling, and Cabernet Sauvignon. Major wineries are Henry Estate and Girardet Wine Cellars, known for their Pinot Noir and Chardonnay.

The Rogue River Valley is warmer still; therefore, Cabernet Sauvignon and Merlot often perform better than Pinot Noir there. Chardonnay is the leading white wine, but Pinot Gris is becoming popular. Bridgeview Vineyards, the region's largest winery, is doing an admirable job with Pinot Gris as well as Pinot Noir. Four other vineyards to watch are Ashland Vineyards, Valley View Winery, Sarah Powell Wines, and Foris Vineyards — the latter a specialist in Merlot and Cabernet Sauvignon.

Wine on the Desert: Washington State

Although Washington and Oregon are neighboring states, their wine regions have vastly different climates due to the location of the vineyards relative to the Cascade Mountains, which cut through both states from north to south.

On Washington's western, or coastal, side, the climate is maritime — cool, plenty of rain, and a lot of vegetation. (In Oregon, almost all the vineyards are located on the coastal side.) East of the mountains, Washington's climate is continental, with hot, very dry summers and cold winters. Most of Washington's vineyards are situated in this area, in the vast, sprawling Columbia and Yakima Valleys. Because it's so far north, Washington also has the advantage of long hours of sunlight, averaging an unusually high 17.4 hours of sunshine during the growing season.

Washington's winemakers have found that with irrigation, many grapes can flourish in the Washington desert. The Bordeaux varieties — Merlot, Cabernet Sauvignon, Cabernet Franc, Sauvignon Blanc, and Sémillon — are the name of the game. Syrah is coming up fast, and Chenin Blanc and the ever-present Chardonnay also are doing well.

Washington first became well-known for the quality of its Merlots. (One winery, Columbia Crest, makes the largest-selling Merlot in the United States in the over-$8 price category.) Lately, Washington's Syrah wines are gaining many of the accolades. In fact, Washington may be the single best region in the United States for this exciting wine. Cabernet Sauvignon and Cabernet Franc are also excellent varietal wines in Washington.

Washington does have a few vineyards west of the Cascades, around Puget Sound, where Riesling and Gewürztraminer grow well. In fact, many of the larger wineries, such as Chateau Ste. Michelle and Columbia Winery, are located in the Puget Sound area, near the thriving city of Seattle (but they obtain almost all their grapes from the Columbia and Yakima Valleys). Running a business is a bit easier in Seattle than in the desert! Chateau Ste. Michelle, along with the even larger Columbia Crest (both under the same corporate ownership), are the giants in the state; they account for over 50 percent of all Washington's wines at present. Two other large Washington wineries are The Hogue Cellars and Washington Hills Cellars.

Like Oregon, Washington got off to a late start in the wine business. With the exception of Chateau Ste. Michelle and Columbia Winery, both founded in the 1960s, practically none of the current wineries existed as late as 1980. In 1981, Washington had 19 wineries; today, more than 400 wineries are in business, making Washington the second-largest wine producer of premium wines in the United States.

The types of wine produced in Washington have also dramatically changed during the past decade. In 1993, about two thirds of Washington's wines were white, one third red. Reflecting Americans' changing tastes in wine, Washington's wines are now about 60 percent red, 40 percent white.

Washington's wine regions

Washington has one gigantic AVA, **Columbia Valley,** which encompasses five other AVAs within its macro-appellation (listed in order of their general importance):

- ✓ **Yakima Valley:** This region is the second largest in acreage, behind the huge Columbia Valley itself; more wineries are actually located here than in the rest of Columbia Valley.

- ✓ **Walla Walla Valley:** Although only 5 percent of the state's *vinifera* grapes grow here, this fast-growing region in the southeast corner of Washington is home to some of the state's top wineries, such as Leonetti Cellar, Woodward Canyon, Waterbrook Winery, Canoe Ridge Vineyard, and L'Ecole # 41.

- ✓ **Red Mountain:** A relatively new (2001) AVA, the tiny Red Mountain area is actually within the Yakima Valley AVA, but its red clay soil and high altitude earned it a separate appellation. About nine wineries, including Hedges and Kiona Vineyards, concentrate on red varieties: Cabernet Sauvignon, Merlot, Cabernet Franc, and Syrah. Some great vineyards are also located here.

- ✓ **Horse Heaven Hills:** Recognized as a separate AVA in 2005, this area in the southernmost part of the Columbia Valley, just north of the Columbia River, has long been known as an ideal location for Cabernet Sauvignon. Many of Washington's leading wineries, including Chateau Ste. Michelle, use grapes from vineyards here.

- ✓ **Wahluke Slope:** A brand-new (2006) AVA, the Wahluke Slope is one of the state's warmer appellations, known for its Merlot and Cabernet Sauvignon, and home to Snoqualmie Vineyards.

A Washington oddity

When was the last time you had a Lemberger? No, we don't mean the cheese! Lemberger is a little-known grape variety from Germany that's also grown in Austria, where it's called Blaufränkisch. Don't feel bad if you haven't heard of it, because few people in the United States — outside of Washington — have tasted it. Lemberger is a hardy red variety that does well in the Yakima Valley; it makes a fruity but dry, inexpensive wine in the Beaujolais or Dolcetto school. Hoodsport, Covey Run, Kiona Vineyards, and Hogue Cellars are four good producers of Lemberger — the wine! Hogue Cellars calls their version "Blue Franc."

Other AVAs include tiny **Rattlesnake Hills,** a sub-appellation of Yakima Valley, and **Columbia Gorge,** a beautiful area in southwest Washington crossing into Oregon, which actually has an equal number of both Oregon and Washington wineries. The Lake Chelan Region, in Northern Columbia Valley, with 12 wineries, has been proposed as an AVA. More than 50 wineries are located in the **Greater Puget Sound/Seattle Area** AVA, which encompasses the Puget Sound Islands; in this cool, moist climate, Pinot Gris and Pinot Noir are leading varieties, as well as Riesling and Gewürztraminer. About nine wineries, including Arbor Crest, are located in the Spokane Area in eastern Washington.

Who's who in Washington

No, we're not talking about cabinet members and senators here! The following are our recommended wine producers in Washington, grouped alphabetically, along with some of their best wines:

- **Andrew Will Cellars:** Cabernet Sauvignon, Merlot
- **Arbor Crest Wine Cellars:** Sauvignon Blanc, Chardonnay, Riesling
- **Badger Mountain Winery:** Chardonnay, Cabernet Franc
- **Barnard Griffin Winery:** Sémillon, Chardonnay, Fumé Blanc, Merlot
- **Betz Family Winery:** Cabernet Sauvignon, Merlot blend, Syrah
- **Bookwalter Winery:** Cabernet Sauvignon, Merlot
- **Canoe Ridge Vineyard:** Merlot, Cabernet Sauvignon
- **Chateau Ste. Michelle:** Merlot, Cabernet Sauvignon, Chardonnay (especially Cold Creek Vineyard of all three), "Eroica" Riesling (with Dr. Loosen)

- **Chinook Winery:** Sauvignon Blanc, Sémillon, Chardonnay

- **Col Solare:** Meritage (mainly Cabernet Sauvignon; a Chateau Ste. Michelle/ Piero Antinori collaboration)

- **Columbia Crest Winery:** Reserve Red (Cabernet-Merlot blend), Sémillon, Syrah, Merlot, Cabernet Sauvignon, Sémillon-Chardonnay

- **Columbia Winery:** Cabernet Sauvignon, Cabernet Franc, Syrah, Merlot (especially Red Willow Vineyard of all four)

- **Covey Run Winery:** Chardonnay, Lemberger

- **DeLille Cellars:** Chaleur Estate (Bordeaux-style blend), Chaleur Estate Blanc (Sauvignon Blanc-Sémillon blend), D2 (second label of Chaleur Estate), Harrison Hill (Cabernet Sauvignon), Syrah

- **Gordon Brothers Cellars:** Chardonnay, Merlot, Cabernet Sauvignon

- **Hedges Cellars:** Red Mountain Reserve (Bordeaux-style blend), Cabernet/Merlot, Fumé/Chardonnay, Three Vineyard Red

- **The Hogue Cellars:** Merlot, Cabernet Sauvignon (Reserve), Blue Franc (Lemberger), Chenin Blanc, Sémillon-Chardonnay, Sémillon

- **Hoodsport Winery:** Lemberger, Sémillon

- **Hyatt Vineyard:** Merlot, Cabernet Sauvignon

- **Januik Winery:** Merlot, Cabernet Sauvignon

- **Kiona Vineyards:** Lemberger, Cabernet Sauvignon, Merlot

- **L'Ecole #41:** Merlot (Seven Hills), Cabernet Sauvignon, Sémillon

- **Leonetti Cellar:** Cabernet Sauvignon (especially Seven Hills Vineyard), Merlot, Sangiovese

- **Long Shadows Winery:** Merlot, Syrah, Riesling

- **Matthews Cellars:** Merlot, Yakima Valley Red (Bordeaux-style blend)

- **McCrea Cellars:** Chardonnay, Syrah

- **Northstar:** Merlot

- **Owen-Sullivan Winery:** Syrah, Cabernet Franc, Merlot

- **Pepper Bridge Winery:** Cabernet Sauvignon, Merlot

- **Preston Wine Cellars:** Cabernet Sauvignon, Merlot (Reserves)

- **Quilceda Creek Vintners:** Cabernet Sauvignon

- **Sagelands Vineyard:** Cabernet Sauvignon, Merlot

- **Seven Hills******:** Merlot, Cabernet Sauvignon

- **Snoqualmie Vineyards:** Cabernet Sauvignon, Merlot, Syrah

- **Tamarack Cellars:** Merlot, Cabernet Sauvignon, Firehouse Red
- **Tefft Cellars:** Sangiovese, Cabernet Sauvignon
- **Thurston Wolfe Winery:** Syrah
- **Washington Hills Cellars:** Cabernet Sauvignon, Merlot, Chardonnay, Sémillon, Cabernet Franc ("Apex" is this winery's premium label; it also uses the "W. B. Bridgman" label)
- **Waterbrook Winery:** Cabernet Sauvignon, Merlot, Chardonnay, Cabernet Franc, Sauvignon Blanc
- **Woodward Canyon Winery:** Chardonnay, Cabernet Sauvignon, Merlot

****Seven Hills Winery is actually just across the border in Oregon, but the vineyard is in Walla Walla Valley, Washington.*

The Empire State

New York City may be the capital of the world in many ways, but its state's wines don't get the recognition they deserve, perhaps because of California's overwhelming presence in the U.S. market. New York ranks as the third largest wine producing state in the United States. Brotherhood America's Oldest Winery, Ltd., the oldest continuously operating winery in the United States, opened its doors in New York's Hudson Valley in 1839. And the largest wine company in the world, Constellation, has its headquarters in the Finger Lakes region of western New York.

Upstate, downstate

New York's most important region is the Finger Lakes, where four large lakes temper the otherwise cool climate. This AVA produces about two-thirds of New York's wines. The other two important regions are the Hudson Valley, along the Hudson River north of New York City, and Long Island, which has three AVAs: North Fork of Long Island (the most important); the Hamptons, on the island's South Fork; and Long Island itself, using grapes from all over Long Island.

In the early days (prior to 1960), most of New York's wines were made from native American varieties, such as Concord, Catawba, Delaware, and Niagara, as well French-American hybrid grapes such as Seyval Blanc, Baco Noir, and Maréchal Foch.

Common wisdom held that the relatively cold New York winters could not support *Vitis vinifera* varieties. But a Russian immigrant, the late, great Dr. Konstantin Frank, proved all the naysayers wrong when he succeeded in growing Riesling (followed by many other vinifera varieties) in 1953 in Hammondsport, in the Finger Lakes region. (The first wines from vinifera grapes were actually made in 1961 at his winery, Dr. Frank's Vinifera Wine Cellars.) His son, Willy Frank, who recently passed away, ran one of the most successful wineries in the state, with an entire line of fine vinifera wines and excellent sparkling wines; the winery carries on today under the leadership of Dr. Franks's grandson, Fred.

In 1973, Alec and Louisa Hargrave got the idea that Long Island's North Fork (about a two-hour drive east of New York City) had the ideal climate and soil for vinifera grapes. Today, Long Island has 32 wineries and is still growing. Like Washington state, Long Island seems particularly suited to Merlot, but Chardonnay, Riesling, Cabernet Sauvignon, Cabernet Franc, and Sauvignon Blanc are also grown, plus some Gewürztraminer, Pinot Noir, and numerous other varieties.

Who's who in New York

The New York wine industry has grown from 19 wineries in 1976 to over 170 today, most of them small, family-run operations. The following are lists of recommended producers in New York's three major wine regions, listed alphabetically.

The Finger Lakes Region

Anthony Road Wine Company
Casa Larga Vineyards
Dr. Frank's Vinifera Wine Cellars
    (and its affiliate, Chateau Frank,
    for sparkling wines)
Fox Run Vineyards
Glenora Wine Cellars
Hazlitt 1852 Vineyards
Hermann J. Wiemer Vineyard
Heron Hill Vineyards
Hunt Country Vineyards

Knapp Vineyards
Lakewood Vineyards
Lamoreaux Landing Wine Cellars
Lucas Vineyards
McGregor Vineyard
Prejean Winery
Standing Stone Vineyards
Swedish Hill Vineyard
Wagner Vineyards
Widmer's Wine Cellars

Hudson River Valley Region

Adair Vineyards
Baldwin Vineyards
Benmarl Vineyards
Brotherhood Winery
Cascade Mountain Vineyards

Clinton Vineyards
Magnanini Winery
Millbrook Vineyards
Rivendell Winery

Long Island Region (North Fork, other than noted)

Bedell Cellars	Martha Clara Vineyards
Castello di Borghes Vineyard	Old Brookville-Banfi (Nassau County)
Channing Daughters (Hamptons)	Osprey's Dominion
Corey Creek Vineyards	Palmer Vineyards
Duck Walk Vineyards (Hamptons)	Paumanok Vineyards
Jamesport Vineyards	Peconic Bay Vineyards
Laurel Lake Vineyards	Pelligrini Vineyards
Lenz Winery	Pindar Vineyards
Lieb Family Cellars	Pugliese Vineyards
Loughlin Vineyards	Raphael
Macari Vineyards	Wolffer Estate (Hamptons)

Oh, Canada

Ask many wine lovers in the United States about Canadian wines, and you'll probably get a blank stare in response. Canada's wines are known mainly to Canadians, who consume the bulk of their country's production.

The 1990s brought incredible growth to the Canadian wine industry: The number of wineries grew from 30 to over 400 today. Wine is made in four of Canada's provinces, but Ontario has bragging rights as the largest producer, with over 100 wineries. British Columbia ranks second. Quebec and Nova Scotia also produce wine.

To identify and promote wines made entirely from local grapes (some Canadian wineries import wines from other countries to blend with local production), the provinces of Ontario and British Columbia have established an appellation system called VQA, Vintners' Quality Alliance. This system regulates the use of provincial names on wine labels, establishes which grape varieties can be used (vinifera varieties and certain hybrids), regulates the use of the terms *icewine, late harvest,* and *botrytised* (see Chapter 11 for an explanation of these terms), and requires wines to pass a taste and laboratory test.

Ontario

Ontario's vineyards are cool-climate wine zones, despite the fact that they lie on the same parallel as Chianti Classico and Rioja, warmer European wine regions discussed in Chapters 10 and 14. Sixty percent of the production is white wine, from Chardonnay, Riesling, Gewürztraminer, Pinot Blanc, Auxerrois, and the hybrids Seyval Blanc and Vidal. Red wines come from Pinot Noir, Gamay, Cabernet Sauvignon, Cabernet Franc, Merlot, and the hybrids Maréchal Foch and Baco Noir.

Ontario's VQA rules permit the use of the appellation Ontario and also recognize three *Designated Viticultural Areas* (DVAs), listed in order of importance:

- ✔ **Niagara Peninsula:** Along the south shore of Lake Ontario

- ✔ **Pelee Island:** Eleven miles south of the Canadian mainland, in Lake Erie, Canada's most southerly vineyards

- ✔ **Lake Erie North Shore:** The warmest of Ontario's viticultural areas

Because winter temperatures regularly drop well below freezing, icewine, made from grapes naturally frozen on the vine, is a specialty of Ontario. It is gradually earning the Canadian wine industry international attention, particularly for the wines of Inniskillin Winery. VQA regulations are particularly strict regarding icewine production, as it has developed into the leader of the Canadian wine exports.

British Columbia

The rapidly growing wine industry of British Columbia now boasts more than 70 wineries. Production is mainly white wine — from Chardonnay, Gewürztraminer, Pinot Gris, Pinot Blanc, and Riesling — but red wine production is increasing, mainly from Pinot Noir and Merlot.

The Okanagan Valley in southeast British Columbia, where the climate is influenced by Lake Okanagan, is the center of wine production; Misssion Hill is a leading winery. VQA rules recognize five Designated Viticultural Areas, listed in order of importance:

- ✔ Okanagan Valley
- ✔ Similkameen Valley
- ✔ Fraser Valley
- ✔ Vancouver Island
- ✔ Gulf Islands

Part V
Wine's Exotic Face

The 5th Wave   By Rich Tennant

"Brother Dom Perignon, everyone really enjoys your sparkling mayonnaise and blanc de turnip soup, but could there not be something else you could make with these grapes?"

In this part . . .

There's life beyond Chardonnay and Merlot! In fact, there's a whole world of truly delicious wines to drink not so much at the table as at parties, on the patio before dinner, or by the fire after dinner. These wines include the most glamorous wine in the world — Champagne! — as well as bubbly wines from other regions, and the classic wines called Sherry and Port. (Nobody doesn't love Port.)

In the two chapters that follow, we tell you how these magical wines are made, which brands to look for, and when to drink the wines (including tips on how to use them in a meal — for an exotic touch).

Chapter 14

Champagne and Other Sparklers

. . . .

. . . .

*I*n the universe of wine, sparkling wines are a solar system unto themselves. They're produced in just about every country that makes wine, and they come in a wide range of tastes, quality levels, and prices. Champagne, the sparkling wine from the Champagne region of France, is the brightest star in the sky, but by no means the only one.

Sparkling wines are distinguished (and distinguishable) from other wines by the presence of bubbles — *carbon dioxide* — in the wine. In the eyes of most governments, these bubbles must be a natural by-product of fermentation in order for a wine to be officially considered a sparkling wine.

In many wine regions, sparkling wines are just a sideline to complement the region's table wine production, but in some places, sparkling wines are serious business. At the top of that list is France's Champagne region (where sparkling wine was — if not invented — made famous). Italy's Asti wine zone is another important region, as is France's Loire Valley, northeastern Spain, and parts of California. Australia, New Zealand, and South Africa are also now making some interesting sparklers.

The cool rule

Many sparkling wine regions are very cool areas, where grapes don't ripen sufficiently for *still* (non-sparkling) wine production. Vinified normally, the wines of these regions would be extremely high in acid, disagreeably tart, and very thin; the reds would lack color. But the elaborate process of sparkling wine production (the *traditional method* of production as practiced in the Champagne region, and described later in this chapter) turns the climate's deficits into virtues, and transforms the ugly duckling grapes into graceful swans.

All That Glitters Is Not Champagne

Champagne, the sparkling wine of Champagne, France, is the gold standard of sparkling wines for a number of reasons:

- ✓ Champagne is the most famous sparkling wine in the world; the name has immediate recognition with everyone, not just wine drinkers.

- ✓ A particular technique for making sparkling wine was perfected in the Champagne region.

- ✓ Champagne is not only the finest sparkling wine in the world, but also among the finest wines in the world of any type.

Within the European Union, only the wines of the Champagne region in France can use the name Champagne. Elsewhere, because of Champagne's fame, the name *champagne* appears on labels of all sorts of sparkling wines that don't come from the Champagne region and that don't taste like Champagne. Wineries call their bubbly wines "champagne" to make them more marketable, and despite tighter regulations regarding the use of the term, many wineries in the United States may still use "champagne" on their labels. Many wine drinkers also use the word "champagne" indiscriminately to refer to all wines that have bubbles.

Ironically, much of the sparkling wine sold in the United States that's called "champagne" is not even made with the same techniques as true Champagne. Most imitation champagnes are made by a technique that takes only a few months from beginning to end (compared to a few years to make Champagne), is less costly, and works more effectively on an industrial scale.

Whenever we use the word Champagne, we are referring to true Champagne, from the region of the same name; we use the generic term *sparkling wine* to refer to bubbly wines collectively, and sparkling wines other than Champagne.

Sparkling Wine Styles

All sparkling wines have bubbles, and nearly all of them are either white or pink (which is far less common than white). That's about as far as broad generalizations take us in describing sparkling wines.

Some sparkling wines are downright sweet, some are bone dry, and many fall somewhere in the middle, from medium-dry to medium-sweet. Some have toasty, nutty flavors and some are fruity; among those that are fruity, some are just nondescriptly grapey, while others have delicate nuances of lemons, apples, cherries, berries, peaches, and other fruits.

The sparkling wines of the world fall into two broad styles, according to how they're made, and how they taste as a result:

✔ Wines that express the character of their grapes; these wines tend to be fruity and straightforward, without layers of complexity.

✔ Wines that express complexity and flavors (yeasty, biscuity, caramel-like, honeyed) that derive from winemaking and aging, rather than expressing overt fruitiness.

How sweet is it?

Nearly all sparkling wines are not technically dry, because they contain measurable but small amounts of sugar, usually as the result of sweetening added at the last stage of production. But all sparkling wines don't necessarily taste sweet. The perception of sweetness depends on two factors: the actual amount of sweetness in the wine (which varies according to the wine's style) and the wine's balance between acidity and sweetness.

Here's how the balance factor operates. Sparkling wines are usually very high in acidity, because the grapes, having grown in a cool climate, weren't particularly ripe at harvest. The wine's carbon dioxide also gives an acidic impression in the mouth. But the wine's sweetness counterbalances its acidity and vice versa. Depending on the actual amount of sugar and the particular acid/sugar balance a sparkling wine strikes, the wine may taste dry, very slightly sweet, medium sweet, or quite sweet.

Champagne itself is made in a range of sweetness levels, the most common of which is a dry style called *brut* (see "Sweetness categories" later in this chapter). Sparkling wines made by the *traditional method* used in Champagne (see "How Sparkling Wine Happens" later in this chapter) are made in the same range of styles as Champagne.

Inexpensive sparkling wines tend to be medium sweet in order to appeal to a mass market that enjoys sweetness. Wines labeled with the Italian word *spumante* tend to be overtly sweet. (See the section "Italian spumante: Sweet or dry," later in this chapter.)

How good is it?

When you taste a sparkling wine, the most important consideration is whether you like it — just as for a still wine. If you want to evaluate a sparkling wine the way professionals do, however, you have to apply a few criteria that don't apply to still wines (or are less critical in still wines than in sparkling wines). Some of those criteria are

- **The appearance of the bubbles.** In the best sparkling wines, the bubbles are tiny and float upward in a continuous stream from the bottom of your glass. If the bubbles are large and random, you have a clue that the wine is a lesser-quality sparkler. If you don't see many bubbles at all, you could have a bad bottle, a poor or smudged glass, or a wine that may be too old.

  Tiny variations in glassware can drastically affect the flow of bubbles. If the wine in your glass looks almost flat, but another glass of wine from the same bottle is lively with bubbles, blame the glass and not the wine. (In this case, you should be able to *taste* the bubbles, even if you can't *see* many of them.) See Chapter 8 for our recommendations about glasses for Champagne and other sparkling wines.

- **The feel of the bubbles in your mouth.** The finer the wine, the less aggressive the bubbles feel in your mouth. (If the bubbles remind you of a soft drink, we hope you didn't pay more than $5 for the wine.)

- **The balance between sweetness and acidity.** Even if a bubbly wine is too sweet or too dry for your taste, to evaluate its quality you should consider its sweetness/acid ratio and decide whether these two elements seem reasonably balanced.

- **The texture.** Traditional-method sparkling wines should be somewhat creamy in texture as a result of their extended lees aging. (See the next section for an explanation of *traditional method* and *lees*.)

- **The finish.** Any impression of bitterness on the finish of a sparkling wine is a sign of low quality.

How Sparkling Wine Happens

When yeasts convert sugar into alcohol, carbon dioxide is a natural by-product. If fermentation takes place in a closed container, that prevents this carbon dioxide from escaping into the air, the wine becomes sparkling. With nowhere else to go, the carbon dioxide (CO_2) becomes trapped in the wine in the form of bubbles.

Most sparkling wines actually go through *two* fermentations: one to turn the grape juice into still wine without bubbles (that's called a *base wine*) and a subsequent one to turn the base wine into bubbly wine (conveniently called the *second fermentation*). The winemaker has to instigate the second fermentation by adding yeasts and sugar to the base wine. The added yeasts convert the added sugar into alcohol and CO_2 bubbles.

Beginning with the second fermentation, the longer and slower the winemaking process, the more complex and expensive the sparkling wine will be. Some sparkling wines are ten years in the making; others are produced in only a few months. The slow-route wines can cost more than $100 a bottle, while bubblies at the opposite end of the spectrum can sell for as little as $4.

Although many variations exist, most sparkling wines are produced in one of two ways: through *second fermentation in a tank,* or through *second fermentation in a bottle.*

Tank fermentation: Economy of scale

The quickest, most efficient way of making a sparkling wine involves conducting the second fermentation in large, closed, pressurized tanks. This method is called the *bulk method, tank method, cuve close* (meaning *closed tank* in French), or *charmat method* (after a Frenchman named Eugene Charmat, who championed this process).

Sparkling wines made in the charmat (pronounced *shar mah*) method are usually the least expensive. That's because they're usually made in large quantities and they're ready for sale soon after harvest. Also, the grapes used in making sparkling wine by the charmat method (Chenin Blanc, for example) are usually *far* less expensive than the Pinot Noir and Chardonnay typically used in the *traditional* or *champagne method* described in the next section.

The following occurs in the charmat method:

 ✔ A base wine is seeded with sugar and yeast, and it ferments. The carbon dioxide created by the fermentation becomes trapped in the wine, thanks to the closed tank, pressure within the tank, and cold temperature.

 ✔ The wine — now a dry sparkling wine with higher alcohol than the base wine had — is filtered (under pressure) to remove the solid deposits (the *lees*) from the second fermentation.

 ✔ Before bottling, some sweetness is added to adjust the wine's flavor, according to the desired style of the final wine.

The whole process can take just a few weeks. In some exceptional cases, it may be extended to a few months, allowing the wine to rest between the fermentation and the filtration.

Bottle fermentation: Small is beautiful

The charmat method is a fairly new way of producing sparkling wines, dating back barely 100 years. The more traditional method is to conduct the second fermentation in the individual bottles in which the wine is later sold.

Champagne has been made in this way for over 300 years and, according to French regulations, can be made in no other way. Many other French sparkling wines produced outside of the Champagne region use the same process but are allowed to use the term *crémant* in their names rather than *champagne*. The best sparkling wines from Spain, California, and elsewhere also use Champagne's traditional method.

The technique of conducting the second fermentation in the bottle is called the *classic* or *traditional method* in Europe; in the United States, it's called the *champagne method* or *méthode champenoise*.

Bottle fermentation (or, more correctly, second fermentation in the bottle) is an elaborate process in which every single bottle becomes an individual fermentation tank, so to speak. Including the aging time at the winery before the wine is sold, this process requires a minimum of fifteen months and usually takes three years or more. Invariably, bottle-fermented sparkling wines are more expensive than tank-fermented bubblies.

The elements of bottle fermentation are as follows:

✔ Each bottle is filled with a mixture of base wine and a sugar-and-yeast solution, closed securely, and laid to rest in a cool, dark cellar.

✔ The second fermentation slowly occurs inside each bottle, producing carbon dioxide and fermentation lees.

✔ As the bottles lie in the cellar, the interaction of the lees and the wine gradually changes the wine's texture and flavor.

✔ Eventually — 12 months to several years after the second fermentation — the bottles undergo a process of shaking and turning so that the lees fall to the neck of each upside-down bottle.

✔ The lees are flash-frozen in the neck of each bottle and expelled from the bottle as a frozen plug, leaving clear sparkling wine behind.

✔ A sweetening solution (called a *dosage*) is added to each bottle to adjust the flavor of the wine, and the bottles are corked and labeled for sale.

Actually, the classic method as practiced in Champagne involves several processes that occur way before the second fermentation. For example, the pressing to extract the juice from the grapes must be gentle and meticulous to prevent the grapeskins' bitter flavors — and their color, in the case of black grapes — from passing into the juice. Another step crucially important to the quality of the sparkling wine is blending various wines after the first fermentation to create the best composite base wine for the second fermentation.

After the first fermentation, each Champagne house has hundreds of different still wines, because the winemaker keeps the wines of different grape varieties and different vineyards separate. To create his base wine, or *cuvée*, he blends these wines in varying proportions, often adding some *reserve wine* (older wine purposely held back from previous vintages). More than 100 different wines can go into a single base wine, each bringing its own special character to the blend. What's particularly tricky about blending the base wine — besides the sheer number of components in the blend — is that the winemaker has to see into the future and create a blend *not* for its flavor today but for how it will taste in several years, after it has been transformed into a sparkling wine. The men and women who blend sparkling wines are true artists of the wine world.

Taste: The proof of the pudding

Tank-fermented sparklers tend to be fruitier than traditional-method sparkling wines. This difference occurs because in tank fermentation, the route from grape to wine is shorter and more direct than in bottle fermentation. Some winemakers use the *charmat,* or tank, method because their goal is a fresh and fruity sparkling wine. Asti, Italy's most famous sparkling wine, is a perfect example. You should drink charmat-method sparklers young, when their fruitiness is at its max.

Second fermentation in the bottle makes wines that tend to be less overtly fruity than charmat-method wines. Chemical changes that take place as the wine develops on its fermentation lees diminish the fruitiness of the wine and contribute aromas and flavors such as toastiness, nuttiness, caramel, and yeastiness. The texture of the wine can also change, becoming smooth and creamy. The bubbles themselves tend to be tinier, and they feel less aggressive in your mouth than the bubbles of tank-fermented wines.

Champagne and Its Magic Wines

Champagne. Does any other word convey such a sense of celebration? Think of it: Whenever people, in any part of the world, want to celebrate, you may hear them say, "This calls for Champagne!" ("This calls for iced tea!" just isn't quite the same.)

Champagne, the real thing, comes only from the region of Champagne (*sham pahn yah*) in northeast France. Dom Pérignon, the famous monk who was cellar master at the Abbey of Hautvillers, didn't invent Champagne, but he did achieve several breakthroughs that are key to the production of Champagne as we now know it. He perfected the method of making white wine from black grapes, for example, and, most importantly, he mastered the art of blending wines from different grapes and different villages to achieve a complex base wine. (See the previous section to find out what "base" wine is.)

Champagne is the most northerly vineyard area in France. Most of the important Champagne *houses* (as Champagne producers are called) are located in the cathedral city of Rheims (French spelling, *Reims*) — where 17-year-old Joan of Arc had Prince Charles crowned King of France in 1429 — and in the town of Epernay, south of Rheims. Around Rheims and Epernay are the main vineyard areas, where three permitted grape varieties for Champagne flourish. These areas are

- The Montagne de Reims (south of Rheims), where the best Pinot Noir grows
- The Côte des Blancs (south of Epernay), home of the best Chardonnay
- The Valleé de la Marne (west of Epernay), most favorable to Pinot Meunier (a black grape) although all three grape varieties grow there

Most Champagne is made from all three grape varieties — two black and one white. Pinot Noir contributes body, structure, and longevity to the blend; Pinot Meunier provides precocity, floral aromas, and fruitiness; and Chardonnay offers delicacy, freshness, and elegance.

What makes Champagne special

The cool climate in Champagne is marginal for grape growing, and the grapes struggle to ripen sufficiently in some years. Even in warmer years, the climate dictates that the grapes are high in acidity — a sorry state for table wine but perfect for sparkling wine. The cool climate and the region's chalky, limestone soil are the leading factors contributing to Champagne's excellence.

Three other elements help distinguish Champagne from all other sparkling wines:

- ✔ The number and diversity of vineyards (over 300 *crus*, or individual vineyards), which provide a huge range of unique wines for blending
- ✔ The cold, deep, chalky cellars — many built during Roman times — in which Champagnes age for many years
- ✔ The 300 years of experience the *Champenois* (as the good citizens of Champagne are called) have in making sparkling wine

The result is an elegant sparkling wine with myriad tiny, gentle bubbles, complexity of flavors, and a lengthy finish. Voilá! Champagne!

Non-vintage Champagne

Non-vintage (NV) Champagne — any Champagne without a vintage year on the label — accounts for 85 percent of all Champagne. Its typical blend is two-thirds black grapes (Pinot Noir and Pinot Meunier) and one-third white (Chardonnay). Wine from three or more harvests usually goes into the blend. And remember, the wines from 30 or 40 different villages (or more) from each year can also be part of the blend. The Champagne winemaker is by necessity a master blender.

Each Champagne house blends to suit its own house style for its non-vintage Champagne. (For example, one house may seek elegance and finesse in its wine, another may opt for fruitiness, and a third may value body, power, and longevity.) Maintaining a consistent house style is vital because wine drinkers get accustomed to their favorite Champagne's taste and expect to find it year after year.

Most major Champagne houses age their non-vintage Champagne for two and a half to three years before selling it, even though the legal minimum for non-vintage is just 15 months. The extra aging prolongs the marrying time for the blend and enhances the wine's flavor and complexity. If you have good storage conditions (see Chapter 16), aging your non-vintage Champagne for one to three years after you purchase it usually improves the flavor, in our opinion.

Most non-vintage Champagnes sell for $25 to $50 a bottle. Often, a large retailer buys huge quantities of a few major brands, obtaining a good discount that he passes on to his customers. Seeking out stores that do a large-volume business in Champagne is worth your while.

Vintage Champagne

Historically, only in about five of every ten years has the weather in Champagne been good enough to make a Vintage Champagne — that is, the grapes were ripe enough that some wine could be made entirely from the grapes of that year without being blended with reserve wines from previous years. Since 1995, the climate in Champagne (and throughout Europe) has been much warmer than normal, and Champagne producers have been able to make Vintage Champagne almost every year. (2001 was the one exception).

Even in the 1980s, Champagne had exceptionally good weather; many houses made Vintage Champagne every year from 1981 to 1990, with the exception of 1984 and 1987. The early '90s were more typical; four years — 1991, 1992, 1993, and 1994 — were unremarkable, and few producers made vintage-dated Champagne.

The Champagne region has had a string of really fine vintages since 1995, especially the 1996 vintage. The three years that followed — 1997, 1998, and 1999 — all have been good. Both 2000 and 2003 were no more than average (too hot, especially 2003), but 2002 and 2004 are fine vintages (with 2002 the best since 1996), and 2005 is variable. Champagne lovers should seek out 1996 Vintage Champagnes; 1996 is exceptional, one of the best long-lived vintages ever!

Champagne houses decide for themselves each year whether to make a Vintage Champagne. Factors that might come into consideration — besides the quality of the vintage — include the need to save some wine instead to use as reserve wines for their non-vintage Champagnes (85 percent of their business, after all), and/or whether a particular vintage's style suits the "house style." For example, although 1989 was a rather good vintage, a few houses decided that Champagnes made from this vintage would be too soft (low in acidity) and/or too precocious (lacking longevity) for them, and did not choose to make a Vintage Champagne in 1989.

Refrigerator blues

Don't leave your Champagne — or any other good sparkling wine — in your refrigerator for more than a week! Its flavor will become flat from the excessively cold temperature. Also, long-term vibrations caused by the cycling on and off of the refrigerator motor are not good for any wine — especially sparkling wine. (See Chapter 16 for more on storing your wine properly.)

The minimum aging requirement for Vintage Champagne is three years, but many houses age their Vintage Champagnes four to six years in order to enhance the wines' flavor and complexity. Vintage Champagnes fall into two categories:

✔ Regular vintage, with a price range of $45 to $70 a bottle; these wines simply carry a vintage date in addition to the name of the house.

✔ Premium vintage (also known as a *prestige cuvée* or *tête de cuvée*), such as Moët & Chandon's Dom Pérignon, Roederer's Cristal, or Veuve Clicquot's La Grande Dame; the typical price for prestige cuvées ranges from $75 to $150 per bottle, with a few even more expensive.

Vintage Champagne is almost always superior to non-vintage for the following reasons:

✔ The best grapes from the choicest vineyards are put into Vintage Champagne (this is *especially* so for prestige cuvées).

✔ Usually, only the two finest varieties (Pinot Noir and Chardonnay) are used in Vintage Champagne. Pinot Meunier is saved mainly for non-vintage Champagne.

✔ Most Champagne houses age Vintage Champagnes at least two years more than their non-vintage wines. The extra aging assures more complexity.

✔ The grapes all come from a year that's above average, at least — or superb, at best.

Vintage Champagne is more intense in flavor than non-vintage Champagne. It is typically fuller-bodied and more complex, and its flavors last longer in your mouth. Being fuller and richer, these Champagnes are best with food. Non-vintage Champagnes — usually lighter, fresher, and less complicated — are suitable as apéritifs, and they are good values. Whether a Vintage Champagne is worth its extra cost or not is a judgment you have to make for yourself.

Blanc de blancs and blanc de noirs

A small number of Champagnes derive only from Chardonnay; that type of Champagne is called *blanc de blancs* — literally, "white (wine) from white (grapes)." A blanc de blancs can be a Vintage Champagne or a non-vintage. It usually costs a few dollars more than other Champagnes in its category. Because they are generally lighter and more delicate than other Champagnes, blanc de blancs make ideal apéritifs. Not every Champagne house makes a blanc de blancs. Four of the best all-Vintage Champagnes, are Taittinger Comte de Champagne, Billecart-Salmon Blanc de Blancs, Deutz Blanc de Blancs, and Pol Roger Blanc de Chardonnay.

Blanc de noirs Champagne (made entirely from black grapes, often just Pinot Noir) is rare but does exist. Bollinger's Blanc de Noirs *Vieilles Vignes Francaises* ("old vines") is absolutely the best, but it is very expensive ($400 to$450) and hard to find. The 1985 Bollinger Blanc de Noirs is one of the two best Champagnes we've ever had; the other is the 1928 Krug.

Rosé Champagne

Rosé Champagnes — pink Champagnes — can also be vintage or non-vintage. Usually, Pinot Noir and Chardonnay are the only grapes used, in proportions that vary from one house to the next.

Winemakers create a rosé Champagne usually by including some red Pinot Noir wine in the blend for the base wine. A few actually vinify some of their red grapes into pink wines, the way that you would make a rosé still wine, and use that as the base wine. Colors vary quite a lot, from pale onion-skin to salmon to rosy pink. (The lighter-colored ones are usually dryer.)

Rosés are fuller and rounder than other Champagnes and are best enjoyed with dinner. (Because they have become associated with romance, they're popular choices for wedding anniversaries and Valentine's Day.)

Who's drinking Champagne

Not surprisingly, France leads the world in Champagne consumption, drinking 58 percent of all the Champagne produced. The United Kingdom is the leading foreign market for Champagne. The United States is second, and Germany is third, followed by Belgium and Italy. But the United States buys the most prestige cuvée Champagne, especially Dom Pérignon.

Like blanc de blancs Champagnes, rosés usually cost a few dollars more than regular Champagnes, and not every Champagne house makes one. Some of the best rosés are those of Roederer, Billecart-Salmon, Gosset, and Moët & Chandon (especially its Dom Pérignon Rosé).

For some people, rosé Champagne has a bad connotation because of the tons of sweet, insipid, cheap pink wines — sparkling and otherwise — on the market. But rosé Champagne is just as dry and has the same high quality as regular (white) Champagne.

Sweetness categories

Champagnes always carry an indication of their sweetness on the label, but the words used to indicate sweetness are cryptic: extra dry is not really dry, for example. In ascending order of sweetness, Champagnes are labeled

- **Extra brut, brut nature,** or **brut sauvage:** Totally dry
- **Brut:** Dry
- **Extra dry:** Medium dry
- **Sec:** Slightly sweet
- **Demi-sec:** Fairly sweet
- **Doux:** Sweet

The most popular style for Champagne and other serious bubblies is brut. However, the single best-selling Champagne in the United States, Moët & Chandon's White Star, actually is an extra dry Champagne. Brut, extra dry, and demi-sec are the three types of Champagne you find almost exclusively nowadays.

Recommended Champagne producers

The Champagne business — especially the export end of it — is dominated by about 25 or 30 large houses, most of whom purchase from independent growers the majority of grapes they need to make their Champagne. Of the major houses, only Roederer and Bollinger own a substantial portion of the vineyards from which they get their grapes — a definite economic and quality-control advantage for them.

Madame Lily Bollinger's advice on drinking Champagne

When Jacques Bollinger died in 1941, his widow, Lily Bollinger, carried her famous Champagne house through the difficult years of the German occupation of France. She ran the company until her death in 1977. Bollinger prospered under her leadership, doubling in size. She was a beloved figure in Champagne, where she could be seen bicycling through the vineyards every day. In 1961, when a London reporter asked her when she drank Champagne, Madame Bollinger replied:

"I only drink Champagne when I'm happy, and when I'm sad. Sometimes I drink it when I'm alone. When I have company I consider it obligatory. I trifle with it if I am not hungry and drink it when I am. Otherwise I never touch it — unless I'm thirsty."

The redoubtable Madame Lily Bollinger died at the age of 78, apparently none the worse for all that Champagne.

Moët & Chandon is by far the largest Champagne house. In terms of worldwide sales, other large brands are Veuve Clicquot, Mumm, Vranken, Laurent-Perrier, Pommery, Nicolas Feuillate, and Lanson. The following lists name some of our favorite producers, grouped according to the style of their Champagne: light-bodied, medium-bodied, or full-bodied. (For an understanding of the term *body* as it applies to wine, see Chapter 2.)

Light, elegant styles

Laurent-Perrier	G.H. Mumm
Taittinger	Bruno Paillard
Ruinart	Perrier-Jouët
Jacquesson	J. Lassalle*
Pommery	Billecart-Salmon
Piper-Heidsieck	

Medium-bodied styles

Charles Heidsieck	Deutz
Pol Roger	Cattier*
Moët & Chandon	Philipponnat

Full-bodied styles

Krug	Alfred Gratien*
Louis Roederer	Delamotte
Bollinger	Salon*
Gosset	Paul Bara*
Veuve Clicquot	

* Small producer; may be difficult to find.

The following list names, in rough order of preference, Champagne houses whose vintage and prestige cuvées have been in top form lately. For more info on Champagne, see Ed McCarthy's *Champagne For Dummies* (Wiley).

- **Louis Roederer:** Cristal
- **Krug:** Grande Cuvée, Vintage, NV Rosé, Clos du Mesnil
- **Bollinger:** Grande Année, Blanc de Noirs Vieilles Vignes
- **Moët & Chandon:** Dom Pérignon
- **Charles Heidsieck:** Blanc des Millenaires
- **Veuve Clicquot:** Vintage, La Grande Dame
- **Gosset:** Celebris, Celebris Rosé, NV Grande Réserve
- **Philipponnat:** Clos des Goisses
- **Pol Roger:** Cuvée Sir Winston Churchill
- **Salon:** Vintage Blanc de Blancs
- **Taittinger:** Comtes de Champagne, Comtes de Champagne Rosé
- **Billecart-Salmon:** Blanc de Blancs, Cuvée Elisabeth Salmon Rosé
- **Deutz:** Cuvée William Deutz, Cuvée William Deutz Rosé
- **Pommery:** Cuvée Louise, Cuvée Louise Rosé
- **Jacquesson:** Signature, Signature Rosé
- **Laurent-Perrier:** Grand Siècle
- **Ruinart:** Dom Ruinart Blanc de Blancs
- **Perrier-Jouët:** Fleur de Champagne Blanc de Blancs, Fleur de Champagne, Fleur de Champagne Rosé
- **Lanson:** Noble Cuvée
- **Piper-Heidsieck:** Champagne Rare
- **Alfred Gratien:** Cuvée Paradis (NV)
- **Cattier:** Clos du Moulin (NV)

Other Sparkling Wines

Wineries all over the world have emulated Champagne by adopting the techniques used in the Champagne region. Their wines differ from Champagne, however, because their grapes grow in terroirs different from that of the Champagne region and because, in some cases, their grapes are different varieties.

Still other sparkling wines are made by using the tank fermentation rather than the bottle fermentation method specifically to attain a certain style, or to reduce production costs.

French sparkling wine

France makes many other sparkling wines besides Champagne, especially in the Loire Valley, around Saumur, and in the regions of Alsace and Burgundy. Sparkling wine made by the traditional method (second fermentation in the bottle) often carries the name *Crémant,* as in Crémant d'Alsace, Crémant de Loire, Crémant de Bourgogne, and so on. Grape varieties are those typical of each region (see Chapter 9).

Some of the leading brands of French sparkling wines are Langlois-Château, Bouvet Ladubay, Gratien & Meyer (all from the Loire Valley), Brut d'Argent, Kriter, and Saint Hilaire. These wines sell for $10 to $15 and are decent. They're perfect for parties and other large gatherings, when you may want to serve a French bubbly without paying a Champagne price. For more info on French sparkling wines, take a look at our book *French Wine For Dummies* (Wiley).

American sparkling wine

Almost as many states make sparkling wine as make still wine, but California and New York are the most famous for it. Two fine producers of New York State sparkling wines in the traditional method are Chateau Frank and Lamoreaux Landing, both under $20.

One sparkling wine, Gruet, deserves special mention because it hails, improbably, from New Mexico. Owned by France's little-known Champagne Gruet, the New Mexican winery makes three excellent bubblies: a NV Brut and NV Blanc de Noirs, both about $18, and a Vintage Blanc de Blancs, $24.

California bubbly is definitely a different wine from Champagne and tastes fruitier even when made by a Champagne house, using the same methods and the same grape varieties as in Champagne. Good California sparkling wines, the ones made in the traditional Champagne method, cost as little as $15 on up to $40 or more.

Most of California's finest sparkling wines do not call themselves Champagne, but the less-expensive, best-selling ones do. In that second category, Korbel, at about $15, is the only brand that is actually fermented in the bottle.

We recommend the following California sparkling wine producers, listed in our rough order of preference within each category:

U.S.-owned

- ✔ **Iron Horse:** In Green Valley, the coolest part of Sonoma (temperature-wise, that is), Iron Horse is clearly making some of California's finest sparkling wine. Look for its better cuvées, such as the Wedding Cuvée, Russian Cuvée, and Vrai Amis, for about $25. Iron Horse's top-of-the-line sparkler, the Late Disgorged Blanc de Blancs, is truly superb, comparable in quality to fine Champagne; it's about $45.

- ✔ **J:** Not content with making some of America's most popular Cabernet Sauvignons and Chardonnays, the Jordan winery in Sonoma now also makes one of the best sparkling wines in the country. Almost all its grapes come from the cool Russian River Valley. Quite fruity and fairly delicate, the wine comes in a knockout bottle and sells for about $30.

- ✔ **S. Anderson:** In Napa Valley, S. Anderson continues to produce one of the finest lines of sparkling wines in the U.S. for about $25 to $30; look especially for its Blanc de Noirs.

- ✔ **Handley Cellars:** Up in Anderson Valley in Mendocino County, Milla Handley makes some excellent, quite dry sparkling wines; her Rosé Brut is a beauty, at about $25.

French- or Spanish-owned

- ✔ **Roederer Estate:** Louis Roederer is such a fine Champagne house that we're not surprised at the smashing success that its Anderson Valley winery, near the town of Mendocino, has achieved. Some critics think it's California's best. Wines include a good-value Brut ($24), a delicate rosé ($30) that's worth seeking out, and outstanding premium cuvées, L'Ermitage and L'Ermitage Rosé ($45).

- ✔ **Mumm Cuvée Napa:** Mumm has established itself as one of California's best sparkling wine houses. Much of its production comes from the cool Carneros District; look especially for the Winery Lake Brut and the cherry-like Blanc de Noirs. The price range is $25 to $30.

- ✔ **Domaine Carneros:** Taittinger's California winery makes an elegant, high-quality brut ($24 to $26) in cool Carneros. Its premium cuvée, Le Rêve, a $50 blanc de blancs, is stunning.

- ✔ **Domaine Chandon:** This Napa Valley winery is part of the Moët & Chandon empire. A must-stop for its restaurant alone, Chandon continues to make solid, consistent sparkling wines at reasonable prices ($15 to $18). Look especially for its premium Etoile (about $35), one of the most elegant sparkling wines in the United States, and the delicious Etoile Rosé ($38).

✔ **Gloria Ferrer:** Spain's Freixenet has built a beautiful winery in windswept Carneros. Most of its wines are priced right ($18 to $25) and are widely available. The winery is definitely worth a visit.

✔ **Scharffenberger:** From the cool Anderson Valley, Scharffenberger, now owned by Champagne Louis Roederer, makes a Chardonnay-based Brut that's especially fine ($18 to $20).

Italian spumante: Sweet or dry

Spumante is simply the Italian word for "sparkling." It often appears on bottles of American wines that are sweet, fruity spin-offs of Italy's classic Asti Spumante. Actually, Italy makes many fine, dry spumante wines and a popular, slightly sparkling wine called *Prosecco,* as well as sweet spumante. For more info on Italian sparkling wines, check out our book *Italian Wine For Dummies* (Wiley).

Asti and Moscato d'Asti

Asti is a delicious, fairly sweet, exuberantly fruity sparkling wine made in the Piedmont region from Moscato grapes, via the tank method. It's one bubbly that you can drink with dessert (fantastic with wedding cake!).

Because freshness is essential in Asti, buy a good brand that sells well. (Asti is not vintage-dated, and so there's no other way to determine how old the wine is.) We recommend Fontanafredda (about $14 to $15), Martini & Rossi ($12), and Cinzano (about $10).

For Asti flavor with fewer bubbles, try Moscato d'Asti, a delicate and delicious medium-dry vintage-dated *frizzante* (slightly sparkling) wine that makes a refreshing apéritif. It's also good with dessert and is a great brunch wine. And it has just 5 to 7 percent alcohol! Vietti makes a good one, called Cascinetta, for about $14. Other good producers of Moscato d'Asti are Dante Rivetti, Paolo Sarocco, and Ceretto, whose wine is called Santo Stefano; all these sell for $14 to $16. Again, freshness is essential. With Moscato d'Asti, let the vintage date guide you; buy the youngest one you can find.

Dry spumante

Using the traditional method, Italy produces a good deal of dry sparkling wine in the Oltrepò-Pavese and Franciacorta wine zones of Lombardy, and in Trentino. Italy's dry sparkling wines are very dry with little or no sweetening dosage. They come in all price ranges:

- Affordable wines include Gancia Brut ($10) and Berlucchi Cuvée Imperiale Brut ($15).

- Good mid-priced wines are Ferrari Brut and Banfi Brut (at about $23).

- Four upscale (and very good) bruts, all $35 to $40 and up, are Bellavista, Cà del Bosco, Giulio Ferrari, and Bruno Giacosa Extra Brut. Giacosa, well-known for his outstanding Barbarescos and Barolos, makes 100-percent-Pinot Noir Brut in his spare time, for kicks. Like everything else he produces, it's superb.

Prosecco

This quintessential Italian sparkling wine has become all the rage in parts of the United States, thanks to the fact that so many Italian restaurants serve it by the glass. Prosecco comes from Prosecco grapes grown near Venice and Treviso. It's a straightforward, pleasant apéritif, low in alcohol (about 11 to 12 percent), and it comes in dry, off-dry, and sweet styles. Prosecco is mainly a frizzante wine, but it also comes as a spumante (fully sparkling), or even as a non-sparkling wine (which we don't recommend; it's better with bubbles). Most Prosecco bears the DOC appellation of either Valdobbiadene or Conegliano (or, in some cases, both), which are two villages in the Veneto.

Prosecco is the perfect wine to have with Italian antipasto, such as pickled vegetables, calamari, anchovies, or spicy salami. Its fresh, fruity flavors cleanse your mouth and get your appetite going for dinner. And Prosecco is eminently affordable: It retails for $12 to $18 a bottle. Recommended producers (alphabetically) include Astoria, Bisson, Canevel, Carpenè Malvolti, Mionetto, Nino Franco, Valdo, Zardetto, and Zonin.

Spanish sparkling wines (Cava)

What if you want to spend about $10 or less for a decent sparkling wine? The answer is Spain's sparkling wine, Cava, which sells mainly for $8 to $12 a bottle. Almost all of it comes from the Penedés region, near Barcelona.

Cava is made in the traditional method, fermented in the bottle. But most Cavas use local Spanish grapes. As a result, they taste distinctly different (a nicely earthy, mushroomy flavor) from California bubblies and from Champagne. Some of the more expensive blends do contain Chardonnay.

Two gigantic wineries dominate Cava production — Freixenet (pronounced *fresh net*) and Codorniu. Freixenet's frosted black Cordon Negro bottle has to be one of the most recognizable wine bottles in the world. Other Cava brands to look for are Mont Marçal, Paul Cheneau, Cristalino, Marqués de Monistrol, and Segura Viudas. Juve y Camps, a vintage-dated, upscale Cava, is a worthwhile buy at $16.

Southern stars

Australia, New Zealand, and South Africa now make some very fine sparkling wines in the traditional method. Australia boasts a really good $10 sparkler called Seaview Brut; for something completely unusual, try Seaview's deep red sparkling Shiraz, about $12. Among New Zealand bubblies, one of the finest is that of Highfield Estate in Marlborough. The South African sparkling brut that has really impressed us comes from the Boschendal Estate in the Franschhoek Valley and is called Le Grand Pavillion (about $13 to $15). Traditional-method South African sparkling wines carry the words *Cap Classique* on their labels.

Buying and Serving Bubbly

Sparkling wine is best cold, about 45°F (7° to 8°C), although some people prefer it less cold (52°F; 11°C). We like the colder temperature because it helps the wine hold its effervescence — and the wine warms up so quickly in the glass, anyway. Because older Champagnes and Vintage Champagnes are more complex, you can chill them less than young, non-vintage Champagne or sparkling wine.

Never leave an open bottle of sparkling wine on the table unless it's in an ice bucket (half cold water, half ice) because it will warm up quickly. Use a sparkling wine stopper to keep leftover bubbly fresh for a couple of days—in the fridge, of course.

If you're entertaining, you should know that the ideal bottle size for Champagne is the *magnum,* which is equivalent to two bottles. The larger bottle enables the wine to age more gently in the winery's cellar. Magnums (or sometimes double magnums) are usually the largest bottles in which Champagne is fermented; all really large bottles have had finished Champagne poured into them, and the wine is therefore not as fresh as it is in a magnum or a regular bottle.

Baby Champagnes are "in"

Although Champagnes in small bottles — 375 ml half-bottles and 187 ml splits — normally don't stay as fresh as Champagne in larger bottles, size becomes less an issue when the bottles sell quickly. A few savvy Champagne houses have a novel way of selling their bubblies in the United States: Attractively package the Champagnes in small bottles, and make them readily available in nightclubs and bars where young people congregate. A few years ago, Pommery introduced its "POP," a bright blue split (187 ml) that comes with a straw so that you can even drink it right out of the bottle. It's an extra-dry non-vintage Champagne, not quite as dry as a brut, which suits the casual occasions when this wine is drunk. Not to be outdone, Piper-Heidsieck followed with a bright red split of its non-vintage brut, which it calls "Baby Piper." Both Champagnes have been selling very well. Perrier-Jouët is now aggressively marketing its half-bottles and splits; ditto Lanson with its half-bottle. More houses will surely follow.

Although Champagne is a serious wine, it obviously offers plenty of opportunity for fun!

Be wary of half-bottles (375 ml) and — chancier yet — splits (187 ml)! Champagne in these small bottles is often not fresh. If you're given a small bottle of Champagne or any sparkling wine as a wedding favor, for example, open it at the first excuse; do not keep it around for a year waiting for the right occasion!

Champagne and other good, dry sparkling wines are extremely versatile with food — and they are the essential wine for certain kinds of foods. For example, no wine goes better with egg dishes than Champagne. Indulge yourself next time that you have brunch. And when you're having spicy Asian cuisine, try sparkling wine. For us, no wine matches up better with spicy Chinese or Indian food!

Fish, seafood, pasta (but not with tomato sauce), risotto, and poultry are excellent with Champagne and sparkling wine. If you're having lamb (pink, not well-done) or ham, pair rosé Champagne with it. With aged Champagne, chunks of aged Asiago, aged Gouda, or Parmesan cheese go extremely well.

Don't serve a dry brut (or extra dry) sparkling wine with dessert. These styles are just too dry. With fresh fruit and desserts that are not too sweet, try a demi-sec Champagne. With sweeter desserts (or wedding cake!), we recommend Asti. (For more info on Champagne with food, see Chapter 14 in *Champagne For Dummies*.)

Ten excuses to indulge

1. You have a bottle on hand.

2. Your demanding boss just left for vacation, or better yet, changed jobs.

3. The noisy neighbors next door finally moved out.

4. You finished your income taxes.

5. It's Saturday.

6. The kids left for summer camp (or college).

7. You just found $20 in your old coat pocket.

8. You didn't get a single telephone solicitation all day.

9. The wire muzzle over the cork makes a great cat toy.

10. You have just finished revising a wine book!

Chapter 15

Wine Roads Less Traveled: Fortified and Dessert Wines

In This Chapter

▶ The world's most versatile wine

▶ 80 grapes for one wine

▶ A wine that lasts 200 years

▶ Liquid gold from rotted grapes

The wines we lump together as *fortified wines* and *dessert wines* aren't mainstream beverages that you want to drink every day. Some of them are much higher in alcohol than regular wines, and some of them are extremely sweet (and rare and expensive!). They're the wine equivalent of really good candy — delicious enough that you can get carried away if you let yourself indulge daily. So you treat them as treats, a glass before or after dinner, a bottle when company comes, a splurge to celebrate the start of your diet — tomorrow.

Pleasure aside, from a purely academic point of view, you owe it to yourself to try these wines. Seriously! Learning about wine is hard work, but it's also a lot of fun.

Timing Is Everything

Many wines enjoyed before dinner, as apéritif wines, or after dinner, as dessert wines, fall into the category of *fortified wines* (called *liqueur wines* by the European Union, or EU; see Chapter 4 for an explanation of EU terms). Fortified wines all have alcohol added to them at some point in their production, giving them an alcohol content that ranges from 16 to 24 percent.

The point at which alcohol is added determines whether the wines are naturally sweet or dry.

- ✔ When fortified with alcohol *during* fermentation, the wines are sweet, because the added alcohol stops fermentation, leaving natural, unfermented sugar in the wine. (See Chapter 1 for an explanation of fermentation.) Port is the classic example of this process.

- ✔ When fortified *after* fermentation (after all the grape sugar has been converted to alcohol), the wines are dry (unless they're subsequently sweetened). Sherry is the classic example of this process.

Some of the wines we call dessert wines don't have added alcohol. Their sweetness occurs because the grapes are at the right place at the right time — when noble rot strikes. (See the discussion of German wines in Chapter 11.) Other dessert wines are sweet because winemakers pick very ripe (but not rotten) grapes and dry them before fermentation to concentrate their juice, or they let the grapes freeze — just other ways of turning grape juice into the nectar of the gods.

Sherry: A Misunderstood Wine

The late comedian Rodney Dangerfield built a career around the line, "I get no respect!" His wine of choice should have been Sherry, because it shares the same plight. Sherry is a wine of true quality and diversity, but it remains undiscovered by most of the world. In a way, we're not sorry, because the price of good Sherry is attractively low.

The Jerez triangle

Sherry comes from the Andalucía region of sun-baked, southwestern Spain. The wine is named after Jerez *(her ETH)* de la Frontera, an old town of Moorish and Arab origin where many of the Sherry *bodegas* are located. *(Bodega* can refer to the actual building in which Sherry is matured or to the Sherry firm itself.)

Actually, the town of Jerez is just one corner of a triangle that makes up the Sherry region. Another corner is Puerto de Santa María, a beautiful, old coast town southwest of Jerez, and home to a number of large bodegas. The third point of the triangle, Sanlúcar de Barrameda (also on the coast but northwest of Jerez), is so blessed with sea breezes that the lightest and driest of Sherries, *manzanilla,* can legally be made only there. Aficionados of Sherry swear that they can detect the salty tang of the ocean in manzanilla *(mahn zah NEE yah).*

Traveling from Sanlúcar to Jerez, you pass vineyards with dazzling white soil. This soil is *albariza,* the region's famous chalky earth, rich in limestone from fossilized shells. Summers are hot and dry, but balmy sea breezes temper the heat.

The Palomino grape — the main variety used in Sherry — thrives only here in the hot Sherry region on albariza soil. Palomino is a complete failure for table wines because it is so neutral in flavor and low in acid, but it's perfect for Sherry production. Two other grape varieties, Pedro Ximénez *(PAY dro he MAIN ehz)* and Moscatel (Muscat), are used for dessert types of Sherry.

The phenomenon of flor

Sherry consists of two basic types: *fino* (light, very dry) and *oloroso* (rich and full, but also dry). Sweet Sherries are made by sweetening either type.

After fermentation, the winemaker decides which Sherries will become finos or olorosos *(oh loh ROH sohs)* by judging the appearance, aroma, and flavor of the young, unfortified wines. If a wine is to be a fino *(FEE no),* the winemaker fortifies it lightly (until its alcohol level reaches about 15.5 percent). He strengthens future olorosos to 18 percent alcohol.

At this point, when the wines are in casks, the special Sherry magic begins: A yeast called *flor* grows spontaneously on the surface of the wines destined to be finos. The flor eventually covers the whole surface, protecting the wine from oxidation. The flor feeds on oxygen in the air and on alcohol and glycerin in the wine. It changes the wine's character, contributing a distinct aroma and flavor and rendering the wine thinner and more delicate in texture.

Flor doesn't grow on olorosos-to-be, because their higher alcohol content prevents it. Without the protection of the flor (and because the casks are never filled to the brim), these wines are exposed to oxygen as they age. This deliberate oxidation protects olorosos against further oxidation — for example, after you open a bottle.

Communal aging

Both fino and oloroso Sherries age in a special way that's unique to Sherry making.

The young wine isn't left to age on its own (as most other wines would) but is added to casks of older wine that are already aging. To make room for the young wine, some of the older wine is emptied out of the casks and is added to casks of even older wine. To make room in those casks, some of the wine is transferred to casks of even older wine, and so on. At the end of this chain, four to nine generations away from the young wine, some of the finished Sherry is taken from the oldest casks and is bottled for sale.

This system of blending wines is called the *solera* system. It takes its name from the word *solera* (floor), the term also used to identify the casks of oldest wine.

As wines are blended — younger into older, into yet older, and eventually into oldest — no more than a third of the wine is emptied from any cask. In theory, then, each solera contains small (and ever-decreasing) amounts of very old wine. As each younger wine mingles with older wine, it takes on characteristics of the older wine; within a few months, the wine of each generation is indistinguishable from what it was before being refreshed with younger wine. Thus, the solera system maintains infinite consistency of quality and style in Sherry.

Because the casks of Sherry age in dry, airy bodegas above ground (rather than humid, underground cellars like most other wines), some of the wine's water evaporates, and the wine's alcoholic strength increases. Some olorosos aged for more than ten years can be as much as 24 percent alcohol, compared to their starting point of 18 percent.

Two makes twelve

So far, so good: two types of Sherry — delicate fino aged under its protective flor, and fuller oloroso, aged oxidatively — and no vintages, because the young wines are blended with older wines. But now Sherry begins to get a bit confusing. Those two types are about to branch into at least twelve. New styles occur when the natural course of aging changes the character of a Sherry so that its taste no longer conforms to one of the two categories. Deliberate sweetening of the wine also creates different styles.

Among dry Sherries, these are the main styles:

- **Fino:** Pale, straw-colored Sherry, light in body, dry, and delicate. Fino Sherries are always matured under flor, either in Jerez or Puerto de Santa María. They have 15 to 17 percent alcohol. After they lose their protective flor (by bottling), finos become very vulnerable to oxidation spoilage, and you must therefore store them in a cool place, drink them young, and refrigerate them after opening. They're best when chilled.

- **Manzanilla:** Pale, straw-colored, delicate, light, tangy, and very dry fino-style Sherry made only in Sanlucar de Barrameda. (Although various styles of manzanilla are produced, *manzanilla fina,* the fino style, is by far the most common.) The temperate sea climate causes the flor to grow thicker in this town, and manzanilla is thus the driest and most pungent of all the Sherries. Handle it similarly to a fino Sherry.

- **Manzanilla pasada:** A manzanilla that has been aged in cask about seven years and has lost its flor. It's more amber in color than a manzanilla fina and fuller-bodied. It's close to a dry amontillado (see the next item) in style, but still crisp and pungent. Serve cool.

- **Amontillado:** An aged fino that has lost its flor in the process of cask aging. It's deeper amber in color and richer and nuttier than the previous styles. *Amontillado (ah moan tee YAH doh)* is dry but retains some of the pungent tang from its lost flor. True amontillado is fairly rare; most of the best examples are in the $25 to $40 price range. Cheaper Sherries labeled "amontillado" are common, so be suspicious if it costs less than $15 a bottle. Serve amontillado slightly cool and, for best flavor, finish the bottle within a week.

- **Oloroso:** Dark gold to deep brown in color (depending on its age), full-bodied with rich, raisiny aroma and flavor, but dry. Olorosos lack the delicacy and pungency of fino (flor) Sherries. They're usually between 18 and 20 percent alcohol and can keep for a few weeks after you open the bottle because they have already been oxidized in their aging. Serve them at room temperature.

- **Palo cortado:** The rarest of all Sherries. It starts out as a fino, with a flor, and develops as an amontillado, losing its flor. But then, for some unknown reason, it begins to resemble the richer, more fragrant oloroso style, all the while retaining the elegance of an amontillado. In color and alcohol content, palo cortado *(PAH loe cor TAH doh)* is similar to an oloroso, but its aroma is quite like an amontillado. Like amontillado Sherry, beware of cheap imitations. Serve at room temperature. It keeps as well as olorosos.

Sweet Sherry is dry Sherry that has been sweetened. The sweetening can come in many forms, such as the juice of Pedro Ximénez grapes that have been dried like raisins. All the following sweet styles of Sherry are best served at room temperature:

- **Medium Sherry:** Amontillados and light olorosos that have been slightly sweetened. They are light brown in color.

- **Pale cream:** Made by blending fino and light amontillado Sherries and lightly sweetening the blend. They have a very pale gold color. Pale cream is a fairly new style.

- **Cream Sherry:** Cream and the lighter "milk" Sherries are rich *amorosos* (the term for sweetened olorosos). They vary in quality, depending on the oloroso used, and can improve in the bottle with age. These Sherries are a popular style.

- **Brown Sherry:** Very dark, rich, sweet, dessert Sherry, usually containing a coarser style of oloroso.

- **East India Sherry:** A type of Brown Sherry that has been deeply sweetened and colored.

- **Pedro Ximénez** and **Moscatel:** Extremely sweet, dark brown, syrupy dessert Sherries. Often lower in alcohol, these Sherries are made from raisined grapes of these two varieties. As varietally labeled Sherries, they are quite rare today. Delicious over vanilla ice cream (really!).

Nut'n Sherry

The aroma of fino Sherry is often compared with almonds. Amontillados are said to smell like hazelnuts, and olorosos smell like walnuts. And, by the way, the named nuts make ideal accompaniments to each particular sherry.

Some wines from elsewhere in the world, especially the United States, also call themselves "Sherry." Many of these are inexpensive wines in large bottles. Occasionally you can find a decent one, but usually they're sweet and not very good. Authentic Sherry is made only in the Jerez region of Spain and carries the official name, *Jerez-Xérès-Sherry* (the Spanish, French, and English names for the town) on the front or back label.

Serving and storing Sherry

The light, dry Sherries — fino and manzanilla — must be fresh. Buy them from stores with rapid turnover; a fino or manzanilla that has been languishing on the shelf for several months will not give you the authentic experience of these wines.

Although fino or manzanilla can be an excellent apéritif, be careful when ordering a glass in a restaurant or bar. Never accept a glass from an already-open bottle unless the bottle has been refrigerated. Even then, ask how long it has been open — more than two days is too much. After you open a bottle at home, refrigerate it and finish it within a couple of days.

We like to buy half-bottles of fino and manzanilla so that we don't have leftover wine that oxidizes. These, and all Sherries, can be stored upright. Try not to hold bottles of fino or manzanilla more than three months, however. The higher alcohol and the oxidative aging of other types of Sherry (amontillado, oloroso, palo cortado, all the sweet Sherries) permit you to hold them for several years.

Manzanilla and fino Sherry are ideal with almonds, olives, shrimp or prawns, all kinds of seafood, and those wonderful tapas in Spanish bars and restaurants. Amontillado Sherries can accompany tapas before dinner but are also fine at the table with light soups, cheese, ham, or salami (especially the Spanish type, *chorizo*). Dry olorosos and palo cortados are best with nuts, olives, and hard cheeses (such as the excellent Spanish sheep-milk cheese, Manchego). All the sweet Sherries can be served with desserts after dinner or enjoyed on their own.

Recommended Sherries

Sherries are among the great values in the wine world: You can buy decent, genuine Sherries for $7 or $8. But if you want to try the best wines, you may have to spend $15 or more. The following are some of our favorite Sherries, according to type.

Fino

All these fino Sherries are about $15 to $18:

- ✔ González Byass's Tío Pepe *(TEE oh PAY pay)*
- ✔ Pedro Domecq's La Ina *(EEN ah)*
- ✔ Emilio Lustau's Jarana *(har AHN ah)*
- ✔ Valdespino's Inocente

Manzanilla

- ✔ Hidalgo's La Gitana (a great buy at $12; $9 for 500 ml bottle); also, Hidalgo's Manzanilla Pasada, about $20

Amontillado

You find a great number of cheap imitations in this category. For a true amontillado, stick to one of the following brands:

- ✔ González Byass's Del Duque (the real thing, at $48; half-bottle, $27)
- ✔ Emilio Lustau (any of his amontillados labeled Almacenista, $35 to $40)
- ✔ Hidalgo's Napoleon (about $18)
- ✔ Osborne's Solera A.O.S. ($40)

Oloroso

- ✔ González Byass's Matusalem ($48; half-bottle, $27)
- ✔ Emilio Lustau (any of his olorosos labeled Almacenista, $35 to $40)
- ✔ Osborne's "Very Old" ($38)

Palo cortado

You find many imitations in this category, too. True palo cortados are quite rare.

- ✔ González Byass's Apostoles ($48; half-bottle, $27)
- ✔ Emilio Lustau (any of his palo cortados labeled Almacenista, $35 to $40)
- ✔ Hidalgo's Jerez Cortado (about $35)

Cream

- ✔ Sandeman's Armada Cream (about $12 to $13)
- ✔ Emilio Lustau's Rare Cream Solera Reserva ($25 to $27)

East India, Pedro Ximénez, Moscatel

- ✔ Emilio Lustau (a quality brand for all three Sherries; all about $25)
- ✔ González Byass's Pedro Ximénez "Noe" ($48; half-bottle, $27)

Montilla: A Sherry look-alike

Northeast of the Sherry region is the Montilla-Moriles region (commonly referred to as Montilla), where wines very similar to Sherry are made in fino, amontillado, and oloroso styles. The two big differences between Montilla *(moan TEE yah)* and Sherry are

- ✔ Pedro Ximénez is the predominant grape variety in Montilla.
- ✔ Montillas usually reach their high alcohol levels naturally (without fortification).

Alvear is the leading brand of Montilla. Reasonably priced (about $14), these wines are widely available, as Finos or Amontillados.

Marsala, Vin Santo, and the Gang

Italy has a number of interesting dessert and fortified wines, of which Marsala (named after a town in western Sicily) is the most famous. Marsala is a fortified wine made from local grape varieties. It comes in numerous styles, all of which are fortified after fermentation, like Sherry, and aged in a form of the solera system. You can find dry, semi-dry, or sweet versions and amber, gold, or red versions, but the best Marsalas have the word *Superiore* or — even better — *Vergine* or *Vergine Soleras* on the label. Marsala Vergine is unsweetened and uncolored, and is aged longer than other styles.

Marco De Bartoli is the most acclaimed producer of dry-style Marsala. His 20-year-old Vecchio Samperi (about $50 for a 500 ml bottle) is an excellent example of a dry, apéritif Marsala. Pellegrino, Rallo, and Florio are larger producers of note. (For more info on Marsala and all other Sicilian fortified or dessert wines, see Chapter 11 in *Italian Wine For Dummies.*)

Two fascinating dessert wines are made on small islands near Sicily from dried grapes. One is Malvasia delle Lipari, from the estate of the late Carlo Hauner. This wine has a beautiful, orange-amber color and an incredible floral, apricot, and herb aroma ($25 to $27 for a half-bottle). The other is Moscato di Pantelleria, a very delicious sweet wine. De Bartoli is one of the best producers; look for his Bukkuram Passito Pantelleria (about $70 for a 500 ml bottle).

The region of Tuscany is rightfully proud of its Vin Santo *(vin SAHN toh),* a golden amber wine made from dried grapes and barrel-aged for several years. Vin Santo can be dry, medium-dry, or sweet. We prefer the first two — the dry style as an apéritif, and the medium-dry version as an accompaniment to the wonderful Italian almond cookies called *biscotti.*

Many Tuscan producers make a Vin Santo; four outstanding examples of Vin Santo (conveniently available in half-bottles as well as full bottles) are from Avignonesi (very expensive!), Badia a Coltibuono, Castello di Cacchiano, and San Giusto a Rentennano.

Port: The Glory of Portugal

Port is the world's greatest fortified red wine.

The British invented Port, thanks to one of their many wars with the French, when they were forced to buy Portuguese wine as an alternative to French wine. To insure that the Portuguese wines were stable enough for shipment by sea, the British had a small amount of brandy added to finished wine, and early Port was the result. The English established their first Port house, Warre, in the city of Oporto in 1670, and several others followed.

Ironically, the French, who drove the British to Portugal, today drink three times as much Port as the British! But, of course, the French have the highest per capita consumption of wine in the world.

Home, home on the Douro

Port takes its name from the city of Oporto, situated where the northerly Douro River empties into the Atlantic Ocean. But its vineyards are far away, in the hot, mountainous Douro Valley. (In 1756, this wine region became one of the first in the world to be officially recognized by its government.) Some of the most dramatically beautiful vineyards anywhere are on the slopes of the upper Douro — still very much a rugged, unspoiled area.

<table>
</table>

Port-O

The term Port has been borrowed even more extensively around the world than "Sherry" has. Many countries outside the EU make sweet, red wine in the Port style and label it as Port. Some of it can be quite good, but it's never as fine as the genuine article that is made only in Portugal. The trick in identifying authentic Portuguese Port is to look for the word *Porto,* which always appears on the label.

Port wine is fermented and fortified in the Douro Valley, and then most of it travels downriver to the coast. The large shippers' wine is finished and matured in the Port lodges of Vila Nova de Gaia, a suburb of Oporto, while most small producers mature their wine in the Valley. From Oporto, the wine is shipped all over the world.

To stop your wine-nerd friends in their tracks, ask them to name the authorized grape varieties for Port. (There are more than 80!) In truth, most wine lovers — even Port lovers — can't name more than one variety. These grapes are mostly local and unknown outside of Portugal. For the record, the five most important varieties are *Touriga Nacional, Tinta Roriz* (Tempranillo), *Tinta Barroca, Tinto Cão,* and *Touriga Franca.*

Many Ports in a storm

Think Sherry is complicated? In some ways, Port is even trickier. Although all Port is sweet, and most of it is red, a zillion styles exist. The styles vary according to the quality of the base wine (ranging from ordinary to exceptional), how long the wine is aged in wood before bottling (ranging from 2 to 40-plus years), and whether the wine is from a single year or blended from wines of several years.

Following is a brief description of the main styles, from simplest to most complex:

- ✔ **White Port:** Made from white grapes, this gold-colored wine can be off-dry or sweet. We couldn't quite figure out why it existed — Sherries and Sercial Madeiras (discussed later in this chapter) are better as apéritifs and red Ports are far superior as sweet wines — until someone served us white Port with tonic and ice one day. Served this way, white Port can be a bracing warm-weather apéritif.

- **Ruby Port:** This young, non-vintage style is aged in wood for about three years before release. Fruity, simple, and inexpensive (around $12 for major brands), it's the best-selling type of Port. If labeled *Reserve* or *Special Reserve,* the wine has usually aged about six years and costs a few dollars more. Ruby Port is a good introduction to the Port world.

- **Vintage Character Port:** Despite its name, this wine is not single-vintage Port — it just tries to taste like one. Vintage Character Port is actually premium ruby blended from higher-quality wines of several vintages and matured in wood for about five years. Full-bodied, rich, and ready-to-drink when released, these wines are a good value at about $17 to $19. But the labels don't always say *Vintage Character;* instead, they often bear proprietary names such as Founder's Reserve (from Sandeman); Bin 27 (Fonseca); Six Grapes (Graham); First Estate (Taylor Fladgate); Warrior (Warre); and Distinction (Croft). As if *Vintage Character* wouldn't have been confusing enough!

- **Tawny Port:** Tawny is the most versatile Port style. The best tawnies are good-quality wines that fade to a pale garnet or brownish red color during long wood aging. Their labels carry an indication of their average age (the average age of the wines from which they were blended) — 10, 20, 30, or over-40 years. Ten-year-old tawnies cost about $30, 20-year-olds sell for $45 to $50, and 30- and over-40-year-old tawnies cost a lot more ($90 to well over $100). We consider 10- and 20-year-old tawnies the best buys; the older ones aren't always worth the extra bucks. Tawny Ports have more finesse than other styles and are appropriate both as apéritifs and after dinner. Inexpensive tawnies that sell for about the same price as ruby Port are usually weak in flavor and not worth buying.

A serious tawny Port can be enjoyed in warm weather (even with a few ice cubes!) when a Vintage Port would be too heavy and tannic.

- **Colheita Port:** Often confused with Vintage Port because it's vintage-dated, colheita is actually a tawny from a single vintage. In other words, it has aged (and softened and tawnied) in wood for many years. Unlike an aged tawny, though, it's the wine of a single year. Niepoort is one of the few Port houses that specializes in colheita Port. It can be very good but older vintages are quite expensive (about $100). Smith Woodhouse and Delaforce offer colheita Portos for $50 or less.

- **Late Bottled Vintage Port (LBV):** This type *is* from a specific vintage, but usually not from a very top year. The wine ages four to six years in wood before bottling and is then ready to drink, unlike Vintage Port. Quite full-bodied, but not as hefty as Vintage Port, it sells for about $18 to $23.

- **Vintage Port:** The pinnacle of Port production, Vintage Port is the wine of a single year blended from several of a house's best vineyards. It's bottled at about two years of age, before the wine has much chance to shed its tough tannins. It therefore requires an enormous amount of bottle aging to accomplish the development that didn't occur in wood. Vintage Port is usually not mature (ready to drink) until about 20 years after the vintage.

Because it's very rich and very tannic, this wine throws a heavy sediment and *must* be decanted, preferably several hours before drinking (it needs the aeration). Vintage Port can live 70 or more years in top vintages.

Most good Vintage Ports sell for $75 to $100 when they're first released (years away from drinkability). Mature Vintage Ports can cost well over $100. Producing a Vintage Port amounts to a *declaration of that vintage* (a term you hear in Port circles) on the part of an individual Port house.

✔ **Single Quinta Vintage Port:** These are Vintage Ports from a single estate *(quinta)* that is usually a producer's best property (such as Taylor's Vargellas and Graham's Malvedos). They're made in good years, but not in the best vintages, because then their grapes are needed for the Vintage Port blend. They have the advantage of being readier to drink than declared Vintage Ports — at less than half their price — and of usually being released when they're mature. You should decant and aerate them before serving, however. (Some Port houses, incidentally, are themselves single estates, such as Quinta do Noval, Quinta do Infantado, and Quinta do Vesuvio. When such a house makes a vintage-dated Port, it's a Vintage Port, as well as a single quinta Port. But that's splitting hairs.)

Storing and serving Port

Treat Vintage Ports like all other fine red wines: Store the bottles on their sides in a cool place. You can store other Ports either on their sides (if they have a cork rather than a plastic-topped cork stopper) or upright. All Ports, except white, ruby, and older Vintage Ports, keep well for a week or so after opening, with aged-stated tawny capable of keeping for a few weeks.

You can now find Vintage Ports and some Vintage Character Ports, such as Fonseca Bin 27, in half-bottles — a brilliant development for Port lovers. Enjoying a bottle after dinner is far easier to justify when it's just a half-bottle. The wine evolves slightly more quickly in half-bottles, and considering the wine's longevity, that may even be a bonus!

It's worth a try!

Don't let all the complicated styles of Port deter you from picking up a bottle and trying it. If you've never had Port before, you're bound to love it — almost no matter which style you try. (Later, you can fine-tune your preference for one style or another.) Port is, simply, delicious!

Another Portuguese classic

One of the great dessert wines made mainly from the white or pink Muscat grape is Setúbal *(SHTOO bahl)*. Produced just south of Lisbon, Setúbal is made similarly to Port, with alcohol added to stop fermentation. Like Port, it's a rich, long-lasting wine. The most important producer is J. M. da Fonseca.

Serve Port at cool room temperature, 64°F (18°C), although tawny Port can be an invigorating pick-me-up when served chilled during warm weather. The classic complements to Port are walnuts and strong cheeses, such as Stilton, Gorgonzola, Roquefort, Cheddar, and aged Gouda.

Recommended Port producers

In terms of quality, with the exception of a few clunker producers, Port is one of the most consistent of all wines. We've organized our favorite Port producers into two categories — outstanding and very good — in rough order of preference. As you might expect, wines in the first group tend to be a bit more expensive. Our rating is based mainly on Vintage Port but can be generally applied to all the various Port styles of the house.

Outstanding

Taylor-Fladgate
Fonseca
Graham
Quinta do Noval "Nacional" (made from ungrafted vineyards; see Chapter 3)

Dow
Smith-Woodhouse
Cockburn *(COH burn)*

Very Good

Ramos Pinto
Warre
Quinta do Noval
Niepoort
Croft
Sandeman
Quinta do Infantado
Quinta do Vesuvio
Rozes

Ferreira
Cálem
Churchill
Delaforce
Gould Campbell
Martinez
Osborne
Offley

Recent good vintages of Vintage Port to buy include 2000, 1994, 1992, and 1991, with both 2003 (just released) and 2004 (will be released beginning in 2007) showing promise for the future. (For a complete list of Vintage Port vintages, see Appendix C.)

Long Live Madeira

The legendary wine called Madeira comes from the island of the same name, which sits in the Atlantic Ocean nearer to Africa than Europe. Madeira is a subtropical island whose precarious hillside vineyards rise straight up from the ocean. The island is a province of Portugal, but the British have always run its wine trade. Historically, Madeira could even be considered something of an American wine, for this is the wine that American colonists drank.

Madeira can lay claim to being the world's longest-lived wine. A few years ago, we were fortunate enough to try a 1799 Vintage Madeira that was still perfectly fine. Only Hungary's Tokaji Azsu (see Chapter 11, "The Re-emergence of Hungary") can rival Vintage Madeira in longevity, and that's true only of Tokaji Azsu's rarest examples, such as its Essencia.

Although Madeira's fortified wines were quite the rage 200 years ago, the island's vineyards were devastated at the end of the nineteenth century, first by mildew and then by the phylloxera louse. Most vineyards were replanted with lesser grapes. Madeira has spent a long time recovering from these setbacks. In the 19th century, more than 70 companies were shipping Madeira all over the world; now, only six companies of any size exist: Barbeito, H. M Borges, Henriques & Henriques, Justino Henriques, the Madeira Wine Company (the largest by far, a consolidation of four old companies — Blandy's, Cossart Gordon, Leacock's, and Miles), and Pereira d'Oliveira.

The very best Madeira wines are still those from the old days, vintage-dated wines from 1920 back to 1795. Surprisingly, you can still find a few Madeiras from the nineteenth century. The prices aren't outrageous, either ($300 to $400 a bottle), considering what other wines that old, such as Bordeaux, cost. (Refer to Chapter 16 for sources of old Madeira.)

Timeless, indestructible, and tasty

The best Madeira comes in four styles, two fairly dry and two sweet. The sweeter Madeiras generally have their fermentation halted somewhat early by the addition of alcohol. Drier Madeiras have alcohol added after fermentation.

A curiosity of most Madeira production is a baking process called the *estufagem (es too FAH jem),* which follows fermentation. The fact that Madeira improves with heat was discovered back in the seventeenth century. When trading ships crossed the equator with casks of Madeira as ballast in their holds, the wine actually improved! Today's practice of baking the wine at home on the island is a bit more practical than sending it around the world in a slow boat.

In the estufagem process, Madeira spends a minimum of three months, often longer, in heated tanks, in *estufas* (heating rooms). Any sugars in the wine become caramelized, and the wine becomes thoroughly *maderized* (oxidized through heating) without developing any unpleasant aroma or taste.

A more laborious and considerably more expensive way of heating Madeira is the *canteiro* method, in which barrels are left in warm lofts of or exposed to the sun (the weather stays warm year-round) for as long as three years. The same magical metamorphosis takes place in the wines. The *canteiro* method is best for Madeira because the wines retain their high acidity, color, and extract much better in the slow, natural three-year process; only the finer Madeiras use this method of aging.

Endless finish

Technically, almost all the best Madeira starts as white wine, but the heating process and years of maturation give it an amber color. It has a tangy aroma and flavor that's uniquely its own, and as long a finish on the palate as you'll find on the planet. When Madeira is made from any of the island's five noble grapes (listed later in this section), the grape name indicates the style. When Madeira doesn't carry a grape name — and most younger Madeiras don't — the words *dry, medium-dry, medium-sweet,* and *sweet* indicate the style.

Vintage Madeira must spend at least 20 years in a cask, but in the old days, the aging was even longer. Some of the most memorable wines we've ever tasted were old Madeiras, and so we're afraid we might get carried away a bit, beginning any time now. Their aroma alone is divine, and you continue tasting the wine long after you've swallowed it. (Spitting is out of the question.) Words truly are inadequate to describe this wine.

If you can afford to buy an old bottle of vintage-dated Madeira (the producer's name is relatively unimportant), you'll understand our enthusiasm. And maybe some day when Madeira production gets back on its feet, every wine lover will be able to experience Vintage Madeira. In the meantime, for a less expensive Madeira experience, look for wines labeled *15 years old, 10 years old,* or *5 years old.* Don't bother with any other type, because it will be unremarkable, and then we'll look crazy.

You never have to worry about Madeira getting too old. It's indestructible. The enemies of wine — heat and oxygen — have already had their way with Madeira during the winemaking and maturing process. Nothing you do after it's opened can make it blink.

If a Madeira is dated with the word *Solera* — for example, "Solera 1890" — it is *not* a Vintage Madeira but a blend of many younger vintages whose original barrel, or solera, dates back to 1890. Solera-dated Madeiras can be very fine and are generally not as expensive — nor as great — as Vintage Madeiras. But Solera Madeiras are becoming obsolete today. In their place is a new style of Madeira, called *Colheita* or Harvest. This style is modeled after *Colheita* Porto (see "Colheita Port" in the "Many Ports in a Storm" section in this chapter) in that colheita Madeira is a single vintage-dated Madeira wine. Colheita Madeira doesn't have to spend a minimum of 20 years aging in cask, as does Vintage Madeira, but only five — or seven for the driest, Sercial. (For example, the 1994 colheita Madeira debuted in 2000 at only six years of age.) Colheita Madeira is much less expensive than vintage Madeira. Most of the six major Madeira shippers are now selling colheita; sales of vintage-dated Madeira have doubled since the introduction of this style.

Vintage, colheita, and solera-dated Madeiras are made from a single grape variety and are varietally labeled. The grapes include five noble white grape varieties and one less noble red variety. (Another noble red variety, Bastardo, is no longer used for commercial production.) Each variety corresponds to a specific style of wine; we list them from driest style to sweetest.

- ✔ **Sercial:** The Sercial grape grows at the highest altitudes. Thus, the grapes are the least ripe and make the driest Madeira. The wine is high in acidity and very tangy. Sercial Madeira is an outstanding apéritif wine with almonds, olives, or light cheeses. Unfortunately, true Sercial is quite rare today.

- ✔ **Verdelho:** The Verdelho grape makes a medium-dry style, with nutty, peachy flavors and a tang of acidity. It's good as an apéritif or with consommé.

- ✔ **Bual (or Boal):** Darker amber in color, Bual is a rich, medium-sweet Madeira with spicy flavors of almonds and raisins and a long, tangy finish. Bual is best after dinner. Like Sercial, true Bual is rare today.

- ✔ **Malmsey:** Made from the Malvasia grape, Malmsey is dark amber, sweet, and intensely concentrated with a very long finish. Drink it after dinner.

Two rare varieties, whose names you may see on some very old bottles, are

- ✔ **Terrantez:** Medium-sweet, between Verdelho and Bual in style, this is a powerful, fragrant Madeira with lots of acidity. For some Madeira lovers, Terrantez is the greatest variety of all. Unfortunately, very little Terrantez is available today; Henriques & Henriques still produces it. Drink it after dinner.

> ✔ **Bastardo:** This is the only red grape of the noble varieties. Old Bastardos from the last century are mahogany-colored and rich, but not as rich as the Terrantez.

The less-noble red Tinta Negra Mole variety is the dominant grape for today's Madeira production (used for over 85 percent of Madeira wines), because it grows more prolifically than the five noble varieties (Sercial, Verdelho, Bual, Malmsey, and Terrantez) without the diseases to which they are prone. Also, it is less site-specific; it can grow anywhere on the island, unlike the noble varieties, which grow in vineyards close to the sea where the urban sprawl of Funchal, Madeira's capital city, impinges on them. Previously, the less-regarded Tinta Negra Mole wasn't identified as a variety on bottles of Madeira but now, the huge Madeira Wine Company is beginning to varietally-label Tinta Negra Mole Madeiras.

Sauternes and the Nobly Rotten Wines

Warm, misty autumns encourage the growth of a fungus called *botrytis cinerea* in vineyards. Nicknamed *noble rot,* botrytis concentrates the liquid and sugar in the grapes, giving the winemaker amazingly rich juice to ferment. The best wines from botrytis-infected grapes are among the greatest dessert wines in the world, with intensely concentrated flavors and plenty of acidity to prevent the wine from tasting excessively sweet.

The greatest nobly rotten wines are made in the Sauternes district of Graves (Bordeaux) and in Germany (see Chapter 11), but they are also produced in Austria and California, among other places.

Sauternes: Liquid gold

Sauternes is a very labor-intensive wine. Grapes must be picked by hand; workers pass through the vineyard several times — sometimes over a period of weeks — each time selecting only the botrytis-infected grapes. Yields are low. Harvests sometimes linger until November, but now and then bad weather in October dashes all hopes of making botrytis-infected wine. Often, only two to four vintages per decade make decent Sauternes (but the 1980s decade was exceptional, and so far, the 2000s decade has been phenomenal; see the vintage chart in Appendix C).

Consequently, good Sauternes is expensive. Prices range from $45 to $50 a bottle up to $300 (depending on the vintage) for Château d'Yquem *(d'ee kem)*. The greatest Sauternes, d'Yquem has always been prized by collectors (see Chapter 16). It was the only Sauternes given the status of *first great growth* in the 1855 Bordeaux Classification (see Chapter 9).

Sauternes is widely available in half-bottles, reducing the cost somewhat. A 375 ml bottle is a perfect size for after dinner, and you can buy a decent half-bottle of Sauternes or Barsac, a dessert wine similar to Sauternes, like Château Doisy-Védrines *(dwahs ee veh dreen)* or Château Doisy-Daëne *(dwahs ee dah en)* for $25 to $30.

Mining the gold

The Sauternes wine district includes five communes in the southernmost part of Graves (one of them named Sauternes). One of the five, Barsac, is entitled to its own appellation; Barsac wines are slightly lighter and less sweet than Sauternes. The Garonne River and the Ciron, an important tributary, produce the mists that encourage *botrytis cinerea* to form on the grapes.

The three authorized grape varieties are Sémillon, Sauvignon Blanc, and Muscadelle — although the latter is used by only a few chateaux, and even then in small quantities. Sémillon is the king of Sauternes. Most producers use at least 80 percent of Sémillon in their blend.

Wine that is called "Sauterne" (no final "s") is produced in California and other places. This semisweet, rather insipid wine is made from inexpensive grapes and usually sold in large bottles. It bears absolutely no resemblance to true, botrytis-infected Sauternes, from Sauternes, France. California does make late-harvest, botrytis-infected wines, mainly Rieslings, and while they are far better than California Sauterne (and even worth trying), they are very different wines from the botrytis wines of Sauternes or of Germany.

Recommended Sauternes

All the Sauternes in the following list range from outstanding to good. (Wines specifically from Barsac are labeled as such.) In Sauternes, vintages are just as important as in the rest of Bordeaux; check our vintage recommendations in Appendix C.

Outstanding

- **Château d'Yquem:** Can last for 100 years or more
- **Château de Fargues:** Owned by d'Yquem; almost as good as d'Yquem, at one-third the price ($100)

✔ **Château Climens (Barsac):** At $75, a value; near d'Yquem's level

✔ **Château Coutet (Barsac):** A great buy ($55 to $60)

Excellent

✔ **Château Suduiraut:** On the brink of greatness ($60 to $65)

✔ **Château Rieussec:** Rich, lush style ($65 to $70)

✔ **Château Raymond-Lafon:** Located next to d'Yquem (about $60)

Very Good

✔ **Château Lafaurie-Peyraguey**

✔ **Château Latour Blanche**

✔ **Château Guiraud**

✔ **Château Rabaud-Promis**

✔ **Château Sigalas-Rabaud**

✔ **Château Nairac (Barsac)**

✔ **Château Doisy-Védrines (Barsac)**

✔ **Château Doisy-Daëne (Barsac)**

✔ **Château Clos Haut-Peyraguey**

Good

✔ **Château Bastor-Lamontagne**

✔ **Château Rayne Vigneau**

✔ **Château d'Arche**

✔ **Château de Malle**

✔ **Château Suau (Barsac)**

✔ **Château Lamothe-Guignard**

✔ **Château Romieu-Lacoste (Barsac)**

✔ **Château Liot (Barsac)**

✔ **Château Doisy-Dubroca (Barsac)**

✔ **Château Filhot**

Letting baby grow

Sauternes has such balance of natural sweetness and acidity that it can age well (especially the better Sauternes mentioned here) for an extraordinarily long time. Unfortunately, because Sauternes is so delicious, people often drink it young, when it's very rich and sweet. But Sauternes is really at its best when it loses its baby fat and matures.

After about ten to fifteen years, Sauternes's color changes from light gold to an old gold-coin color, sometimes with orange or amber tones. At this point, the wine loses some of its sweetness and develops flavors reminiscent of apricots, orange rind, honey, and toffee. This stage is the best time to drink Sauternes. The better the vintage, the longer Sauternes takes to reach this stage, but once there, it stays at this plateau for many years — sometimes decades — and very gradually turns dark amber or light brown in color. Even in these final stages, Sauternes retains some of its complex flavors.

In good vintages, Sauternes can age for 50 to 60 years or more. Château d'Yquem and Château Climens are particularly long-lived. (We recently had a half-bottle of 1893 Château d'Yquem that was glorious!)

Sauternes is best when served cold, but not ice cold, at about 52° to 53°F (11°C). Mature Sauternes can be served a bit warmer. Because the wine is so rich, Sauternes is an ideal companion for *foie gras* although, ordinarily, the wine is far more satisfying after dinner than as an apéritif. As for desserts, Sauternes is excellent with ripe fruits, lemon-flavored cakes, or pound cake.

Sauternes look-alikes

Many sweet, botrytis-infected wines similar to Sauternes exist; they sell for considerably less money than Sauternes or Barsacs. These wines are not as intense or as complex in flavor, but they are fine values at $15 to $25.

Directly north and adjacent to Barsac is the often overlooked Cérons wine region. You can probably convince many of your friends that a Cérons, served blind, is a Sauternes or Barsac. From the Entre-Deux-Mers district of Bordeaux, look for wines with the Cadillac, Loupiac, or Sainte-Croix-du-Mont appellations — all less expensive versions of Sauternes and Monbazillac from farther afield.

Part VI
When You've Caught the Bug

The 5th Wave   By Rich Tennant

"I want something that will go well with a retired admiral, a best-selling author, and a media wonk."

In this part . . .

The incubation period of the wine bug is unpredictable. Some people no sooner express interest in wine than they become engrossed in the subject. Other people exhibit mild symptoms for many years before succumbing to the passion. (And believe it or not, a lot of people are immune.)

But as soon as you've been bitten by the wine bug, you know it. You find yourself subscribing to magazines that your friends never heard of, making new friends with whom you have little in common other than an interest in wine, boycotting restaurants with substandard wine lists, and planning vacations to wine regions!

However quickly you got to this stage, the following four chapters provide fuel for your fire.

Chapter 16

Buying and Collecting Wine

. . . .

In This Chapter

▶ Playing hardball with hard-to-get-wines

▶ Keeping your own little black book of wine retailers

▶ Shopping virtually

▶ Collecting wine

▶ Helping your wine stay healthy

. . . .

You read about a wine that sounds terrific. Your curiosity is piqued; you want to try it. But your local wine shop doesn't have the wine. Neither does the best store in the next town. Or maybe you decide to balance your wine collection by buying some mature wines. But the few older wines you can find in wine shops aren't really what you want.

How do other wine lovers manage to get their hands on special bottles of wine when you can't?

Wines That Play Hard to Get

There's a catch-22 for wine lovers who have really caught the bug: The more desirable a wine is, the harder it is to get. And the harder it is to get, the more desirable it is.

Several forces conspire to frustrate buyers who want to get their hands on special bottles. First, some of the best wines are made in ridiculously small quantities. We wouldn't say that quantity and quality are necessarily incompatible in winemaking, but at the very highest echelons of quality, there usually isn't much quantity to go around.

We once bought six bottles of a grand cru red Burgundy produced by a small grower, Hubert Lignier. We learned that Lignier made only 150 cases of that wine, and 50 of those cases came to the United States. We found it incredible that we could buy half a case of such a rare wine for ourselves, leaving only 49.5 cases to satisfy the whole rest of the country! Right time, right place.

Today, many small-production wines sell *on allocation,* which means that distributors restrict the quantity that any one store can purchase, sometimes limiting stores to as few as six bottles of a particular wine. Most stores, in turn, limit customers to just one or two bottles. Certain wines are allocated in such a way that they're available primarily at restaurants.

The issue of allocations brings us to the second factor preventing equal opportunity in wine buying: Wine buying is a competitive sport. If you're there first, you get the wine, and the next guy doesn't. (We've been on the short end of that deal plenty of times, too.)

Buying highly rated wines is especially competitive. When a wine receives a very high score from critics, a feeding frenzy results among wine lovers, not leaving much for Johnnies-come-lately. (See Chapter 17 for information on wine critics and Chapters 18 and 21 for more on wine ratings.)

A final factor limiting availability of some wines is that wineries usually sell each wine just once, when the wine is young. In the case of many fine wines, such as top Bordeaux wines, the wine isn't at its best yet. But most wine merchants can't afford to store the wine for selling years later. This means that aged wines are usually hard to get.

Playing Hardball

When the wine plays hard-to-get, you have to play hardball; you have to look beyond your normal sources of supply. Your allies in this game are wine auction houses, wine shops in other cities, and, in the case of domestic wines, the wineries themselves.

Buying wines at auctions

The clear advantage of buying wine through auction houses is the availability of older and rarer wines. In fact, auction houses are the principal source of mature wines — their specialty. (In general, you can obtain younger wines at better prices elsewhere.) At auctions, you can buy wines that are practically impossible to obtain any other way. Many of these wines have been off the market for years — sometimes decades!

The main disadvantage of buying wine at auction is that you don't always know the storage history — or *provenance* — of the wine you're considering buying. The wine may have been stored in somebody's warm apartment for years. And if the wine does come from a reputable wine collector's temperature-controlled cellar, and thus has impeccable credentials, it will sell for a very high price.

Also, almost all auction houses charge you a buyer's premium, a tacked-on charge that's 10 or 15 percent of your bid. In general, prices of wine at auctions range from fair (rarely, you even find bargains) to exorbitant.

If you're personally present at an auction, be careful not to catch auction fever. The desire to win can motivate you to pay more for a wine than it's worth. Carefully thought-out, judicious bidding is in order. To plan your attack, you can obtain a catalog for the auction ahead of time, usually for a small fee. The catalog lists wines for sale by lots (usually groupings of three, six, or twelve bottles) with a suggested minimum bid per lot.

Improving your odds of getting a *good*, old bottle

Acquiring and drinking old wines requires you to be a bit of a gambler. But you *can* reduce the odds against buying a bottle well past its peak by following a few easy tips:

✔ Buy from reputable wine merchants and auction houses. They often know the history of their older wines, and most likely acquired the wines from sources that they trust.

✔ Trade bottles only with wine-savvy friends who know the storage history of their wines.

✔ Stick to well-known wines with a proven track record of longevity.

✔ Inspect the wine if you can. Look at the *ullage* (the airspace between the wine and the cork). Ullage of an inch or more can be a danger sign indicating that evaporation has occurred, either from excessive heat or lack of humidity — both of which can spoil the wine. (On a very old wine, say 35 or more years old, an inch of ullage is quite acceptable, though.) Another sign of poor storage is leakage or stickiness at the top of the bottle, suggesting that wine has seeped out through the cork.

✔ Inspect the wine's color, if the bottle color permits. A white wine that is excessively dark or dull, or a red wine that has become quite brown, can be oxidized and too old. (Shine a penlight flashlight through the bottle to check the color of red wines.) But some red wines and Sauternes can show quite a bit of brown and still be very much alive. If you're not sure about the color, get advice from someone who knows about older wines before plunking down your money.

✔ If you buy at auction by telephone or online, ask the seller to inspect the bottle and describe its fill level and color.

✔ Be wary if the price of the bottle seems too low. Often, what appears to be a bargain is a damaged or over-the-hill wine.

✔ Ask wine-knowledgeable friends or merchants about the particular wines that you are considering buying. Frequently, someone will be familiar with them.

✔ Say a prayer, take out your corkscrew, and plunge in. Live dangerously!

New York is currently one of the hottest wine auction markets around. (You can either sell or buy wines at auction.) Four large retail stores lead the crusade: Morrell & Company, Sherry-Lehmann, Zachy's, and Acker, Merrall & Condit. (Contact information for all these stores is listed in the section, "Some U.S. wine stores worth knowing," later in this chapter.) Sotheby's Auction House (212-606-7050, www.sothebys.com/wine) also holds wine auctions, under the direction of Serena Sutcliffe, MW; Christie's Auction House (212-636-2270, www.christies.com) is also a major player.

In Illinois, The Chicago Wine Company (708-647-8789, www.tcwc.com) and Hart Davis Hart (312-482-9996; www.hdhwine.com) are leading auction houses. In California, leaders include Butterfield's Auction House (800-223-2854, ext. 3550, www.butterfields.com), The Rare Wine Company (800-999-4342, www.rarewineco.com), and Christie's Los Angeles (310-385-2603).

You can also bid for wine online. Winebid.com (www.winebid.com) conducts auctions at its Web site. Acker, Merrall & Condit, a wine shop in New York City that conducts live auctions, also conducts an auction online at www.ackerwines.com during the first 12 days of each month; these auctions feature odd lots not suitable for the shop's live auctions.

Buying wine by catalog or Internet

A real plus to buying wine online or perusing wine shop catalogs and ordering from your armchair is, of course, the convenience (not to mention the time savings). Most major wine retail stores have good Web sites and issue a wine catalog two or more times a year to customers on their mailing lists; just give a call to obtain a free catalog.

Other advantages of buying wine long-distance include the availability of scarce wines and (sometimes) lower prices than you might pay in your home market.

Sometimes, the *only* way to buy certain wines is by catalog, because sought-after wines made in small quantities aren't available in every market. If a wine you want is available locally, but you don't live in a market where pricing is competitive, you may decide that you can save money by ordering the wine from a retailer in another city — even after the added shipping costs.

One minor disadvantage of buying wine by catalog or online is that an adult usually must be available to receive the wine. Also, because wine is perishable, you have to make certain that it's not delivered to you during hot (above 75°F/24°C) or cold (below 28°F/-2°C) weather. Spring and autumn are usually the best times for wine deliveries.

Crossing state lines

Because wine contains alcohol, it doesn't move as freely through commercial channels as other products do. Each state must decide whether to permit wineries and stores outside its borders to ship wine to its residents or not, and under which conditions. By requiring consumers to buy wine only from local, licensed retail stores or wineries, a state government can be sure it's getting all the tax revenue it's entitled to on every wine transaction in its jurisdiction.

A ruling by the U.S. Supreme Court in 2005 shot down some of the restrictions that individual states had placed on wine shipments to consumers from businesses in other states, and sent lawmakers in many states scurrying to rewrite their regulations. As of mid-2006, the dust created by the Supreme Court decision had not yet settled.

Most wine shops and wineries are sympathetic to out-of-state customers, but out-of-state deliveries are risky for their businesses, depending on the regulations in their state and the destination state. The risk is all theirs, too; the store or winery can lose its license, while all the buyer loses is any wine that's confiscated by the authorities.

If you want to buy wine from an out-of-state winery or merchant, discuss the issue with the people there. If shipping to you isn't legal, they can sometimes find a solution for you, such as holding the wine for you to pick up personally, or shipping to a friend or relative in a legal state.

Buy all the wine you want when you visit a winery: Different rules apply, and wine drinkers may legally ship home wines that they purchase during visits to out-of-state wineries.

Some U.S. wine stores worth knowing

We can't possibly list *all* the leading wine stores that sell wine by catalog, newsletter, or online. But the following purveyors are some of the best. Most of them either specialize in catalog sales or in certain kinds of fine wine that can be difficult to obtain elsewhere. We name the stores' main wine specialties here:

- Acker, Merrall & Condit, New York, NY; ☎ 212-787-1700; www.ackerwines.com — Burgundy, California Cabernets

- Astor Wines & Spirits, New York, NY; ☎ 212-674-7500; www.astorwines.com — French, California, Spanish

- Brookline Liquor Mart, Allston, MA; ☎ 617-734-7700; www.BLMWine.com — Italian, Burgundy, Rhône

- Burgundy Wine Company, New York, NY; ☎ 212-691-9244; www.burgundywinecompany.com — Burgundy, fine California Chardonnay and Pinot Noir, Rhône

✔ Calvert Woodley, Washington, D.C.; ☎ 202-966-4400;
www.calvertwoodley.com — California, Bordeaux, other French

✔ Chambers Street Wines, New York, NY; ☎ 212-227-1434;
www.chambersstreetwines.com — Loire, biodynamic/organic wine

✔ The Chicago Wine Company, Niles, IL; ☎ 847-647-8789;
www.tcwc.com — Bordeaux, Burgundy, California

✔ Corti Brothers, Sacramento, CA; ☎ 800-509-3663; www.cortibros.biz —
Italian, California, dessert wines

✔ D & M Wines & Liquors, San Francisco, CA; ☎ 800-637-0292;
www.dandm.com — Champagne

✔ Garnet Wines, New York, NY; ☎ 800-872-8466; 212-772-3211;
www.garnetwine.com — Bordeaux, Champagne (great prices)

✔ Hart Davis Hart Wine Co., Chicago, IL; ☎ 312-482-9996;
www.hdhwine.com — Bordeaux, Burgundy

✔ Kermit Lynch Wine Merchant, Berkeley, CA; ☎ 510-524-1524;
www.kermitlynch.com — French country wines, Burgundy, Rhône

✔ Le Dū's Wines, New York, NY; ☎ 212-924-6999; www.leduwines.com —
French, Italian, small estates

✔ MacArthur Liquors, Washington, D.C.; ☎ 202-338-1433;
www.bassins.com — California, Burgundy, Bordeaux, Italian,
Rhône, Alsace, Australian, German, Vintage Port

✔ McCarthy & Schiering, Seattle, WA; ☎ 206-524-9500 or 206-282-8500;
www.mccarthyandschiering.com — Washington, Oregon

✔ Marin Wine Cellar, San Rafael, CA; ☎ 415-456-9463;
www.marinwinecellar.com — Bordeaux (especially fine, rare, old)

✔ Mills Wine & Spirit Mart, Annapolis, MD; ☎ 410-263-2888;
www.millswine.com — Bordeaux, other French, Italian

✔ Morrell & Co., New York, NY; ☎ 212-688-9370; www.morrell.com —
California, Italian, French

✔ North Berkeley Wines, Berkeley, CA; ☎ 800-266-6585;
www.northberkeleyimports.com — French, Italian

✔ PJ's Wine Warehouse, New York, NY; ☎ 212-567-5500; www.pjwine.com —
Italian, Spanish

✔ Pop's Wines & Spirits, Island Park, NY; ☎ 516-431-0025;
www.popswine.com — California, Italian, Bordeaux, Long Island

✔ The Rare Wine Company, Sonoma, CA; ☎ 800-999-4342;
www.rarewineco.com — Italian, French, Port, Madeira

✔ Rosenthal Wine Merchant, New York, NY; ☎ 212-249-6650;
www.madrose.com — Burgundy, Rhône, Loire, Italian

- ✔ Royal Wine Merchants, New York, NY; ☎ 212-689-4855; www.royalwinemerchants.com — French (especially rare Bordeaux), Italian, Burgundy, hard-to-find wines

- ✔ Sam's Wine & Spirits, Chicago, IL; ☎ 800-777-9137; www.samswine.com — French, Italian, California

- ✔ Sherry-Lehmann, New York, NY; ☎ 212-838-7500; www.sherry-lehmann.com — Bordeaux, Burgundy, California, Italian

- ✔ Twenty-Twenty Wine Merchants, West Los Angeles, CA; ☎ 310-447-2020; www.2020wines.com — Bordeaux (especially rare, old), California, Burgundy

- ✔ Vino, New York, NY; ☎ 212-725-6516; www.vinosite.com — Italian

- ✔ Wally's, Los Angeles, CA; ☎ 888-9-WALLYS; www.wallywine.com — Italian, California, French, Champagne

- ✔ The Wine Club, Santa Ana, CA, ☎ 800-966-5432; San Francisco, CA, ☎ 800-966-7835; www.thewineclub.com — Bordeaux, California

- ✔ Zachy's, Scarsdale, NY; ☎ 866-922-4971; www.zachys.com — Bordeaux, Burgundy

Wine online

The major Web sites for purchasing wine online are those of actual bricks-and-mortar wine shops, and we list most of them in the preceding section "Some U.S. wine stores worth knowing." Here are another few Internet sites worth checking out when you want to purchase wine online.

- ✔ Wine Access (www.wineaccess.com): This site calls itself a "wine shopping community" and in fact it is a mall of sorts, where you can purchase wine from numerous participating wine shops across the United States or from participating wineries. The site contains a section where you can read about trends and also enables you to subscribe to some newsletters.

- ✔ K&L Wines (www.klwines.com): A critically-acclaimed Web site from a California retailer; is easy to navigate and features a very comprehensive inventory, knowledgeable commentary and a blog.

- ✔ Wine-Searcher (www.wine-searcher.com): This site searches for wines that you name and lists stores and prices for them, including merchants outside the United States.

- ✔ The Wine Web (www.wineweb.com). A site that enables you to buy wine through participating retailers or wineries.

Buying time: Wine futures

Every so often you may notice ads in the newspaper or in wine catalogs urging you to buy *futures* of certain wines (usually Bordeaux, but sometimes California wines). The ads suggest that, to ensure getting a particular wine at the lowest price, you should buy it now for future delivery. In other words, "Give us your money now; you'll get the wine in due course, probably sometime next year when the winery releases it."

Generally, we recommend that you don't buy futures. Often the wine will be the same price, or only slightly higher, when it hits the market. To save little or nothing, you will have tied your money up for a year or more, while the store has made interest on it or spent it. Stores have gone bankrupt. And during recessionary economies in the past, some people who bought wine

futures actually paid more for their wine than they would have paid if they had waited for the wine to arrive before purchasing it.

Futures are useful only in two situations: For wines that are made in such small quantity that you're pretty sure the wine will sell out before it reaches the stores; and for a wine that receives an extraordinarily high rating in the wine press before its release, assuring that its price could double and even triple by the time the wine reaches the market.

Here's the bottom line: Buy futures only when you must have a particular wine and buying futures may be the only way you can get it. For most wines, though, keep your wallet in your pocket until the wine is actually available.

The Urge to Own: Wine Collecting

Most people consume wines very quickly after buying them. If this is your custom, you have plenty of company. But many people who enjoy wine operate a bit differently. Oh, sure, they buy wine because they intend to drink it; they're just not exactly sure *when* they'll drink it. And until they do drink it, they get pleasure out of knowing that the bottles are waiting for them. If you count yourself in this second group, you're probably a wine collector at heart. The chase, to you, is every bit as thrilling as the consummation.

If you're a closet wine collector, developing a strategy of wine buying can prevent a haphazard collection of uninteresting or worthless bottles from happening to you. (Even if you never intend to have a wine collection, it's worthwhile to put at least a little thought into your wine purchases.)

The first step in formulating a wine-buying strategy is to consider

✔ How much wine you drink

✔ How much wine you want to own (and can store properly)

✔ How much money you're prepared to spend on wine

✔ What types of wine you enjoy drinking

Unless you strike a balance on these issues, you can end up broke, bored, frustrated, or in the vinegar business!

Balancing your inventory

Unless your intention is to fill your cellar with wines that bring you the greatest return on investment when you later sell them — in other words, unless you aren't interested in actually drinking the wines you own — you should like a wine before buying it. (We're not talking about all those bottles you buy while you're playing the field and experimenting with new wines — just those that you're thinking of making a commitment to by buying in quantity.) Liking a wine before you buy it sounds like the plainest common sense, but you'd be surprised at how many people buy a wine merely because somebody gave it a high rating!

A well-planned wine inventory features a range of wines. It can be heavy in one or two types of wine that you particularly enjoy, but it has other types of wine, too. If you like California Cabernet Sauvignons, for example, you may decide to make them your specialty. But consider that you may grow weary of them if you have nothing else to drink night after night. By purchasing other wines as well, you can have the fun of exploring different types of wine.

Table wines, of course, are the bulk of most wine collections. But it's a good idea to have a few apéritif wines — such as Champagne or dry Sherry — and dessert wines — such as Port or sweet white wines — so that you're prepared when occasions arise. (If you're like us, you'll invent plenty of occasions to open a bottle of Champagne!)

Another hallmark of a balanced collection is a healthy selection of both inexpensive wines ($8 to $18 a bottle) that can be enjoyed on casual occasions and important wines that demand a special occasion. Purchasing only expensive wines is unrealistic. You need wines that you can open at any time, with anyone.

You also want to purchase wines that are ready to drink and those that require additional aging. We give you some pointers about doing so in the next two sections.

Is the sky the limit?

Some wine collectors own more than 10,000 bottles! This might be called taking one's hobby to the extreme. We believe that a collection of 1,000 to 1,500 bottles is definitely sufficient to handle anyone's needs nicely. Then again, 100 bottles isn't so bad, either!

Everyday wines

What you stock as everyday wines will depend on your personal taste. Our candidates for everyday white wines include

- Simple white Burgundies, such as Mâcon-Villages or St.Véran
- Sauvignon Blancs from New Zealand, France (Sancerre and Pouilly-Fumé), and California
- Pinot Gris/Pinot Grigio from Oregon, Alsace, and Italy
- Italian Pinot Bianco
- Flavorful Italian whites such as Vermentino, Verdicchio, or Falanghina
- Grüner Veltliner from Austria
- Riesling from Germany, Austria, or Alsace
- Moschofilero from Greece
- Albariños from Spain

For everyday red wines, we especially like Italian reds such as Barbera, Dolcetto, Montepulciano d'Abruzzo, Valpolicella, and simple (under $20) Chianti. These red wines are enjoyable young, versatile enough to go well with the simple, flavorful foods many people eat everyday, and sturdy enough to age for a couple of years if you don't get around to them (that is, they won't deteriorate quickly).

Other everyday red wines we recommend include Beaujolais, Côtes du Rhône, and lighter-bodied (under $15) Bordeaux.

Age-worthy wines

In planning your own wine collection, include some age-worthy wines that you buy in their youth when their prices are lowest. Many of the better red wines, such as Bordeaux, Barolo, and Hermitage, often aren't at their best for at least ten years after the vintage — and some of them are difficult to find once they are ready to drink. Aging is also the rule for some fine white Burgundies (such as Corton-Charlemagne), better white Bordeaux, Sauternes, German Rieslings and late-harvest wines, and Vintage Port, which usually requires about 20 years of aging before it matures!

Age-worthy white wines we recommend include

- ✔ Above all, grand cru and premier cru white Burgundies — such as Corton-Charlemagne, Bâtard- and Chevalier-Montrachets, Meursault, and Chablis Grand Crus
- ✔ Better (over $30) white Bordeaux
- ✔ Great German and Austrian Rieslings
- ✔ Alsace Rieslings or Gewurztraminers

See Chapters 9 and 11 for explanations of these wines.

Among the many long-lived red wines, some likely candidates for *cellaring* (the term for letting wines mature) are

- ✔ Fine Bordeaux
- ✔ Grand cru and premier cru Burgundies
- ✔ Big Italian reds, such as Barolo, Barbaresco, Chianti Classico Riserva, Brunello di Montalcino, Taurasi, and Super-Tuscan blends
- ✔ From Spain: Rioja, Ribeira del Duero, and Priorato wines
- ✔ From California: Better Cabernet Sauvignons (and Cabernet blends)
- ✔ From the Rhône: Hermitage, Côte Rôtie, and Cornas
- ✔ Portugal's Barca Velha, and other good Douro table wines
- ✔ Australia's Grange (Penfolds), the Henschke Shiraz wines, such as Hill of Grace, and other super-premium Shirazes

Other age-worthy wines include

- ✔ Finer Champagnes (usually Vintage Champagnes and prestige cuvées; see Chapter 14)
- ✔ The finest dessert wines, such as late-harvest German Rieslings (see Chapter 11), French Sauternes, sweet Vouvrays from the Loire Valley (see Chapter 9), Vintage Port, and Madeira. (See Chapter 15 for Sauternes, Port, and Madeira.)

The charm of an aged wine

Aged wines are a thing apart from young wines — and some wines don't really reach their full expression until they have aged. Try drinking a highly acclaimed young red Bordeaux, say a 1996 Château Lafite-Rothschild. You taste a mouthful of tannin, and although the wine has concentration, you probably wonder what all the fuss is about. Try it in 10 to 15 years; the assertive tannins have softened, a wonderful bouquet of cedar, tobacco, and black currants emerges from the glass, and a natural sweetness of flavor has developed.

As a fine wine matures in the bottle, a series of chemical and physical changes occur. These changes are poorly understood, but their effects are evident in the style of a mature red wine:

✔ The wine becomes paler in color.

✔ Its aroma evolves from the fruity aromas (and often oakiness) it had when young to a complex leathery and earthy bouquet.

✔ Its tannic, harsh texture diminishes, and the wine becomes silky.

Mature wines seem to be easier to digest, and they go to your head less quickly. (Perhaps that's because we tend to drink them slowly, with reverence.) Besides visceral pleasure, they offer a special emotional satisfaction. Tasting an aged wine can be like traveling back in time, sharing a connection with people who have gone before in the great chain of humanity.

Organization is peace of mind

When you're not only a wine drinker but also a wine collector, you become aware that you need to keep track of all your wine so that

✔ You can find a bottle quickly when you're looking for it.

✔ You know what you own. (Many a bottle has gone over the hill because the owner forgot that he had it!)

✔ You can show off your wine collection to your friends (something like showing your baby's pictures).

You can keep track of your wine in many different ways. A wine inventory on paper should include a list of the specific wines in your collection, the number of each, and the location.

Cataloging our wine collection by computer turned out to be a lot easier than we expected. We used a database program (Filemaker, specifically) on our Mac to create the file. We set up a field for each of the following items:

- ✔ Vintage
- ✔ Producer
- ✔ Wine name
- ✔ Appellation
- ✔ Region
- ✔ Country
- ✔ Type (red, white, rosé, sparkling, apéritif, or dessert)
- ✔ Quantity owned
- ✔ Price paid (per bottle)
- ✔ Value (the latest estimated worth, per bottle)
- ✔ Size of bottle (to indicate 1.5-liter magnums, half-bottles, and so on)

Two summary fields provide the total number of bottles in our inventory at any moment (or the total of any segment of our inventory, such as our red Bordeaux) as well as the current value of our inventory.

A Healthy Environment for Your Wines

If you've decided to collect wine — or if you discover that a wine collection is happening to you — please take heed: Poorly stored wines make disappointment after disappointment inevitable.

If you plan to keep wines indefinitely, you really need a wine storage facility with controlled temperature and humidity. This is especially important if you live where the temperature exceeds 70°F (21°C) for any length of time. Without proper storage, you may be tempted to drink those fine wines long before they reach their best drinking period (known in wine circles as infanticide), or worse yet, the wines may die an untimely death in your closet, garage, or warm cellar.

The passive wine cellar

You may be fortunate enough to have conditions suitable for what is called a passive wine cellar (if you've recently inherited a castle in Scotland, for example).

If the place where you intend to store your wine is very cool (below 60°F, 15.5°C) and very damp (75 percent humidity or higher) year-round, you can be the lucky owner of a passive cellar. (It's called passive because you don't have to do anything to it, such as cool it or humidify it.) Usually, only deep cellars completely below ground level with thick stones or comparable insulation can be completely passive in temperate climates. Passive cellars are certainly the ideal way to store wines. And you can save a lot of money on their upkeep, to boot.

If you don't have a space that's already ideal for a passive wine cellar, you might decide that you can dig one. For instructions on building your own passive wine cellar, see Richard M. Gold's authoritative book, *How and Why To Build a Passive Wine Cellar,* Third Edition (Sandhill Publishers).

If you can't be passive, be bullish

Most of us are neither lucky enough to have a passive wine cellar nor fortunate enough to be able to create one without extraordinary expense and trouble (bulldozers, wrecking crews, and so on). But second best — an artificially cooled and/or humidified room — is far better than nothing.

The following are key features of a good wine storage area:

- ✔ The temperature stays cool — ideally, in the 53° to 59°F range (12° to 16°C).

- ✔ The temperature is fairly constant — wide swings in temperature are not good for the wine.

- ✔ The area is damp or humid, with a minimum of 70 percent humidity and a maximum of 95 percent (mold sets in above 95 percent).

- ✔ The area is free from vibrations, which can travel through the wine; heavy traffic and motors cycling on and off — such as in refrigerators or washers/dryers — are detrimental to your wine.

- ✔ The area is free from light, especially direct sunlight; the ultraviolet rays of the sun are especially harmful to wine.

- ✔ The storage area is free from chemical odors, such as paints, paint remover, and so on.

We built a room in our cellar for wine storage. Whatever area you use, your wine will keep well provided that the space has a climate control unit and is properly insulated (see the following sections in this chapter).

The issue of humidity

Some wine collectors are not particularly concerned about the humidity level of their cellars. High humidity causes mold, they argue, and disfigures labels. But dry air can dry the cork and allow the airtight seal to deteriorate, enabling oxygen to get in or causing your wine to evaporate or leech out around the cork, resulting in excessive *ullage* (space between the wine and the cork). The greater the ullage, the greater the chance of your wine's becoming oxidized.

Because we recommend humidity between 70 and 95 percent, we believe that air conditioners, which dehumidify the air to about 50 percent, are not suitable for wine storage areas.

Buy a hygrometer (an instrument that measures humidity) for your wine storage area. Our hygrometer gives us both the percentage of humidity and a digital reading of the temperature — information so valuable that we check it almost daily. (Hygrometers are available through wine accessory catalogs, such as The Wine Enthusiast, Pleasantville, NY, ☎ 800-356-8466.)

Avoid refrigerators for wine storage. Don't leave good wine or Champagne in the refrigerator for more than a week; not only is the refrigerator motor harmful, but the excessively cold temperature (as low as 35°F, 1.6°C) tends to numb and flatten the flavors of the wine.

Climate control

Professional cooling units are available. (Find them advertised in wine accessory catalogs and wine magazines.) These are climate-control devices that humidify the air of a room as well as cool it. These units come in various capacities to suit rooms of different dimensions. Many require professional installation; they cost from $600 to $2,400, depending on their capacity.

Depending on where you live, you may not need to run your cooling unit all year. We live in the northeastern United States and keep ours going from about mid-May to October. The additional expense for electricity comes to about $20 a month for four to five months — well worth it when we consider the value of the wine we're protecting. During the winter months when the air gets dry, we often run a humidifier in our wine room.

Wine racks

Racking systems vary from elaborate redwood racks to simple metal or plastic types. The choice of material and configuration really hinges on how much you want to spend and your own personal taste.

Large, diamond-shaped wooden (or synthetic composition) racks are popular because they efficiently store up to eight bottles per section and make maximum use of space (see Figure 16-1). Such racks also permit the easy removal of individual bottles.

Figure 16-1: Diamond-shaped wine rack.

© Akira Chiwaki

A rack configuration that gives each wine its own cubbyhole is more expensive; if you're checking out such racks, consider whether any of your oversized bottles (such as bulbous sparkling wine bottles) may be too large to fit the racks. (And consider whether your half-bottles may be too small!)

Some collectors prefer to store their wine in the wines' original wooden crates. (Many classic wines, such as Bordeaux and Vintage Port, come in these crates; you can also usually pick up empty wooden crates in wine stores.) The crates are beneficial for storing wine because the wine remains in a dark environment inside the case, and the temperature changes very slowly thanks to the mass of wine bottles packed together in the closed case. Retrieving a bottle from the bottom row of the case can really be inconvenient, though.

Cardboard boxes aren't suitable for wine storage. The chemicals used in the manufacture of the cardboard can eventually affect the wine. Also, the cardboard boxes become damaged, in time, from the moisture in the air, assuming that you're maintaining a proper humidity in your cellar.

Insulation

Far more important than your choice of racks is your choice of insulation.

We definitely do not recommend fiberglass insulation because it will absorb the moisture created by your cooling unit. We've heard of cases in which the weight of the moisture inside the insulation actually caused parts of ceilings to come tumbling down, creating quite a mess.

The ideal insulation is a 3-inch-thick, thermoplastic resin called polyurethane. It's odorless, doesn't absorb moisture, and makes a fine seal. Even when a cooling unit isn't running, temperatures will change extremely slowly in most wine rooms with this kind of insulation.

Wine caves for apartment dwellers

If you live in a house that has either a cellar or a separate area for your wine, consider yourself fortunate. What if you have no space — for instance, if you live in an apartment?

As an apartment dweller, you have three choices:

- Leave your wine in a friend's or relative's house (provided that he has adequate storage facilities — and that you trust him or her not to drink your wine!).
- Rent storage space in a refrigerated public warehouse.
- Buy a wine cave — also known as a wine vault — a self-contained, refrigerated unit that you plug into an electrical outlet.

We find the first two options barely acceptable because they don't give you immediate access to your wine. It's downright inconvenient to make a trip every time you want to get your hands on your own wine. And both of these options rob you of the pleasure of having your wines readily available in your home where you can look at them, fondle the bottles, or show them off to your friends.

If we lived in an apartment, we'd definitely own a wine cave. Many wine caves resemble attractive pieces of furniture, either vertical or horizontal credenzas. Some have glass doors, and all of them can be locked.

Wine caves range in size and capacity from a tiny unit that holds only 24 bottles to really large units that hold up to 2,800 bottles, with many sizes in between. Prices range from $300 to about $8,000. You find wine caves advertised extensively in wine accessory catalogs and in the back pages of wine magazines.

If you plan to build a wine cellar or buy a wine cave, allow for expansion in your wine collection. Like most waistlines, wine cellars inevitably grow larger with the passing years.

Chapter 17

Continuing Education for Wine Lovers

*L*earning about wine is like space travel: Once you get going, there's no end in sight. Fortunately for those who choose to be educated wine drinkers, learning about wine is a fascinating experience, full of new flavors, new places, and new friends.

Although we teach others about wine, we are also avid students of wine. We can't imagine that we'll ever reach the point where we say, "Now we know enough about wine; we can stop here." So off we go to another vineyard, to another wine tasting, or deep into the pages of another wine magazine. Every step brings not only more knowledge but also more appreciation of this amazing beverage.

Back to the Classroom

The best way to learn about wine and to improve your wine-tasting skills is to take a wine course. Wine classes provide the ideal combination of authoritative instruction and immediate feedback on your tasting impressions.

If you live in a medium-sized or large city, you're sure to find several wine courses offered by private individuals, by universities, by local school districts as adult-education extension programs, or by local wine shops or restaurants.

Most wine courses are *wine appreciation* courses — they don't teach you how to make wine, they don't usually provide you with professional credentials, and they're not accredited. (Some professional-level courses and courses offered at an actual university can be exceptions.) The purpose of most wine courses is to provide both information about wine and practice in tasting wine. (For information on professional wine credentials, see "One wine school in action" and "What do the initials MW mean?" later in this chapter.)

Introductory classes deal with wine grape varieties and how to taste wine, while more advanced classes discuss in depth the various wine regions of the world or the wines of a particular region. Instructors are usually experienced professionals who work in the wine trade or who write about wine.

Brand promotion and education often enjoy too cozy a relationship in the wine field. Many wine instructors, such as distributor salespeople or winery reps, have a vested interest in the brands of wine that they offer as tasting samples in class. As long as the instructor has expertise beyond his or her own brands, you can still benefit from the instruction. But you should request disclosure of any commercial affiliations at the first class. And when possible, consider taking classes from independent instructors instead.

One wine school in action

The following announcement is a shameless plug: We run a wine school in New York City called International Wine Center (www.internationalwinecenter. com). We offer the programs of the Wine & Spirit Education Trust (WSET®), the leading international wine education organization; they're geared towards people in the wine trade but are open to anyone who is serious about learning.

Unlike courses geared only toward wine drinkers — where entertainment is as much a goal as education — courses for wine professionals are more comprehensive, and the information covered is more technical. For example, our WSET courses cover three levels of study (from beginner to very advanced) and range from 8 to 40 sessions in length; each course has a textbook, self-study materials, and an examination. Students who pass the exam corresponding to their level of study earn a certificate that gives them professional credentials.

But whether they target wine lovers or those in the trade, most wine classes have a lot in common. A typical class usually lasts about two hours; students listen to a lecture on a particular topic and taste six to eight wines related to that topic. The instructor encourages questions. References to maps of wine regions or sketches on the blackboard punctuate the discussion.

At most wine classes, each student sits before a place setting of wine glasses — ideally one glass per wine to be tasted. Water and crackers are available to help students clear their palates between tastes of wine. Next to each student should be a large plastic cup for dumping leftover wine. Each student should receive a printed list of the wines being tasted, as well as other material about the subject of that particular class session.

For the name of a wine school or an individual who offers wine programs in your area, contact the Society of Wine Educators, Washington, DC (☎ 202-347-5677), which has members throughout the United States, Canada, and some other countries. The Society offers wine instructors the opportunity to become Certified Wine Educators, and those who pass that exam are entitled to identify themselves with the initials CWE — a credential to look for when choosing a wine course.

Wine tastings of all shapes and sizes

Wine tastings are events designed to give enthusiasts the opportunity to sample a range of wines. The events can be very much like classes (seated, seminar-like events), or they can be more like parties (tasters milling around informally). Compared to a wine class, the participants at a wine tasting are more likely to have mixed levels of knowledge. Tastings don't come in beginner, intermediate, and advanced levels — one size fits all.

Wine tastings are popular because they override the limitations of sampling wine alone, at home. How many wines can you taste on your own (unless you don't mind throwing away nine-tenths of every bottle)? How many wines are you willing to buy on your own? And how much can you learn tasting wine in isolation — or with a friend whose expertise is no greater than yours?

At wine tastings, you can learn from your fellow tasters, as well as make new friends who share your interest in wine. Most importantly, you can taste wine in the company of some individuals who are more experienced than you, which is a real boon in training your palate.

We have led or attended literally thousands of wine tastings in our lives — so far. And it's fair to say that we've learned something about wine at almost all of them.

To attend a wine tasting in your area, contact your wine merchant. Your local shop may sponsor wine-tasting events occasionally (apart from the informal sampling opportunities in the store itself) and should also be aware of wine schools or other organizations that conduct wine tastings in your area.

What do the initials MW mean?

You may have noticed that one of the co-authors of this book has "Master of Wine" (often shortened to "MW") after her name. Wine professionals receive this title — which is the most respected wine credential in the world — by passing a grueling three-part exam. The Institute of Masters of Wine awards the credential; it offers preparatory programs and/or exams in Australia, the United States, the United Kingdom, and continental Europe. A high level of knowledge, experience in the wine trade, and completion of any locally-available wine courses, such as the WSET programs, are the normal prerequisites. As of this writing, there are 251 Masters of Wine in the world (22 in North America).

For more information, visit the Institute online at www.masters-of-wine.org.

When in Rome . . .

If you've never been to a wine tasting, we should warn you that a few matters of etiquette apply at most tastings. Familiarizing yourself with this etiquette will help you feel more comfortable. Otherwise, you're likely to be appalled by what you see or hear. Why are those people behaving like that?!

To spit or not to spit?

Remember we mentioned a large, plastic cup that each student in a wine class has for dumping out his leftover wine? Well, we lied. (We wanted to ease you into what we realize may be a shocking concept.) The cup is really for students to *spit out the wine* after tasting it.

Professional wine tasters long ago discovered that if they swallow every wine they taste, they're far less thoughtful tasters by the time they reach wine nine or ten. So spitting became acceptable. In working wineries, professional tasters sometimes spit right onto the gravel floor or into the drains. In more elegant surroundings, they spit into a *spittoon,* usually a simple container like a large plastic cup (one per taster) or an ice bucket that two or three tasters share.

At first, some tasters are naturally loath to spit out wine. Not only have they been brought up to believe that spitting is uncouth, but they've also paid good money for the opportunity to taste the wines. Why waste them?

Well, you can drink all your wine at a wine tasting, if you wish — and some people do. But we don't advise that you do, for the following reasons:

- ✔ Evaluating the later wines is difficult if you swallow the earlier ones. The alcohol you consume clouds your judgment.

- ✔ Swallowing is not really necessary in order to taste the wine fully. If you leave the wine in your mouth for eight to ten seconds (see Chapter 2), you are able to taste it thoroughly — without having to worry about the effects of the alcohol.

- ✔ If you are driving to the tasting, you're taking a risk driving home afterwards if you drink instead of spit. The stakes are high — your life and health, others' lives, and your driver's license. Why gamble?

The simple solution: Spit out the wine. Just about all experienced wine tasters do. Believe it or not, spitting will seem to be a very normal thing to do at wine tastings after a while. (And, in the meantime, it's one sure way to appear more experienced than you are!)

If you know that you can't bring yourself to spit, be sure to have something substantial to eat before going to a wine tasting. You absorb alcohol more slowly on a full stomach — and the simple crackers and bread at most wine tastings aren't sufficient to do the trick.

What's with the sound effects?

Do you have to make that loud slurping or gurgling noise that you hear "serious" wine tasters make at tastings?

Of course you don't. But drawing air into your mouth does enhance your ability to taste the wine (as explained in Chapter 2). With a little practice, you can gurgle without making loud, attention-getting noises.

Horizontal or vertical?

Two of the goofiest expressions in the world of wine apply to wine tastings. Depending on the nature of the wines featured, wine-tasting events can be categorized as *vertical tastings* or as *horizontal tastings.* These categories have nothing to do with the position of the tasters themselves — they're usually seated, and they're never lying down (that went out of fashion after the Romans).

A vertical tasting is a wine tasting featuring several vintages of the same wine — Château Latour in each vintage from 1988 to 1998, for example. A horizontal tasting examines wines of a single vintage from several different wineries; usually the wines are of a similar type, such as 2002 Napa Valley Cabernet Sauvignons.

There's no particular name for tastings with less disciplined themes, but we suggest *paisley.*

More fine points of wine etiquette

Because smell is such an important aspect of wine tasting, courteous tasters try not to interfere with other tasters' ability to smell. This means

- ✔ Smoking (anything) is a complete no-no at any wine tasting.
- ✔ Using any scent (perfume, after-shave lotion, scented hair spray, and so on) is unacceptable. These foreign odors can really interfere with your fellow tasters' ability to detect the wine's aroma.

Courteous wine tasters also don't volunteer their opinions about a wine until other tasters have had a chance to taste the wine. Serious tasters like to form their opinions independently and are sure to throw dirty looks at anyone who interrupts their concentration.

Most of these wine-tasting etiquette guidelines apply to wine classes as well — and are also relevant when you visit wineries around the world.

Dinner with the winemaker

A popular type of wine event is the winemaker dinner, a multicourse dinner at which a winemaker or winery executive is the guest of honor. Wine drinkers pay a fixed price for the meal and taste various wines from the featured winery that are matched to each course.

As far as learning goes, winemaker dinners rank below seminar-style wine tastings but above many informal, reception-style tastings. These dinners offer the chance to taste wines under ideal circumstances — with food — but we find that most speakers disseminate very little information of any value and give you little opportunity to ask questions.

Blind man's bluff

One of the favorite diversions of wine tasters is tasting wines blind. Before you conjure up thoughts of darkened rooms, blindfolded tasters, or other forms of hanky-panky, let us explain that the tasters are not blind, the bottles are. Or anyway, the bottles have their faces covered.

In *blind tastings,* the tasters don't know the identities of the wines. The theory behind this exercise is that knowing the identities may prejudice the tasters to prefer (or dislike) a particular wine for its reputation rather than for "what's in the glass," as they say. Sometimes, extremely skilled tasters taste wines blind and try to identify them, in an effort to sharpen their tasting skills even further.

If you don't know enough about wine to be prejudiced by the labels, there's little point in tasting blind. Nevertheless, there's something about blind tasting that really helps you focus your concentration on what you're tasting — and that's always good practice.

In their potential for fun, however, winemaker dinners are right up there at the top of the list — even if you don't get to sit next to the winemaker.

Visiting the wineries

One of the best — and most fun-filled — ways to learn about wine is to actually visit wine regions and, if possible, speak to the winemakers and producers about their wines. You get to immerse yourself in the region you visit — experiencing the climate firsthand, seeing the soil and the hills, touching the grapes, and so on. You can walk through the vineyards if you wish, visit nearby towns or villages, eat the local food, and drink the wine of the region.

You discover that there's something special about the people who devote their lives to making wine. Maybe it's their creativity or their commitment to bringing pleasure to the world through their labor. Whatever the reason, they are exceptional people. We have found some of our dearest friends in wine regions throughout the world.

Appointments definitely in order

When you do plan to visit a winery, you usually need to call or write ahead for an appointment.

The major exceptions are a few of the large wineries in California that offer scheduled tours or self-guided visits. Many wineries in the United States do have tasting rooms that are open every day during the busy tourism months and on weekends during the winter. In these tasting rooms, you can sample wines (sometimes for a small fee), buy wine, and buy souvenirs such as T-shirts or sweatshirts with the logo of the winery imprinted on them.

If you visit wineries that are less geared toward tourism — which is the case in most of the rest of the wine world — you can simply sample the wines, talk to the winemaker or proprietor when he's available (you *have* made an appointment, right?), take an informal tour of the winery, and buy some wine if you wish (an especially nice idea if the wine isn't available back home).

Don't know the language? No problema

Don't let your limited (or nonexistent) ability to speak the local language prevent you from visiting wine regions. These days, English is the nearly universal language of the wine world. Even if the person you're visiting doesn't speak English, he invariably has someone available (his wife, his son, or his dog) who does. Besides, wine itself is a universal language. A smile and a handshake go a long way towards communicating!

Armchair Travel

Traveling around the world takes time and money. Alternatively, you can travel through the wine world from the comfort of your living room, letting the written word carry you to faraway wine regions. Many retail wine stores sell wine magazines, newsletters, and books. You can also find wine books in or near the cooking section of most book stores.

Recommended books

The following books are some of *the* established tomes; they take you into great depth on particular aspects of wine.

General knowledge

Hugh Johnson and Jancis Robinson, MW, *World Atlas of Wine,* Fifth Edition, London, Mitchell Beazley, 2001. Johnson and Robinson, both English, are probably the world's most respected wine writers. Complete with detailed maps of all the world's wine regions, this book is essential for any serious wine lover's library. (*Hugh Johnson's Wine Companion* and *Pocket Encyclopedia of Wine* are two additional worthwhile books by Hugh Johnson.)

Oz Clarke, *Oz Clarke's New Encyclopedia of Wine,* New York, Harcourt, 1999. Oz Clarke is undoubtedly the wine world's most prolific wine writer — the Stephen King of winedom. This comprehensive encyclopedia is well organized and up-to-date. A great wine reference book. *(Oz Clarke's Encyclopedia of Grapes* is also worthwhile.)

Jancis Robinson, MW (editor), *The Oxford Companion to Wine,* Second Edition, Oxford, Oxford University Press, 1999. An encyclopedic reference book that sets the standard in the wine field. We would expect no less from Robinson, one of the truly brilliant wine writers. This book is a "must" for all serious students of wine. A Third Edition is scheduled for 2006 publication. (Also check out Robinson's *Vines, Grapes, and Wines,* published by Alfred A. Knopf.)

Bordeaux

Robert M. Parker, Jr., *Bordeaux,* Fourth Edition, New York, Simon & Schuster, 2003. Robert Parker is certainly America's — if not the world's — most famous wine writer. He earned his reputation for his knowledge of Bordeaux; he was also the first writer to use the 100-point wine rating system. This fourth edition covers all major Bordeaux wines from 1961 to 2002, with info on wines dating back to 1945 — an essential book for any Bordeaux lover. (Anther book by Parker worth having is *The Wines of the Rhône Valley,* Second Edition, 1997.)

David Peppercorn MW, *Wines of Bordeaux,* Revised Edition, London, Mitchell Beazley, 2004. England's David Peppercorn is rightfully regarded as one of the great Bordeaux experts. In this succinctly written wine guide, Peppercorn offers his own ratings of Bordeaux wines, when to drink them, and which ones are particularly good values.

Burgundy and the Rhône Valley

Anthony Hanson, MW, *Burgundy,* London, Mitchell Beazley, 2004. Hanson has written a succinct, excellent work on this very complicated wine region.

Clive Coates, MW, *Côte d'Or,* Berkeley, University of California Press, 1997. This may be the prolific Mr. Coates' best book yet on his favorite wine region. Coates, another one of the fine corps of British wine writers, covers all the major districts of the Côte d'Or (which is the home of all the great red and white Burgundy wines; see Chapter 9), reviews all the producers, and provides detailed information on vintages. A thorough reference book on Burgundy. (Also worth reading is Coates' book on Bordeaux, *Grands Vins,* and his *The Wines of France.*)

Remington Norman, MW, *Rhône Renaissance,* San Francisco, The Wine Appreciation Guild Ltd., 1997. This is a much-needed book on a region that has gone through major changes in recent years.

Champagne

Ed McCarthy, *Champagne For Dummies,* New York, Wiley, 1999. Your *Wine For Dummies* co-author, a Champagne specialist, has written this comprehensive guide to the world of Champagne, including a section on touring Champagne and a directory of Champagne houses.

Tom Stevenson, *World Encyclopedia of Champagne & Sparkling Wine,* Revised Edition, San Francisco, The Wine Appreciation Guild Ltd., 2003. England's Tom Stevenson knows more about Champagne than the Champenois themselves! A complete look at Champagne and all the major sparkling wines of the world.

Richard Juhlin, *4000 Champagnes,* Paris, Flammarion, 2005. Juhlin, an extremely knowledgeable Swedish lover of Champagne, gives his own very personalized views of the Champagne houses. Thorough and comprehensive.

Old and rare wines

Michael Broadbent, MW, *Michael Broadbent's Vintage Wine,* New York, Harcourt, 2002. No one has tasted more great wines, especially old and rare ones, than England's Michael Broadbent. This guide to vintage wines going back to the nineteenth century concentrates on Bordeaux, Sauternes, and Burgundy. This is a book for the advanced wine buff. Great stuff from one of the world's greatest French wine connoisseurs.

France

Ed McCarthy and Mary Ewing-Mulligan, MW, *French Wine For Dummies,* New York, Wiley Publishing, Inc., 2001. Every French wine region is covered, with special emphasis on Bordeaux, Burgundy, and the Rhône Valley. Dare we say, "Eminently readable"?

James Turnbull, *Fine French Wines,* Paris, Flammarion, 2003. Turnbull selects and describes 220 of France's outstanding wines, covering just about every wine region. An excellent survey for the French wine connoisseur.

Andrew Jefford, *The New France,* London, Mitchell Beazley, 2002. A fresh look at the classic wine regions of France.

Italy

Mary Ewing-Mulligan, MW, and Ed McCarthy, *Italian Wine For Dummies,* New York, Wiley Publishing, Inc., 2001. Every Italian wine region and every major Italian wine is covered, with special emphasis on Piedmont, Tuscany, Northeastern Italy, and Southern Italy.

Daniele Cernilli and Marco Sabellico, *The New Italy,* London, Mitchell Beazley, 2000. This regional approach to Italy's wines has sections on notable producers in each region, many of whom are new or recent.

Burton Anderson, *Burton Anderson's Best Italian Wines,* London, Little Brown, 2001. Anderson, originally from Minnesota but now living in Tuscany, is one of the world's most highly regarded writers on Italian wines. The recommendations in this book carry the ring of authority that only one with Anderson's vast experience can deliver.

Germany

Stuart Pigott, *The Wine Atlas of Germany,* London, Mitchell Beazley, 1996. Although British, Pigott lives in Germany and is regarded as one of the leading experts writing about the intricacies of German wine. The series editor of this atlas is Hugh Johnson, another German wine lover and a man who knows something about putting together wine atlases. An excellent reference for German wines.

Spain

Jeremy Watson, *The New and Classical Wines of Spain,* Barcelona, Montagud Editores, 2002. Watson has performed a great service in providing the wine world with a modern, comprehensive reference on one of the world's great wine countries.

California

Stephen Brook, *Wines of California,* London, Mitchell Beazley, 2002. A respected British writer gives us a refreshing look at California's wines in this easy-to-read, 200-page guide. The major part of the book is a directory of wineries, listed alphabetically and succinctly described, with each rated on a scale of one to five stars.

Australia and New Zealand

Oz Clarke, *Oz Clarke's Australian Wine Companion,* London, Websters International Publishers, 2004. The author's passion for Australian wines is enough to convert anyone. The book's authoritative information and clear maps are also top-notch.

James Halliday, *Wines of Australia,* London, Australia, Mitchell Beazley, 2003. A compact but expert guide to the wine regions of Australia from the prolific James Halliday, wine writer, winemaker, and barrister.

Michael Cooper, *Wine Atlas of New Zealand,* Auckland, Hodder, Moa Beckett, 2002. Cooper is arguably the world's leading authority on New Zealand's wines. This comprehensive tome is required reading for all New Zealand wine lovers.

Wine magazines and newsletters

Wine magazines and newsletters can provide more topical information about wine than books can. They keep you up-to-date on the current happenings in the wine world, give you timely tasting notes on newly released wines, profile the currently hot wines and winemakers, and so on. Also, the classified ads in the back of most wine magazines are a good way to hear about wine-related equipment for sale, wine tours, and other useful offers.

Some magazines that we recommend include

- ✔ *Decanter:* One of the oldest and one of the best, this magazine covers the world but is especially strong on French and Italian wines. *Decanter* also frequently issues supplements on major wine regions as part of your subscription. It's published monthly in London. ☎ 800-875-2997 (U.S.) or 1444-475675 (U.K.); www.decanter.com.

- ✔ *Wine Spectator:* Much of the current wine news is in the *Spectator,* but it also includes rather extensive coverage of the world's major wine regions, with plenty of tasting notes. This magazine is published twice monthly. ☎ 800-752-7799; www.winespectator.com.

✔ *Wine Enthusiast:* A colorful, newsy monthly that includes an extensive wine-buying guide. It is published monthly in Elmsford, New York. ☎ 800-829-5901; www.winemag.com.

✔ *Wine & Spirits:* This high-class magazine offers comprehensive, thoughtful coverage of wine and spirits. Extensive tasting notes are always included. It's published eight times a year in New York, NY. ☎ 888-695-4660; www.wineandspiritsmagazine.com.

Wine newsletters usually express the personal opinion of one authoritative writer. They contain mainly wine-tasting notes, whereas magazines contain feature-length articles along with tasting notes. One nice thing about many newsletters is that they accept no advertising; thus, they can maintain (in theory, at least) more impartiality than magazines. Most wine newsletters are intended for the intermediate to advanced wine buff.

✔ *The Wine Advocate:* Robert M. Parker, Jr., is an attorney turned wine critic. His approach to wine is methodical and thorough, complete with ratings of wine on a 100-point scale. Clear and easy to read with lots of charts and wine-buying tips, *The Wine Advocate* is a must-read for all serious wine lovers (not for the complete beginner); it covers the world's major wine regions but is especially strong on French wines. Published bimonthly. P.O. Box 311, Monkton, Maryland 21111. ☎ 410-329-6477; www.eRobertParker.com.

✔ *International Wine Cellar:* Steve Tanzer combines thoughtful articles, interviews with major wine figures, and extensive tasting notes to make an intelligent guide for the advanced wine buff. Published bimonthly in New York. Tanzer Business Communications, Inc., P.O. Box 20021, New York, NY 10021. ☎ 800-WINE-505; www.internationalwinecellar.com.

Internet newsletters and interesting sites

If you're thirsty for wine knowledge, you can spend hours learning about wine from Internet sites. Most wineries and some wine importers have their own sites, as do several wine magazines. Other sites feature groups of wineries. Here are some of our favorite places to read about, or chat about, wine online.

✔ **Wine Review Online** (www.winereviewonline.com): Robert Whitley, a San Diego-based wine writer and radio wine show host, is publisher of this new, free, bi-monthly newsletter, edited by Michael Franz. Contributors include a very experienced group of wine writers from all over the United States, including both authors of this book. Free.

- **Burghound.com** (www.burghound.com): In a short period of time, Allen Meadows' comprehensive, quarterly review of red and white Burgundies has become *the* most respected newsletter covering perhaps the most challenging wines of all to evaluate. Each issue averages 150 pages. A "must-read" for Burgundy lovers. $125/year.

- **Jancis Robinson.com** (www.jancisrobinson.com): This site features articles and commentary from England's leading wine journalist, as well as lively, active chat boards with international participation. Subscribers gain access to her purple pages, where they can even search Robinson's authoritative *Oxford Wine Companion*. $119/year.

- **Piedmont Report** (www.piedmontreport.com): Antonio Galloni, a Piedmontese wine lover, publishes a quarterly newsletter on his favorite Italian wine region, with special emphasis on Barolo and Barbaresco. $60/year.

- **WineSpectator.com** (www.winespectator.com): Here you can look up descriptions and ratings of just about any wine that *The Wine Spectator* magazine has ever reviewed. You also can find articles that have appeared in the magazine, menus pairing food and wine, travel and dining articles, and more. $50/year, or $75 for both the magazine and full Web site access.

- **Robert Parker Online** (www.erobertparker.com): Features wine reviews and articles from the world's most powerful wine critic and his team. Subscribers to the site can access these reviews, but even non-subscribers can view Parker's vintage chart and a very useful page of links to sites such as institutional wine promotion boards. $99/year.

- **Decanter.com** (www.decanter.com): *Decanter* magazine's site is full of information about wine, and strong on breaking news. Free.

- **Wine Lovers' Page** (www.wineloverspage.com): One of the original wine Web sites, founded in 1994. It features online discussion groups, tasting notes, and feature articles. Free.

- **Wine Anorak** (www.wineanorak.com): An online magazine from writer Jamie Goode with a distinctly British flavor. Strong in technical information about wine. Free.

- **Appellation America** (wine.appellationamerica.com): When you want to learn specifically about North American wines, this site will give you plenty of information about grape varieties and regional characteristics. Free.

Just about every wine region and wine producing country also has an official Web site where you can read about the wines of that area. Obviously these site are too numerous to list here. One site that will take you quickly to the region or country of your choice is www.winelinks.ch.

Chapter 18

Describing and Rating Wine

• •

In This Chapter

▶ Ways to be a more thoughtful taster

▶ Tips for writing tasting notes

▶ Numeric shorthand for wine quality

• •

*W*hen we first got excited about wine, we tried to share our enthusiasm with a relative who appeared to have some interest in the subject (well, he drank a glass now and then). Each time we served a wine, we'd talk about it in great detail. But he wasn't interested. "I don't want to talk about wine — I just want to drink it!" he proclaimed.

On some fundamental level where wine is just a generic beverage, it's certainly possible to drink wine without talking about it. But if you're the kind of person who likes to talk about food, or if you've been bitten by the wine bug, you know that it's difficult (if not impossible) to enjoy wine without talking about it at least a little. Wine is a social pleasure that's enhanced by sharing with others.

Ironically, the experience of a wine is highly personal. If you and three other people taste the same wine at the same time, each of you will have your own impression of that wine based on personal likes and dislikes, physiology, and experience. Maybe some day, if humans learn how to link their minds through WiFi, someone else will be able to experience your experience of a wine — but until then, your taste is singular. The only way you can share your impressions with others is through conversation.

Words Cannot Describe . . .

Language is our main vehicle for communicating our entire experience of life. Our vocabulary of taste is undeveloped, however. When we were young, we were taught a visual vocabulary: what is green, yellow, gold, and orange — and for that matter, what is pine green, jungle green, olive green, forest green, and sea green (thanks, Crayola!). No one ever taught us the precise difference in the words *bitter, astringent,* and *tart.* Yet to talk about wine taste, we use these words as if we all agree on what they mean.

Any discussion of wine's taste is particularly complicated, because wine is a complex beverage that gives us multiple taste sensations:

- Olfactory sensations (all those flavors we perceive by smelling them in our mouths — as we discuss in Chapter 2)

- Basic taste sensations (sweetness, sourness, and bitterness)

- Tactile sensations (the bite of astringency, for example, as well as the prickliness, roughness, smoothness, or other textural impressions of a wine in our mouths)

- Sensations on the holistic level, a synthesis of all the wine's characteristics taken together

For example, say we just tasted an oaked Sauvignon Blanc from California. We may perceive the wine as intense in herbaceous and fruity aromas, with melon-like flavor (olfactory impressions), very slightly sweet, yet with firm acidity (basic taste impressions), smooth and rich (tactile impressions), a vibrant wine with personality to spare (holistic impression). What sounds like some insufferable wine snob showing off is actually just some poor wine lover trying his best to report the taste data the wine is sending him.

You've probably gotten many a laugh from wine descriptions you've read. At face value, they sound preposterous: *Unctuous, with butter and vanilla flavors that coat the sides of your mouth. Supple and smooth, showing some fatness in the mouth, and a long finish.* (Wait! They forgot to say wet and "liquidy.") Imperfect medium that language is, however, it's the only way we have of communicating the taste of wine.

What the words are worth

Once, we engaged in a humbling yet fascinating exercise. Several wine writers were given a wine to taste, along with eight published tasting notes from other writers, only one of which corresponded to that wine. We were asked to identify that tasting note, as well as the note that seemed the most inappropriate. The description we all voted *least* appropriate for the wine turned out to be the description taken from the back label of the wine bottle! Not one of us had correctly matched the description's words to our taste experience. Again, with another wine, we each discovered that *our* taste and *their* words failed to correspond. Our only possible conclusions were either that we can't taste very well, writers can't write very well (present company included), or that communicating taste is a hopeless exercise.

Reading wine descriptions (or *tasting notes,* as they're often called) in wine newsletters or magazines can be as difficult as writing them. We must admit that our eyes often glaze over when we try to read tasting notes. And we're not alone. Frank Prial, former wine columnist of *The New York Times,* once wrote that ". . . a stranger's tasting notes, to me anyway, are about as meaningful as a Beijing bus schedule."

When It's Your Turn to Speak

Describing your experience or impression of a wine involves two steps: First, you have to form the impression; second, you have to communicate it.

When you drink wine with friends purely for enjoyment and appreciation — over dinner, for example — simple impressions and silly comments are perfectly appropriate. If a wine strikes you as unusually full and voluptuous, why *not* say that it's like Anna Nicole? If a wine seems tight and unyielding, go ahead and call it Ebenezer Scrooge. Everyone will know exactly what you mean.

In other circumstances, though, such as when you're attending a wine-tasting event, you probably want to form more considered impressions of each wine so that you can participate in the discussion and gain the most from the event. To form a considered impression, you need to taste thoughtfully.

Organizing your thoughts

The language you use to describe a wine starts with your own thoughts as you taste the wine. Thus, the process of tasting a wine and the process of describing it are intertwined.

Although wine tasting involves examining wine visually and smelling it as well as tasting it, those first two steps are a breeze compared to the third. When the wine is in your mouth, the multiple taste sensations — flavors, texture, body, sweetness or dryness, acidity, tannin, balance, length — occur practically all at once. In order to make sense of the information you receive from the wine, you have to impose some order on the impressions. (Turn to Chapter 2 for information on the steps involved in examining, smelling, and tasting wine.)

One way of organizing the impressions a wine sends you is to classify those impressions according to the nature of the "taste":

- ✔ The wine's *aromatics* (the olfactory data, all the flavors you smell in your mouth)

- ✔ The wine's *structure* (its alcohol/sweetness/acid/tannin makeup and its basic tastes — the wine's bricks and mortar, so to speak)

- ✔ The wine's *texture* (the tactile data, how the wine feels in your mouth; texture is a function of the wine's structural components — a high acid, dry, low-alcohol white wine may feel thin or sharp, for example, whereas a high-alcohol red wine with low tannin may feel soft and silky)

Another way of organizing the impressions a wine sends you is by the sequence of your impressions, as we describe in Chapter 2. The words that tasters use to describe the sequence are

- ✔ **Attack:** The first impression of the wine, which may involve sweetness, dryness, richness or thinness of texture, or even fruitiness (although most of the wine's flavors register a few moments later).

- ✔ **Evolution:** The development of the wine in your mouth. You can think of this stage in two parts: the *mid-palate impression,* a phase when you tend to notice the wine's acidity, get a first impression of its tannin (in red wines) and notice its flavors and their intensity; and the *rear-palate impression,* which involves the degree of persistence that the wine's flavors have across the length of your mouth, the amount and nature of the wine's tannins, and any indication of a burning sensation from overly high alcohol.

- ✔ **Finish** or **aftertaste:** Flavors or impressions that register after the wine has been spat or swallowed. Both the duration of the aftertaste and its nature are noteworthy. A long finish is commendable, for example, and a bitter one is not. A suggestion of concentrated fruit character on the finish often indicates that a wine is age-worthy.

Writing tasting notes

Some people have a special ability to remember tastes. But other people need to take notes in order to remember what they tasted, let alone what they thought of it. If you have the slightest difficulty remembering the names of wines, jot down the names of wines you try and like so that you can enjoy them — or similar wines — again.

To taste, perchance to drink

In wine circles, tasting and drinking are two different activities. Tasting involves thoughtful evaluation of a wine's quality, flavors, texture, aging potential, and so on; if more than a couple of wines are being tasted comparatively, usually tasters spit the wine out (as we mention in Chapter 17) in order to keep their thinking clear. Drinking, on the other hand, involves consumption and sheer appreciation, without any particular analysis of the wine other than the judgment that you like it. (If you don't like it, you don't drink it.)

Unless you're a professional in the wine business, you don't ever have to taste a wine seriously; you can just drink it. However, many wine drinkers have discovered that wine tasting can be a fun way to learn more about wine.

It's a good idea to write comments about wines that you taste, too. Even if you're one of those lucky few who can remember everything you taste, we recommend that you write tasting notes now and then because the exercise of taking notes helps discipline your tasting methods.

When we take notes on wines, we automatically write the letters

- ✔ *C* (for color and appearance in general)
- ✔ *N* (for nose)
- ✔ *T* (for taste, or mouth impressions)

We put one below the other, under the name of each wine on our tasting sheet, leaving space to record our impressions.

When we taste, we take each wine as it comes: If a wine is very aromatic, we write lots of things next to *N,* but if the aroma is understated we can just write *subtle* or even *not much.* When we taste the wine, we approach it sequentially, noting its attack and evolution, and we hold the wine long enough to note its balance and texture, too. Then (having spat), we often taste the wine again to determine what else it may be saying. Sometimes at that point we arrive at a summary description of the wine, like *a huge wine packed with fruitiness that's ready to drink now,* or *a lean, austere wine that will taste better with food than alone.* Our tasting notes are a combination of fragmented observation — *high acid, very crisp* — and summary description.

At first, your own notes will be brief. Just a few words, like *soft, fruity* or *tannic, hard* are fine to remind you later what the wine was like. And as an evaluation of overall quality, there's absolutely nothing wrong with *yum!*

Describing wine: Purism versus poetry

Some people have the idea that there's a right way and a wrong way to describe wine. Many *enologists* (people who have earned a degree in the science of winemaking), for example, usually favor a scientific approach to describing wine. This approach relies on descriptors that are objective, quantifiable, and reproducible — such as the level of acidity in a wine (which is measurable) or specific aroma and flavor descriptors (reproducible in laboratory tests). They dislike fanciful or unspecific terms, such as *rich, generous,* or *smooth.*

Other people who aren't scientists (ourselves included) believe that strictly scientific descriptions usually fail to communicate the spirit of a wine. We're all for noting the relative acidity, tannin, and alcohol levels of a wine, but we won't stop there; we like to describe the overall personality of a wine, even if we have to use language that's more personal than universal.

Sometimes, if a wine is really a great wine, tasters stumble into the most controversial realm of wine description: poetry. We never *try* to come up with picturesque metaphorical descriptions for wines, but sometimes a wine just puts the words in our mouths. One memorable wine in our early days of tasting was a 1970 Brunello di Montalcino that we described as a rainbow in the mouth, its flavors so perfectly blended that each one is barely perceptible individually. Recently a friend of ours described a glass of great but young Vintage Port as "like rubbing a cat in the wrong direction."

If a wine inspires you to such fanciful description, by all means go with it; only a cold-blooded scientist would resist. The experience of that wine will become memorable through the personal words you use to name it.

But beware of anyone who is moved to poetry over every wine. The vast majority of wines are prosaic, and their descriptions should be, too.

And when you do lapse into metaphor over a wine, don't necessarily expect others to understand what you mean or even to approve. Literal types will be all over you, demanding to know what a rainbow tastes like and how a wine can possibly resemble a cat.

In the end, the experience of wine is so personal that the best any of us can do is to *try* to describe the experience to others. Your descriptions will be meaningful to people who share your approach and your language, especially if they're tasting the wine along with you. But someone else picking up your notes will find them incomprehensible. Likewise, you'll find some wine descriptions you read incomprehensible. Such is the nature of the exercise.

Rating Wine Quality

When a wine critic writes a tasting note, he usually accompanies it with a point score, a judgment of the wine's quality on a scale of 20 or 100. You see these numbers plastered all over the shelves in your wine shop and in wine advertisements.

Because words are such a difficult medium for describing wine, the popularity of number ratings has spread like wildfire. Many wine lovers don't bother to read the descriptions in a critic's wine reviews — they just run out to buy the wines with the highest scores. (Hey, they're the best wines, right?) Wines that receive high scores from the best-known critics sell out almost overnight as the result of the demand generated by their scores.

Numbers do provide a convenient shorthand for communicating a critic's opinion of a wine's quality. But number ratings are problematic, too, for a number of reasons:

- ✔ The sheer precision of the scores suggests that they're objective, when in fact they represent either the subjective opinion of an individual critic or the combined subjective opinions of a panel of critics.

- ✔ Different critics can apply the same scale differently. For example, some may assign 95 points only to wines that are truly great compared to all wines of all types, while others could assign the same score to a wine that is great in its own class.

- ✔ The score probably reflects an evaluation of a wine in different circumstances than you will taste it. Most critics rate wines by tasting them without food, for example, while most wine drinkers drink wine with food. Also, the wine glass the critic uses can be different from what you use, and even this detail can affect the way the wine presents itself.

- ✔ Number scores tell you absolutely nothing about how the wine tastes.

This last point, for us, is the most important. You may hate a wine that's rated highly — and not only that, but you may end up feeling like a hopeless fool who can't recognize quality when it's staring him in the face. Save your money and your pride by deciding what kinds of wine you like and then trying to figure out from the words whether a particular wine is your style — *regardless of the number rating*. This advice is the principle behind our book *WineStyle* (Wiley); we urge you to read it, so that you can articulate what you like.

Despite the pitfalls of number ratings, you may be inclined to score wines yourself when you taste — and we encourage you to do that. Numbers can be very meaningful to the person assigning them.

To start, decide which scale you'll use. We suggest a scale with 100 as the highest score, because it is more intuitive than a scale ending in 20. (Most 100-point scales are actually only 50-point scales, with 50 points, not zero, representing the poorest conceivable quality.)

After deciding your scale, create several groupings of points, and write down the quality level that each group represents. It can be something like this:

- 95–100: Absolutely outstanding; one of the finest wines ever
- 90–94: Exceptional quality; excellent wine
- 85–89: Very good quality
- 80–84: Above-average quality; good
- 75–79: Average commercial quality (a "C" student)
- 70–74: Below average quality
- Below 70: Poor quality

Until you get the hang of using this system, you may just want to give each wine a range rather than a precise score, such as 80–84 (good) or 85–89 (very good). As you gain experience in tasting wine and rating wine quality, you become more opinionated and your scores will naturally become more precise.

Just remember that like every other critic, you have your own taste preferences that inevitably influence your scores, no matter how objective you try to be. Don't fall into the trap of thinking that all your wine friends should agree with you.

Chapter 19

Marrying Wine with Food

· ·

In This Chapter

▶ Predictable reactions between wines and foods

▶ Guiding principles for matchmakers

▶ Classic combos that still work

· ·

*E*very now and then, we encounter a wine that stops us dead in our tracks. It's so sensational that we lose all interest in anything but that wine. We drink it with intent appreciation, trying to memorize the taste. We wouldn't dream of diluting its perfection with a mouthful of food.

But 999 times out of 1,000, we drink our wine with food. Wine is meant to go with food. And good food is meant to go with wine.

Good. We've settled that. Wine goes with food, and food goes with wine. Any questions?

Of course we're being facetious. There are thousands of wines in the world, and every one is different. And there are thousands of basic foods in the world, each different — not to mention the infinite combinations of foods in prepared dishes (what we really eat). In reality, food-with-wine is about as simple an issue as boy-meets-girl.

The Dynamics of Food and Wine

Every dish is dynamic — it's made up of several ingredients and flavors that interact to create a (more or less) delicious whole. Every wine is dynamic in exactly the same way. When food and wine combine in your mouth, the dynamics of each change; the result is completely individual to each dish-and-wine combination. (Dare we also mention that we each use our individual palates to judge the success of each combination? No wonder there are no rules!)

When wine meets food, several things can happen:

- The food can exaggerate a characteristic of the wine. For example, if you eat walnuts (which are tannic) with a tannic red wine, such as a Bordeaux, the wine tastes so dry and astringent that most people would consider it undrinkable.

- The food can diminish a characteristic of the wine. Protein diminishes the impression of tannin, for example, and an overly-tannic red wine — unpleasant on its own — could be delightful with rare steak or roast beef.

- The flavor intensity of the food can obliterate the wine's flavor or vice versa. If you've ever drunk a big, rich red wine with a delicate filet of sole, you've had this experience firsthand.

- The wine can contribute new flavors to the dish. For example, a red Zinfandel that's gushing with berry fruit can bring its berry flavors to the dish, as if another ingredient had been added.

- The combination of wine and food can create an unwelcome third-party flavor that wasn't in either the wine or the food originally; we get a metallic flavor when we eat plain white-meat turkey with red Bordeaux.

- The food and wine can interact perfectly, creating a sensational taste experience that is greater than the food or the wine alone. (This scenario is what we hope will happen every time we eat and drink, but it's as rare as a show-stopping dish.)

Fortunately, what happens between food and wine is not haphazard. Certain elements of food react in predictable ways with certain elements of wine, giving us a fighting chance at making successful matches. The major components of wine (alcohol, sweetness, acid, and tannin) relate to the basic tastes of food (sweetness, sourness, bitterness, and saltiness) the same way that the principle of balance in wine operates: Some of the elements exaggerate each other, and some of them compensate for each other. (See the discussion of balance in Chapter 2.)

The fifth wheel

Common wisdom was that humans can perceive four basic tastes: sweet, sour, salty, and bitter. But people who study food have concluded that a fifth taste exists, and there may be many more than that. The fifth taste is called umami (pronounced *oo MAH me*), and it's associated with a savory character in foods. Shellfish, oily fish, meats, and cheeses are some foods high in umami taste.

Umami-rich foods can increase the sensation of bitterness in wines served with them. To counteract this effect, try adding something salty (such as salt itself) or sour (such as vinegar) to your dish. Although this suggestion defies the adage that vinegar and wine don't get along, the results are the proof of the pudding.

Here are some ways that food and wine interact, based on the components of the wine. Remember, each wine and each dish has more than one component, and the simple relationships we describe can be complicated by other elements in the wine or the food. Whether a wine is considered tannic, sweet, acidic, or high in alcohol depends on its dominant component. (See "Describing Taste" in Chapter 2.)

Tannic wines

Tannic wines include most wines based on the Cabernet Sauvignon grape (including red Bordeaux), northern Rhône reds, Barolo and Barbaresco, and any wine — white or red — that has become tannic from aging in new oak barrels. These wines can

- ✔ Diminish the perception of sweetness in a food
- ✔ Taste softer and less tannic when served with protein-rich, fatty foods, such as steak or cheese
- ✔ Taste less bitter when paired with salty foods
- ✔ Taste astringent, or mouth-drying, when drunk with spicy-hot foods

Sweet wines

Some wines that often have some sweetness include most inexpensive California white wines, White Zinfandel, many Rieslings (unless they're labeled "dry" or "trocken"), and medium-dry Vouvray. Sweet wines also include dessert wines such as Port, sweetened Sherries, and late-harvest wines. These wines can

- ✔ Taste less sweet, but fruitier, when matched with salty foods
- ✔ Make salty foods more appealing
- ✔ Go well with sweet foods

Acidic wines

Acidic wines include most Italian white wines; Sancerre, Pouilly-Fumé, and Chablis; traditionally-made red wines from Rioja; most dry Rieslings; and wines based on Sauvignon Blanc that are fully dry. These wines can

- ✔ Taste less acidic when served with salty foods
- ✔ Taste less acidic when served with slightly sweet foods
- ✔ Make foods taste slightly saltier
- ✔ Counterbalance oily or fatty heaviness in food

High-alcohol wines

High alcohol wines include many California wines, both white and red; southern Rhône whites and reds; Barolo and Barbaresco; fortified wines such as Port and Sherry; and most wines produced from grapes grown in warm climates. These wines can

✔ Overwhelm lightly flavored or delicate dishes

✔ Go well with slightly sweet foods

Birds of a Feather, or Opposites Attract?

Two principles can help in matching wine with food: the complementary principle and the contrast principle. The complementary principle involves choosing a wine that is similar in some way to the dish you plan to serve, while the contrast principle (not surprisingly) involves combining foods with wines that are dissimilar to them in some way.

The characteristics of a wine that can either resemble or contrast with the characteristics of a dish are

✔ **The wine's flavors:** Earthy, herbal, fruity, vegetal, and so on

✔ **The intensity of flavor in the wine:** Weak flavor intensity, moderately flavorful, or very flavorful

✔ **The wine's texture:** Crisp and firm, or soft and supple

✔ **The weight of the wine:** Light-bodied, medium-bodied, or full-bodied

---

"A châque son gout" — personal taste rules

We once happened to discuss food pairings for red Bordeaux wine with the owner of one of the five first growths of Bordeaux (see Chapter 9 for an explanation of first growths). "I don't like Bordeaux with lamb," the distinguished gentleman proclaimed. We were confused; "But Bordeaux and lamb is a classic combination!" we said. "No, I don't agree," he answered, holding his ground. After a moment, he added, "Of course, I don't like lamb."

You probably use the complementary principle often without realizing it: You choose a light-bodied wine to go with a light dish, a medium-bodied wine to go with a fuller dish, and a full-bodied wine to go with a heavy dish. Some other examples of the complementary principle in action are

- ✔ **Dishes with flavors that resemble those in the wine.** Think about the flavors in a dish the same way you think about the flavors in wine — as families of flavors. If a dish has mushrooms, it has an earthy flavor; if it has citrus or other elements of fruit, it has a fruity flavor (and so on). Then consider which wines would offer their own earthy flavor, fruity flavor, herbal flavor, spicy flavor, or whatever. The earthy flavors of white Burgundy complement risotto with mushrooms, for example, and an herbal Sancerre complements chicken breast with fresh herbs.

- ✔ **Foods with texture that's similar to that of the wine.** A California Chardonnay with a creamy, rich texture could match the rich, soft texture of lobster, for example.

- ✔ **Foods and wines whose intensity of flavor match.** A very flavorful Asian stir-fry or Tex-Mex dish would be at home with a very flavorful, rather than a subtle, wine.

The contrast principle seeks to find flavors or texture in a wine that aren't in a dish but that would enhance it. A dish of fish or chicken in a rich cream and butter sauce, for example, may be matched with a dry Vouvray, a white wine whose crispness (thanks to its uplifting, high acidity) would counterbalance the heaviness of the dish. A dish with earthy flavors such as portobello mushrooms and fresh fava beans (or potatoes and black truffles) may contrast nicely with the pure fruit flavor of an Alsace Riesling.

You also apply the contrast principle every time you decide to serve simple food, like unadorned lamb chops or hard cheese and bread, with a gloriously complex aged wine.

In order to apply either principle, of course, you have to have a good idea of what the food is going to taste like and what various wines taste like. That second part can be a real stumbling block for people who don't devote every ounce of their free energy to learning about wine. The solution is to ask your wine merchant. A retailer may not have the world's greatest knack in wine and food pairings (then again, he or she might), but at least he should know what his wines taste like.

The Wisdom of the Ages

No matter how much you value imagination and creativity, there's no sense reinventing the wheel. In wine-and-food terms, it pays to know the classic pairings because they work, and they're a sure thing.

Here are some famous and reliable combinations:

- ✔ Oysters and traditional, unoaked Chablis
- ✔ Lamb and red Bordeaux (we like Chianti with lamb, too)
- ✔ Port with walnuts and Stilton cheese
- ✔ Salmon with Pinot Noir
- ✔ Amarone with Gorgonzola cheese
- ✔ Grilled fish with Vinho Verde
- ✔ Foie gras with Sauternes or with late-harvest Gewürztraminer
- ✔ Braised beef with Barolo
- ✔ Dry amontillado Sherry with soup
- ✔ Grilled chicken with Beaujolais
- ✔ Toasted almonds or green olives with fino or manzanilla Sherry
- ✔ Goat cheese with Sancerre or Pouilly-Fumé
- ✔ Dark chocolate with California Cabernet Sauvignon

Look for various additional suggestions on wine and food pairings scattered throughout Chapters 9 through 15 of this book.

TIP

Wine from Venus, food from Mars

Sooner or later you're bound to experience food-and-wine disaster — when the two taste miserable together. We've had many opportunities to test our solution to food-and-wine disaster, and it works: As long as the wine is good and the food is good, eat one first and drink the other afterwards — or vice versa.

Part VII
The Part of Tens

The 5th Wave — By Rich Tennant

"This one's earthy but light, with undertones of blackberry, vanilla, and Scotchgard."

In this part . . .

This is the place to turn for quick answers and easy solutions. The next time a friend tells you that expensive wines are always better, the next time you're wondering when to drink that special wine, the next time someone tells you that Champagnes don't age — check out the advice in this part.

Chapter 20

Answers to Ten Common Questions about Wine

. . . .

*I*n our years of teaching about wine and helping customers in wine shops, we've noticed that the same questions about wine pop up again and again. Here are our answers.

What's the best wine?

This is probably the question customers ask most frequently in wine shops. The retailer usually responds with a barrage of questions, such as

- ✔ "Do you prefer red wines or white wines?"
- ✔ "How much do you want to spend for a bottle?"
- ✔ "Are you planning to serve the wine with any particular dish?"

As all these questions suggest, the "best wine" depends on your taste and circumstances. There's no single "best wine" for everyone.

Hundreds of very good wines can be found in most wine shops. Thirty years ago, there were far fewer — but winemaking and grapegrowing know-how has progressed dramatically, to the point that there are now few poor wines.

You won't necessarily like every one of those good wines, however. There's simply no getting around the fact that taste is personal. If you want to drink a good wine that's right for you, you have to decide what the characteristics of that wine could be. And then get advice from a knowledgeable retailer.

When should I drink this wine?

Wine retailers frequently hear this question from customers, too. The answer, for most wines, is "Any time now."

The great majority of wines are ready to drink when you buy them. Some of them may improve marginally if you hold them for a year or so (and many of them will maintain their drinkability), but they won't improve enough for you to notice, unless you're a particularly thoughtful and experienced taster.

Some fine wines are an exception: They not only benefit from aging but also they *need* to age, in order to achieve their potential quality. For example, assuming that the wines are well stored (turn to Chapter 16 for specifics of wine storage):

- You can usually count on 20 to 30 years (or more) of life from top-quality red Bordeaux wines in good years such as 1982, 1986, 1989, 1990, 1995, 1996, 2000, or the upcoming 2005 (available in late 2007 and 2008). *Note:* many 1982s are ready to drink now.

- The best Barolos, Barbarescos, and Brunello di Montalcinos can age for 20 to 30 years in good vintages.

- The best white Burgundies and white Bordeaux improve with 10 to 15 years of aging or more, in good vintage years.

- Most of today's red Burgundies, with the *possible* exception of the 1996 and 2002 vintages, should be consumed within 10 to 15 years (the less expensive ones even earlier).

For a listing of good vintage years and the approximate stage of readiness of the wines from those years, refer to Appendix C. For the names of some specific producers in each category whose wines we recommend, refer to Chapters 9 and 10.

Is wine fattening?

A glass of dry wine contains 80 to 85 percent water, 12 to 14 percent ethyl alcohol, and small quantities of tartaric acid and various other components. Wine contains no fat.

A 4-ounce serving of dry white wine has about 104 calories, and 4 ounces of red wine has about 110 calories. Sweeter wines contain about 10 percent more calories depending on how sweet they are; fortified wines also contain additional calories because of their higher alcohol.

What grape variety made this wine?

Most New World wines (from the Americas, Australia, and other continents besides Europe) tell you what grape variety they're made from right on the front label — it's often the very name of the wine — or on the back label. Traditional European wines blended from several grape varieties usually don't give you that information a) because the winemakers consider the name of the place more important than the grapes, anyway, and b) because often the grapes they use are local varieties whose names few people would recognize.

If you really want to know what grape varieties make a Soave, Valpolicella, Châteauneuf-du-Pape, Rioja, Côtes du Rhône, or other blended European wines, you'll generally have to look it up. (See our charts in Chapters 9, 10, and 11.)

Which vintage should I buy?

This question assumes that you have a choice among several vintages of the same wine. Most of the time, however, you don't. Nearly every wine is available in only one vintage, which is referred to as the *current* vintage.

For white wines, the current vintage represents grapes that were harvested as recently as nine months ago or as long as three years ago, depending on the type of wine; for red wines, the current vintage is a date one to four years ago.

Classified-growth red Bordeaux wines (see Chapter 9) are a notable exception: Most wine shops feature several vintages of these wines. A few other fine wines — such as Burgundies, Barolos, or Rhône wines — may also be available in multiple vintages, but often they're not because the quantities produced are small and the wines sell out.

A red Rioja or a Chianti Classico may appear to be available in multiple vintages, but if you read the label carefully, you see that one vintage of the Rioja could be a *crianza* (aged two years before release), another may be a *reserva* (aged three years), and another may be a *gran reserva* (aged five years) — so they are each actually different wines, not multiple vintages of the same wine. Likewise, a Chianti may be available in an aged riserva version as well as a non-riserva style.

Most of the time, for most wines, the vintage to buy is the vintage you *can* buy — the current vintage. For the exceptional cases, consult our vintage chart in Appendix C.

Are there any wines without sulfites?

Sulfur dioxide exists naturally in wine as a result of fermentation. It also exists naturally in other fermented foods, such as bread, cookies, and beer. (Various sulfur derivatives are also used regularly as preservatives in packaged foods.)

Winemakers use sulfur dioxide at various stages of the winemaking process because it stabilizes the wine (preventing it from turning to vinegar or deteriorating from oxygen exposure) and safeguards its flavor. Sulfur has been an important winemaking tool since Roman times.

Very few winemakers refrain from using sulfur dioxide, but some do. Your wine shop may carry a few wines whose sulfite content is so low that their labels do not have to carry the phrase *Contains Sulfites* (which the U.S. government requires on the label of any wine that contains more than 10 parts per million of sulfites).

If you wish to limit your consumption of sulfites, dry red wines should be your first choice, followed by dry white wines. Sweet wines contain the most sulfur dioxide. For more info, turn to Chapter 1.

What are organic wines?

The new standards of organic agriculture established by the U.S. Department of Agriculture in 2002 contain two categories for wine:

- *Wine made from organically grown grapes;* these are wines whose grapes come from certified organic vineyards.
- *Organic wine;* these wines come from organically grown grapes and are also produced organically, that is, without the addition of chemical additives such as sulfur dioxide during winemaking.

These categories apply to imported wines sold in the United States as well as to domestic wines. Many more brands, by far, fall into the first category than the second, because most winemakers do use sulfur dioxide in making their wines. (See the previous section for the reasons.)

But not all wines from organically grown grapes are labeled as such. Some winemakers who are deeply committed to organic farming prefer to promote and sell their wines based on the wines' quality, not the incidental feature of their organic farming. For them, organic farming is a means to an end — better grapes, and therefore better wine — rather than a marketing tool. Also, the fact that a national definition of *organic* did not exist in the past disinclined some wineries from using that word.

Now that formal categories exist, many more producers who farm organically will perhaps begin using the "O" word on their labels. But the number of wines in the more rigid *Organic wine* category will probably remain small, because of the sulfur dioxide restriction.

What is a wine expert?

A wine expert is someone with a high level of knowledge about wine in general, including grape growing, winemaking, and the various wines of the world. A wine expert also has a high degree of skill in tasting wine.

Until fairly recently, most wine experts in the United States gained their expertise through informal study, work experience, or experience gained as *amateurs* (lovers) of wine. Although accredited wine courses did exist, they were university programs in *enology* (winemaking) and *viticulture* (grapegrowing) — valuable for people who plan to become winemakers or grape growers, but scientific overkill for people whose goal is breadth of knowledge about wine.

Today, many people become wine experts through the programs of the Wine & Spirit Education Trust (or WSET®; www.wset.co.uk), or various professional sommelier organizations, which include examinations at the end of study. Some examinations entitle successful students to use initials after their names, such as CWE (Certified Wine Educator), MS (Master Sommelier) or MW (Master of Wine). MW is the oldest and most difficult credential for wine experts to earn.

How do I know when to drink the special older wines I've been keeping?

Unfortunately, no precise answer to this question exists because all wines age at a different pace. Even two bottles of the same wine that are stored under the same conditions can age differently.

When you have a specific wine in mind, you can get advice in several different ways:

- ✔ Consult the comments of critics like Robert Parker, Michael Broadbent, or Steve Tanzer, who almost always list a suggested drinking period for wines they review in their newsletters and books (listed in Chapter 17); their educated guesses are usually quite reliable.

- ✔ Contact the winery; in the case of fine, older vintages, the winemaker and his staff are usually happy to give you their opinion on the best time to drink their wine — and they typically have more experience with the wine than anyone else.

- ✔ If you have several bottles of the same wine, try one from time to time to see how the wine is developing. Your own taste is really the best guide — you may enjoy the wine younger, or older, than the experts.

Do old wines require special handling?

Like humans, wine can become somewhat fragile in its later years. For one thing, it doesn't like to travel. If you must move old wine, give it several days' rest afterwards, before opening the bottle. (Red Burgundies and other Pinot Noirs are especially disturbed by journeys.)

Older wines, with their delicate bouquet and flavors, can easily be overwhelmed by strongly flavored foods. Simple cuts of meat or just hard cheeses and good, crusty bread are usually fine companions for mature wines.

If you're going to drink an older wine, don't over-chill it (whether it's white or red). Older wines show their best at moderate temperatures. Temperatures below 60°F (15.5°C) inhibit development in the glass.

Decant red wines or Vintage Ports to separate the clear wine from any sediment that formed in the bottle. (For tips on decanting, see Chapter 8.) Stand the bottle up two or three days before you plan to open it so that the sediment can drift to the bottom. An important concern in decanting an old wine is giving the wine *too* much aeration: A wine in its last stages will deteriorate rapidly upon exposure to air, often within a half hour — sometimes in 10 or 15 minutes.

When you decant an old wine, taste it immediately and be prepared to drink it rapidly if it shows signs of fading.

Chapter 21

Ten Wine Myths Demystified

●●●

*A*s you leaf through the pages of this chapter, you'll probably recognize several of the myths we mention. They all represent common thinking — and common misinformation — about wine. We set the record straight.

The best wines are varietal wines

Many people applaud varietal wines — wines that are named after a grape variety, such as Chardonnay or Merlot — because when you buy a varietal wine, you supposedly know what you're getting. (Actually, for most American wines, only 75 percent of the wine has to come from the named variety, and for most other wines, only 85 percent — so you don't know *exactly* what you're getting.) But the presence of a grape variety name on the label, even a top-quality variety such as Cabernet Sauvignon, tells you nothing about the quality of the wine.

Varietal wines range in quality from ordinary to excellent. Wines named in other ways (for their region of production or with a fantasy name) also range in quality from ordinary to excellent. Varietal wines in general are no better and no worse than other wines.

Wine has to be expensive to be good

For wine, as for many other products, a high price often indicates high quality. But the highest quality wine isn't always the best choice, for the following reasons:

- ✔ Your taste is personal, and you may not like a wine that critics consider very high in quality.
- ✔ Not all situations call for a very high quality wine.

We certainly can enjoy even an $8 wine in many circumstances. At large family gatherings, on picnics, at the beach, and so on, an expensive, top-quality wine can be out-of-place — too serious and important.

Likewise, the very finest wines are seldom the best choices in restaurants — considering typical restaurant prices. Instead, we look for the best value on the wine list (keeping in mind what we are eating) or experiment with some moderately priced wine that we haven't tried before. (There will *always* be some wines that you haven't tried.)

Quality isn't the only consideration in choosing a wine. Often, the best wine of all for your taste or for a certain situation will be inexpensive.

Dark-colored reds are the best red wines

Many red wines today are extremely deep in color, almost to the point of being black rather than red. An opaque appearance in a red wine suggests that the wine's aromas and flavors are as concentrated as its color is, and for that reason, some people have begun to equate deep color with high quality.

While it's true that some very great red wines have deep color, other great red wines do not. Wines made from lightly pigmented grape varieties such as Pinot Noir, Nebbiolo and Sangiovese, for example, will never be naturally opaque in color, and yet they can certainly be great. (And if winemakers strive to get the grapes super-ripe, which can deepen the wine's color, the wine is likely to be dark at the expense of finesse in its flavors.)

Winemakers today have ways of artificially deepening the color of red wines, and therefore even cheap, everyday wines can be deep in color if the winemaker wants to make them that way. Don't be fooled into thinking that dark equals high quality.

The tendency to make red wines as dark in color as possible often backfires: the resulting wine may be over-ripe, overly tannic, too high in extract, and/or too high in alcohol. Regard very-dark colored wines as a warning signal: You may love some of them, but on the other hand, you may find others to be overdone or over-manipulated.

White wine with fish, red with meat

As guidelines go, this isn't a bad one. But we said *guideline,* not rule. Anyone who slavishly adheres to this generalization deserves the boredom of eating and drinking exactly the same thing every day of his life! Do you want a glass of white wine with your burger? Go ahead, order it. You're the one who's doing the eating and drinking, not your friend and not the server who's taking your order.

Even if you're a perfectionist who's always looking for the ideal food and wine combination, you'll find yourself wandering from the guideline. The best wine for a grilled salmon steak is probably red — like a Pinot Noir or a Bardolino — and not white at all. Veal and pork do equally well with red or white wines, depending on how the dish is prepared. And what can be better with hot dogs on the grill than a cold glass of rosé?

No one is going to arrest you if you have white wine with everything, or red wine with everything, or even Champagne with everything! There are no rules. (We offer a few additional suggestions for possible wine-food pairings in Chapter 19.)

Numbers don't lie

It's natural to turn to critics for advice. We do it all the time, when we're trying to decide which movie to see, when we're choosing a new restaurant to try, or when we want to know what someone else thinks of a particular book.

In most cases, we weigh the critics' opinions against our own experience and tastes. Say a steak house just got three stars and a fabulous review from the dining critic. Do we rush to the telephone to make a reservation? Not if we don't like red meat! When the movie critics give two thumbs up, do we automatically assume that we'll like the movie — or do we listen to their commentary and decide whether the movie may be too violent, silly, or serious for us? You know the answer to that.

Yet many wine drinkers, when they hear that a wine just got more than 90 points, go out of their way to get that wine. The curiosity to try a wine that scores well is understandable. But the rigid belief that such a wine a) is necessarily a great wine, and b) is a wine you will like, is simply misguided.

The critics' scores are nothing more than the critics' professional opinion — and opinion, like taste, is *always* personal. (Chapter 18 tells you more about scoring wine.)

Vintages always matter/ vintages don't matter

The difference between one vintage and the next of the same wine is the difference between the weather in the vineyards from one year to the next (barring extenuating circumstances such as replanting of the vineyard, new ownership of the winery, or the hiring of a new winemaker). The degree of vintage variation is thus equivalent to the degree of weather variation.

In some parts of the world the weather varies a lot from year to year, and *for wines from those regions,* vintages certainly do matter. In Bordeaux, Burgundy, Germany, and most of Italy, for example, weather problems (frost, hail, ill-timed rain, or insufficient heat) can affect one vintage for the worse, while the next year may have no such problems. Where a lot of weather variation exists, the quality of the wine can swing from mediocre to outstanding from one year to the next.

In places where the weather is more predictable year after year (like much of California, Australia, and South Africa), vintages can still vary, but the swing is narrower. Serious wine lovers who care about the intimate details of the wines they drink will find the differences meaningful, but most people won't.

Another exception to the "Vintages always matter" myth is inexpensive wine. Top-selling wines that are produced in large volume are usually blended from many vineyards in a fairly large area. Swings in quality from year to year are not significant.

Wine authorities are experts

Wine is an incredibly vast subject. It involves biochemistry, botany, geology, chemistry, climatology, history, culture, politics, laws, and business. How can anyone be an expert in all that? To compound the problem, some people in authoritative positions within the wine field may have had little, if any, education, training, or background in wine before being given jobs by wine companies or columns by publishers, and "ordained" wine authorities almost overnight.

Also, different aspects of wine appeal to different people. Depending on what they particularly like about wine, people tend to specialize in some of wine's disciplines at the expense of others. (Now you know why it takes two of us to write this book.)

Don't expect any one person to be able to answer all your questions about wine in the most accurate and up-to-date manner. Just like doctors and lawyers, wine professionals specialize. They have to.

Old wines are good wines

The idea of rare old bottles of wine being auctioned off for tens of thousands of dollars apiece, like fine art, is fascinating enough to capture anyone's imagination. But valuable old bottles of wine are even rarer than valuable old coins because, unlike coins, wine is perishable.

The great majority of the world's wines don't have what it takes to age for decades. Most wines are meant to be enjoyed in the first one to five years of their lives. Even those wines that have the potential to develop slowly over many years will achieve their potential only if they are properly stored. (See Chapter 16 for information on storing wines.)

The purpose of wine is to be enjoyed — usually, sooner rather than later.

Great wines are supposed to taste bad when they're young

If this myth were true, wouldn't that be convenient for anyone who made poor wine! "It's a great wine," the winery owner could argue. "It's *supposed* to taste bad when it's young."

In the past, some of the great wines of the world, like red Bordeaux, were so tough and tannic that you really couldn't drink them until they had a few decades under their belts. As recently as the 1975 vintage of Bordeaux, some collectors believed that the undrinkability of the young wines was proof positive of their age-worthiness.

Winemakers today believe that a great wine must be in balance when it's young in order to be a balanced wine when it's old. (Refer to Chapter 2 for a discussion of balance.) Although the tannins in old wines usually soften and/or drop out in the form of sediment, most wines today that are extraordinarily tannic when young don't have enough fruit character to last until their tannins fade.

A wine can be in balance without being ready to drink. A great wine can have enormous tannin when it's young, along with its enormous fruit. It may be balanced, even if it's still embryonic. You may be able to appreciate the wine's balance when it's young; you may even enjoy the wine to some degree; but its true greatness is years away, thanks to the wine's ability to develop flavor complexity and greater harmony of its components with age.

Champagnes don't age

We don't know who started this myth; to the contrary, Champagne *does* age well! Depending on the particular year, Vintage Champagne can age especially well. We have enjoyed two outstanding 1928 Vintage Champagnes, Krug and Moët & Chandon's Dom Pérignon, neither of which showed any sign of decline. The oldest Champagne that we've ever tasted, a 1900 Pol Roger, was also in fine shape.

But Champagne demands excellent storage. If kept in a cool, dark, humid place, many Champagnes can age for decades, especially in the great vintages. They lose some effervescence but take on a complexity of flavor somewhat similar to fine white Burgundy. Champagnes in magnum bottles (1.5 l) generally age better than those in regular size (750 ml) bottles.

If you want to try some very fine, reliable, older bottles of Vintage Champagne, look for either Krug or Salon in the 1964, 1969, 1973, or 1976 vintage. If stored well, they will be magnificent. Dom Pérignon is also reliable — the 1961 and 1969 DPs are legendary.

The following houses produce Champagnes known to age well:

- ✔ **Krug:** All their Champagnes are remarkably long-lived.
- ✔ **Pol Roger:** Especially Cuvée Sir Winston Churchill.
- ✔ **Moët & Chandon:** Cuvée Dom Pérignon, ageless when well stored.
- ✔ **Louis Roederer:** Cristal, Cristal Rosé, and Vintage Brut all age well.
- ✔ **Jacquesson:** Signature and Vintage Blanc de Blancs.
- ✔ **Bollinger:** All their Champagnes, especially the Grande Année.
- ✔ **Gosset:** Grand Millésime and Celebris.
- ✔ **Salon:** Remarkable Blanc de Blancs; needs at least 15 years of aging.
- ✔ **Veuve Clicquot:** La Grande Dame and the Vintage Brut.
- ✔ **Taittinger:** Their Blanc de Blancs (Comtes de Champagne).
- ✔ **Billecart-Salmon:** The Blanc de Blancs.
- ✔ **Pommery:** Cuvée Louise.
- ✔ **Laurent-Perrier:** Cuvée Grand Siècle.
- ✔ **Philipponnat:** Clos des Goisses.

Recent great vintages for Champagne are 1996, 1990, 1988, 1985, and 1982.

Part VIII

Appendixes

The 5th Wave   By Rich Tennant

THE TEXAS RANGERS SEND DAVY CROCKETT FOR SUPPLIES

Remember the Almaden!

San Antonio Wines

In this part . . .

Here we give you some useful tools of the trade, like a vintage chart, an extensive pronunciation guide to wine terms and names, and a glossary of wine terms. We were going to include a listing of every winery in the world that makes Chardonnay, but we ran out of space.

Appendix A

Pronunciation Guide to Wine Terms

• •

*N*othing will set a wine snob on your case more quickly than a mispronounced name of a famous wine or wine region. In order not to give snobs their smug satisfaction, we provide pronunciations of dozens of words here, for easy reference. This list is not exhaustive, however; the pronunciations of other, less common names and terms appear throughout the book. Accented syllables, if any, are indicated with capital letters.

Name or term = Pronunciation	*Name or term = Pronunciation*
Agiorghitiko = *eye your YEE tee koe*	Auxey-Duresses = *awk say deh ress*
Aglianico del Vulture = *ah lee AHN ee coh del VUL toor ay*	Barbaresco = *bar bah RES co*
	Barbera = *bar BEAR ah*
Albariño = *ahl bah REE nyoh*	Barolo = *bah RO lo*
Aligoté = *ah lee go tay*	Batard-Montrachet = *bah tar mon rah shay*
Aloxe-Corton = *ah luss cor tohn*	Beaujolais = *boh jhoe lay*
Alsace = *al zass*	Beaulieu (Vineyards) = *bo l'yuh*
(Alto)-Adige = *AH dee jhae*	Bianco di Custoza = *bee AHN coh dee cus TOEZ ah*
amontillado = *ah mon tee YAH doh*	
Anjou = *ahn jhew*	Blanchot = *blahn shoh*
Arneis = *ahr NASE*	botrytis = *boh TRY tis*
Assyrtiko = *ah SEER tee koe*	Bougros = *boo groh*
Au Bon Climat = *oh bone klee maht*	Bourgogne = *boor guh nyuh*
Auslese = *OUSE lay seh*	Bourgueil = *bor guh'y*
Auxerrois = *aus ser whah*	*(continued)*

Name or term = Pronunciation
Brouilly = *broo yee*
Brunello di Montalcino = *brew NEL lo dee mon tahl CHEE no*
brut = *brute*
Cabernet Sauvignon = *cab er nay saw vee nyon*
Canaiolo = *cahn eye OH loh*
Carmignano = *car mee NYAH no*
Chablis = *shah blee*
Chardonnay = *shar doh nay*
Chassagne-Montrachet = *shah san yuh mon rah shay*
(Château de) Fieuzal = *fee oo zahl*
(Château) Grillet = *gree yay*
(Château) Haut-Brion = *oh bree ohn*
(Château) Lafite-Rothschild = *lah feet roth sheeld*
(Château) Margaux = *mahr go*
(Château) Mouton-Rothschild = *moo tohn roth sheeld*
(Château) Petrus = *peh troos*
(Château) Trotanoy = *trot ahn wah*
Châteauneuf-du-Pape = *shah toe nuf dew pahp*
Chénas = *shay nahs*
Chenin Blanc = *shen in blahnk*
Chevalier-Montrachet = *sheh vah lyay mon rah shay*
Chianti = *key AHN tee*
(Chianti) Rufina = *ROO fee nah*
Chinon = *she nohn*

Name or term = Pronunciation
Chiroubles = *sheh roob leh*
Clos du Val = *clo dew val*
Colheita = *col YAI tah*
Condrieu = *cohn dree uh*
Corton-Charlemagne = *cor tawn shahr luh mahn*
Côte de Beaune = *coat deh bone*
Côte Chalonnaise = *coat shal oh naze*
Côte d'Or = *coat dor*
Côte de Nuits = *coat deh nwee*
Côte de Nuits-Villages = *coat deh nwee vee lahj*
Côte Rôtie = *coat roe tee*
Côtes du Ventoux = *coat due vahn too*
cuvée = *coo vay*
Dolcetto = *dohl CHET oh*
(Domaine) Leroy = *lay wah*
Eisele Vineyard = *EYE seh lee*
Entre-Deux-Mers = *ahn truh duh mair*
Fleurie = *fluh ree*
Fourchaume = *for chahm*
Friuli-Venezia Giulia = *free OO lee veh NETZ ee ah JOO lee ah*
Galicia = *gah LEETH ee ah*
Garrafeira = *gar ah FAIR ah*
Gattinara = *gah tee NAH rah*
Gavi = *GAH vee*
Genevrières = *jen ev ree aire*

Name or term = Pronunciation	*Name or term = Pronunciation*
Gewürztraminer = *geh VAIRTZ trah mee ner*	Moët = *moh ett*
Gigondas = *jhee gohn dahs*	Mont de Milieu = *mon deh meh lyew*
Givry = *jee vree*	Montagny = *mon tah nyee*
grands crus classés = *grahn crew clas say*	Montepulciano d'Abruzzo = *mon tae pul chee AH noh dah BRUTE so*
Graves = *grahv*	Monthélie = *mohn teh lee*
Grenouilles = *greh n'wee*	Montlouis = *mon loo wee*
Grüner Veltliner = *GREW ner VELT lee ner*	Montmains = *mon man*
halbtrocken = *HAHLB tro ken*	Montrachet = *mon rah shay*
Haut-Médoc = *oh may doc*	Moschofilero = *mos cho FEEL eh roe*
Hermitage = *er mee tahj*	Mosel-Saar-Ruwer = *MOH zel-zar-ROO ver*
Juliénas = *jool yay nahs*	Moulin-á-Vent = *moo lahn ah vahn*
Languedoc-Roussillon = *lahn gweh doc roo see yawn*	Moulis = *moo lees*
Les Clos = *lay cloh*	Müller-Thurgau = *MUU lair TOUR gow*
Les Forêts = *lay for ay*	Muscadet = *moos cah day*
Les Preuses = *lay preuhz*	Muscat = *moos caht*
Liebfraumilch = *LEEB frow milsh*	Nahe = *NAH heh*
Listrac = *lee strahk*	Nantais = *nahn tay*
Loire = *lwahr*	Nebbiolo = *neb bee OH lo*
Mâcon-Villages = *mac cawn vee lahj*	Neuchatel = *NOI sha tel*
Malvasia = *mal va SEE ah*	Niebaum-Coppola = *NEE baum COPE poh lah*
Margaux = *mahr go*	Niederosterreich = *nee der OZ ter ryke*
Médoc = *meh doc*	Nuits-St.-Georges = *nwee san jorg*
Menetou-Salon = *meh neh too sah lohn*	Orvieto = *or vee AE toh*
Mercurey = *mer cure ay*	Pauillac = *poy yac*
Merlot = *mer loh*	Pays d'Oc = *pay ee doc*
Meursault = *muhr so*	Penedés = *pen eh DAIS*

(continued)

Name or term = Pronunciation
Pernand-Vergelesses = *pair nahn vair juh less*
Perrier-Jouët = *per ree yay joo ett*
Pessac-Léognan = *pay sac lay oh nyahn*
Pfalz = *fallz*
Pinot Bianco = *pee noh bee AHN coh*
Pinot Blanc = *pee noh blahnk*
Pinot Grigio = *pee noh GREE joe*
Pinot Gris = *pee noh gree*
Pinot Noir = *pee noh nwahr*
Pinotage = *pee noh TAHJ*
Pouilly-Fuissé = *pwee fwee say*
Pouilly-Fumé = *pwee foo may*
premier cru = *prem yay crew*
Priorato = *pree oh RAH to*
Puligny-Montrachet = *poo lee nyee mon rah shay*
Qualitätswein = *KAL ee tates vine*
Quincy = *can see*
Quinta = *KEEN ta*
Regnie = *ray nyay*
Reuilly = *reuh yee*
Rheingau = *RYNE gow*
Rheinhessen = *RYNE hess ehn*
Rías Baixas = *REE ahse BYCE ahse*
Ribera del Duero = *ree BEAR ah del doo AIR oh*
Ribolla Gialla = *ree BOHL lah JAHL lah*
Riesling = *REESE ling*

Name or term = Pronunciation
Rioja = *ree OH hah*
Rueda = *roo AE dah*
Rully = *rouh yee*
Saint-Amour = *sant ah more*
Saint-Aubin = *sant oh ban*
Saint-Nicolas-de-Bourgueil = *san nih coh lahs deh bor goye*
Saint-Romain = *san ro man*
Saint-Véran = *san veh rahn*
Sancerre = *sahn sair*
Sangiovese = *san joe VAE sae*
Saumur = *soh muhr*
Sauvignon Blanc = *saw vee nyon blahnk*
Savennieres = *sah ven nyair*
Savigny-lès-Beaune = *sah vee nyee lay bone*
Scheurebe = *SHOY reb beh*
Semillon = *SEM eh lon* (Australian)
Sémillon = *seh mee yohn* (French)
Sèvre-et-Maine = *sev'r et mehn*
Soave = *so AH vay*
Spanna = *SPAH nah*
Spätlese = *SHPATE lay seh*
spumante = *spoo MAHN tay*
St-Estèphe = *sant eh steff*
St-Julien = *sant jhoo lee ehn*
St.-Emilion = *sant ay meal yon*
Steiermark = *STY er mark*

Name or term = Pronunciation
Tempranillo = *tem prah NEE yoh*
Tinto = *TEEN toe*
Tocai Friulano = *toe KYE free ou LAH noh*
Tokaj-Hegyalja = *toe KYE heh JAH yah*
Torgiano = *tor gee AH no*
Tre Venezie = *trae veh NETZ ee ae*
Trebbiano = *treb bee AH noh*
Trentino-Alto Adige = *tren TEE noh-AHL toh AH dee jhae*
trocken = *TRO ken*
Vacqueyras = *vah keh rahs*
Vaillons = *vye yon*
Valais = *vah lay*
Valmur = *vahl moor*
Valpolicella = *val po lee CHEL lah*
Vaudésir = *voh deh zeer*
Vendange Tardive = *vahn dahnj tahr deev*

Name or term = Pronunciation
Veneto = *VEN eh toh*
Verdejo = *ver DAY ho*
Verdicchio = *ver DEE key oh*
Vernaccia di San Gimignano = *ver NOTCH cha dee san jee mee NYAH noh*
Vinho = *VEEN yo*
Vinho Verde = *VEEN yo VAIRD*
(Vino) Nobile di Montepulciano = *NO be lay dee mon tay pul chee AH no*
Viognier = *vee oh nyay*
Vosne-Romanée = *vone roh mah nay*
Vouvray = *voo vray*
Wachau = *va COW*
Weissburgunder – *VICE boor gun der*
Wien = *vee EN*
Willamette (Valley) = *wil LAM ette*
Xinomavro = *ksee NO mav roe*

Appendix B

Glossary of Wine Terms

• •

*H*ere, for handy reference, are definitions of dozens of the most common wine terms and wine-tasting terms.

acidity: A component of wine, generally consisting of tartaric acid (a natural acid in grapes) and comprising approximately 0.5 to 0.7 percent of the wine by volume.

aerate: To expose wine to air in preparation for drinking it, usually with the intention of allowing the most attractive aromas to reveal themselves in an older wine, or softening the harshness of a younger wine.

alcohol level: The percentage of alcohol by volume that a wine has; most white wines have an alcohol level between 9 and 14 percent, and most red wines have an alcohol level between 12 and 14 percent.

American oak: Oak wood from a U.S. forest, of the species *quercus alba,* and the barrels made from such wood; some wine-makers in certain wine regions (such as Spain and Australia) favor American oak for aging their wines.

ample: A descriptor for wines that give the impression of being full and expansive in your mouth.

AOC: Abbreviation for *Appellation d'Origine Contrôlée,* sometimes shortened to *Appellation Contrôlée* and abbreviated as AC; translates to *protected place name;* France's official category for its highest-ranking types of wine, whose name, origin, grape varieties, and other defining factors are regulated by law.

appellation: Name; often used to mean the official geographic origin of a wine, which is part of a wine's official name.

aroma: The smell of a wine. Some purists use the term *aroma* only for the straightforward, youthful smells of a wine, and use the term *bouquet* for the more complex smells of an aged wine. But we use *aroma* as a general term for all wine smells.

aromatic: A descriptor for a wine that has a pronounced smell, used particularly in reference to fruity and floral smells. Some white grape varieties are also dubbed *aromatic* because they are strong in aroma compounds.

aromatic compounds: Those substances in wine — derived from the grapes, from winemaking, or from aging — that are responsible for a wine's aromas and flavors.

astringent: A descriptor for the mouth-puckering, pore-tightening tactile character of some wines, caused by tannin, acid, or the combination of both. Generally not a positive trait.

attack: The first impression a wine gives you when you taste it. A wine's attack is related to sensations in the front of your mouth.

balance: The interrelationship of a wine's alcohol, residual sugar, acid, and tannin; when no one component stands out obtrusively in your mouth, a wine is said to be well-balanced; wines can also have balance between their aromas/flavors and their structure.

barrel: A relatively small wooden container for fermenting and/or aging wine, generally 60 gallons in size and generally made of oak.

barrel-aged: A term that applies to wines that are fermented in containers of inert material, such as stainless steel, and subsequently placed into wooden barrels for a period of maturation; the term also applies to the maturation period of wines that also fermented in the barrel.

barrel-fermented: A term that applies to white wines that are fermented in oak barrels; the oaky character of such wines is generally more subtle than that of wines that have been merely barrel-aged.

big: A general descriptor for wines that are either very full or very intense.

black fruits: A general term for wine aromas and flavors that suggest blackberries, blueberries, black cherries, blackcurrants, or other black fruits.

black grapes: Wine grapes that have a reddish or blue pigmentation in their skins; used to make red wine.

blend: To mix together two or more individual lots of wine, usually wines from different grape varieties (but also applies to wines from different vineyards, different regions, or different vintages); a wine derived from the juice of different grape varieties is called a blend.

bodega: A winery in Spain; also the Spanish word for a building where wine is stored.

body: The impression of a wine's weight in your mouth. A wine's body is generally described as light, medium, or full.

bottle-age: Maturation of a wine after it has been bottled; most wines undergo a short period of bottle-age at the winery before release; fine wines can require additional bottle-age from the consumer.

bouquet: Evolved, mature aromas.

bright: Indicates a wine whose characteristics are perceived as vivid by the senses. A wine can be visually bright, or it can have bright aromas and flavors; in both cases, the opposite is dull.

cask: A relatively large wooden container for making or storing wine.

castello: Italian for *castle;* refers to a wine estate.

cedary: Having aromas or flavors that resemble the smell of cedar wood.

character: An anthropomorphic attribute of wines that give the impression of having substance and integrity.

charry: Having aromas or flavors that suggest burnt wood or charred wood.

chateau: A French name for a grand winery estate, commonly used in the Bordeaux region as well as other regions.

classico: An Italian term applicable to certain DOC or DOCG wines whose vineyards are situated in the original, classic part of the territory for that particular type of wine.

clone: A subvariety of a grape variety; a vine, or set of genetically identical vines, that exhibits characteristics specific to it as compared to other vines of the same variety.

colheita: Vintage, in Portuguese.

commune: A village, and its surrounding vineyard territory.

compact: A descriptor for wines that give the impression of being intense but not full.

complex: Having a multiplicity of aromas and flavors

concentrated: A descriptor for wines with aromas and flavors that are dense rather than dilute.

concentration: A characteristic of wines whose flavors or fruit character are tightly knit as opposed to being dilute or watery.

cosecha: Vintage, in Spanish.

crisp: A wine that feels clean and slightly brittle in your mouth; the opposite of "soft." Crispness is usually the result of high acidity, and crisp wines therefore are usually relatively light in body and go well with food.

decant: To transfer wine from a bottle to another container, either for the purpose of aerating the wine or to separate a red wine from its sediment.

depth: A characteristic of fine wines that give the impression of having many layers of taste, rather than being flat and one-dimensional; a positive trait.

dilute: A descriptor for wines whose aromas and flavors are thin and watery, as opposed to concentrated; a negative characteristic.

district: A geographic entity more specific than a region and less specific than a commune.

DO: Abbreviation for *Denominación de Origen,* which translates to *place name;* Spain's official category for wines whose name, origin, grape varieties, and other defining factors are regulated by law. Also an abbreviation for Portugal's highest official wine category, *Denominação de Origem,* translated similarly and having the same meaning.

DOC: Abbreviation for *Denominazione di Origine Controllata,* which translates to *controlled place name;* Italy's official category for wines whose name, origin, grape varieties, and other defining factors are regulated by law.

DOCG: Abbreviation for *Denominazione di Origine Controllata e Garantita,* which translates to *controlled and guaranteed place name;* Italy's official category for its highest-ranking wines.

domaine: A French term for wine estate, commonly used in the Burgundy region.

dry: A wine that is not sweet. The word *dry* can also describe the texture of a wine that feels rough in your mouth, as in *dry texture* or *dry mouthfeel.* But when used alone, it refers specifically to lack of sweetness.

dull: A wine whose expression is muddled and unclear. This term can apply to a wine's appearance, to its aromas and flavors, or to its general style. It is a negative characteristic.

earthy: Having aromas and flavors that suggest earth, such as wet soil, dry earth, certain minerally aromas, and so forth. This term is sometimes used as a euphemism for wines that are rustic and lack refinement.

elegance: An attribute of wines that express themselves in a fine or delicate manner as opposed to an intense or forceful way — considered a positive trait.

estate: A property that grows grapes and produces wines from its own vineyards; wines labeled *estate-bottled* are made from vineyards owned by (or in some cases, under the direct control of) the same entity that owns the winery and makes the wine; use of the term is regulated by law in most areas.

fermentation: The natural process by which the sugar in grape juice is transformed into alcohol (and the juice is thus transformed into wine) through the action of yeasts.

finish: The final impressions a wine gives after you have swallowed it or spat it out; aftertaste.

firm: A descriptor for wines that are not soft, but are not harsh and tough; generally relates to the tannic content of a red wine or the acidity of a white wine.

flabby: A perjorative term used to describe wines that taste too soft, generally due to a lack of acidity or tannin.

flavor intensity: The degree to which a wine's flavors are pronounced and easily observable.

flavors: Aromatic constituents of a wine that are perceived in the mouth.

fleshy: A descriptor for a rich textural or tactile impression of some wines.

fortified wine: A wine that has had alcohol added to it.

French oak: Oak wood from the forests of France, of the species *quercus robur,* considered the finest type of oak for aging most white wines; the barrels made from such wood.

fruit character: Those characteristics of a wine that derive from the grapes, such as a wine's aromas and flavors.

fruity: Having aromas and flavors suggestive of fruit. This is a broad descriptor; in some cases the fruity aroma or flavor of a wine can be described more precisely as suggestive of fresh fruit, dried fruit, or cooked fruit, or even more precisely as a specific fresh, dried, or cooked fruit, such as fresh apples, dried figs, or strawberry jam.

full: A descriptor for wines that give the impression of being large and weighty in your mouth. A wine's fullness can derive from high alcohol or from other aspects of the wine. A wine can be pleasantly full or too full, depending on one's taste preferences.

garrafeira: A Portuguese term for a reserva wine with specific aging requirements — for red wines, at least three years of aging in oak and bottle before release.

generous: A descriptor for wines whose characteristics are expressive and easy to perceive; usually describes fuller, rounder styles.

gran reserva: On Spanish red wines, a term indicating a wine that has aged at least five years before release, at least two of which were in oak.

grape tannin: Those tannins in a red wine that come from the grapes from which the wine was made, usually from the grapes' skins.

grape variety: A distinct type of grape within a species.

harmonious: A flattering descriptor of wines that are not only well balanced but also express themselves in a particularly graceful manner.

herbal: Having aromas and flavors that suggest herbs, such as fresh herbs, dried herbs, or specific herbs (rosemary, thyme, tarragon, and so forth).

intense: Usually used in reference to a wine's aromas and flavors, to describe the volume of those aromas or flavors — how strong the smell of lemon is in the wine, for example.

lees: Grape solids and dead yeast cells that precipitate to the bottom of a wine vessel after fermentation.

length: A characteristic of fine wines that give a sustained sensory impression across the length of the tongue.

maceration: The process of soaking the skins of red grapes in their grape juice to leach the skins' color, tannin, and other substances into the juice.

malolactic fermentation: A natural conversion of harsh malic acid into milder lactic acid, which weakens the total acidity of a wine; an optional process in white wine production.

maturation: The aging period at the winery during which a wine evolves to a state of readiness for bottling; the process of development and evolution that fine wines undergo after they are bottled.

medium-dry: A term to indicate the perceived sweetness of wines that are very slightly sweet.

medium-sweet: A term to indicate the perceived sweetness level of wines that are sweeter than medium-dry, but not fully sweet.

minerally: Having aromas or flavors that suggest minerals (as opposed to organic substances such as plants or animals). This is a broad descriptor; in some cases the minerally aroma or flavor of a wine can be described more precisely as suggestive of chalk, iron, steel, and so forth.

new oak: Oak barrels that are used for the first time to make a particular wine; can also refer to a group of barrels that includes first-use to third-use barrels.

New World: Collective term for those winemaking countries of the world that are situated outside of Europe.

nutty: Having aromas or flavors that suggest nuts. This is a broad descriptor; in some cases the nutty aroma or flavor of a wine can be described more precisely as suggestive of roasted nuts, toasted nuts, nut butter, or cashews, almonds, hazelnuts, and so forth.

oaky: Having characteristics that derive from oak, such as toastiness, smokiness, a charry smell or flavor, vanilla aroma, or a higher tannin level than the wine might ordinarily have. Usually these oaky characteristics occur as the wine ages in oak barrels, but in very inexpensive wines they may have been added as an actual flavoring.

off-dry: A generalized term for wines that are neither fully dry nor very sweet.

old oak: Oak barrels or casks that are old enough to have lost most of their oaky character, generally three years old and older.

old vines: An unregulated term for grape vines whose fruit quality presumably is quite good due to the fact the vines are old — generally 40 years old or older — and therefore produce a very small crop of concentrated grapes.

Old World: Collective term for the wine-making countries of Europe.

palate: A term used by wine tasters as a synonym for "mouth," or to refer to the characteristics of a wine that manifest in the taster's mouth.

petrol: Having aromas or flavors that suggest diesel fuel; can be a positive trait.

phylloxera: A parasite louse that feeds on the roots of Vitis vinifera grape vines, resulting in the vines' premature death.

plummy: Having aromas or flavors that suggest ripe plums.

powerful: An anthropomorphic descriptor for wines that convey an impression of strength and intensity.

pretty: An anthropomorphic descriptor for wines that are attractive for their delicacy and finesse.

primary aromas: Fresh aromas in a wine that derive from the grapes used to make that wine.

red grapes: Wine grapes that have a deep reddish or blue pigmentation in their skins; also called black grapes.

region: A geographical entity less specific than a district, but more specific than a country; for Italian wines, the term "region" applies to the political entity as well as to the wine zones within that area.

reserva: On a Spanish wine, a term indicating that the wine has aged longer at the winery (usually some specified combination of oak aging and bottle aging) than a non-reserva version of the same type of wine; red reserva wines must age at least three years (with a year in oak) before release. On a Portuguese wine, a wine of superior quality from a single vintage.

reserve: A designation for wines that are presumably finer than the non-reserve (normal) version of the same wine; use of the term is unregulated in the United States and in France.

residual sugar: Sugar remaining in the wine after fermentation.

rich: A descriptor of wines that offer an abundance of flavor, texture, or other sensory perceptions.

riserva: Italian word for "reserve," indicating a wine that has aged longer before release from the winery than a non-reserve version of the same type of wine, and suggesting higher quality; the period of time a wine must age to earn the term "riserva" (and sometimes the conditions of that aging) is defined by individual DOC regulations for each wine that may use this term.

round: A descriptor for wines that are perceived in the mouth to be neither flat nor angular. Roundness relates to the wine's structure — that is, its particular makeup of acid, tannin, sweetness, and alcohol, which dictates texture and mouthfeel.

second-label wine: A less-expensive, second wine (or a second brand of wine) made by a winery from grapes or wine not considered worthy of the winery's primary label.

sediment: The solid residue in a bottle of red wine that forms as the wine matures.

serious: A metaphorical descriptor for a wine that is of high quality, as opposed to a popularly styled, mass-market wine.

silky: Having a supple, smooth texture.

single-vineyard wine: A wine that is made from the grapes of a single (presumably exceptionally good) plot of land, and that usually carries the name of the vineyard on its label; the term is unregulated in that "vineyard" is not defined as to size or ownership.

skin contact: The process during which the juice of grapes rests in contact with the grape skins; in red wine, the process by which the wines absorb color, tannin, and other substances; not normally used in white wine production, but occasionally used to enhance the aromatic character of the wine.

smoky: Having aromas or flavors that suggest smoke or smoked wood.

smooth: Descriptor for a wine whose texture is not rough or harsh.

soft: Textural descriptor for a wine whose alcohol and sugar (if any) dominate its acidity and tannin, resulting in a lack of hardness or roughness.

stemmy: Descriptor for red wines that give the impression of having dry, raspy, woody tannins, as if from the stems of grape bunches.

stems: The woody part of a grape bunch, which are high in tannin; usually the stems are removed and discarded prior to fermentation.

stony: Having minerally aromas or flavors that suggest stones. In some cases the stony aroma or flavor of a wine can be described more precisely as suggestive of wet stones.

structural components: Principally, a wine's alcohol, acid, tannin, and sugar (if any).

structure: That part of a wine's taste that derives from perception of the wine's structural elements.

style: The set of characteristics through which a wine manifests itself.

supple: A descriptor for wines that seem fluid in texture in the mouth, without roughness or sharpness; a positive trait.

süssreserve: German for _sweet reserve;_ unfermented grape juice that is added to a white wine to increase the wine's residual sugar and sweetness.

sweetness: The impression of sugary taste in a wine, which can be due to the presence of residual sugar or to other sweet-tasting substances in the wine, such as alcohol.

tannic: A word used to describe wines that seem to be high in tannin.

tannin: A substance in the skins, stems, and seeds of grapes; a principal component of red wines, which — unlike white wines — are made by using the grape skins. Tannin also is a component of oak barrels.

tarry: Having aromas or flavors that suggest fresh tar.

tart: A descriptor for aromas or flavors of under-ripe fruit. This term can also apply to a wine that is too high in acid.

taste: A general term for the totality of impressions a wine gives in the mouth; more specifically, the primary tastes found in wine: sweetness, sourness, and bitterness.

terroir: A French word that is the collective term for the growing conditions in a vineyard, such as climate, soil, drainage, slope, altitude, topography, and so on.

texture: A wine's consistency or feel in the mouth.

thin: A word used to describe wines that are lacking in substance.

tight: A descriptor for wines that seem to be inexpressive. This term can apply to a wine's aromas and flavors, or to its structure.

underbrush: Aromas or flavors that suggest wet leaves, dampness, and slight decay; a welcome note in many older reds.

varietal: A wine named for the sole or the principal grape variety from which it was made.

varietal character: The characteristics of a wine that are attributable to the grape variety from which it was made.

vegetal: Having aromas or flavors that suggest vegetables, such as green peppers or asparagus; these can be pleasant or not, depending on the taster.

vin de pays: French phrase for *country wine;* legally, a category of French wine that holds lower status than AOC wines.

vinification: The activity of making grape juice into wine.

vintage: The year in which a wine's grapes grew and were harvested; sometimes used as a synonym for the grape harvest.

viticulture: The activity of growing grapes.

Vitis vinifera: The species to which most of the world's wine grapes belong.

weight: The impression of a wine's volume in the mouth.

wood tannin: Those tannins in a wine that are attributable to the barrels in which the wine aged, as opposed to the grapes.

yeasts: One-cell microorganisms responsible for transforming grape juice into wine.

Appendix C

Vintage Wine Chart: 1985–2004

• •

*A*ny vintage wine chart must be regarded as a rough guide — a general, average rating of the vintage year in a particular wine region. Remember that many wines will always be exceptions to the vintage's rating. For example, some wine producers will manage to find a way to make a decent — even fine — wine in a so-called poor vintage.

WINE REGION	1985	1986	1987	1988	1989	1990	1991	1992	1993	1994
Bordeaux										
Médoc, Graves	85c	90b	75c	85b	90c	90c	75c	75d	80c	85c
Pomerol, St-Emil	85c	85b	75d	85b	90c	95c	60d	75d	80c	85b
Sauternes/Barsac	80c	90b	70c	95a	90b	95a	70d	65d	65d	75c
Burgundy										
Côte de Nuits	85c	65d	75d	80c	85c	90c	85c	70d	80c	75d
Côte Beaune	85c	70d	80d	85c	85c	90c	70c	80c	75d	75d
Burgundy White	85c	90c	80c	80c	90c	85c	70d	85c	70d	75d
Rhône Valley										
Northern Rhône	85c	80c	80c	90c	90b	90c	90c	75c	60d	85c
Southern Rhône	85c	75d	60d	85c	95b	95c	65d	75d	80d	85d
Other Wine Regions										
Alsace	90c	80d	80d	85c	95c	95c	75c	85c	85c	90c
Champagne	95c	80c	NV	90b	85c	95c	NV	NV	80c	NV
Germany	85c	80c	80c	90c	90c	95c	85c	80c	85c	90c
Rioja	80c	80c	80d	85c	90c	85c	75c	85c	85c	90c
Vintage Port	85b	NV	NV	NV	NV	NV	90a	95a	NV	95a
Italy										
Piedmont	90c	85c	80c	90b	95a	90c	75c	70d	80c	75d
Tuscany	95c	80d	75d	90c	70d	90c	75d	70d	80d	80d
California North Coast										
Cab. Sauvignon	90c	80c	85c	75c	80c	90c	95b	90c	85c	95c

WINE REGION	1995	1996	1997	1998	1999	2000	2001	2002	2003	2004
Bordeaux										
Médoc, Graves	90b	90a	85b	85a	85a	95a	85a	85b	85a	85a
Pomerol, St-Emil	90b	85a	85b	95a	85a	95a	85a	85b	80a	85a
Sauternes/Barsac	85b	85b	85b	85a	85a	85a	95a	90a	90a	80a

WINE REGION	1995	1996	1997	1998	1999	2000	2001	2002	2003	2004
Burgundy										
Côte de Nuits	90b	90a	90c	80c	90b	85c	80b	90a	85a	85a
Côte Beaune	85b	90b	85c	80c	90b	75c	75c	90a	80b	80b
Burgundy White	90b	90b	85c	80c	85c	85c	85c	90b	80b	85b
Rhône Valley										
Northern Rhône	90b	85c	90c	90a	95a	85b	90a	75c	95a	80c
Southern Rhône	90b	80d	80d	95b	90b	95b	95a	60d	90b	85c
Other Wine Regions										
Alsace	85c	85c	85c	90c	85c	90c	90c	85c	75c	90b
Champagne	85b	100a	85b	85c	85c	80c	NV	90a	?	?
Germany	85c	90b	85c	90b	85c	70d	90b	90b	85b	90a
Rioja	90c	85c	85c	80d	85c	85c	95b	75d	85c	90b
Vintage Port	NV	NV	85a	NV	NV	90a	NV	NV	90a?	90a?
Italy										
Piedmont	85b	95a	85c	90a	95a	90b	95a	75c	80b	85a?
Tuscany	85b	75c	90c	85c	95c	85c	95b	75c	80b	85a?
California North Coast										
Cab. Sauvignon	90b	90b	90c	85c	85b	75c	95a	90b	90b	85b

Key:

100 = Outstanding	75 = Average	a = Too young to drink
95 = Excellent	70 = Below Average	b = Can be consumed now,
90 = Very Good	65 = Poor	but will improve with time
85 = Good	50–60 = Very Poor	c = Ready to drink
80 = Fairly Good		d = May be too old
		NV = Non-vintage year

WINE REGION	Recent Past Great Vintages (prior to 1985)
Bordeaux	
Médoc, Graves	1959, 1961, 1970, 1982
Pomerol, St-Emil	1961, 1964, 1970, 1975, 1982
Burgundy	
Côte de Nuits-Red	1959, 1964, 1969, 1978
Côte Beaune-Red	1959, 1969
Burgundy, White	1962, 1966, 1969, 1973, 1978
Rhône Valley	
Northern Rhône	1959, 1961, 1966, 1969, 1970, 1972 (Hermitage), 1978
Southern Rhône	1961, 1967, 1978
Other Wine Regions	
Alsace	1959, 1961, 1967, 1976, 1983
Champagne	1961, 1964, 1969, 1971, 1975, 1979, 1982
Sauternes	1959, 1962, 1967, 1975, 1983
Germany	1959, 1971, 1976
Rioja (Spain)	1964, 1970, 1981, 1982
Vintage Port	1963, 1966, 1970, 1977, 1983
Italy	
Piedmont	1958, 1964, 1971, 1978, 1982
Tuscany	1967, 1970 (Brunello di Montalcino), 1971
California North Coast	
Cabernet Sauvignon	1951, 1958, 1968, 1970, 1974, 1978

Index

• *C* •

• D •

• E •

• **Q** •

• **R** •

• Z •

BUSINESS, CAREERS & PERSONAL FINANCE

0-7645-5307-0

0-7645-5331-3 *†

Also available:
- Accounting For Dummies †
  0-7645-5314-3
- Business Plans Kit For Dummies †
  0-7645-5365-8
- Cover Letters For Dummies
  0-7645-5224-4
- Frugal Living For Dummies
  0-7645-5403-4
- Leadership For Dummies
  0-7645-5176-0
- Managing For Dummies
  0-7645-1771-6

- Marketing For Dummies
  0-7645-5600-2
- Personal Finance For Dummies *
  0-7645-2590-5
- Project Management For Dummies
  0-7645-5283-X
- Resumes For Dummies †
  0-7645-5471-9
- Selling For Dummies
  0-7645-5363-1
- Small Business Kit For Dummies *†
  0-7645-5093-4

HOME & BUSINESS COMPUTER BASICS

0-7645-4074-2

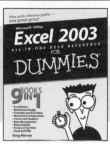

0-7645-3758-X

Also available:
- ACT! 6 For Dummies
  0-7645-2645-6
- iLife '04 All-in-One Desk Reference
  For Dummies
  0-7645-7347-0
- iPAQ For Dummies
  0-7645-6769-1
- Mac OS X Panther Timesaving
  Techniques For Dummies
  0-7645-5812-9
- Macs For Dummies
  0-7645-5656-8

- Microsoft Money 2004 For Dummies
  0-7645-4195-1
- Office 2003 All-in-One Desk Reference
  For Dummies
  0-7645-3883-7
- Outlook 2003 For Dummies
  0-7645-3759-8
- PCs For Dummies
  0-7645-4074-2
- TiVo For Dummies
  0-7645-6923-6
- Upgrading and Fixing PCs For Dummies
  0-7645-1665-5
- Windows XP Timesaving Techniques
  For Dummies
  0-7645-3748-2

FOOD, HOME, GARDEN, HOBBIES, MUSIC & PETS

0-7645-5295-3

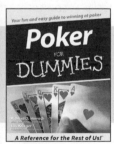

0-7645-5232-5

Also available:
- Bass Guitar For Dummies
  0-7645-2487-9
- Diabetes Cookbook For Dummies
  0-7645-5230-9
- Gardening For Dummies *
  0-7645-5130-2
- Guitar For Dummies
  0-7645-5106-X
- Holiday Decorating For Dummies
  0-7645-2570-0
- Home Improvement All-in-One
  For Dummies
  0-7645-5680-0

- Knitting For Dummies
  0-7645-5395-X
- Piano For Dummies
  0-7645-5105-1
- Puppies For Dummies
  0-7645-5255-4
- Scrapbooking For Dummies
  0-7645-7208-3
- Senior Dogs For Dummies
  0-7645-5818-8
- Singing For Dummies
  0-7645-2475-5
- 30-Minute Meals For Dummies
  0-7645-2589-1

INTERNET & DIGITAL MEDIA

0-7645-1664-7

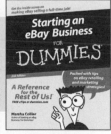

0-7645-6924-4

Also available:
- 2005 Online Shopping Directory
  For Dummies
  0-7645-7495-7
- CD & DVD Recording For Dummies
  0-7645-5956-7
- eBay For Dummies
  0-7645-5654-1
- Fighting Spam For Dummies
  0-7645-5965-6
- Genealogy Online For Dummies
  0-7645-5964-8
- Google For Dummies
  0-7645-4420-9

- Home Recording For Musicians
  For Dummies
  0-7645-1634-5
- The Internet For Dummies
  0-7645-4173-0
- iPod & iTunes For Dummies
  0-7645-7772-7
- Preventing Identity Theft For Dummies
  0-7645-7336-5
- Pro Tools All-in-One Desk Reference
  For Dummies
  0-7645-5714-9
- Roxio Easy Media Creator For Dummies
  0-7645-7131-1

* Separate Canadian edition also available
† Separate U.K. edition also available

SPORTS, FITNESS, PARENTING, RELIGION & SPIRITUALITY

0-7645-5146-9

0-7645-5418-2

Also available:
- Adoption For Dummies
  0-7645-5488-3
- Basketball For Dummies
  0-7645-5248-1
- The Bible For Dummies
  0-7645-5296-1
- Buddhism For Dummies
  0-7645-5359-3
- Catholicism For Dummies
  0-7645-5391-7
- Hockey For Dummies
  0-7645-5228-7

- Judaism For Dummies
  0-7645-5299-6
- Martial Arts For Dummies
  0-7645-5358-5
- Pilates For Dummies
  0-7645-5397-6
- Religion For Dummies
  0-7645-5264-3
- Teaching Kids to Read For Dummies
  0-7645-4043-2
- Weight Training For Dummies
  0-7645-5168-X
- Yoga For Dummies
  0-7645-5117-5

TRAVEL

0-7645-5438-7

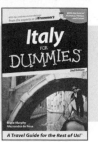

0-7645-5453-0

Also available:
- Alaska For Dummies
  0-7645-1761-9
- Arizona For Dummies
  0-7645-6938-4
- Cancún and the Yucatán For Dummies
  0-7645-2437-2
- Cruise Vacations For Dummies
  0-7645-6941-4
- Europe For Dummies
  0-7645-5456-5
- Ireland For Dummies
  0-7645-5455-7

- Las Vegas For Dummies
  0-7645-5448-4
- London For Dummies
  0-7645-4277-X
- New York City For Dummies
  0-7645-6945-7
- Paris For Dummies
  0-7645-5494-8
- RV Vacations For Dummies
  0-7645-5443-3
- Walt Disney World & Orlando For Dummies
  0-7645-6943-0

GRAPHICS, DESIGN & WEB DEVELOPMENT

0-7645-4345-8

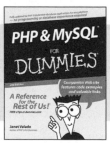

0-7645-5589-8

Also available:
- Adobe Acrobat 6 PDF For Dummies
  0-7645-3760-1
- Building a Web Site For Dummies
  0-7645-7144-3
- Dreamweaver MX 2004 For Dummies
  0-7645-4342-3
- FrontPage 2003 For Dummies
  0-7645-3882-9
- HTML 4 For Dummies
  0-7645-1995-6
- Illustrator CS For Dummies
  0-7645-4084-X

- Macromedia Flash MX 2004 For Dummies
  0-7645-4358-X
- Photoshop 7 All-in-One Desk
  Reference For Dummies
  0-7645-1667-1
- Photoshop CS Timesaving Techniques
  For Dummies
  0-7645-6782-9
- PHP 5 For Dummies
  0-7645-4166-8
- PowerPoint 2003 For Dummies
  0-7645-3908-6
- QuarkXPress 6 For Dummies
  0-7645-2593-X

NETWORKING, SECURITY, PROGRAMMING & DATABASES

0-7645-6852-3

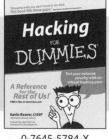

0-7645-5784-X

Also available:
- A+ Certification For Dummies
  0-7645-4187-0
- Access 2003 All-in-One Desk
  Reference For Dummies
  0-7645-3988-4
- Beginning Programming For Dummies
  0-7645-4997-9
- C For Dummies
  0-7645-7068-4
- Firewalls For Dummies
  0-7645-4048-3
- Home Networking For Dummies
  0-7645-42796

- Network Security For Dummies
  0-7645-1679-5
- Networking For Dummies
  0-7645-1677-9
- TCP/IP For Dummies
  0-7645-1760-0
- VBA For Dummies
  0-7645-3989-2
- Wireless All In-One Desk Reference
  For Dummies
  0-7645-7496-5
- Wireless Home Networking For Dummies
  0-7645-3910-8

HEALTH & SELF-HELP

0-7645-6820-5 *†

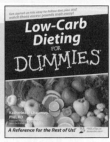

0-7645-2566-2

Also available:

- Alzheimer's For Dummies
  0-7645-3899-3
- Asthma For Dummies
  0-7645-4233-8
- Controlling Cholesterol For Dummies
  0-7645-5440-9
- Depression For Dummies
  0-7645-3900-0
- Dieting For Dummies
  0-7645-4149-8
- Fertility For Dummies
  0-7645-2549-2

- Fibromyalgia For Dummies
  0-7645-5441-7
- Improving Your Memory For Dummies
  0-7645-5435-2
- Pregnancy For Dummies †
  0-7645-4483-7
- Quitting Smoking For Dummies
  0-7645-2629-4
- Relationships For Dummies
  0-7645-5384-4
- Thyroid For Dummies
  0-7645-5385-2

EDUCATION, HISTORY, REFERENCE & TEST PREPARATION

0-7645-5194-9

0-7645-4186-2

Also available:

- Algebra For Dummies
  0-7645-5325-9
- British History For Dummies
  0-7645-7021-8
- Calculus For Dummies
  0-7645-2498-4
- English Grammar For Dummies
  0-7645-5322-4
- Forensics For Dummies
  0-7645-5580-4
- The GMAT For Dummies
  0-7645-5251-1
- Inglés Para Dummies
  0-7645-5427-1

- Italian For Dummies
  0-7645-5196-5
- Latin For Dummies
  0-7645-5431-X
- Lewis & Clark For Dummies
  0-7645-2545-X
- Research Papers For Dummies
  0-7645-5426-3
- The SAT I For Dummies
  0-7645-7193-1
- Science Fair Projects For Dummies
  0-7645-5460-3
- U.S. History For Dummies
  0-7645-5249-X

Get smart @ dummies.com®

- **Find a full list of Dummies titles**
- **Look into loads of FREE on-site articles**
- **Sign up for FREE eTips e-mailed to you weekly**
- **See what other products carry the Dummies name**
- **Shop directly from the Dummies bookstore**
- **Enter to win new prizes every month!**

* Separate Canadian edition also available

† Separate U.K. edition also available

Available wherever books are sold. For more information or to order direct: U.S. customers visit www.dummies.com or call 1-877-762-2974.
U.K. customers visit www.wileyeurope.com or call 0800 243407. Canadian customers visit www.wiley.ca or call 1-800-567-4797.